MARYLAND

CALENDAR OF WILLS

1726-1732

VOLUME 6

Jane Baldwin Cotton

WILLOW BEND BOOKS
2007

WILLOW BEND BOOKS
AN IMPRINT OF HERITAGE BOOKS, INC.

Books, CDs, and more—Worldwide

For our listing of thousands of titles see our website
at
www.HeritageBooks.com

Published 2007 by
HERITAGE BOOKS, INC.
Publishing Division
65 East Main Street
Westminster, Maryland 21157-5026

Originally published 1920

All rights reserved. No part of this book may be reproduced or transmitted in any form or by any means, electronic or mechanical, including photocopying, recording or by any information storage and retrieval system without written permission from the author, except for the inclusion of brief quotations in a review.

International Standard Book Number: 978-0-940907-09-6

MARYLAND CALENDAR OF WILLS

Burneyat (Burnyeat), John, Talbot Co.,
26th April, 1726;
3rd Aug., 1726.

To kinsman **William White** (second son to bro.-in-law **William White**, of afsd. co., planter) and hrs., "Killingsworth," in Bullenbrook Hundred, n. side gr. Choptank R.; bou. by father, **William Barneyeat**, of **William Jones**.
" kinsman **Charles Gorsuch** and bros.-in-law **James** and **William White**, personalty.
" 4 kinsfolk (meaning the 2 sons and 2 daus. of **William White** afsd.), residue of estate.
Ex.: Bro.-in-law **William White**.
Test: William Thomas, Richard Humphrey, William Madrey, Joseph Wray. 19, 1.

Warner, George, planter, Kent Co.,
15th day, 6th mo., 1725;
18th June, 1726.

To 2 sons, **George** and **Joseph**, dwell. plan. ——— equally.
" dau. **Sarah**, personalty.
" wife **Sarah**, extx., ⅓ personal estate, residue to afsd. child. equally at age of 21; shd. all 3 child. die without issue, real estate to bro. **Joseph** and hrs.; shd. wife die before child. are of age, bros. **Thomas Rasin** and **Joseph Warner** to be exs. and ed. child. as Quakers.
Test: Geo. Dunkan, Samuel Smith, David Hull, Richd. Bentham. 19, 2.

Bally, William, Prince George's Co.,
22nd March, 1724-5;
26th March, 1725.

To **Jon.** (son of **Francis Toulson**), 750 A. on Douge Ck., in Muddy Hole, Stafford Co., Va.
" **Mary** (dau. of **William Cogwill**) and hrs., 270 A. on Muddy Hole, joining land of Richd. Wist.
" **Francis Toulson**, ex., residue of estate.
Test: John Bronor (Branner), Jacob Jackson, Walter Bayne.
19, 4.

Simmons, Jonathan, Prince George's Co.,
9th Jan., 1724;
1st Dec., 1726.

To wife **Elizabeth,** extx., dwell. plan. —— during life, at her decease to son **Jonathan.**
" son **Joseph** and daus. **Eliza, Mary** and **Ann,** personalty.
" son **Richard** and daus. **Rebecca, Ainie, Sarah** and **Marjory,** equal portions of personal estate, wife's thirds being deducted; sd. son to have his portion at age of 21, daus. at marriage.
Test: Joseph Brown, Richard Loder, Walter Dallas. 19, 5.

Watson, William, planter, Prince George's Co.,
22nd Jan., 1722;
30th Nov., 1726.

To sons **William** and **James** and their hrs., real estate equally; wife **Jane** to have use of ⅛ thereof during life.
" wife **Jane** and sons afsd., exs., personal estate equally.
Overseers: Son-in-law **John Thomas** and John George.
Test: John Spencer, Elizabeth (Shearnead) Spencer, Peter Brightwell. 19, 6.

Dawkins (Dawkings, Dakins), William, Calvert Co.,
30th May, 1726;
30th Sept., 1726.

To son **James** and hrs., 299 A. "Chelton" and "Smith," bou. of Robert Gilley.
" wife **Ann,** extx., pt. of dwell. plan. —— during life in lieu of her dower.
" son **Bennet** and hrs., eastern pt. of dwell. plan., and after his mother's decease her portion; and personalty.
" son **William** and hrs., n. pt. of afsd. tract; and personalty.
" dau. **Mary Pattason** and hrs., pt. of "Dorrington," adj. John Hues, and 47 A. of "Inlargement of Dorrington"; and personalty.
" dau. **Penelope** and hrs., residue of "Dorrington" and 28 A. of "Inlargement of Dorrington"; shd. she die before age of 21 and without issue, to pass to child., viz. **Bennet, William, Mary Pattason** and **Elizabeth;** and personalty.
" dau. **Elizabeth** and hrs., 200 A. "Joseph his Place"; shd. she die without issue or before age of 21, to pass to child., viz. **Bennet, William, Mary Pattason** and **Penelope;** and personalty.
" dau. **Ann Hellen** and hrs., personalty.

To 4 child., viz. Bennet, William, Elizabeth and Penelope,
residue of estate, after wife's thirds are deducted.
Test: William Blackburn, William Walker, William Gray.
19, 7.

Orrell, Mary, widow, Dorchester Co., 4th Sept., 1726; 26th Nov., 1726.

To dau. Mary and hrs., lot No. 6 in Cambridge, bou. by husband, John Orrell, of Thomas Taylor; and personalty.
" dau. Martha, personalty had of John Stewart.
Exs.: Govert Loockerman and Thomas Nevett to sell lots Nos. 3 and 4 for maintenance of 3 youngest child.—Glidwell, Francis and Elizabeth.
Test: James Woolford (Woollford), John Stewart, Mary Stewart. 19, 10.

Smoot, William, planter, Charles Co., 9th Nov., 1726; 18th Nov., 1726.

To son Thomas, personalty; to be in charge of Mark Penn, ex., until 21 yrs. of age, and to receive 2 yrs. schooling.
" son William, personalty; to be in charge of John Wilder until 21 yrs. of age, and to receive 2 yrs. schooling. Sd. Wilder to receive with son William half what remains.
Test: Thomas Morris, Elizabeth Weeden, Thomas Hawton.
19, 12.

Turvy, Edward, Charles Co., 30th Aug., 1726; 16th Sept., 1726.

To sons Thomas, William and John, entire estate; sd. sons to be of age at 18.
Ex.: John Wilder.
Test: Francis Brown, Jonathan Nichols (Nicholds), Timothy Dunaway. 19, 14.

Wilkinson, William, merchant, Charles Co., 4th Nov., 1725; 29th Aug., 1726.

To dau. Sophia Wilkinson (alias Sophia Hicks), 86 A. bou. of Phillip Willocy; 86 A. adj., bou. of Hugh Williams; both ad. tracts in Prince George's Co.; and personalty, including ½ revenue from mill.
" grandson William, personalty, including ½ revenue from mill, and debts due testator in London.
" grandson Francis and granddau. Susanna, personalty.

To dau. **Sophia** and 3 grandchild. afsd., 600 A. "The Enclosure," Patuxent, bou. of John Craycroft. Shd. there be any dispute, to get the money (£140) of the widow Craycroft, Prince George's Co.

" **Thomas Grant**, gentleman, Prince George's Co., personalty; joint ex. with dau. **Sophia**.

Test: Bigger Head, John Burch (Birch), John Thomas.

Codicil: 17th Aug., 1726. A legacy to grandson **William** revoked.

Test: Jona. Davies, Bigger Head, Charles Craycroft.

19, 16.

Lynes, William, ditcher, Cecil Co., 16th Nov., 1726; 30th Nov., 1726.

To John Tilton, 300 A. "Cedar Swamp," s. side Egg Harbour, surveyed by Danl. Leads.

" John Numberson, personal estate.

Test: Alexander Mecandlis, Isaac Corwen, Richard Yates.

19, 19.

Tilden, Marmaduke, Kent Co., 24th May, 1726; 19th Oct., 1726.

To wife ———, extx., ⅓ of estate not hereafter bequeathed, use of dwell. plan. ——— during minority of son **Marmaduke**; shd. sd. son die before age of 21, sd. plan. to wife during her widowhood; shd. son **Marmaduke** die during minority or without issue, to pass successively to daus. **Jane, Mary**, son **Charles** and dau. **Martha** and their hrs.

" son **Charles** and hrs., plan. on Langford's Bay; he dying without issue, the profits afsd. plan. divided among afsd. 3 daus.; shd. any of daus. die without issue, survivors to enjoy portion of deceased; shd. all daus. die without issue, to pass to son **Marmaduke** and hrs. During minority of son **Charles** 3 daus. to receive rents from sd. plan. until they marry or arrive at age of 20.

" sons **Marmaduke** and **Charles** and daus. **Jane, Mary** and **Martha**, personalty and residue of estate equally.

Overseers: James Harris, Esq., and bro. **John**.

Test: Simon Wilmer, Ann Wilmer, John Tilden. 19, 20.

Spalding, John, Charles Co., 18th Jan., 1724-5; 14th Sept., 1726.

To wife **Priscilla**, dwell. plan. "Collier Tone Manner" during life; at her decease to. young. son **Charles** and hrs.; he

dying without issue, to son **John** and hrs.; also certain
personalty during life, at her decease, to pass to son
Charles; he dying during minority or without issue, to
other children.
To son **John** and hrs., 100 A. of "Batchelors Rest," in
Clement's Bay Forest; he dying without issue, to sons
William and **Bassell** and their hrs.; also pt. of "Five
Brothers," and "St. Giles," St. Mary's Co.
" sons **William** and **Bassell** and their hrs., 200 A. "Greens
Inheritance," nr. Port Tobba.; also tract on Beavour Dam
Mannour, St. Mary's Co.
" son **John**, dau. **Mary**, sons **William** and **Bassell** (at age
of 18), personalty.
" wife afsd., ⅛ of personalty, residue to 5 child.; son
John to have charge of education of child.
Exs.: Wife and son **John**.
Test: Wm. Spalding, George Burch (Birch), Elizab. Morris,
Brian Macdanell (Magdonill). 19, 23.

Hagan (Hargan), Mary, Charles Co., 8th Apr., 1721; 4th Feb., 1726.

To son **William**, ex., entire estate.
Test: Thos. Webster, Thos. Jameson. 19, 26.

Carty, Maurice, innholder, Kent Co., 2nd Dec., 1726; 8th Dec., 1726.

To son **Maurice** and hrs., tract in Kent Co.
" dau. **Margt.** and hrs., "Smith's Range," Queen Anne's Co.
" dau. **Susannah** and hrs., tract in Quaker Neck, Kent Co.,
formerly belonging to John and Joseph Everett.
" dau. **Mary** and hrs., tract at head of Chester, Q. A. Co.,
formerly John French's.
" servts. Jonathan Whitworth and Mary, his wife, and
William Stanley, remainder of their time.
" wife **Susanna**, extx., residue of estate.
Test: Thos. Wilkins, John Griffith, Jonathan Whitworth.
19, 27.

Middleton, Luckner, planter, Kent Co., 2nd Nov., 1726; 3rd Dec., 1726.

To sons **Luckner** and **John**, exs., and their hrs., real estate;
son **John** to have land on w. side of Branch with dwell.
plan.; shd. either of sd. sons die without issue, his
portion to son **Studly** and hrs.
Test: Robert Ford, Joseph Hull, Ferdinando Hull. 19, 29.

Rawlings, Daniel, Calvert Co., 29th Dec., 1726; 20th Jan., 1726-7.

To youngest son **Daniel** and hrs., dwell. plan. ―――― on St. Leods Ck. and 200 A. "Rawling's Choice."
" son-in-law **John Clare** and **Elizabeth,** his wife, deed of gift dated 12 Nov., 1722, of 143 A. "Rawlings Choyce," pt. of "Great Elton Head Mannour," confirmed.
" dau. **Ann** and hrs., 157 A. of "Rawling's Choice."
" eldest son **Isaac** and hrs., 500 A., the residue of "Rawling's Choice."
" dau. **Mary Hollaway,** personalty.
" 5 child. afd., residue of estate; shd. any die before possessed of estate and without issue, survivors to divide portion of deceased.
Exs.: Son **Isaac** and **John Clare.**
Test: John Parran, William Day, Alexander Parran.
19, 31.

Miles, John, Sr., St. Mary's Co., 3rd Jan., 1726-7; 23rd Jan., 1726-7.

To wife **Mary,** dwell. plan., 54 A. ――――, during life.
" son **John,** ex., and hrs., "Summerfield" and "Westfield"; and personalty.
" son **Henry** and hrs., 92 A. "Cornelius's"; dwell. plan. at decease of his mother ――――; 4,000 lbs. tob. to be expended for land; and personalty.
" daus. **Mary, Margaret, Elizabeth, Priscilla** and **Anne,** and bros. **Nicholas** and **Edward,** personalty.
" dau. **Elineor Sinnott,** 2,000 lbs. tob. in full of her pt. of estate.
" wife afsd. and 7 child., viz. **John, Mary, Margaret, Elizabeth, Henry, Priscilla** and **Anne,** residue of estate.
Test: Edwd. Cole, Charles Joy, Thos. Oglesby. 19, 34.

Massy, Nicholas, Queen Anne's Co., 13th Apr., 1724; 8th Jan., 1726.

To grandson **Daniel,** personalty.
" wife **Mary,** dwell. plan. ―――― during life, at her decease to 5 sons, viz. **Peter, Thomas, William, James** and **Nicholas.** To wife and sd. 5 sons, residue of personalty.
Exs.: Sons **Peter** and **Thomas.**
Test: Emanuel Hust, Stephen Miars (Miors), Ann Miars (Miors). 19, 37.

Coursey, Elizabeth, Wye R., Queen Anne's Co., widow of William Coursey of sd. co. 25th March, 1725; 6th Oct., 1726.

To kinswoman Mary, wife of Thomas Hynson Wright; sister Sarah, wife of Jacob Covington; kinswomen Sarah, wife of Arthur Emory, Jr.; Elizabeth, wife of Thomas Wilkinson; Thomas, son of Thomas Marsh, of Kent Island, deceased, personalty.
" servt. Elizabeth Willington, nine months of her time.
" kinsman William Turbutt and hrs., remaining lands had of deceased husband not already sold or devised.
" Michael, Anna and Mary, child. of sd. William Turbutt; and John, Thomas and Mary, child. of John Coursey, of sd. co., deceased, residue of personal estate at age of 21 or day of marriage.
Exs.: William Turbutt, Thomas Hynson Wright and Mary his wife.
Test: Vincent Hemsley, David Lesage, Elizabeth Willington.
Codicil: 15 Aug., 1726. To Elizabeth, wife of Thomas Wilkinson, personalty; same test. 19, 38.

Covington, Jacob, Queen Anne's Co., 21st Aug., 1726; 22nd Oct., 1726.

To daus.-in-law Margaret, wife of Nicholas Lowe, of Talbot Co., gent.; Sarah, wife of Arthur Emory, Jr., personalty.
" 2 daus.-in-law Mary, wife of Thomas Hynson Wright, and Sarah Emory afsd., household goods, etc., equally.
" kinswoman Mary, wife of Robert Noble, of Talbot Co., ½ of all stock; other ½ to afsd. Mary Wright and Sarah Emory; shd. sd. Sarah die without issue, her portion to revert to afsd. Mary Wright.
Wife Sarah, extx., to have use of estate during her widowhood.
Test: Mary Benton, Vincent Hemsley. 19, 43.

Hardy, James, Sr., 17th Sept., 1722; 12th Oct., 1727.

To son Robert and hrs., tract ———— and 1s.
" son James and hrs., residue of "Barber Rest" and 50 A. "Barber and Dison."
" sons John, Joseph and Ben and their hrs., land at Barren Ck. equally.
" daus. Sarah Smith, Ann Oliver and Er. Nickalson, personalty.
" child., viz. James, John, Phillis, Rachell, Joseph and Ben, residue of estate.
" wife ————, extx., her thirds during life.

8   MARYLAND CALENDAR OF WILLS

Test: Thos. Humphris, Jr., John Soslin, Roger Phillips, John Howard.
Codicil: 25th July, 1726. Dau. Phillis to have but 1s., dau. Mary to have her pt.; by reason of wife's decease, sons Joseph and Ben to care for their bro. James till 18 yrs. of age.
Ex.: Son James.
Test: Thos. Humphris, Thos. Heasy, John Goslee, Thos. Goslee (Gostea). 19, 46.

Nicholson (Nickallson), Richard, Jr., 10th June, 1726; 7th Nov., 1726.

To son Richard, daus. Mary, Filles and Bette, personalty.
" wife ———, personalty.
" child. afsd., residue of estate equally.
Test: James Nicholson, Fillis Nicholson, Thomas Humphry (Humphris). 19, 49.

Outen (Outten), Thomas, Somerset Co., 3rd Jan., 1725; 19th Nov., 1726.

To William Selby and hrs., tract adj. "Simpaltun."
" wife ———, extx., use of dwell. plan. ——— during her widowhood; shd. she marry, use of ½ thereof; ⅓ personal estate absolutely.
" son Thomas and hrs., dwell. plan. ——— bequeathed by father, John Outten, to possess ½ thereof at age of 18, the whole after his mother's decease.
" son Samuel, personalty when of age.
" child., viz. John, Thomas, Samuel, Elizabeth and Abraham, residue of personalty equally.
Test: George Truitt, Abraham Outten, Samuel Truitt.
19, 51.

Mathewes (Mathews), William, Somerset Co., 4th Oct., 1726; 12th Dec., 1726.

To eldest son William, sons Samuel, Teague and John and their hrs., "Edwin" and certain marsh land (for desc. and div. see will).
" sons William and Samuel afsd. and their hrs., "Ellis Lott."
" Jacob Adams, certain marsh land.
" son David and hrs., 110 A. "Worthless."
" dau. Sarah, personalty.
" four youngest child., viz. David, Elizabeth, Rachell and Martha, residue of personal estate.

Wife **Mary**, extx., not to be disturbed in poss. of Manner plantation or personal estate during widowhood.
Test: Jacob Addams, Robert Tayler, Thomas Maddox.
19, 53.

Phillips, Jane, Somerset Co., 15th June, 1726; 15th Sept., 1726.

To 2 youngest child., **Dorothy** and **James**, personalty left by dec'd husband, **Richard Phillips**, to pay for schooling.
" son **Richard** and 3 eldest daus., **Ann, Sarah** and **Betty,** personalty.
" 8 child. —— thirds equally. Child. to be kept together until 2 youngest sons are educated and bound to a trade.
Ex.: John Jones.
Test: Jonathan Bound, Thomas Stevens. 19, 57.

Hutchings, George, Somerset Co., 29th Dec., 1726; 16th Jan., 1726-7.

To son **William** and dau. **Mary**, entire estate.
Exs.: Adam Heath, Thos. Humphris.
Test: John Harddy, John Richards. 19, 58.

Denson, William, planter, Wicocomoco, Somerset Co., 28th Nov., 1726; 4th Jan., 1726-7.

To sons **William** and **John** and dau. **Mary Nesham**, 1s. each.
" granddau. **Mary Nesham**, personalty.
Wife **Elizabeth** and dau. **Elizabeth**, exs. and residuary legatees.
Test: George Goddard, Benj. Cottman. 19, 59.

Stoddert (Stoddart), James, Prince George's Co., 29th March, 1726; 31st May, 1726.

To wife **Elizabeth**, ⅓ of "Southampton" during life, "Daniell's" in Pamunkey Neck, adj. Hill plantation of Mr. Pile; and personalty.
" son **James** and hrs., "Southampton," Pamunkey Ck., wife's thirds excepted; n. pt. of "The Pasture"; he making over to son **William** and hrs. his interest s. of a certain line.

To son **John** and hrs., land at Smith's Point, Charles Co.; tract on upper side Coles Ck.; interest in land at Nanjemy held in partnership with William Hutchison; and personalty.
" son **William** and hrs., pt. of "The Pasture" and "Addition" in Pamunkey Neck; 300 A. "Friendship," on Fall Run; and personalty.
" sons **Benj.** and **Thomas** and their hrs., 1,260 A. of "Friendship"; shd. sd. sons die during minority, their portion of sd. tract to be divided among 3 sons, viz. **James, John** and **William**; and personalty.
" afsd. child. ——— residue of personal estate, after wife's thirds are deducted.
Wife **Elizabeth** and sons **James, John** and **William**, exs., empowered to sell 1,878 A. at Mount Calvert and "Rocky Creek" for benefit of personal estate.
Test: Peter Dent, Martha Clalan, William White. 19, 61.

Miles, Thomas, Prince George's Co.,
2nd day, 6th mo., 1725;
23rd Nov., 1726.

To 2 sons, **Thomas** and **John**, and their hrs., lands in A. A. Co., at hd. of Lyons Ck.; shd. either son die during minority, survivor to inherit portion of dec'd.
" son **Thomas** afsd., personalty at age of 18.
" dau. **Sarah** (the now wife of Samuel Plummer) and dau. **Elizabeth**, personalty.
" wife **Elizabeth**, extx., and 2 child. by her, viz. **John** and **Rachell**, residue of estate.
Test: William Coale, Saml. White, Benjamin White.
19, 65.

Stimton (Stimson), Solomon, planter, Prince George's Co.,
9th Jan., 1726-7;
26th Jan., 1726-7.

To son **Solomon**, £30.
" son **Benjamin**, 50 A. where he now lives and £30.
" son-in-laws **William** and **Thomas Elder**, personalty.
" wife **Elizabeth**, extx., son **Jeremiah**, daus. **Sarah** and **Mary**, personal estate equally.
" dau. **Ann**, £5.
" wife **Elizabeth** and hrs., rights in land adj. Charles Bevans; shd. any of child. die during minority, their portion to be divided among all child. equally.
Test: Thos. Chartur (Chartor), Paul Talbart (Tabart), Elizabeth Morris. 19, 67.

Daniel, Elizabeth, Prince George's Co.,
17th Jan., 1725;
11th Feb., 1726-7.

To John Carroll, Mary Croxall, Susana Neal, Richard Croxall, Ann Neal, Mrs. Joanna Croxall, Charles Neal, Mrs. Ann Neal and Arthur Neal, personalty (some of which des. as being in John Hooper's hands).
Exs.: Richard Croxall and John Carroll, Prince George's Co. planters.
Test: Thomas Howard, Leonard Piles, Kathrine Carte.
19, 69.

Hays (Hayes), John, Baltimore Co., 9th Jan., 1726-7;
30th Jan., 1726.

To son **John Stansbury** and hrs., entire real estate; and personalty.
" dau. **Elizabeth Lenex,** personalty and 50s.
Test: Stephen Body, John Hillen, Aron Fox, John Weeks (Wickes). 19, 70.

Merriken, Joshua, Baltimore Co., 6th Nov., 1726;
8th March, 1726.

To wife **Dianna,** extx., ½ land ——— during life; shd. unborn child be a son, to be named "Joshua" and possess afsd. tract at wife's decease. ½ personal estate during widowhood; shd. she marry, a child's portion.
" son **Hugh** and hrs., ½ afsd. land; shd. either of afsd. sons die without issue, survivor to inherit portion of decease, neither son having power to sell or mortgage their portions. To both sons afsd. "George's Hill."
" dau. **Ann** and hrs., outward pt. of "Merrikeen's Inheritance."
" dau. **Mary** and hrs., 200 A. "Merrikeen's Outlet," hd. of Bush R. (for desc. see will).
" unborn child (if a girl, to be named "Diana") and hrs., "Merrikeen's Branches," nr. land of John Weasly.
Test: Edward Day, Samuel Baker, William Bradford, Alexdr. Maccomus. 19, 72.

Mathews, William, Talbot Co., 28th Oct., 1726;
31st Oct., 1726.

To wife ———, extx., entire estate.
Test: Rev. Daniell Maynader, Charles Markland, David Robinson. 19, 75.

Moulton, Walter, planter, Talbot Co., 1st Nov., 1722;
1st March, 1726.

To wife **Lydea,** extx., and hrs., entire estate.
Test: John Smith, Margret Barker, William Barker.
19, 76.

Kingsbury, James, doctor of physick, Calvert Co.,
2nd Feb., 1724;
25th Jan., 1726-7.

Entire estate in Maryland or England deeded to wife **Elizabeth.**
Test: John Thomas, Thos. Brooke, Jr., Richard Stevens (Stephens). 19, 78.

Kent, William, planter, Calvert Co., 28th Dec., 1726;
27th Feb., 1726-7.

To son **Joseph** and hrs., pt. of "Timberwell," given testator by his grandfather, **Wm. Wadsworth,** being the plantation where John Dalby now lives; and personalty. Pt. of land given sd. son called "The Neck," adj. to Richard Stallinges, not to be cleared until sd. son is of age at 18 yrs.
" Richard Deale (who m. Martha, dau. of John Bowling) and hrs., pt. of "Timberwell," which afsd. **Wm. Wadsworth** bequeathed to sd. John Bowling, there being a consid. received for same.
" unborn child if a son, residue of real estate and personalty at age of 18; shd. sd. child be a dau., sd. lands to son **Joseph** and hrs.
" wife **Elizabeth,** extx., residue of personal estate. Shd. wife die, son **Joseph** to care of mother-in-law **Frances Wilson**; after her decease, bro.-in-law **John Veatch,** guardian to sd. son, who is to have 3 years' schooling.
Test: John Dalby, Saml. Galloway, Richd. Stallinges.
19, 80.

Hume, James, Calvert Co., 26th Dec., 1726;
6th Feb., 1726-7.

To dau. **Anne** and hrs., ½ of real estate.
" unborn child, other ½ of sd. land; shd. both child. die without issue, sd. lands to wife **Sarah,** extx., and hrs.
Test: Francis Hollinshead, John Austin (Austen), Jacob Stallings. 19, 83.

Henly, Darby, Calvert Co., 4th Oct., 1726;
22nd March, 1726-7.

To son **Darby,** ex., dwelling house and 30 A. "Mary's Widdower" adj.
" son **John,** 50 A., the half of "Island Neck"; and personalty.
" son **Edmond,** "Addition to Island Neck," where he now dwells; and personalty.
" dau. **Ann Elliott,** personalty.
Test: George Elliott, Ann Elliott, Mitchell (Michll) Phillips.
19, 84.

Osburn, Thomas, Charles Co., 10th Nov., 1726;
20th Feb., 1726.

To Elizabeth and Mary, daus. of Will Hoskins, personalty.
" son **Joseph** and hrs., entire real and ½ personal estate; sd. son dying without issue, to pass to wife ——— and hrs. Sd. son to care of Will Hoskins, and Richd. Harrison, to receive estate at age of 21.
Wife **Elizabeth,** extx. and residuary legatee.
Test: Richard Price, Robert Minion, Daniel Coffe. 19, 86.

Polk (Polke), William, Dorchester Co.,
25th Nov., 1726;
21st Feb., 1726-7.

To son **John,** dwell. plan. ———.
" John Pollet, tract now belonging to Manner plantation, conditionally.
" eldest dau. **Jane** and hrs., 2 tracts adj., viz. "Lowridge" and "Polks Folley."
" youngest dau. **Ann** and hrs., 50 A. at hd. of Dame Quarter Ck.
" wife ———, extx., use of lands during widowhood; shd. child. die without issue, sd. lands to revert to wife ——— and hrs.
Test: Francis Hayward, Jr., John Aing, Sarah Samuels (Saminuels). 19, 87.

Carter, John, blacksmith, Dorchester Co.,
15th Aug., 1726;
15th March, 1726.

To sons **James** and **John** and their hrs., each 102 A. of "Barnet Purches," bou. of Thomas Barnen, lying in freshes of Great Choptank R., after their mother's decease; personalty and 1s. each.

To 4 daus., viz. **Mary, Elizabeth, Ann** and **Rachell**, personal estate at decease of wife ———.
Exs.: Wife **Elizabeth** and son **James**.
Test: Thomas Rumball, Thomas Kidder, James Kidder.
19, 88.

Nuner, Thomas, cooper, Dorchester Co.,
8th April, 1722;
15th March, 1726-7.

To wife **Mary**, extx., dwell. plan. ——— during life; ⅓ personal estate absolutely.
" daus. **Elizabeth Rice, Sarah, Ann** and **Mary**, personalty.
" son-in-law **James Conner**, 50 A. of "Nuner's Lott," nr. w. side Blackwater R.
" daus. **Ann** and **Mary** and their hrs., residue of personal estate; dwell. plan. ——— at decease of wife; and 50 A. of "Nuner's Lott."
Test: John Meekins, Josias Mace, Mary Mace.
Note: Extx. being dec'd, adm. granted by a power of atty. for Sarah Nuner, next of kin, to Capt. Henry Hooper.
19, 91.

Foster, John, Dorchester Co., 9th Nov., 1725;
22nd March, 1726.

To dau. **Rebecca** and hrs., residue of "Exchange" at hd. of Transquaking.
" dau. **Susannah Dawson** and hrs., land where she now dwells.
" dau. **Mary Fooks** and hrs., land adj. dau. **Susannah's**.
" dau. **Pheby** and hrs., land adj. **Mary Fooks'**.
" daus. **Susannah Dawson, Mary Fooks** and **Ann Deane**, 5s. each.
" daus. **Sarah, Rebecca** and **Pheby**, personalty.
" son **Thomas**, personalty; to pay to his sister **Sarah** after decease of wife ——— £4 3s. yearly.
Wife **Mary** and son **Thomas** exs. and residuary legatees of personal estate.
Overseer: Henry Ennalls, Sr.
Testator directs that he be buried in Friends Graveyard, Transquaking.
Test: Wm. Murray, Thomas Ennalls, Bartholemew Ennalls.
19, 93.

Johns (Johnes), Hugh, Baltimore Co.,
22nd March, 1726-7;
1st April, 1727.

To son **Hugh** and hrs., "Horton's Fortune."
" son **Benjamin** and hrs., "Hobson's Choyce."
" sons **Hugh** and **Benjamin**, daus. **Charity, Mary, Clary** and youngest dau. **Ann**, personal estate equally.
Ex.: Benjamin Bowing.
Test: Lloyd (Loyd) Harris, George Walker, Abraham Lake (Leak), John Cole, Jr. 19, 96.

Norton, John, planter, Baltimore Co., —— —— ——;
3rd April, 1727.

To son **William,** 1s.
" 2 sons, **John** and **Richard,** and their hrs., entire real estate.
" sons **John** and **Richard,** and daus. **Ann, Elizabeth** and **Mary,** personal estate equally; shd. any die before of age, survivors to divide portion of dec'd. Son **Richard** to be free at 18 yrs. Patrick Butler at discretion of his mother.
Exs.: Wife **Elizabeth** and son **John;** wife to have use of great dwelling house during life.
Test: John Moorcock (Morecock), Susannah Moorcock, Thomas Stone.
Note: Widow claims her thirds. 19, 97.

Bordley, Thomas. Esq., Annapolis, 29th June, 1726;
14th Jan., 1726.

(Youngest son of Rev. Stephen Bordley, clerk, late prebendary of St. Paul's and rector of St. Mary's, Newington, London, starting on a voyage to London.)
To son **Stephen** and hrs., all real estate in Annapolis, except that hereinafter disposed of; 1,300 A. "Sand Gate"; 100 A. "Grime's Addition," up Severn; "The Discovery" on the Branches of Petuxent R. and "Gueists Plains" adj., cont. in all 1,340 A.
" son **William** and hrs., "Painters Rest" with "The Addition" thereto, cont. 1,900 A., Cecil Co., at hd. of Sasafrax R.; house and lot in Annapolis, wherein Jno. Jordain lives, bou. of Mr. Thomas Bladen.
" son **John** and hrs., all real estate in Kent Co., about 2,000 A., viz. "The Fancy," "Bordley's Beginning," "Partnership," "The Adventure," "The Grumble."

To son **Thomas** and hrs., share of "Augustine Mannor," Cecil Co., surveyed for his mother's grandfather, **Augustine Herman**; "Bordley's Choyce," Prince George's Co.; shd. son **Thomas** die during minority and without issue, portion of "Augustine Mannor" to surviving child. of present wife.

" sons **John** and **Thomas** and their hrs., 4 lots whereon the Brewhouse, Malthouse and other houses stood, Nos. 92, 93, 104, 105.

" son **Matthias** and hrs., 2,000 A. "Backland," Prince George's Co.; 5 A. adj. to Calvert St. and Bloomsberry Square, Annapolis, to include Dowcras Tanyard.

" dau. **Elizabeth** and hrs., 500 A. residue of "Backland," to be laid out by the guardians of son **Matthias**; house and lot where Benjamin Getchell and wife now live, also where Thos. Jobson and wife live.

" unborn child, tract in Prince George's Co. taken up with Benj. Gaither; 5 A. convenient to n.w. of Tabernacle St., Annapolis, so as not to incommode a settlement upon beautiful hill adj.

" wife **Arianna**, extx., use of real estate during minority of child; ⅓ personal estate absolutely, residue to child. equally; child. to have good education.

" daus.-in-law **Sarah, Margaret** and **Augustina Frisby**, personal estate of their father ———.

" sisters **Mary** and **Elizabeth**, in Newcastle upon Tyne, all claims against them.

" cousins **Thomas** and **Stephen**, personalty.

Shd. any of child. die during minority and without issue, survivors to divide portion of dec'd, except in case of "Augustine Mannor." Charges in suits bet. Forward and Cockey of one pt. and testator to be pd. out of estate.

Overseers: Bro. **James Harris**, Esq., and **John Beale**, Esq. Shd. wife die overseers to act as exs.

Test: Elizabeth Beale, Anne Denton, Richard Clagett, Phillip Plafay, Thos. Worsley. 19, 99.

Wilson, Josiah, Prince George's Co.,
9th Dec., 1726;
14th March, 1726-7.

To wife **Eliz.**, extx., and hrs., 1 share of "Land Over," other share to son **Henry** and hrs.

" son **Henry**, daus. **Martha** and **Margret**, personalty.

"Buttington," Prince George's Co., and "Orphans' Gift," Baltimore Co., to be sold by Edward Sprigg and R. Crabb

for payment of debts. Saml. Magruder and John Middleton to be secured against loss, they being securities for balance due to bros. and sisters (unnamed) from father's ——— estate. The residue from sd. lands to daus. **Martha** and **Margret**.
Test: Ann Gittings, John Gittings, Thos. Truelove. 19, 105.

Harris, Thomas, planter, Prince George's Co.,
24th Jan., 1726-7;
29th March, 1727.

To wife **Mary**, extx., and hrs., personalty, and with John Greenup dwell. plan. ——— and real estate equally.
Test: Allen Lock, Francis Turner, Edw. Sprigg. 19, 107.

Nicholas, Griffith, Cecil Co., 5th Dec., 1726;
2nd Jan., 1726-7.

To grandson **Samuel Wilde, Jr.,** and hrs., real estate on e. side Great Elk R., inc. grist mill; to possess estate at age of 21.
" grandchild. **Joseph** and **Margaret Holland** and their hrs., dwell. plan. ———, late in tenure of Thomas Wilde, when of age.
" grandchild. **Mary** and **Margaret Nicholas** and their hrs., 100 A. nr. North East, where Griffith Nicholas, Jr., lived; to possess same when of age.
" wife **Margaret,** £50.
" granddau. **Sarah Wilde,** £20 when of age.
" Church of Christ, meeting at the Iron Hills, nr. Christianah Ck., Newcastle on Delaware, £10.
" **Elisha Thomas,** £5.
" 2 child. of son **Griffith Nicholas** ———, daus. **Mary Wilde** and **Sarah Holland** and their child. ———, personal estate and a tract ——— bou. of Isaac Miller equally.
" son-in-law **Samuel Wilde, Sr.,** ex., personalty and income from estate, real and personal, during minority of legatees. Ex. instructed to fulfill all bequests made by son **Abel Nicholas,** dec'd., from personal estate before div.
Test: Thomas Rees, Evan David, Lewis John. 19, 108.

Atkey (Atkay, Attkey), John, Cecil Co.,
1st July, 1723;
25th Jan., 1726.

To grandson **John Coppin** and hrs., pt. of dwell. plan. ———, formerly laid out for Thomas Smithson, now in poss. of Cornelius Van Sante.

To **James** (youngest son of dau. **Pennington**) tract ——— laid out for John Smithson, now in poss. of John Stoops; shd. sd. **James** die during minority, to next son of sd. dau.; she failing male issue, to sd. dau. and hrs.
" John Chambers, overseer, his debts.
" wife **Anne**, residue of dwell. plan. ——— during life, and certain personalty; at her decease to daus. **Angelico Coppins** (**Coppens**) and **Mary Pennington** and their hrs. Also to wife and dau. **Angelico** afsd., residue of personalty, legacies to following excepted.
" **John Asfurd** (**Ashfurd**) at age; child. of John Chambers afsd., dau. **Pennington** and John Welsh, personalty.
Exs.: Wife, dau. **Angelico** and son-in-law **John Coppens**.
Test. directs that his grave be paled in, that certain personalty be expended for education of dau. **Pennington's** child., and that during 12 yrs., in the minority of grandson **James Pennington**, 40s. rent from plantation bequeathed him be expended yearly for books for poor children.
Test: James Panton, Cornelius Vansand (Vansandt), Nehemiah Martin. 19, 112.

Burbage, John, Sr., weaver, Somerset Co.,
20th Dec., 1726;
24th March, 1727.

To eldest son **Edward**, personalty.
" youngest son **John**, ex., and hrs., residue of estate, real and personal.
Test: John Cavenough, Isay. Bredell, Danet Penoyre.
19, 115.

Fenton, Moses, Somerset Co., 21st Sept., 1723;
24th March, 1727.

To dau. **Elizabeth McDonell**, alias **Fenton**, 12d.
" wife **Margrett**, extx., use of real and personal estate during life; at her decease to 4 daus., viz. **Naomi, Margrett, Sarah** and **Agnes**.
" 4 grandchild., **Margrett, Moses, Elizabeth** and **Naomi McDonell, Robert Jenkins Henry** and **John Henry**, personalty. John Blare's child. (unnamed) to be paid what their father left them, his debts being first deducted.
Test: Isaac Piper (Pypor), David Dreden, Robert Mills.
19, 117.

Hall, James, Somerset Co., 16th March, 1726;
4th April, 1727.
To father and mother (unnamed), use of certain personalty, at their decease to bro. **Pheanix.**
" bros. **Phenix, Thomas** and **William, Nehemiah, Benjamin, Leath, Israel** and **Mary Elizabeth Holland** (Hollon), and wives of bros. **Phenix** and **William,** personalty.
" all bros., residue of personal estate.
Ex.: Bro. **William.**
Test: John Purnell (Purnall), Abraham Outten, Benjamin Holland. 19, 119.

Fountaine, Marcy, Somerset Co., 9th Nov., 1726;
6th April, 1727.
To son **Nicklis** and hrs., dwell. plan. ———; wife **Mary** to have a home thereon during life.
" son **Samuel** and male hrs., 130 A. "Barros Lott" bou. of John Davis. Mary, widow of John Fountaine, to have a living on it during her widowhood; "New Found Land" and "Fishing Island," both on s. side Manoken R.; wife **Mary** and afsd. Mary Fountaine to have certain privileges. Sd. sons not to mortgage or sell lands.
" son **Thomas,** personalty.
" wife **Mary,** certain personalty during life, at her decease to sons **Nicklis** and **Samuel** afsd. and dau. **Brichett**; and ⅓ residue of personal estate; remaining ⅔ to all child.
———, and grandson **Risden Fountaine.** Two youngest child., **Batty** and **Estar,** to enjoy what their mother has shd. she die a widow.
Exs.: Wife **Mary** and son **Nicklis.**
Test: Daniel Maddux, Nicholas Fountaine, Robert Pitts (Pitt). 19, 121.

Bozman, Blandina, Somerset Co., 30th Sept., 1724;
7th April, 1727.
To daus. **Ann** and **Bridgett,** extxs., and their hrs., personal estate.
Test: Jno. Jones, Thomas Lawes, Robt. Jones. 19, 123.

Polke (Pollock), Magdalen, 7th April, 1726;
20th March, 1727.
To son **Joseph,** ex., and hrs., "Moning," in kingdom of Ireland, County Donegall, parish of Leford.
Test: David Polk, William Pollett, Magdalen Pollett (Polet).
19, 125.

Ferson, Percy, Charles Co., 20th Jan., 1726;
18th April, 1727.

To 3 child. **Eliza., Sarah** and **Sophia,** exs., personal estate equally.
" dau. **Elizabeth,** residue of lease, at her death to next eldest.
Overseer: Raphael Neale.
Test: Jona. Nichols, Wm. Oarde, Jane Ferson.   19, 126.

Ashcom, Charles, gent., St. Mary's Co.,
20th Nov., 1725;
23rd March, 1726-7.

To wife **Judith,** extx., daus. **Martha, Susannah** and **Elizabeth** (at age of 16) and son **Samuel,** Joyce Haines, Richard Ward Key and Philip Key, personalty.
" 4 child. afsd., testator's share in personal estate of bro. **John,** dec'd.; division to be made at time that James Greenfeild's child. take their pt. of the estate.
" dau. **Martha** and hrs., 100 A. "Ashcom's Mary Greenfeild," adj. Harris Hows; she dying without issue, to dau. **Susannah** and hrs.; she failing issue, to dau. **Elizabeth** and hrs.
" son **Samuel** and hrs., "Point Patience" and dwell. plan. "Marsh Neck"; sd. son dying without issue, to 3 daus. equally. Also land in Calvert Co. and "Town Neck" (pt. of dwell. plan. ———) in lieu of legacy from his grandmother Mrs. **Martha Dansey,** shd. he not accept, then to 3 daus. afsd. equally.
" **Elizabeth Shelley,** personalty out of debt due from her husband ———.
" wife and 4 child., residue of personal estate equally.
Overseers: Jeremiah Sheredine and Phillip Key; the latter to act as ex. shd. wife die during minority of child., and until they are of age to receive what is herein or by testator's mother devised to them.
Test: Grace Clelan, Magdalen Tomlinson, Richard Deaver (Deavour), Thomas Truman Greenfeild, Ellis Slater.
19, 127.

Stanford, John, planter, Dorchester Co.,
17th April, 1725;
6th April, 1727.

To eldest son **John** and hrs., 43 A. "Benjamin's Mass" and "Stanford's Addition," and pt. of "London," adj.; wife **Elizabeth** to have use of sd. lands during minority of son

John; he dying without issue, to his bro. and sisters surviving; and personalty.
To dau. **Elizabeth** and hrs., pt. of "London" (for desc. see will); and personalty.
" son **William** and hrs., pt. of "London"; and personalty.
" dau. **Margaret** and hrs., "Stanfords Perventur," adj. "London"; she dying without issue, to her sister **Elizabeth** and hrs.; shd. both die, to their 2 bros. equally; and personalty.
" wife **Elizabeth**, extx., use of afsd. lands and residue of personal estate; shd. she marry, her dower only.
Test: Alexander Strahon, John Marchant, John Ford (Foord), William Stanford, Charles Stanford. 19, 132.

Johnson, Henry (nunc.), Dorchester Co.,
12th May, 1727.

Ex.: Mr. Thomas Stewart.
Test: Richard Webster, Abraham Woodall. (Mrs. Grace Woollford and Anthony Lamb also present.) 19, 135.

Polk, Robert, planter, Dorchester Co., 21st Feb., 1725; 10th May, 1727.
To son **Thomas** and hrs., "Venture"; wife ——— to have use of same during her widowhood; and personalty.
" son **Robert** and hrs., "Hazard"; and personalty; to be free at age of 14.
" bro. **Joseph** and hrs., pt. of "Forlorn Hope" surveyed for Augustin Stanford; "Ballehack," nr. hd. of Pidgeon House Ck.
" 5 daus. ———, residue of personal estate, wife's ——— thirds being first deducted. Daus. **Grace** and **Mary** to be free at their mother's marriage, otherwise at age of 16.
Test: William Polk, Daniel Harrison, Robert Polk. 19, 136.

Parker, Richard, joyner, Talbot Co., 17th Nov., 1726; 25th Nov., 1726.

(Otherways of Citty of Philadelphia.)
To James Horney, of Talbot Co., personalty, some of which in poss. of Sarah Higgs, of sd. co.
Test: Robert Goldsborough, Jr., Rebecca Hopkins, Robert Jones. 19, 139.

Bowdle, Thomas, planter, Talbot Co., 31st Oct., 1726;
30th Nov., 1726.

    To 2 sons **Joseph** and **Thomas,** unborn child, and wife **Mary,** personal estate equally; sons afsd. to live with wife until 18 yrs. of age.

    Exs.: Wife **Mary** and son **Joseph.**

    Test: Wm. White, John Feston (Feaston), John Carr.
                                                   19, 140.

Lowe, John, Talbot Co.,
                26th day, 11th mo. (Jan.), 1726;
                8th March, 1726.

    To son **John** and hrs., 110 A. of "Graften's Mannour," bet. hd. of Grates Ck. and Wm. Lambden's, Jr.; also tract at hd. of Muddy Cove (for desc. see will).

    " daus. **Mary** and **Elizabeth,** personalty.

    " son **Thomas** and hrs., dwell. plan. ———, being pt. of "Graften's Mannour"; "Piney Neck"; and personalty.

    " 4 child. afsd., residue of personal estate.

    Exs.: Son **John** and dau. **Mary,** who are empowered to pay to the meeters at the Bay Side £3.

    Test: John Kemp (Kimp), William Kemp (Kimp), William Lamdin, Jr., Thomas Smith.   19, 141.

Copeland, Samuel, Prince George's Co.,
                27th Jan., 1726;
                23rd Feb., 1726-7.

    To wife **Barbary,** ⅓ of personal estate, at her decease to 2 only child. ———.

    " only dau. **Cathrine,** ⅓ of real and personal estate.

    Overseers: Edward Swann and Thomas Swan, Jr.

    Test: Thomas Swan (Swann), Edward Swan, Thomas Swan (Swann), Jr.

    Note: Testator des. himself as member of Church of England.   19, 144.

Dyer, Thomas, marriner, Cecil Co.,
                15th Jan., 1726;
                23rd March, 1726-7.

    To Joseph Brascup, personalty.

    Ex.: Philemon Lloyd, of Queen Anne's Co. Value of estate to be transmitted to wife **Elizabeth,** of Kenton, County Devon, Great Britain.

    Test: John Lloyd, Timothy Carty, Thomas Randolph.
                                                  19, 147.

Carpenter, John, Queen Anne's Co., 6th Nov., 1721; 4th April, 1727.
To son William and hrs., entire estate, real and personal; sd. son dying during minority, to pass to son John, ex., and hrs.
Test: Augustin Thompson, Sarah Thompson, James Horsley.
19, 148.

Connor, Nathaniel, planter, Queen Anne's Co., 29th Sept. 1726; 27th March, 1727.
To granddau. Mary Brown, personal estate; sd. estate to be in charge of wife Sarah, extx., during her widowhood, at her marriage to care of son-in-law Mathew Brown or Letitia, his wife, until granddau. afsd. comes to age of 16 or marries.
Test: Nicholas Swormsted (Swarmstedt), John Osborn.
19, 150.

Harrison, Capt. Joseph, Charles Co., 24th Dec., 1726; 5th May, 1727.
To son **Richard** and hrs., 400 A. "Cow" or "Cool Spring," 300 A. "Richard's Pleasure" and "Holy Spring."
" son **Joseph** and hrs., 427 A. "Amsterdam," 300 A. "Urlinda" ("Verlinda") and 200 A. "Carpenter's Square."
" dau. **Tabathia** and hrs., "Daniel's Quarter" bou. of John Allen, 400 A. "Land's Lane" at Maryland Point.
" wife ———, 300 A. dwell. plan. "Delahayes Chance," 150 A. "Minges Chance," "Woodberries Hope," during her life; at her decease to unborn child.
" godson **Hezekiah** and hrs. (son of Richard and Hester Harrison), 150 A. of "Christian Milford," bou. of John Pilbert.
Sons **Richard** and **Joseph,** dau. **Tabathia** and wife ——— each to pay annually to son **William** 500 lbs. tob. for his maintenance.
Exs.: Wife ———, William Stone, Sr., Thomas Mathews.
Test: Rev. William Maconchie, Richard Harrison, Thomas Wright.
Codicil: 24th Dec., 1726. Exs. empowered to sell 150 A. at Pamunkie, bou. of Wm. Stone, and 88 A. "Harrison's Plain" for benefit of estate.
To bro. **Thomas,** use of plantation whereon mother ——— now lives during his life.
" sons **Richard** and **Joseph** and dau. **Tabitha,** personalty.
" wife ———, residue of personalty.

Exs. and test. same as in above will.
Note: 5th May, 1727. **Virlinda**, relict of afsd. Joseph Harrison, accepts will. 19, 151.

Goodrick, George, planter, Portobacco Parrish, Charles Co.,   27th March, 1727; 15th May, 1727.

To dau. **Christian Butts**, a half crown.
" son **Aron**, dwell. plan. ——— and personalty; to care of son **William** until age of 20.
" sons **Benjamin** and **Robert** and dau. **Ann**, personalty.
" 5 child., viz. **William, Benjamin, Robert, Aron** and **Ann**, residue of estate.
Exs.: 3 eldest sons, **William, Benjamin** and **Robert**.
Test: John Jones, Thos. Reeves, Susannah Heyden.
     19, 155.

Sheredine, Jeremiah, Calvert Co.,   28th Dec., 1726; 2nd May, 1727.

To wife **Martha**, extx., 1 moiety of personal estate and entire real estate during life; at her marriage or death to dau. **Elizabeth** and hrs., to whom is bequeathed residue of personal estate.
Overseer: Benjamin Mackall, gent.
Test: Frans. Hutchins, Ellis Slater, John Booth.   19, 156.

Roland, Robert, Calvert Co.,   8th March, 1726; 6th April, 1726-7.

To **Elizabeth Mackinnys**, extx. (desc. as residing in testator's house), entire estate, except legacies to **Joseph** and **Ann Mackinnys** at legal age.
Test: Sarah Rose.   19, 159.

Barkus, George, Kent Co.,   23rd Feb., 1726; 25th March, 1727.

To wife **Elizabeth**, sons **William, James** and **George**, dau. **Elizabeth**, wife of **Daniel Boulton**; daus. **Hannah, Mary** and **Rebecca**, Charles Baker, William, son of William Clark and Rachell his wife, personalty.
" child. ———, residue of estate; 2 youngest sons to be free at 18.
Exs.: Son **William** and **Daniel Boulton**.
Test: John Newell, John West, Peter Drovine.   19, 160.

Okane (Ocane), John, planter, St. Mary's Co.,
            12th March, 1726-7;
            27th April, 1727.

 To wife **Elizabeth,** ⅓ of 100 A. dwell. plan. ——— during life.
 " mother **Elizabeth Willis,** remaining ⅔ during life.
 " sister **Nappler Mills,** 100 A. afsd. at decease of wife and mother.
 Ex.: Father-in-law **Thomas Scott.**
 Test: John Hayle, John Mills, Jane Reeves.   19, 162.

Ferguison, Alexander,   29th May, 1727;
            6th June, 1727.

 To William Shaw, ex., care of son **James** during minority.
 " wife **Kathrine** and son afsd., entire estate.
 Test: John Daffan, John Green, Robert Salmond.   19, 164.

Ross, Robert, Dorchester Co.,   2nd Jan., 1726-7;
            20th May, 1727.

 To Ann Chapman and John (son of Thomas Brown), personalty.
 " 2 child. **Charles** and **Mary,** entire estate at discretion of Thomas Smith and Thomas Cannon; to be in charge of mother ——— after decease of wife ———. Son to be free at 18, dau. at 16.
 Wife ———, extx.; at her decease bro. **James** to act.
 Test: Thomas Brown, Wm. Bradly, James Hickman.
                   19, 165.

Smith, John, Dorchester Co.,   6th April, 1727;
            20th May, 1727.

 To eldest son **John,** plan. ———.
 " bro. **Thomas,** all silver and gold, to apply same to purchase of land for 2 sons **William** and **Levin;** to see that sons are educated.
 " 2 eldest sons **John** and **William,** personalty.
 Wife **Anne,** extx.
 Test: Mathew Young, Thomas Hickman, Thomas Brown.
                   19, 167.

Howell, Mordecai, shipwright, Cecil Co.,
2nd April, 1727;
28th April, 1727.

To sister **Mary Davis,** personalty.
" bro. **William,** ex., residue of estate.
Test: Sarah Baker, Nathanl. Chapman, John Copson.
19, 168.

Engels (Engls, Inglish), Margrat, Cecil Co.,
10th March, 1727;
24th March, 1726.

To Hugh Wattson, ex., care of estate for benefit of child.
(unnamed); to have charge of child. until of age at 18,
girl at 16 yrs.
Test: John Wright and Hannah Wright.
Note: Hugh Wattson afsd. certified that design of testatrix
was to enable him to discharge his bonds as her security
for admin. of estate of her dec'd husband **Thomas Inglish.**
19, 169.

Piles, Richard, Prince George's Co., 10th April, 1727;
24th April, 1727.

To bro. **Leonard,** ex., interest in estate of father ———,
dec'd, and personalty.
Test: Robert Oram, Jane Oram, Francis Meo, Jno. Carroll.
19, 171.

Piles, Francis, Sr., Prince George's Co., 23rd May, 1726;
24th April, 1727.

To sons **James, John** and **Francis,** daus. **Elizabeth, Anne**
and **Jane,** personalty.
" son **Richard** and hrs., 77 A. "Cockolds Pint," nr. mouth
of w. branch of Patoxon R.; he dying without issue, to
son **Leonard** and hrs.; son **Leonard** dying without issue,
to dau. **Elizabeth** and hrs.
" son **Leonard** and hrs., 150 A. dwell. plan. "Come Unto
Him"; he dying without issue, to dau. **Jane** and hrs. Shd.
dau. **Jane** be left destitute at death of her husband,
Robert Orome, she is to have 40 A. out of sd. tract.
" sons **Leonard,** ex., and **Richard,** residue of personal
estate.
Test: John Deacon (Deakens), William Ridgely, John
Blackwood. 19, 172.

Mackeny, Alexander, Calvert Co., 27th Feb., 1727; 11th May, 1727.

To son **John** and bro.-in-law **James Currant**, personalty.
" wife **Sarah**, extx., ½ residue of estate.
" 2 child. **John** and **Elizabeth**, remaining half. Son **John** and his estate to care of Luke Smith; to have 4 yrs. schooling, and receive estate at age of 19. Jeremiah Currant to have charge of dau. Elizabeth and her estate until of age at 16.
Test: Stephen Spratt, James Burn. 19, 173.

Dangerman, Christopher, Calvert Co., 1st Feb., 1726-7; 11th May, 1727.

To dau. **Rennis Renard Dangerman** and hrs., 80 A. of "Charles' Gift," bou. of Mathew Dorman; and personalty.
" dau. **Elizabeth** and hrs., 114 A. "Taylor's Joy," bou. of Henry Easterling; and personalty.
" dau. **Sufeer (Suferr) Renard Dangerman**, personalty.
" wife **Elizabeth**, extx., dwell. plan. ——— during life; at her decease to dau. Sufeer afsd.; ¼ of residue of personal estate, remaining ¾ to 3 daus. afsd.
Test: Charles Clagett (Clagatt), Robt. High, James Humes.
19, 175.

Busie, Charles, Sr., planter, Calvert Co., 9th April, 1727; 17th June, 1727.

To wife **Dinah**, extx., entire estate during life; except tract ——— other side of Thomas Smith's mill branch to be sold and proceeds divided bet. wife **Dinah** and son **Paul**.
" 2 sons **Samuel** and **Daniel**, residue of real estate at decease of wife; shd. either son die without issue, survivor to inherit portion of dec'd. Son **Daniel** free at 18, shd. wife be dead; son **Samuel** free when crop is finished.
" 5 youngest child., viz. **Samuel, Daniel, Elizabeth, Vilinder** and **Clare**, residue of estate at decease of wife.
" 4 eldest child. **Charles, Susannah Benson, Mary Simpson** and **Sarah** each 1s.
Test: John Norris, Jr., John William, Clare Norris.
19, 177.

Hillen, John, Baltimore Co., 19th March, 1726; 22nd April, 1727.

To son **Solomon**, ex., and hrs., entire estate; wife **Mary** to have use of dwell. plan. ——— during life; shd. son **Solomon** die without issue or during minority, estate to pass as follows:

To godson Daniel Sheredine and hrs., "Shoomakers Hall."
" goddau. Elizabeth Harrett and hrs., 51 A. "Addition to Shoomakers Hall."
" bro.-in-law Thomas Hines and hrs., dwell. plan. "Hazard" at decease of wife.
" 3 sons-in-law Walter, William and Watkins James, personal estate.
Test: Joseph Thurman, Thomas Biddeson, Henry Williamson, Henry Adams. 19, 179.

Randall, Hannah. widow, Baltimore Co.,
23rd Oct., 1726;
31st May, 1727.

To son Christopher, ex., and hrs., "Gutheridge Addition" and "Kinsey's Choyce"; also 100 A. of "Green Spring Punch"; sd. son dying without issue, to dau. Urith and hrs.; sd. dau. dying without issue, to Roger and Aquila Randall (child. of bro.-in-law Christopher).
" dau. Urith and hrs., residue of "Green Spring Punch"; she dying without issue, to son Christopher; he dying without issue, to Roger and Aquila Randall afsd.; and personalty.
" dau.-in-law Cathrine and bro.-in-law Christopher, personalty.
" son Christopher and dau. Urith afsd., personal estate.
Test: William Hamilton, Charles Wells, Mary Arnold (Arnald). 19, 181.

Tubman, Richard, planter, Dorchester Co.,
6th April, 1719;
13th June, 1727.

To wife Elener, extx., ⅓ of estate, real and personal.
" son Richard and hrs., residue of estate; sd. son dying without issue, his portion to pass to wife absolutely. To receive estate at age of 21 yrs.
Overseers: John Griffin, George Staplefort, John Meekins.
Test: Elizabeth Geoftree, Sarah Rage, Hannah Griffin, John Meekins, George Staplefort, John Griffin. 19, 183.

Pagget (Pagett), Benjamin, Charles Co.,
15th April, 1727;
13th June, 1727.

To son William and hrs., "Wallnut Thicket."
" son Benjamin and hrs., "Paggets Purches."
" wife Mary, extx., personal estate.
Test: Henry Acton, Sr., Stephen Cawood, Jr., Henry Acton, Jr. 19, 184.

Doyne, Jesse, Charles Co., 14th Dec., 1726; 26th June, 1727.
To son **Robert** and hrs., 100 A., including dwell. plan. ———, being pt. of 200 A. formerly belonging to bro. **William,** dec'd.; 1,000 A. "Timnah Sarah" left by father **Joshua Doyne** bet. testator and bro. **Ethelbirth,** dec'd.; 200 A. ———, where John Morey lives.
" son **Joseph** and hrs., 100 A. of dwell. plan. ———, pt. where Charles Mattenby now lives; 200 A. (less 19 A. sold to Richard Hutson) formerly belonging to bro. **Dennis,** dec'd.; 550 A. "Rause" left by father to bro. **William,** dec'd.
" Peter Atwood, personalty bou. of Jno. Turrell.
" overseers Wm. Chandler and Charles Sanders, personalty.
Exs.: Sons **Robert** and **Joseph,** to be of age at 18 yrs.
Testator directs he be buried at Chappell Poynt.
Test: John Chalmers, John Hinkson, Francis Adams.

19, 185.

Addison, Thomas, Prince George's Co., 9th April, 1722; 28th June, 1727.
To son **John** and hrs., 1,430 A. "Saint Elizabeth," 512 A. "Discontent," 545 A. "Barnobie," 100 A. "Canton," 226 A. "Force," 340 A. "Gleening," 370 A. "Locust Thicket," 340 A. "Maddox Folly."
" son **Thomas** and hrs., 850 A. "Gisburough," 300 A. "Berry," 260 A. "Pasture," 336 A. "Prevention." A division line to be run through the following 5 tracts, viz. 393 A. "The Union," 209 A. "Barwick upon Tweed," 236 A. "Brother's Joynt Interest," 106 A. "Nonsuch" and 300 A. "North Britton"; pt. to the s.w. of sd. line to son **Thomas** and hrs.
" son **Henry** and hrs., 400 A. "Chichester," 289 A. "Addition," 428 A. of "Freindship," at the Eastern br., owned jointly with Mr. Abington; 400 A. of "Freindship," nr. the falls of Potomack; the pt. of the afsd. 5 tracts to n.e. of division line.
" son **Anthony** and hrs., 400 A. "Whitehaven," 400 A. "Philip and Jacob," 1,200 A. of "Freindship," nr. falls of Potomack.
" daus. **Rebecca Bowles** and **Eleanor Lowe,** £500 each and personalty; shd. afsd. legacy not be paid, the following tracts, viz. 850 A. "Batchelors Harbour," 345 A. "Swan Harbour" and 396 A. of "Strife" held with Mr. Parker at Mattawoman, with £200 to sd. daus. and their hrs. in lieu of £500 each.

30   MARYLAND CALENDAR OF WILLS

    To wife **Eleanor,** extx., ¼ of residue of personal estate; remaining ¾ to her 5 child., viz. **John, Thomas, Henry, Anthony** and **Ann.**
    Overseers: Benj. Tasker, James Bowles, George Noble; shd. wife marry a member of the Church of Rome, overseers to take child. and their estates, and to see that they are educated and brought up in faith of the Church of England. Sons to be of age at 19.
    Test: William Masters, Benjamin Osborne (Osbern), Dr. Patrick Hepburn, Peter Dent.
    Codicil: 2nd Nov., 1725. To sons **Thomas, Henry** and **Anthony** and their hrs., 2,300 A. "Addison's Choice," on Monocosey, equally.
    Test: Notley Rozer, George Noble, John Williams. 19, 188.

Jadwyn (Jadwin), Robert, planter, Talbot Co.,
                                26th Nov., 1726;
                                21st June, 1727.

    To wife **Elizabeth,** extx., use of dwell. plan. "Parkers Range" during life; at her decease to son **Joseph** and hrs.; he dying without issue, to son **Samuel;** ⅛ personal estate absolutely.
    " dau. **Martha,** 30 A. ——— on Tuckahow Ck.
    " child., viz. **Robert, Joseph, Hannah, Rachell, Samuel, Priscilla** and **Solomon,** residue of personal estate. Dau. **Hannah** to care of cousin **Jeremiah Jadwyn** until age of 17 (she being 14 next March). Sons **Samuel** and **Solomon** of age at 18.
    Test: Sarah Ouldfilde, Mary Jadwyns, Bartholemew Greenwood, John Maccdanill. 19, 193.

Dusey (Ducey), Daniel, Calvert Co.,   4th Nov., 1725;
                                    20th July, 1727.

    To dau. **Mary,** personalty.
    Son **Daniel,** ex. and residuary legatee.
    Test: Arthur Jones, Sutton Isaacke. 19, 194.

Jadwyn (Jadwin), Jeremiah, planter, Queen Anne's Co.,
                                  11th Dec., 1726;
                                10th June, 1727.

    To wife **Isabel,** extx., 1,500 lbs. tob. in hands of Cutbud Olifer, 500 lbs. yearly to be paid out of "Hamton" by son **Bartholemew** during life; 50 A. "Hamton's Addition" during life, at her decease to dau. **Ann Montigu** and hrs.; 100 A. "Cow Raing" during life, at her decease to son **Jeremiah** and hrs.; and personal estate during widowhood, shd. she marry, child. afsd. to have an equal share of personal estate. To keep John Parnif during his time of servitude.

To son **Jeremiah** and hrs., 50 A. "Timms Neglect." **Jeremiah Jadwin's** wife **Elizabeth** to keep Elizabeth Parnif during her time of servitude.
Test: Nathaniel Smith, William Hubanks, John Lane.
Note: 7th July, 1727. **Bartholemew Jadwin** assigns all interest in administration to Wm. Swift and Isabella his mother.
Test: Wm. Hemsley.
19, 195.

Falkoner (Falkner), John, Sr., planter, Queen Anne's Co., 20th March, 1726-7; 9th May, 1727.

To wife **Sarah,** extx., entire estate and charge of child. Sons **Thomas, James, William** and **Emanuel** of age at 21 yrs., dau. **Ann** at 18 or marriage.
Test: Michael Hussey, Richard Moore, Jane Manner.
19, 197.

Raily, Richard, St. Mary's Co., 25th April, 1727; 19th July, 1727.

To goddau. **Ann Dean,** bros. **William, John** and **Henry,** personalty.
Bro. **Michael,** ex. and residuary legatee.
Test: Nicholas Sewall, Jr., Owen Guyther, Sarah Guyther.
19, 199.

Head, Ann, St. Mary's Co., 22nd May, 1727; 7th June, 1727.

To husband **Adam,** "Provention" during life; at his decease to two daus. **Eliza. Herbert** and **Prissilla Head** equally. In case of death of sd. dau. without issue, sd. tract to **Eliza. Herbert** and hrs.
Test: Edward Cole, John Holland, Mary More. 19, 200.

Walstone (Wallstone), Thomas, Somerset Co., 7th Jan., 1726; 17th April, 1727.

To son **London,** dau. **Files Rilince,** sons **Boez** and **Joy,** 1s. each.
" wife **Mary,** extx., residue of estate during life; at her decease, real estate to sons **William** and **Thomas.**
Test: John Tull, Sr., John Tull, Jr., Joshua Tull. 19, 200.

King, John, Somerset Co., 22nd March, 1726;
1st May, 1727.

To son **Whittington** and hrs., Mannour plantation, 160 A. on n. side of Mr. Chambers branch, ½ of marsh at Haw Tree, 40 A. Cypress Swamp; and personalty.
" son **John** and hrs., 90 A. adj. mill, with water and bolting mill, residue of marsh at Haw Tree and Cypress Swamp; 100 A. of "Coney Warren"; 50 A. "Woolf Harbour"; 50 A. "Tick Ridge"; and personalty.
" daus. **Elenor** and **Elizabeth**, personalty; to be of age at death of testator.
" 4 child. afsd., residue of personal estate. Sons to be of age at 18.
Exs.: Son **Whittington** and friend Robt. **King**.
Test: Benjamin King, Richard Chambers, Thomas Brewton.
19, 201.

Davis, Sarah, Somerset Co., 13th April, 1727;
9th May, 1727.

To sister **Mary Wallstone**, personalty.
" **George**, son of George Bozman, residue of estate.
Test: Catherine Bozman, Sary Staples. 19, 204.

Polk, James, ship carpenter, Somerset Co.,
8th Nov., 1726;
11th May, 1727.

To son **David** and hrs., dwell. plan. ———; ½ of land and marsh on Pidgeon House (Ck.).
" sons **John** and **James** and their hrs., residue of last named tract.
Testator states that cousin **Charles** ——— is to make over a warrant for 100 A., ½ of which to son **David**, other half to sons **John** and **James**.
" son **Henry** and hrs., 100 A. of marsh on Samuel Jones' island.
" cousin **Edward Roberts**, 100 A. last named tract conditionally.
" sons **Henry, John** and **James** and their hrs., land bou. of Thomas Layfeild, and all bou. of Richd. Taten, both tracts lying on or nr. Black Walnut landing.
" daus. **Mary, Sarah, Margret, Elizabeth, Magdalen, Jane, Ann** and unborn child, £10 each.
" wife ———, use of dwell. plan. ——— during widowhood.

Exs.: Sons David, Henry and John.
Test: William Polk, John Pollet, Mary Pollet. 19, 205.

Morris, Jacob, planter, Somerset Co.,
19th Feb., 1726-7;
23rd May, 1727.

To 2 eldest sons **Mark** and **Jacob** and their hrs., real estate (for div. see will). Son **Mark** dying without issue, his portion to son **Jacob**, and **Jacob's** to next son **Joseph**; shd. **Jacob** die without issue, his pt. to his next bro., and so successively through sons—one not to inherit all land whilst two are alive. Sons **Mark** and **Jacob** to give their bros. ——— schooling, and shd. mother die, be free at 18 yrs.

" daus. **Temperance** and **Jemima**, personalty.
" wife ———, her thirds, residue to child. ———.

Exs.: Wife ——— and sons **Mark** and **Jacob**.
Test: Charles Hill, Joseph Nicholson, John Reddish.
19, 207.

Roach, John, Sr., Somerset Co., 26th Oct., 1725;
1st June, 1727.

To son **William** and hrs., 50 A. "Muling Feild"; 144 A. of "Partner's Desire" on Anomesex; 50 A. marsh "Hopkins' Destiny" conditionally.

" son **John** and hrs., 150 A. "Longtown"; 63 A. "Father's Care"; and 36 A. "Lott" adj. in little Anomesix Neck.

" son **Charles** and hrs., plan. where father ——— dwelt, being 150 A. "Make Peace" and 50 A. "Exchange"; interest of the marshes jointly with son **John**.

" son **Isaac** and hrs., 250 A. "Long Acre."

" son **Stephen** and hrs., 200 A. of "Sumerfeild"; 50 A. "Paul's Folly"; 88 A. "Veil of Misery."

" son-in-law **Benjamin Fooks** and **Catherine** his wife and their hrs., 120 A. of "Long Acre," where they now live.

" 4 youngest child., viz. **Charles, Isaac, Stephen** and dau. **Sabarah**, £10 each when of age.

" wife **Allis**, dwell. plan. ——— during life; at her decease to pass with 300 A. of "Sumerfeild" to son **William** and hrs.; and personalty; ⅓ of residue of estate absolutely.

" child., viz. **Catherine Fooks, William, John, Charles, Sarah Fooks, Isaac, Stephen** and **Sabarah**, remainder of personal estate.

Exs.: Wife **Ales** and son **William** to have charge of son **Isaac's** portion.
Test: John Disheroon, Michael Disheroon, Mary Disheroon, Rebecca Stevens. 19, 208.

Dickeson, Sommersett, Somerset Co.,
13th March, 1726-7;
20th June, 1727.

To dau. **Mary,** son **Charles,** daus. **Sarah** and **Direeter, Samuel Rigin, William Donaho, William Beachham,** personalty. Son **Charles** to be free at age of 18.
" wife **Hannah,** extx., residue of estate.
Test: George Howard, Samuell Dirikeson. 19, 211.

Peper, William, Somerset Co., 19th March, 1726-7;
20th June, 1727.

To son **William** and hrs., 100 A. dwell. plan. "Aqueteth"; he and his estate to care of dau. **Mary** until 18 yrs. of age.
" daus. **Mary** and **Elizabeth,** personalty.
" **John Blisard** and hrs., 100 A. "Pepers Delight."
" **Jacob** and **Cornelius Collick,** each one tract in Sommersett Co., they having patents for sd. lands.
" 3 child. afsd., residue of estate.
Exs.: Dau. **Mary** and **John Blissard.**
Test: George Howard, Samuell Dirikeson (Dirikson).
19, 213.

Richardson, Charles, planter, Allhallowes parish, Somerset Co., 25th April, 1720-1.
18th April, 1727.

To son **Charles** and hrs., pt. of dwell. plan. ——— (for desc. see will).
" son **James** and hrs., plantation where Allexander Stewart now lives, ——— (for desc. see will).
" son **William** and hrs., tract on Hills and County Road, excepting pt. already sold to John Brattan and Robt. Perry; shd. any of 3 sons afsd. die without issue, portion of son first dec'd to son **Samuel** and hrs. Afterwards succession to be as follows: If youngest die without issue, next youngest to succeed him; if eldest, the next younger of sd. 4 sons to succeed him. Testator directs shd. he die within 6 yrs. from date, his bro. **James Brattan** shall take charge of sd. 4 sons and their estates until of age at 18, excepting son **Charles** to be of age at 21 yrs.
" wife **Mary,** ⅓ personal estate; remaining ⅔ to sons, viz. **Robert, Charles, William, Samuel,** dau. **Tabitha** and youngest son **John.**
Exs.: Sons **Robert** and **Charles** and bro. **James Brattan.**
Test: Wm. Bratten, Quanten Bratten, Adam Spence, Jr., Charles Caves. 19, 215.

MARYLAND CALENDAR OF WILLS 35

Patrick, Roger, planter, Somerset Co., 13th April, 1727;
24th June, 1727.

To cousin **Mary,** personalty in poss. of Wm. Pourter and Thos. Collins.
" bro. **Mathew** and hrs., personalty; also acct. in hands of Chas. Holston; shd. sd. bro. bring any account against estate, sd. legacies to 3 cousins, viz. **Mary, Rodger** and **Daniel.**
" 3 cousins afsd. and **Joseph, David** and **Charles Bishop,** personalty.
" 2 cousins, viz. **Rodger** and **Daniel** afsd., residue of estate.

Ex.: Bro.-in-law **William Pourter.**

Test: William Whittington, Elizabeth Whittington, William Whittington, Jr. 19, 218.

Potter, Thomas, planter, Parish of Coventree, Somerset Co., 3rd March, 1726-7;
11th July, 1727.

To wife **Ann,** extx., use of entire estate during life; at her decease to son **Thomas** and hrs., "Moseses Lott," where he now lives; and dwell. plan. "Head of Mitchell's Choyce."
" son **Henry** and hrs., residue of real estate; and personalty.
" daus. **Alee** and **Catherine,** personalty.
" 4 youngest child. (unnamed), residue of personal estate.

Test: Michael Roach, John Conner (Connard), Geo. Gibbs.
19, 220.

Harris, Richard, planter, Wicocomoco R., Somerset Co.,
9th Jan., 1727;
19th July, 1727.

To wife **Jean,** entire estate during life, she to deliver immediately certain personalty to dau. **Temperance.** Acct. with Madam Betty Gale to be settled.
" eldest son **George** and hrs., real estate at decease of wife.

Test: Rev. Mr. Alexander Adams, William Harris, Thomas Howard, George Gibsone.

Codicil: To all child. (unnamed), personal estate equally at decease of wife. Date and test. same. 19, 222.

Rozer, Notley, Prince George's Co., 6th April, 1727; 5th Aug., 1727.

    Estate to be kept in hands of wife **Elizabeth,** extx., until debts are paid, especially debts to John Hyde & Co., mchts. in London.
    To son **Henry** and hrs., dwell. plan. "Admirathoree" ("Admariothoria").
    " dau. **Ann** and hrs., "Dunnington Manor."
    " all child. (including unborn child), residue of estate.
    Test: Henry Darnall, John Whetenhall, Daniel Wattz.
    Codicil: Testator having purposed to raise £2,000 by a lottery for payment of debts, authorizes Thos. Addison and Charles Diggs to carry out the same.
    Test: Henry Darnall, Henry Whetenhall, John Whetenhall.
    19, 224.

Elliot, William, Prince George's Co., 2nd Aug., 1727; 19th Aug., 1727.

    To wife **Mary,** extx., and hrs., entire estate, real and personal.
    Test: Walter Bayne, Thomas Phillips, Richard Blew.
    19, 227.

Demall, John, Prince George's Co., 8th April, 1725; 28th June, 1727.

    To wife **Mary,** extx., and hrs., dwell. plan. ―――― and personal estate both here and in Great Britain.
    Overseer: Cousin **Robert Pottenger.**
    Test: Brock Mockbie, Thomas Wood, Robert Pottenger.
    19, 228.

Nicholson, Charles, Somerset Co., 13th Nov., 1726; 16th Aug., 1727.

    To son **James,** 100 A. surveyed by Southy Whittington, adj. Wolf Pit Swamp.
    " wife **Elizabeth,** dwell. plan. ―――― during life, to revert to son **Mathias;** he dying without issue, to hr. at law.
    " sons **John** and **Joseph,** "Popular Ridge"; shd. either die without issue, portion of dec'd to survivor. Sons **Mathias** and **Joseph** to care of wife until 18 yrs. of age.
    " daus. **Sarah** (of age at 16) and **Mary,** personalty.

Exs.: Wife and son **John.**
Test: Edmond Hough, John Beavans, Joseph Houlston.
Note: 16th Aug., 1727. Elizabeth Nicholson assigns rights of admin. to **John Nicholson.** Test: David Wilson.
19, 229.

Wade, Richard, Charles Co., 7th Aug., 1727; 18th Sept., 1727.

To eldest son Zachariah and hrs., "Lynn" (Lim); "Lynn's Inlargement"; "Douglas Adventure" and "Douglas' Addition"; and personalty after his mother's decease.
" son **Robert** and hrs., "Wade's Adventor," Prince George's Co., and personalty after his mother's decease.
" daus. **Mary Manning** and **Ginnitt Godfrey,** personalty after decease of their mother-in-law.
" daus. **Elizabeth Speeak** and **Theodoshea Speeak** (after their mother's decease), personalty.
Exs.: Sons **Zachariah** and **Robert.**
Test: William Williams, Barbara Barnes, Robert Ferrall (Farrell).
Note: 10th Oct., 1727. **Mary Wade,** widow, renounces above will. 19, 232.

Walker, Thomas, St. Mary's Co., 10th June, 1727; 2nd Aug., 1727.

To son **Thomas** and hrs., plan. ——— at e. side of hd. of St. Clements Bay, where John Brown lives.
" Michael Thompson, interest in lease of 49 A. ———.
" dau. **Susanna** and hrs., plan. ———, where Thos. Howard lives.
" son **Joseph** and hrs., plan. ———, where Jno. Winifrett lives; 40 A. leased land; and residue of real estate; shd. sons and daus. die without issue, portion of dec'd to dau. **Heneretter Clark** and survivors.
" wife **Mary,** extx., ⅓ personal estate, residue to 4 child. equally; shd. wife die, son-in-law **James Clark** to act as ex. Sons to be educated and of age at 21 yrs.
Test: Richard Melton, John Johnson, Edward Clark.
19, 234.

Bullen, Joseph, carpenter, Talbot Co.,
16th Jan., 1721;
5th July, 1727.

To Thomas (son of John Turner), personalty.
" wife Mary, 100 A. "Turner's Hazard" during life; shd. a child be born, to pass to sd. child and hrs., otherwise to Nathan Dobson and hrs.; residue of personal estate.

Exs.: Wife and William Turner.

Test: Aaron Parratt, Tho. Pratt, Joshua Clarke, Edward Turner. 19, 237.

Willson, John, Tuckhow, Queen Anne's Co.,
10th April, 1725;
19th Aug., 1727.

To wife Mary during life, 100 A. "Sawer's Addition"; 100 A. of "Branfield" with plantation whereon Johamas Denosia lived.
" son John and hrs., 100 A. "Sayers Addition"; 150 A. of "Branfeild."
" son Nathan and hrs., 200 A. of "Branfeild."
" dau. Jemima and hrs., 150 A. residue of "Branfeild."
" son Phenies and hrs., 400 A. "Willson's Chance," 100 A. "Lan's Chance," both on White Marsh branch, Dorchester Co.; and personalty.
" daus. **Deborah Dudley, Tamer Dunand** and **Mary Bages** and their hrs., 1,000 A. in the Colony of Salem, on Stowes Ck. or Gravell Run, West Jersey.
" 3 daus. **Dinah Pratt, Sarah** and **Susannah** and their hrs., "Gillford," Kent Co., on Delaware, in territories of Pensilvania, Bishops Br.
" dau. **Ester** and hrs., "Willson's Fancy," Kent Co., on Delaware, nr. Road to Sent Jons (Saint Johns), Pensilvania.

Wife Mary, extx., ½ personal estate; empowered to sell following tracts for benefit of estate: "Harton," bou. of Sqr. Bennett; dwell. plan. "Willson's Addition" and "Good Luck's Range" and "Nod," both near Old Town.

To seven child., viz. **Phineas, Sarah, Susannah, Ester, Nathan, Jemima** and **John,** each an equal share of residue of personal estate as they come of age.

Test: Joseph Clift, Wm. Driskill (Driskell), Wm. Gwynn, John Madden (Maden), John Todd. 19, 239.

Morris, Thomas, Kent Island, Queen Anne's Co.,
20th March, 1726-7;
7th Sept., 1727.
To wife **Mary,** extx., entire estate.
Test: Capt. Wm. Elliott, James Hill. 19, 242.

Holland, William, Baltimore Co., 16th June, 1721;
19th Sept., 1727.
To wife **Elizabeth,** extx., and hrs., entire estate, real and personal, excepting legacies to following:
" **William Andrew** (son of wife's sister **Sarah**), Ann Hackman, Thomas Durbin, Elizabeth Shaw (at age of 16), personalty.
Test: F. Whitehead, William Gallaway, Samuel Durbin, Elizabeth Joy. 19, 243.

Bateman, George, Sr., 16th Sept., 1727;
21st Oct., 1727.
To sons **George** and **Lawrence,** personalty.
" wife **Mary,** extx., ⅓ of estate, residue to all children —— equally.
Test: Raphael Neale, Samuel Simpson. 19, 245.

Neale (Neal), James, Sr., Wolleston Mannor, Charles
Co., 1st April, 1725;
11th Oct., 1727.
To eldest son **James, Jr.,** deed of "Woolleston Mannour" afsd. confirmed; and personalty.
" second son **Henry,** deed of 500 A. "Gills Land" confirmed; and personalty.
" son **Benjamin** and hrs., 500 A. leased to and known by names of Davies, Antho. Smith, Jno. Castles and Tho. Sparkes; sd. son dying without issue, to son **William** and hrs.; and personalty.
" son **William** and hrs., 500 A. leased to Cha. Rocks, Nat. Freeman and Thomas Marrish; and all land at Matta Woman bou. of Geo. Hinson; sd. son dying without issue or during minority, to son **Benj.** and hrs.; and personalty at age of 21.
" wife **Elizabeth** and hrs., interest in 340 A. lying at Upper Machoteck, Va., lately in poss. of Michaell Webb and Benja. Berryman; ½ personal estate.

To daus. **Mary Deaton,** formerly **Vanswerring, Mary Tawney,** formerly **Neale, Ann,** now wife of Mr. **Edward Cole,** and **Margaret,** personalty.
" dau. **Mildred,** £30 at age or marriage.
Exs.: Wife and sons **Benjamin** and **William** to divide residue of personal estate equally.
Test: Walter Story, Thos. Taney, Joseph Alvey.
Codicil: Son **William** and dau. **Mildred** to have no interest in bequests until they give bond to acquit themselves and hrs. of all interest in certain slaves once property of dau. **Elizabeth.** Date and tests same as above will.
19, 246.

Jenkins, Thomas, Charles Co.,   1st Nov., 1726; 31st Oct., 1727.

To son **Edward** and hrs., 160 A. where he now lives, being half of "Pyes Hardshift" bou. of Charles Pye.
" son **William** and hrs., residue of afsd. tract.
" son **George** and hrs., after decease of wife **Ann** 150 A. dwell. plan. "Lynsei" ("Lindsey"); and personalty; also ⅖ of personal estate, exclusive of wife's thirds.
" dau. **Ann Spaulding** and hrs., 100 A. "St. Thomas."
" **Peter Attwood,** granddau. **Sarah Simpson** and **Eliza. Winser,** personalty.
" sons and daus. (after decease of wife), viz. **Edward, William, Elizabeth Edlen** and **Ann Spaulding,** residue of personal estate, wife's thirds excepted.
" dau. **Mary Norris,** 5s.
Exs.: Wife **Ann** and son **George.**
Test: Will Chandler, Patrick Boyle, Marthy Waldy.
19, 251.

Stone, Thomas, Nanjemy Parrish, Charles Co.,   25th May, 1727; 7th Nov., 1727.

To son **David** and hrs., ½ dwell. plan. ——— and personalty.
" grandson **Gerrard Fowke,** personalty.
" wife **Katherine,** extx., ½ dwell. plan. ——— during life; at her decease, to son **David** and hrs., certain personalty absolutely and certain personalty during life to be divided among child. (unnamed). ½ personal estate absolutely, residue to two child. **David** and **Mary** equally.
Test: Rev. Wm. Maconchie, Henry Barnes, Verlinda Boughton.
19, 254.

Harris, John, St. Mary's Co.,   24th Sept., 1727;
3rd Oct., 1727.

To preist ———, 600 lbs. tob. in poss. of Md. Dorothy Smith.
" goddau. Mary Hickee at age or marriage, Wm. Carroll and Thomas Hutchinson, personalty.
Ex.: David Hickee.
Test: Wm. Spalding, John Langley, Thomas Hutchinson.
19, 256.

Jessep (Jessop), William, St. Mary's Co.,
30th Sept., 1726;
2nd Nov., 1727.

To bro. Richard Hopewell, Thomas Kerby, Sr., Cicilly Glyn, Charles King, Jr., personalty.
" child. of exs., residue of estate.
Exs.: Richard Hopewell, Sr., and Charles King.
Test: Thomas Tolley, Peter Cullason, Cecily Glen.
Codicil (nunc.): 30th Oct., 1727. To John Milburn, personalty.
Test: Henry Coram and Deborah, wife of Thos. Kerby.
19, 258.

Jacob, John, Sr., South R., A. A. Co.,   4th June, 1719;
1st Dec., 1726.

To son John and hrs., 100 A. ———, where he now lives, with ½ the orchard adj.
" sons Richard and Samuel and their hrs., residue of real estate in A. A. Co. at decease of their mother; and personal estate equally.
" sons Joseph and Benjamin and their hrs., 200 A. ———, Prince George's Co., now in their poss.
" daus. Elizabeth and Susannah, personalty at decease of their mother.
Ex.: Wife ———.
Test: Richd. Poole, Gillbird Pattison, Joseph Williams.
19, 260.

Hutton, John, A. A. Co.,   15th Nov., 1726;
17th Dec., 1726.

To wife Mary, extx., entire estate.
Test: William Dove, Elez Cowley, Thomas Cowley. 19, 263.

Brice, Sarah, widow, A. A. Co., 13th April, 1725; 30th Dec., 1726.

To dau. **Anne Denton** and hrs., 130 A. "Howard's Inheritance," Severn R., bou. from son **Wm. Worthington,** son-in-law **Nicholas Ridgley** and dau. **Sarah** his wife; £50 in full of her pt. of estate. Neither she nor son-in-law **Vachell Denton** to be charged for any sallery for what was pd. them on acct. of the sd. Anne's father's estate.

" dau. **Rachell,** £130 and personalty.

" son **Charles Worthington,** £300 and personalty.

" granddaus. **Sarah (R.), Rebecca (R.), Rachel (R.), Ruth (R.)** and **Anne Ridgley,** sons **John (W.), Thomas (W.)** and **William Worthington** and wives of sd. sons, sons-in-law **Nicho. Ridgley** and **Vachell Denton,** cousins **James Butcher** and **John Brice,** personalty.

" son **John Brice** and hrs., residue of real estate; and personalty.

" grandchild., viz. son **John Worthington's** child, son **Thos. Worthington's** child. and dau. **Sarah Ridgley's** child., residue of personal estate.

Son **John B.** and dau. **Rachel B.** to be pd. their portion of their father's estate according to bal. remaining in the commissary's office.

Exs.: Sons **Thomas W.** and **John B.**

Test: Cha. Hammond, Robert Jubb, Judith Danenlen.

Codicil: 13th March, 1725. To son **William Worthington** and son-in-law **Vachell Denton,** £30 each. To 2 grandchild. born to sons **John W.** and **Wm. W.** since making of above will an equal share in personal estate.

Test: Robert Jubb, Elizabeth Fleet, Judith Davelen.

19, 264.

Duhadway, Jacob, A. A. Co., 20th Feb., 1723-4; 14th Feb., 1726.

To 2 sons **Jacob** and **Edward** and their hrs., entire real estate.

" child. ———, certain personalty as expressed in will of father-in-law **Edward Parrish.**

" wife **Elizabeth,** extx., ⅓ personal estate, remaining ⅔ to all child. ———, including unborn child, equally.

Overseer: Joseph Galloway.

Test: John Galloway, John Steward, Joseph Galloway, Deborah Edwards.

19, 269.

Mariarte, Daniel, gent., A. A. Co., 18th Jan., 1724-5; 21st Feb., 1726.

To wife **Elinor,** 100 A. "Clarks Folly" (being s. end of "Darnells Groves," Prince George's Co., cont. 300 A.) during life, at her decease to sons **Ninian** and **Arden** equally.
" son **Ninian** and hrs., 100 A. at n. end of afsd. tract.
" son **Arden** and hrs., residue of afsd. tract; shd. either son die without issue, survivor to inherit portion of dec'd; shd. both die without issue, sd. land to 3 daus. **Elinor, Anne** and **Margarett** and their hrs. equally.
" 2 sons afsd., 88 A. "Piney Hedge," e. branch of Potomack.
" wife and 5 child. afsd., personal estate equally.

Exs.: Wife and son **Ninian.**
Test: Joseph Richardson, Sarah Richardson, Mary Powell, Ester Idle (?). 19, 270.

Anderson, John, A. A. Co., 20th Sept., 1725; 31st March, 1727.

To son **Thomas,** dau. **Hannah** and sons **William** and **Benjamin,** personalty.
" dau. **Eliza.,** use of certain personalty during life, at her decease to granddau. **Eliza. Powell** and hrs.

Wife **Eliza.** and son **William,** exs. and residuary legatees.
Test: Thomas Gimber, William MacDaniell (McDaniel), Saml. Battel. 19, 272.

Duhadway, Elizabeth, widow, A. A. Co., 25th day of 1st mo. (March), 1726-7; 17th April, 1727.

To youngest son **Thomas,** entire estate except legacies to following:
" 2 daus. **Mary** and **Margarett,** personalty; son **Thomas** and dau. **Margarett** to care of mother **Mary Parrish;** dau. **Mary** to care of Joseph Richardson and his wife **Rebecca.** Other 2 sons **Jacob** and **Edward** to care of Joseph Galloway, ex.

Test: Joseph Rabbling, Mary Maccubbin, Frances Sands.
19, 273.

Gills (Gyles), John, 20th Jan., 1727; 14th April, 1727.

To son Samuel and hrs., entire real estate; he dying without issue, sd. lands to 3 eldest daus., viz. Rachell, Rebecca and Elizabeth and their hrs. Daus. Rachell and Rebecca to dwell on sd. land until son afsd. is of age; and personalty.
" daus. Rachell, Rebecca, Elizabeth, Mary and Sarah, personalty.
" wife ———, ⅓ residue of personal estate.
Exs.: Wife ——— and eldest dau. Rachell.
Test: William Ford (Foard), John Chocke, Margarett Chocke, George Chocke. 19, 275.

Rawlings, John, planter, A. A. Co., 26th March, 1727; 1st May, 1727.

To 7 child. (unnamed), entire estate divided equally amongst them or the survivors as they arrive at legal age. Exs. to place child. as they think best. Rev. Mr. John Humphrys and Francis Peairpoint to have those they wish to take. Crop begun to be made and shipped to Mr. Jonathan Scarth, mercht., London, at discretion of exs.
Exs.: Richard Warfield and Thomas Worthington.
Test: Francis Peirpoint, Edwd. Gaither, Will. Andrews, Wm. Henwood. 19, 276.

Richardson, William, Somerset Co., 10th May, 1727; 31st July, 1727.

To son John and hrs., "Wilkshear"; and personalty.
" son Samuel and hrs., 300 A. left testator by Matthew Scarbrough, dec'd, at eastmost end of "Scarbroughs Castle"; and personalty.
" son David and hrs., dwell. plan. "Waymouth"; and personalty.
" dau. Annah, personalty, including horse known as her bro. William's (dec'd).
" wife Hannah, ⅓ personal estate absolutely, and use of ⅓ dwell. plan. during life.
" child., residue of personal estate, divided as follows: dau. Annah (at decease of testator), son John (at age of 18), daus. Eliza. and Tabitha (at age of 16), sons Samuel and David (at age of 21).
Exs.: Wife Hannah and son John.
Test: Nathanl. Hopkins, Sr., Dennis Hopkins, Thomas Newton. 19, 280.

Scott, William, Annomessex, Somerset Co.,
7th March, 1724-5;
16th Aug., 1727.

To eldest dau. **Deborah** and hrs., dwell. plan. ———; and personalty.
" youngest dau. **Eliza.** and hrs., plantation where father ——— lived; and personalty.
Exs.: Daus. afsd.
Overseers: Uncle **William Willson,** Thos. Addams and bro. **John.**
Test: Wm. Wilson, Randel Long, Joseph Eames. 19, 283.

Roberts, William, Somerset Co., 1st Jan., 1726-7;
16th Oct., 1727.

To George Martin, bro. **John,** Sarah Martin, bro. **Rensha,** sister **Rachl.,** personalty.
" wife **Elizabeth,** extx., real estate during widowhood, to pass to bro. **Thomas** and hrs.; he dying without issue, sd. lands to dau. ———; wife to share with child (unnamed) residue of personalty.
Test: Thomas Rensha (Rencher), Underwood Rensha (Rencher), George Martin. 19, 285.

Franklyn (Franklin), John, gent., All hallowes Parrish,
Somerset Co., 8th Feb., 1726-7;
24th Nov., 1727.

To Capt. Wm. Fassitt and hrs., ⅓ pt. of 500 A., according to patent in testator's name; and personalty.
" Mr. **Joseph** and hrs., ⅓ of 500 A. ———.
" Jonathan James and hrs., 50 A. ———.
" dau. **Mary Collins,** 200 A. ———, where she now lives, during life; to pass to her 4th son **Thomas Collins** on condition he lives with testator during his life, otherwise sd. land to fall to hrs. at law.
" **Franklin Fassitt** and granddau. **Elizabeth Fassitt,** personalty.
" dau. **Elizabeth Walton,** 1s., and to her child. (unnamed), 12 lbs. in country produce.
" son **Ebenezar,** ex., and hrs., 600 A. "The Exchange," 125 A. "Long Accor," 111 A. marsh; and residue personal estate.
Test: Benjamin Burton, Wm. Turvile, Edward Franklyn, Henry Turner. 19, 286.

Collings, Price, Parish of All hallows, Somerset Co.,
3rd Oct., 1727;
24th Nov., 1727.

To son **Solomon** and hrs., pt. of "Silver Street" and of "Cumberland" (for desc. see will); he dying without issue, to pass to son **Samuel** and hrs.; and personalty.

" son **Price** and hrs., residue of afsd. tracts; sd. son dying without issue, to pass to son **Samuel** and hrs.; and personalty.

" son **Samuel,** personalty.

" wife **Rebecca** and 3 sons afsd., residue of estate equally. Sons **Price** and **Samuel** to care of kinsman **Richard Chambers** until 18 yrs. of age.

Ex.: Abraham Smith.
Test: Ebenezar Crapper, John Williams, James Round.
19, 289.

Pritchard, Obadiah, carpenter, Baltimore Co.,
1st Oct., 1727;
9th Nov., 1727.

To sons **Samuel, Obadiah** and **James,** entire real estate, to make choice in order named.

" dau. **Sarah,** personalty at marriage.

" wife **Margret,** extx., dwell. plan. ——— during life; and ⅓ personal estate, resiude to child. ——— equally.

Test: Thomas Knight, John Boyce, John Clarke, Dorothy Cave. 19, 290.

Guy, David, carpenter, Baltimore Co., 5th Nov., 1727;
25th Nov., 1727.

To servant **John Lawrance** and **John Willmot,** Jr., personalty.

" **Ruth Willmot,** 150 A. taken up in A. A. Co., nr. Seagull branch; 50 A. bou.; a servant **James Relley;** and residue of estate, real and personal.

Ex.: Landlord John Willmot.
Test: Thos. Elton, George Walker, John Lawrance. 19, 292.

Smith, Thomas, Sr., Anderbys Ck., Great Choptank R., Talbot Co., 21st May, 1727;
22nd Nov., 1727.

To wife **Martha,** use of dwell. plan. ——— during life. Son **Peter** to settle on a pt. of "Lamberton's Addition" at age of 21 and to enjoy entire tract at decease of wife; sd. son dying without issue, to pass to sons **Thomas** and **John** and their hrs.

To son **Peter**, personalty.
" child. ———, personal estate equally at decease of wife.
Exs.: John Robinson, Threadhaven Ck.; William Harris, Anderbys Ck.; wife **Martha** and son **Peter** at age of 21 yrs.
Test: Thomas Greenhough, David Matthews, Francis Cook.
19, 293.

Harington (Harrington), John, planter, Talbot Co., 5th Sept., 1727; 22nd Nov., 1727.

To son **John** and hrs., "Hatton's Garden"; and personalty.
" dau. **Elizabeth** and hrs., "Crooked Wik," adj. afsd. tract; and personalty; shd. either child die without issue, survivor to inherit portion of dec'd; shd. both die without issue, estates to pass to sister-in-law **Elizabeth Hatton** and hrs.
" sister-in-law **Elizabeth Hatton** and bro. **Richard,** exs., personalty.
" 2 child. afsd., personal estate equally. Son **John** to care of bro. **Richard** until 19 yrs. of age; dau. **Elizabeth** to care of her aunt **Elizabeth Hatton** until 16 yrs. or marriage; sd. **Elizabeth Hatton** to have tuition and care of cousin **Sarey Coocklin** until 16 yrs. of age. Estate to be responsible for debt due orphans of Timothy Coocklin.
Test: Thomas Ashcraft, John Willes, Susannah Willes.
19, 295.

Forbes, Alexander, Queen Anne's Co., 5th Oct., 1726; 26th Nov., 1727.

To Col. Richard Tilghman and hrs., real estate on Kent Island.
" wife **Sarah,** extx., personal estate.
Test: Wm. Turbutt, James Earle, Jr., Walter Carmichall, Thomas Murphey. 19, 297.

Crapper, Nathaniel, Somerset Co., 2nd Oct., 1727; 13th Jan., 1727-8.

To bro. **Nehemiah,** ex., and hrs., testator's pt. of "Red Lane."
" bro. (unnamed) and sister **Sarah Davy,** personal estate equally. Uncles **Thomas Brereton** and **Richard Chambers** to bury testator as they see convenient.
Test: Thos. Brereton, Mary Brereton, Alex. Hall, Jr. (Eliz. Hall, Jr.). 19, 299.

Bowles, James, merchant, St. Mary's Co.,
13th June, 1727;
3rd Jan., 1727.

To dau. **Elinor** and hrs., "Half Pone" and all land in Scotch Neck where Robert Phillip, Daniel Gur, John Gibbins and Henry Tucker dwell.
" dau. **Mary** and hrs., land where Hector Macleane lived, adj. to John Reads; "Hogg Neck" up along the branch called Break Neck Hill to main road going to church; and land s. side of branch from where Owen Read lived, to hd. line bet. John Hall and Wm. Wilkinson.
" dau. **Jane** and hrs., residue of real estate in St. Mary's Co., viz. dwell. plan. ——— and "Mason's," over St. Thomas' Ck., where Doctr. Magill lives.
" wife **Rebecca,** extx., interest in ¼ of afsd. land during life; to share personal estate with 3 daus. afsd.; shd. another child be born, to have an equal pt. of estate; shd. a son be born, to inherit all real estate.
" uncle **George,** his debt and £20.
" poor relations in England or elsewhere, £50 to be divided by extx.
Test: Wm. Brogden, John Mitchell, Josias Jeffery, Daniel (David) Makgill (Makgilt), Edmund Plowden.   19, 300.

Hall, John, St. Mary's Co.,   29th Nov., 1727;
13th Feb., 1727-8.

To 2 sons **John** and **William,** real estate equally, they to purchase 50 A. for their bro. **Thomas.**
" wife ———, certain personalty above the ⅓ of estate for maintenance of her young child. ———.
" daus. **Elizabeth** and **Mary** and son **Thomas,** personalty.
Exs.: Wife ——— and son **John.**
Test: David Makgill, Grace Makgill.   19, 302.

Cuttance, Josias (nunc.), Charles Co., 13th Jan., 1727;
20th Jan., 1727.

To **John** (son of John Chandler), personalty.
" wife ———, residue of estate.
Test: Doct. Gustavus Brown, Capt. Barton Smoot.   19, 304.

Hanson, George, Kent Co.,   9th Oct., 1727;
30th Nov., 1727.

To son **William** and hrs., 150 A. dwell. plan. ———, being pt. of 525 A. bou. by father **Hance Hanson** of Ebenz.

Blakison; sd. son dying without issue, to pass to dau.
Christina and hrs.; she failing issue, to daus. Mary and
Martha and their hrs. in succession; sd. daus. dying
without issue, to nephew Gustavus (son of Fred. Hanson)
and hrs.; sd. nephew dying without issue, to next surviving child of bro. Fred.; and personalty formerly belonging to bro. William.
To wife Jane, ⅓ personal estate.
" dau. Martha, personalty, formerly her mother's (Sarah Hanson).
" dau. Mary, personalty left testator by Maj. Potts.
" dau. Christina, personalty.
" child. afsd., residue of personal estate. Son William to receive portion at age of 21 or 18 yrs. at discretion of his uncle Fred.; daus. at 16 or day of marriage.
Exs.: Wife Jane and bro. Frederick.
Test: Thomas Macdaniell, Robert Hurd, Sarah Young.
19, 304.

Alebone, Edward, planter, Kent Co., 13th Oct., 1725; 17th Nov., 1725.

To grandson John Davis and hrs., tract bou. of William Haywood and pt. of "Hilling's Adventure"; he dying without issue, to pass to grandson Robert Davis and hrs.
" grandson Robert Davis, 2s. 6d.; shd. both grandsons die without issue, afsd. lands to pass to son-in-law Roger Hailes and dau. Ann, his wife, and their hrs.
" grandson Edward Hailes and granddau. Jane Hailes, personalty at ages of 21 yrs.
" son-in-law Roger Hailes and dau. Ann, his wife, exs., residue of personal estate; and a life interest in dwell. plan. ——— and in "Alebone's Addition"; at their decease to pass to grandson Edward Hailes and hrs.
Test: John Gail, Sr., Thomas Midford, Bullvin Midford, Abraham Redgrave, Sr. 19, 307.

Edds (Eads), Henry, planter, Kent Co., 27th July, 1727; 7th Dec., 1727.

To wife Mary, extx., dwell. plan. ——— during life; and personal estate.
" sons James and Henry and their hrs., dwell. plan. ——— and lands at decease of wife.
" rest of child. (unnamed), 12d. each; shd. wife marry, sons to be free at 18 yrs.
Test: Nich. Smith, Charles Garfet, Anne Garfet. 19, 309.

Hincly, John, Cecil Co., 20th Nov., 1727;
16th Dec., 1727.

To John Buttrum, ex., entire estate.
Test: Thomas Simper, Peter Picott (Peiott). 19, 311.

Smith, Thomas, Dorchester Co., 20th Nov., 1727;
6th Dec., 1727.

To son-in-law **John Brown** and hrs., 50 A. "Richridge"; 87 A. "Popler Ridge"; 50 A. "Thomas Lott," Somerset Co.; and personalty.
" son-in-law **Thomas Brown** and hrs., "Thomas Lott"; and personalty.
" son-in-law **Charles Brown** and hrs., "John Lott"; 50 A. ———; 50 A. "Goodwell"; and personalty.
" son-in-law **James Brown** and hrs., 100 A. "Goulden Grove"; and personalty.
" bro. **Stephen** and hrs., 50 A. ———, warrant for which in poss. of James Hays; and personalty.
" **Robert Poalk** and hrs., 100 A. ———, on Ridge branch.
" godson **Peter Taylor,** "Cornoner," on e. fork Nanticoke R.; and personalty.
" **John** and **William Smith** (sons of bro. **John**), residue of "Laste."
" **Wm. Layton** and hrs., 1 A. ———.
" **Thos. Layton** and hrs., 50 A. ———.
" **Anne Hewes, Thomas Hyws, Mary Williams, Sarah Williams, John Ross, Parcill Ross, Sarah Ross,** personalty.
" wife **Rose,** extx., 80 A. dwell. plan. ——— during life, to pass to son-in-law **John Brown** and hrs.; residue of personal estate during life, at her decease to 3 sons-in-law, **John, James** and **Charles Brown,** equally. Son (sic) **Peter Taylor** to divide land bet. wife and 2 cousins (?) **John** and **William Smith.**
Test: Peter Taylor, Rich. Barton, John Brown, Sarah Ross.
19, 312.

Levinis (Levenis, Levenes), Rice, Dorchester Co.,
19th Nov., 1727;
4th Jan., 1727-8.

To dau. **Elizabeth,** at age of 15, personalty.
" 2 sons **Rice** and **Peter,** real estate divided equally at age of 21.
" wife **Elizabeth,** extx., personal estate.
Test: John Hackney, Peter Minner, John Sharp. 19, 315.

Clarke, John, planter, St. Mary's Co.,
20th Jan., 1727-8;
9th Feb., 1727-8.

To sister **Mary Compton,** Thomas (son of Luke Clarke, dec'd) at age of 21 yrs., Thomas Chaimberlin, John Curbe and Elizabeth Clarke (at age of 16), personalty.

" **Electious** (son of **Adam Clarke**), ½ of leased land "Chaptico Manner," other ½ to bro. **Benjamin** when they shall arrive at age of 21.

Bro. **Adam,** ex. and residuary legatee.

Test: John Johnson Sothoron, Richard Sothoron, Robert Parker. 19, 316.

Skinner, Thomas, Charles Co., 8th Oct., 1727; 19th Feb., 1727.

To wife **Constance,** her portion of estate; and personalty.
" son **Thomas** and hrs., 160 A. of "Milerne"; he dying without issue, to his 2 bros. **William** and **James** and their hrs.
" son **William** and hrs., 160 A. of "Doncaster" and "Aspinnall's Chance"; he dying without issue, to his 2 bros. **Thomas** and **James;** and personalty, to be for himself at 18 yrs.
" son **James** and hrs., 160 A. residue of 3 tracts afsd.; he dying without issue, to his 2 bros. **Thos.** and **William;** and personalty, to be for himself at 18 yrs.
" 3 sons afsd., ⅔ of personal estate equally.

Exs.: Wife and son **Thomas.**

Overseers: Coll. John Fendall and Capt. George Dent.

Test: Anthony Collings, Adam Clinkscales, Charles Mastin. 19, 318.

Crooke, James, Baltimore Co., 5th Oct., 1727; 26th Dec., 1727.

To dau. **Cloe** and hrs., "Bushey Neck" and "Hopewell."
" son **Charles** and hrs., lot No. 79 Wappon St. (now Prince George St.), Annapolis; ½ of lot No. 26 on upper end Prince George St., Annapolis (other pt. sold to Joshua George); "Trvdant," at mouth of Back R. After decease of wife, son **Charles** to care of Charles Calvert, Esq., until age of 21; dau. **Cloe** to care of Thomas Jopson and his wife Susannah until age of 16.

Test: Will Buckner, Luke Raven, Jr., Thomas Bedeson. 19, 321.

Taylor, Lawrance, Baltimore Co., 6th Nov., 1727;
5th March, 1727.

To 2 sons **James** and **Abraham** and their hrs., 200 A. dwell. plan. "Good Speed." Either son dying without issue, survivor to inherit portion of dec'd; shd. both sons die without issue, sd. lands to dau. **Sara** and hrs. Sons to receive estates at age of 19.

" sons afsd. and dau. **Sara,** cattle branded with their marks.

" wife **Agnes,** extx., ⅓ of personal estate; residue to child. afsd. equally.

Test: Richard Haskins, William Cook, John Burton, John Clark. 19, 323.

King, Elizabeth, widow, Talbot Co., 17th Oct., 1726;
26th Dec., 1727.

To grandchild. (unnamed), £5 each.

" granddau. **Elizabeth Hopkins,** sister **Sarah** ———, personalty.

" 4 child. (unnamed), residue of estate.

Ex.: Son **Phillip.**

Test: William Moore, Robert Richalls, Elizabeth Moore.
19, 325.

Purit, William, Talbot Co., 15th Jan., 1727;
7th Feb., 1727.

To grandsons **James Jones** and **William Springar,** eldest dau. **Alice Jones** and dau. **Elizabeth,** grandson **Lewis Jones** and granddau. **Mary Springar,** personalty.

" 2 daus. afsd., extx., residue of personal estate.

Test: John Parr, Rebecca White. 19, 327.

Alford, Matthias, Dorchester Co., 30th Dec., 1727;
6th Feb., 1727-8.

To youngest son **Matthias, Jr.,** and son **James,** personalty; residue of estate (wife's thirds deducted) to 4 sons, viz. **Matthias, Sr., Robert, John** and **William** equally.

" son **Thomas,** 2s.

Exs.: Wife **Mary,** sons **Matthias, Sr.,** and **Robert.**

Test: Jno. Elliot, William Chipley, Ambrose Alford, Joseph Stack. 19, 329.

Turner, John, Dorchester Co., 12th Jan., 1727-8;
13th Feb., 1727-8.

To Timothy Carsy and hrs., 100 A. dwell. plan. "Bachelder's Folly," now "Dubelfork"; sd. Casey to pay James Sawell £5.
Test: Charles Nutter, Jr., Richard Layton, Mary Middalton.
19, 330.

Hurley, Roger, Sr., planter, Dorchester Co.,
1st Jan., 1727;
20th Feb., 1727-8.

To grandchild **Ann,** personalty.
" wife **Mary,** ½ dwell. plan. ——— and ½ "Gollaways" during life; at her decease to son **Derbey** and hrs.; and personalty.
" son **Derbey (Darbey)** and male hrs., ½ dwell. plan. ———, ½ "Gollaways"; and personalty.
" **John Hurly** and hrs., "Thompson's Lott."
" son **Roger** and hrs., "End of All Strife," "Pass Watter"; and personalty; residue of estate to all child. equally.
Exs.: Wife **Mary** and son **Derbey.**
Test: Patrick Quatermus, Isaiah Quatermus, John Carraway.
19th Feb., 1727-8, widow claims her thirds. 19, 332.

Hubbart, Charles, carpenter, Dorchester Co.,
31st Dec., 1727;
13th March, 1727.

To sister **Mary** and hrs., 50 A. "Vinson's Chance," 50 A. "Hubbart's Addition"; she dying without issue, to pass to **Daniel Hubbart** and hrs.; and personalty.
Bro. **Daniel** ex. and residuary legatee.
Test: Thomas Brannock, Sr., Charles Wheeler, John Brannock, Jr., Thomas Brannock, Jr. 19, 334.

Garrett, Amos, merchant, Annapolis, A. A. Co.,
4th Sept. 1714;
——— ——— ———.

(Son of **James** and **Sarah Garrett,** late of Saint Olives St., Southwark, England.)
To child. (unnamed) of sister **Mary Woodward,** £600 divided equally; to be paid at age of 17 or day of marriage.
" sister **Eliz. Ginn,** £600.

To mother **Sarah Garrett**, int. on £1,000 during her life; at her decease int. to be pd. to sister **Eliz.** afsd. or to her child.; shd. she leave none, to child. of sister **Mary** afsd.

" bro.-in-law **Henry Woodward** (husband of sister **Mary**), £300.

" cousin **Henry Facer** and **Elizabeth**, his wife (dau. of **Seth Garrett**), £100 and 1 A. lot No. 8, Annapolis, bou. of widow Mary Slimeedar and since known as the "Hospital House," where a free school is kept.

" kinsman **Thomas Facer**, shoemaker, of A. A. Co. (bro. to **Henry Facer** afsd. hatmaker), £100, sum of his indebtedness; and 1 A. lot No. 82, Annapolis, now in poss. of widow Elinor Chinton, adj. on John Baldwin's lot.

" cousin **James**, of St. Olives, Southwark, hatmaker (son of **Seth Garrett**), and his male hrs., £100, lots Nos. 17 and 15, Annapolis; the one next the water in poss. of Wm. M———, the other in poss. of Edwd. Smith, formerly ——— of Charles Kibburne.

" to kinswoman **Martha Eltington** (aunt of **James Garrett** afsd.), £100; and to her and her male hrs., lot No. 21, Annapolis, bou. of Robt. Quarry, now in poss. of Evan Jones.

" kinsman **James** (son of **Thomas** and **Martha Facer**, late of Rugby, Gr. Britain), £100; and to him and his male hrs., lot No. 31, Annapolis, bou. of Alex. Dehinayassa, now in poss. of Sarah Hickcock and William Brimer.

" niece **Elizabeth** (dau. of **Henry** and **Mary Woodward** afsd.), £300; and to her and her male hrs., 300 A. "Middleneck," "Middleneck Quarter" (150 A. thereof to be conveyed to Hezekiah Haynes on his payment of £60), both sd. tracts being in Cecil Co.; 400 A. "Gillingham," 200 A. "Davis' Pasture," 250 A. "Kendalls Delight," 400 A. "The Enlargement"; the 2 preceding tracts being Patuxent Plantation, the afsd. 4 tracts being in Baltimore Co.

" niece **Mary Woodward**, £300; and to her and her male hrs., 254 A. "Dryars Inheritance," 226 A. of "Littleton," 100 A. "Robin's Camp," 110 A. of "Canon's Delight," 260 A. of "Land of Goshen," 226 A. "Part of Littleton"; sd. 6 tracts in Baltimore Co.

" nephew **William Woodward**, £400; and to him and his male hrs., 300 A. "Hall's Palace," Baltimore Co.; 100 A., 150 A. and 250 A. of "Part of Sewell's Increase," 50 A. "Chilton," 50 A. "The Addition"; 5 tracts afsd. in A. A. Co. Lots Nos. 33 and 34, Annapolis, now in poss. of James Crooke and others.

To niece **Hannah Woodward**, £300; and to her and her male hrs., 580 A. "Maiden Fancy," Prince George's Co.; 150 A. "Great Brushy Neck," 60 A. "Sumerlands Lott," 30 A. "Woodcock's Nest," 70 A. "Clark's Purchase," 384 A. "Range"; 5 tracts afsd. in A. A. Co.

" nephew **Amos Woodward**, £500; and to him and his male hrs., 100 A. "Part of Roper Gray," also "Gentile Craft," 250 A. "Swan Neck," 25 A. "The Addition," 187 A. "Grime's Enlargement," 100 A. "Grime's Stone," 40 A. "Bruton's Hope"; afsd. 6 tracts being in A. A. Co. Lots Nos. 42 and 43 in poss. of Mary Newell, Thomas Andrews and John Freeman.

" nephew **Garrett Woodward**, £500; and to him and his male hrs., 114 A. "Part of Huckleberry Forrest," 262 A. "Hiccory Ridge," 101 A. "Timber Neck," 51 A. "Charles Hills," 120 A. "Todd's Range"; 5 tracts afsd. being in A. A. Co., 200 A., "Majors Choyce," Baltimore Co. The 2 last named tracts to be made over to Sarah Norwood by exs. in case sd. Sarah indemnifies estate for all costs, etc., in admin. of her late husband Samuel Norwood's estate, and delivers a bond signed with her by testator delivered to Benjamin Fordham and Cornelius Howard. Lots Nos. 46 and 104, Annapolis; one being next the market house and in poss. of Ann Noads, No. 104, and the other in poss. of Richard Evans.

" mother **Sarah Garrett** during her life, 13 tracts, viz. 80 A. "Medcalf Chance," 70 A. "Medcalf's Mount," 110½ A. "Honest Man's Lott," 150 A. of "Howard and Porters Range," 26½ A. of "Herreford," 100 A. "Mill Land," 210 A. of "Norwood's Fancy," 200 A. of "Providence," 50 A. of "Soloman (Salmon's) Hills," 19 A. of "Grey Sands," 120 A. of "Canaan," 110 A. "Sturton's Rest," 300 A. of "Millford and Taylors Lott"; afsd. tracts in A. A. Co. Lots No. 45, 61, 62 and 63, Annapolis, including warehouses, house on the hill, "corn house," brick dwelling-house, boathouse, etc. Afsd. tracts, lots, etc., to pass at decease of mother to sister **Elizabeth Ginn** during her life, at her decease to her surviving child.; sd. sister dying without issue, to sister **Mary** and hrs.

" vestry of St. Ann's Church, Annapolis, for maintenance of minister, who is to hold service or read a sermon in the new dwelling-house on plan. bou. of Samuel Dorsey and John Pettycoat, 14 tracts, viz. 225 A. of "Wyatts Ridge," 165 A. "Clark's Enlargement," 100 A. "Residue of Clark's Enlargement," 150 A. "Howard's Interest,"

160 A. pt. of "Upper Taunton," 100 A. of "Burnt Wood," 50 A. "Dorsey's Addition," 50 A. of "Venings Inheritance," 40 A. "Ridgley's Beginning," 80 A. "Howard's Mount," 150 A. "Woodyard," 100 A. "Bare Ridge," 114 A. pt. of "Upper Taunton," 50 A. "Burnt Wood Common"; afsd. tracts being in A. A. Co.; shd. there not be a sermon preached or read for 4 consecutive Sundays in the afsd. house or some other house on pt. of "Wyatt's Ridge" (being 225 A. where Robt. Hewell is overseer), afsd. 14 tracts to pass to mother **Sarah Garrett**, and at her death to sister **Elizabeth Ginn**; also to vestry as afsd. library of Divinity Books.

To mother **Sarah**, bro. and sister **Woodward** and their child., and to sister **Elizabeth Ginn**, £100 for mourning.

Extxs.: Mother and sisters **Mary** and **Elizabeth**.

Overseer: Bro.-in-law **Henry Woodward**.

Test: None given.

Note: Testator directs that he be buried near the new house at the plantation where Robert Hewett lives as overseer; gives most minute directions as to his funeral, tombstone, etc., and instructs his exs. to purchase 1,000 prs. of deerskin gloves to be distributed among his customers, and 1,000 books (such as 200 Bibles and Prayer-books, 100 Taylor's "Holy Living and Dying," "Golden Grace" and "Guide to the Penitent"); sd. books to be distributed by exs. 19, 335.

Elliot, Mary, Prince George's Co., 14th Nov., 1727; 5th March, 1727-8.

To son **Edward Broner**, 1s.

" grandsons **Edward**, **William**, **Thomas** and **John Broner** (sons of son **Edward** afsd.), granddaus. **Elizabeth** and **Abigall Broner** (daus. of son **Edward** afsd.), personalty.

" **Henry Broner** (son of **Wm. Broner**, dec'd) and hrs., 50 A. of "Hunter's Kindness"; and personalty at age of 21; he dying without issue, sd. 50 A. to pass to son **John Broner** and hrs.

Son **John** afsd., ex. and residuary legatee.

Test: Jno. Abengton, Robt. Wade, Sr., Thomas Phillips, Richard Blew. 19, 353.

Hoy, Paul, Prince George's Co., 4th Jan., 1727-8; 20th Feb., 1727.

To eldest son **James** and hrs., pt. of dwell. plan. "Twifor"; and personalty.

To son Dorset and hrs., ½ of "Twifor," bou. of William
Pounce; and personalty.
" son Isaac and hrs., residue of tract bequeathed son
Dorset; and personalty.
" daus. Mary, Margrett (at age of 16), Anne and Martha,
personalty.
" child., residue of estate.
Exs.: Wife ——— and son James. Shd. wife ——— marry,
sons Dorset and Isaac to receive estate at age of 18.
Test: Thomas Dorsett, Jno. Wighte (White), William
Harris.   19, 355.

Pearson, Robert, Prince George's Co.,
          5th Feb., 1727-8;
          5th March, 1727-8.

To William Taylor and his sister Elizabeth, personalty.
Henry Massy, ex. and residuary legatee.
Test: Rev. John Frasor, Lewin Jones.   19, 358.

Page, Ralph, Kent Co.,   30th May, 1727;
          19th March, 1727-8.

To son Ralph, ex., and hrs., dwell. plan. ———, 150 A.
"Page's Purchase," 100 A. "Edwin's Affront," 100 A.
"Edwin's Addition," pt. of "Hazzard" and "Middle
Branch"; sd. son dying without issue, tracts afsd. to
revert to dau. Mary and hrs.; she dying without issue,
to bro.-in-law John Tharp and hrs.
" dau. Mary and hrs., residue of "Middle Branch" bou. of
William Dean, residue of "Hazzard"; sd. dau. dying without issue, to revert to son Ralph and hrs.; he dying
without issue, to John Tharp afsd. and hrs.
" son Ralph and dau. Mary, personal estate equally. Dau.
of age at 16 or marriage.
Test: Thos. Ringgold, James Ringgold, Samuel Tovey,
Priddocks Blackiston.   19, 359.

Pearce, Daniel, Kent Co., 20th June, 1726;
          4th Jan., 1727.

To wife Mary, dwell. plan. ——— with half the lands adj.,
viz. "Verona," "Slip," "Chance" and pt. of "Friendship,"
during life; at her decease to be divided bet. son Andrew
and dau. Sarah; division to be made by James Smyth
and Arthur Miller, Sr.
" dau. Sarah, Arthur, son of Arthur Miller, Sr., and Sarah,
wife of Arthur Miller, personalty.

To son **Andrew** and hrs., 40 A. adj. "Tibbott" given by father ———, dec'd, to sd. son; 200 A. "New Holland," bou. of Wm. Burrar; and personalty lent to Isaac Caulk.
" son-in-law **Thos. Hynson** and **Isabell**, his wife, and their hrs., 200 A. "Castle Carey," at hd. of Island Ck., bou. of Wm. Chivens, 200 A. "Friendship," 400 A. "New Munster," Elk R., Cecil Co.; sd. **Thos.** and **Isabel** dying without issue, sd. lands to revert to son **Andrew** and hrs.
" wife and 3 child., viz. **Isabell, Andrew** and **Sarah**, personal estate equally, allowance to be made for portion already given dau. **Isabell**. Rents from 2 plantations to be used for schooling of son **Andrew** and dau. **Sarah**.
Exs.: Son **Andrew** and **Arthur Miller, Sr.**
Test: Jno. Johnson, Edwd. Fottrell, John Evans. 19, 361.

Reed, Robert, planter, Dorchester Co., 18th Sept., 1727; 2nd Oct., 1727.

To cousin **Wm. Reed**, 1s.
" son-in-law **Samuel Lawson**, ex., and 3 daus.-in-law, viz. **Ann Tucker, Elizabeth Roe** and **Margrett Brachaw**, residue of estate.
Test: Redman Fallen, Ann Jones, Mary Green. 19, 365.

Semmes, James, Charles Co., 5th Aug., 1727; 12th March, 1727-8.

To **William Chandler** and hrs., title in "Burnt Quarter" at Portobacco bou. of sd. Chandler.
" son **Marmaduke** and hrs., "Chandler's Invention" to path leading from Andrew Simpton's quarter to John Ashman's; and personalty.
" wife **Mary**, dwell. plan. ——— during life and residue of "Chandler's Invention"; at her decease to sons **Joseph Milburn Semmes** and **Ignatius** and their hrs.
" 4 daus. **Mary, Ann, Juliana** and **Susannah**, personalty; shd. any of them die during minority, their legacy to pass to sons **Joseph** and **Ignatius** afsd.
" son **James**, personalty.
" child. afsd., residue of estate.
Exs.: Wife and son **Marmaduke**.
Test: Rev. Peter Attwood, Juliana Simpton, Robert Hanson.
Codicil: 7th Aug., 1727. To son **James**, money in Liverpool which Garard Slye is empowered to recover, not to exceed £70; overplus, if any, to wife **Mary**, who is also given ⅓ stock and household stuff.
Test: James Nicoll, Robert Hanson. 19, 366.

Shacklet, Michael, Charles Co., 14th March, 1727; 6th April, 1728.

To dau. **Tabitha,** entire estate. Bro.-in-law and sister, **Thomas Taylor** and **Tabitha,** his wife, to have charge of her and her estate until of age at 16.
Test: Joseph Chunn, Thomas Taylor, Tabitha Taylor.
19, 369.

Thompson, William Mathews (nunc.), Charles Co., 24th March, 1727-8; 25th March, 1728.

To wife ———— and child ————, entire estate; shd. child die before he comes to age of 18, wife ———— to receive his portion.
Test: William Thompson, Ignatius Doyne. 19, 370.

Ball, Benjamin, Kent Island, Queen Anne's Co., 25th Dec., 1727; 29th Jan., 1727-8.

To bro.-in-law **Nathan Richeson (Richison)** and hrs., 100 A. of "Clover fields," originally poss. by Wm. Dawlan.
" wife **Elizabeth,** extx., residue of "Clover fields" during widowhood; shd. she marry, ½ of sd. tract during life; also to wife **Elizabeth** and her hrs., 60 A. "Barren Ridge Addition," Cox Ck.; tract on sd. ck. near plan. of Richard Blunt; and entire personal estate.
" nephews **Daniel** and **Benjamin Richeson** and their hrs., residue of "Clover fields"; shd. either die without issue, portion of dec'd to survivor; shd. both die without issue, to nephews **John Leads** and **John Ball** and their hrs.
" the Quakers, dwelling for their meeting house.
" Rhoda, wife of John Brown, personalty.
Test: Walter Carmichall, William Willson, John Sallaway.
19, 371.

Collier, Mathew, Queen Anne's Co., 24th Jan., 1726-7; 21st March, 1727-8.

To wife **Alice,** dwell. plan. ———— during life; at her decease to William Bishop and hrs.
" bro. **William,** baker, living in Rosemary Lane nr. little Tower Hill, London, £20.
" 2 sisters **Alice** and **Mary,** in Great Britain, £100 each.
" father **Mathew Collier,** £80; shd. he be dec'd, to be pd. to nearest relative.

To son-in-law **John Austin** and dau.-in-law **Margrett Watson**, James Pruet and William Pennington, their debts.
" **Philemon**, son of Christopher Phillips, and **Mary**, dau. of Leon Watson, personalty.
Exs.: Wife and Christopher Phillips.
Test: William Rakes, Savil Jones, Richard Jones.
Codicil: 9th March, 1727-8. Reversion of dwell. plan. ——— to William Bishop, nullafied; wife to dispose of same.
Test: Christopher Winkinson, Andrew Prewett, Margrett Carter. 19,373.

Dormott (Dirmott), Charles, planter, Cecil Co.,
19th Oct., 1727;
16th Nov., 1727.

To wife **Sarah**, extx., entire estate during life; at her decease to dau. **Rachell** and hrs., shd. she survive her mother; shd. they both die, to dau. **Lucia**, wife of **Robert Veazey**.
" dau. **Lucia Veazey** and her dau. **Mary Veazey**, personalty.
Test: Richard Garrett, John Storts, C. Whitley. 19,376.

Loyd (Loyde), Thomas, Prince George's Co. (member of the Church of England), 27th Feb., 1726-7;
28th March, 1728.

To son **Ben**, ex., and hrs., dwell. plan. ———; and personalty.
" son **John** and dau. **Sarah**, personalty.
" 3 child. afsd., residue of personal estate. Son **John** to be for himself at age of 18.
Overseers: James Pettey, Alex. Magruder, Sr.
Test: Alex. Magruder, Henry Buttler (Botcher), Margrett Harrison. 19,379.

Bramell, James, sawer, Prince George's Co.,
8th March, 1727;
27th March, 1728.

To wife **Mary**, extx., 150 A. dwell. plan. "The Refuse" and "Addition to the Golden Rod," with personal estate during life; at her decease to son **James** and dau. **Rebecca**; son **James** to have dwell. plan., dau. **Rebecca** other tract.
Test: Richard Lanham, Anthony Long, James Kendall.
27th March, 1728. **Mary Bramell** renounces as extx. Test: Thomas Lancaster, Robt. Bradly. 19,380.

Bowin, William, Somerset Co., 4th March, 1727-8;
20th March, 1727-8.

To son **Luke** and hrs., dwell. plan. ———.
" sons **Littleton** and **John** and their hrs., plantations where each lives; and personalty.
" son **George,** tract bet. plantation and son **John's.**
" daus. **Martha Purnell, Elizabeth Bredell** and **Anne Ballard,** and granddau. **Esibella Thompson,** personalty.
" 5 child., viz. **John, Luke, George, Joyce** and **Priscillia,** residue of estate. Son **George** and his estate to care of son **John** until of age at 18; shd. either dau. **Joyce** or dau. **Priscillia** die without issue, their portions to pass to sons **John** and **Luke;** 3 sons afsd. to have an equal privilege in marsh land at Saint Martins.

Exs.: Sons **John** and **Luke.**

Test: George Jones, Joseph Truitt, Ed. Round. 19, 382.

Mersey, Alexander, planter, 18th Feb., 1727-8;
20th March, 1727-8.

To son **William** and hrs., tract in Accomoke, nr. Pitca Ck., and 100 A. of the plantation where he now lives, running 40 yds. along the old Town Road; and personalty.
" **Johnson,** son of son **William** afsd., personalty.
" son **Alexander,** ex. and hrs., dwell. plan. ———, 80 or 90 A. in the forest by Josiah Bradley's; and personalty.
" dau. **Comfort** and hrs., tract where John Hinsey lives; and personalty.
" 3 youngest child., viz. **Alex., Esther** and **Comfort,** £6 for their schooling.

Test: Andrew Robertson, Peter Collier, Francis Hamlyn.
19, 385.

Dukes, Thomas, Sr., planter, Somerset Co.,
18th Feb., 1727-8;
20th March, 1727-8.

To son **Melven,** dwell. plan. "What You Will"; to be in care of Thomas Scott until 21 yrs. of age.
" wife **Mary,** extx., use of afsd. plan. during life; and personalty; care of son **John.**

Son **Robert** to care of Teague Donohaw until 21 yrs. of age; sons **William** and **Thomas** at age ———.

Test: Wm. Porter, Sarah Porter, Samuel Cooper. 19, 387.

Innes, Cornelius, Somerset Co., 11th Nov., 1727;
20th March, 1727-8.

To wife Mary, ⅓ of dwell. plan. —— during life; to share personal estate with all child. equally.
" son **Cornelius** and hrs., 200 A. of "Cannaday."
" son **John** and hrs., 200 A. of "Canoday."
" son **Samuel** and hrs., 315 A. "Fearon Hills."
Exs.: Wife **Mary** and son **Cornelius.**
Test: Abraham Smith, Isaac Brittingham, William Morris.
19, 389.

Tull, Sarah, relict of Thomas Tull, Somerset Co.,
26th Nov., 1727;
1st April, 1728.

To son **Thomas,** ex., personalty on condition that he cares for his two bros. **William** and **Isaac,** and his two youngest sisters **Esther** and **Grace** until of age; tract of land or marsh conveyed by Jno. Tull, son **Samuel** to have certain privileges therein.
" sons **William, Isaac** and **Samuel,** daus. **Sarah, Rachel, Esther** and **Grace,** personalty.
" dau. **Mary,** 1s.
Sons **William** and **Isaac** to care of Jeoffrey Long, to receive estates at age of 18.
Test: John Turpen (Turpin), Saml. Handy, Jno. Benson (Benston). 19, 390.

Plunkett, Richard, Somerset Co., 31st March, 1724;
2nd April, 1728.

To **Mathew** (son of George Benston and Rebecca, his wife) and hrs., 50 A. dwell. plan. —— at decease of wife.
" wife **Winnifritt,** extx., entire personal estate.
Test: James Strawbridge, James Pope, George Benston.
19, 393.

Taylor, Thomas, mcht., Talbot Co., —— ——, 1713;
31st Jan., 1727.

To nephew **John** and hrs., 100 A. "Hyer-Dier-Lloyd" bou. of John Bell, 1 house and lot in Cambridge; and personalty.
" son **Jonathan,** ex., and hrs., residue of estate in Great Britain or elsewhere.
Test: Thomas Alexander, Mary Armstrong (at date of probate Mary Hill), Theodorus Bonner. 19, 394.

Lurtey, Nicholas, innholder, Talbot Co.,
19th Feb., 1727-8;
11th March, 1727.

To daus. **Mary Dawson** and **Mary Skinner,** personalty.
" son-in-law **Richard Dawson,** John Bullen's note drawn on him on condition that he make over certain personalty to 2 grandsons **Ralph** and **Nicholas Dawson.**
" dau. **Elizabeth Pemberton** and hrs., dwelling house after decease of wife; and personalty.
" wife **Sarah,** ⅓ of personal estate.
" son **John,** ex., and hrs., "Bridges" and "Elstones Hazard," both on w. side Harrises Ck.; and residue of personal estate.
Test: Alexander Murdy, Elizabeth Stevens, Henry Deane.
19, 397.

Bullen, Margaret, widow, Talbot Co., 8th July, 1727;
16th April, 1728.

To son **Thomas,** ex., and hrs., entire estate.
Test: Ann Parremore, William Perrymore, John Hamilton (Hambleton), Jone Harris. 19, 400.

Robinson, Richard, Dorchester Co., 2nd Feb., 1727;
10th May, 1728.

To Thomas Barnett, 10 A. conditionally.
" son **Solomon** and hrs., residue of real estate in Dorchester Co. after decease of wife **Sarah**; and personalty.
" son **William** and hrs., real estate in Talbot Co. after decease of wife **Sarah.** Sons afsd. to have privileges of lands at age of 21.
" wife **Sarah,** extx., son **William** and dau. **Elinor,** personal estate equally.
Test: Robert Jones, Benony Frazer, Wm. Barker. 19, 401.

Watts (Wats), Grace, Dorchester Co.,

20th March, 1727-8.

To Job (eldest son of Richard Norman), real estate in Dorchester Co.
" sister **Naomy,** Sarah Griffin and Mary Griffin, personalty.
" Richard Norman, residue of estate.
Test: John Rex, Rebecca Nicholls, Philemon Lecompt.
19, 402.

Maxwell, James, gent., Baltimore Co., 4th Jan., 1727;
8th March, 1727.

    To younger son **James** and hrs., plan. on Watertons Ck., including plan. seated by elder son **James.**
    " son **Asahell** and hrs., land bou. of Moses Groom; 27 A. bou. of Robert Cuchin; "Major's Choice" at the land of Nodd.
    " dau. **Ann** and hrs., 500 A. "Yapp," at hd. of Sassafras.
    Test: Josias Middlemore, John Roberts, Thomas Hastwell, Robert Smart.
    Note: Above will not signed.   19, 403.

Redgrave, Abraham, Kent Co.,   15th Jan., 1727;
10th May, 1728.

    To son **Abraham** and dau. **Eliza. Gideons,** personalty.
    " wife **Martha,** sons **John, Isaac, Jacob, Joseph** and **William,** and dau. **Martha,** residue of estate. Sons **Isaac** and **Jacob** to be of age at 18. Portions of sons **Joseph** and **William** and of dau. **Martha** to be in poss. of their mother until of age.
    Exs.: Wife ——— and son **John.**
    Test: Isaac Perkins, William Reech, George Skirven.
    10th May, 1728. Widow claims her thirds.   19, 405.

Porter, Giles, Kent Co.,   9th May, 1720;
3rd May, 1728.

    To **Sarah Deet,** plan. where she lives during widowhood.
    " **George Wetherill,** personalty had of Thomas Thalkstone.
    " **James Hornbee, Mary Lamb, Wm. Brace** and **Oliver Palmer,** personalty.
    " sister **Sarah Jones** and hrs., entire real estate; she dying without issue, to pass to hr. at law.
    Ex.: Bro.-in-law **Grifin Jones.**
    Test: James Kelly, William Spearmint (Spearman), Francis Lamb.   19,407.

Plummer, Thomas, Prince George's Co.,
29th June, 1726;
26th June, 1728.

    To eldest son **Thomas,** 10s.
    " son **Samuel,** 20s.
    " son **James,** 5s.
    " sons **Philimon** and **Jerom,** personalty.

To 5 sons, viz. **George, John, Micajah, Yate** and **Abezar** and their hrs., 4 tracts, viz. "Seaman's Delight," pt. of "Swanson's Lott," "Dundee," "Part of Dundee," and interest in all lands in afsd. co. Sons to dispose of afsd. lands only to sd. 5 bros. or to their bro. **Jerom**; shd. any die without issue, survivors to divide portion of dec'd; shd. wife marry, 3 youngest sons to be of age at 16.

" daus. **Priscilla** and **Phebe**, 10s. each.

" wife **Elizabeth**, extx., residue of personal estate; shd. she die during minority of 3 youngest child., sons **John** and **Jerom** to take care of child. and their estates until of age.

Test: Thomas Stockett, Jr., Thomas Still, Thomas Waitt.

19, 409.

Corricke, Patrick, Charles Co., 10th Feb., 1727-8; 3rd May, 1728.

To dau. **Jone**, 5s.

" 2 sons **James** and **Patrick**, exs., residue of estate.

Test: Stephen Mankin, Hope Capshaw. 19, 411.

Cox, Samuel, St. Michael's Parish, Barbadoes, 10th April, 1724; 5th Feb., 1724-5.

To wife **Elizabeth** and hrs., entire estate; shd. wife die before testator, estate to pass to child. of 3 daus., viz. **Maud Beckles, Elizabeth Grame** and **Sarah Peers**, all of afsd. Island.

Exs.: Wife and sons-in-law Hon. **Thomas Beckles, George Grame** and **Henry Peers**.

Test: Mary Sharpe, Jos. Walker.

Note: Above will recorded at request of John Donelson, of Somerset Co., admin. 19, 413.

Coape, George, planter, Prince George's Co., 5th Aug., 1727; 12th July, 1728.

To dau. **Sarah Cooke**, extx., dwell. plan. ——— during life; at her decease to granddau. **Rachell Hill** and hrs.; and personalty.

" grandson-in-law **William Barnsbee**, grandson **William Cook** and granddau. **Rachell Hill**, personalty.

Test: Benj. Lawrance, Richard Harrison, William Smith.

Note: Above will proved at request of William Barnsbee, bro.-in-law to Rachell Hill. 19, 416.

Smith, James, planter, Queen Anne's Co.,
9th Jan., 1727;
7th May, 1728.

To sons **Joseph, James** and **Henry,** personalty.
" wife **Mabel,** extx., residue of estate; shd. wife marry, sons to be of age at 17.
Test: Sarah Herly, Sarah Bellitior (Belitier), Magdalen Williams. 19, 418.

Brown, Elizabeth, Queen Anne's Co.,
22nd Aug., 1727;
30th May, 1728.

To granddaus. **Rebecca Jackson** and **Mary Sadler,** personalty.
" son-in-law **James Sadler,** ex., personal estate.
Test: John Evans, Susannah Griffith. 19, 419.

Elsbery, Thomas, planter, Queen Anne's Co.,
22nd May, 1728;
7th May, 1728-9.

To wife **Margaret,** extx., 100 A. dwell. plan. ——— during life; at her decease to her son **Henry Burt;** and personal estate.
Test: Patrick Robertson, William Hadden. 19,420.

Boyer, John, planter, Cecil Co., 8th Feb., 1727-8;
11th May, 1728.

To eldest dau. **Elizabeth Thackery** and hrs., 50 A. of dwell. plan. ———, lying along main road leading from Elk R. to Elk R. Ferry at James Kinkeys.
" son **Peter,** ex., and hrs., residue of real estate.
" son **Peter** and 3 younger daus. **Hannah, John** (sic) and **Mary,** personal estate.
Overseer: Edward Johnson.
Test: John Numbers, Richard Lewis, John Lewis. 19, 422.

Harris, Thomas, Sr., planter, Prince George's Co.,
26th April, 1728;
25th June, 1728.

To wife **Rachell,** extx., tract ——— during life; at her decease to son **Samuel** and hrs.; sd. son dying without issue and in poss. of sd. tract, to pass to son **Benjamin** and hrs.; and ⅔ personal estate absolutely; residue to child. equally.
Test: William Daynes, James Tannehill, Thomas Goodman.
19, 424.

Hunter, William, Sr., Prince George's Co.,
6th May, 1728;
25th June, 1728.

To wife **Rebecca**, personal estate during widowhood; at her marriage or death to son **William** and dau. **Mary**, wife of **John Pile (Piles)**.
" grandson **Hunter Piles** and hrs., 150 A. "Huntersfield," residue to other 3 grandchild., viz. **William, John** and **Mary Piles** and their hrs. 1 A. of sd. tract where first wife (unnamed) and some child. are buried (and where testator directs that he be buried) not to be sold.
" grandson **Thomas Hunter**, 1s.
Exs.: Son **William** and Zechariah Wade.
Test: Philip Tennely, John Brawner, James Kendall.
19, 425.

Quinton, Walter, Dorchester Co., 25th March, 1727-8;
17th May, 1728.

To cousin **Edward Hambleton** and hrs., plan. —————— in Talbot Co., where William Carry now lives.
" cousin **Sarah Hambleton** and hrs., 500 A. "Robotham's Raing," Dorchester Co.
" Sisly Saxton, 50 A. "Bunhill Fields" during life; sd. Sisly dying without issue, to revert to donor; and personalty.
" goddau. Margaret Edwards and hrs., "Horsepond Ridge" and "Hambletons Marsh"; she dying without issue, sd. tracts to revert to **Edward Hambleton** and hrs.
" Margaret White and hrs., 130 A. "Neglect."
" Absolom (son of John and Sisly Saxton), Dennis Conway and William White, personalty.
" cousins **Edward, Sarah** and **Margaret Hambleton**, and Alis White, residue of personal estate after wife's —————— thirds are deducted.
Exs.: William and Margaret White and Sarah Hambleton.
Test: Anthony Rawlings, John Sexton, Charles Lowd (Lowde). 19, 427.

Daughity (Daugity), George, planter, Dorchester Co.,
19th March, 1728;
17th May, 1728.

To son **John** and hrs., 50 A. "Horse Ridge."
" son **James** and hrs., 100 A. of "Heron's Lott."
" 2 daus. **Jane** and **Herodias** and their hrs., 50 A. of "Heron's Lott."

To son **Absolom** and hrs., dwell. plan. "Venture."
" 2 daus. **Rebecca** and **Dorkus,** "Popler Land."
Wife **Amey,** extx.
Test: Anthony Rawlings, Jr., Edward Tatlock, Thomas
    Grenaway   19, 430.

Dyer, John, planter, Dorchester Co., 22nd Dec., 1727; 5th June, 1728.

To wife **Martha,** extx., personal estate absolutely and use of dwell. plan. ―――― during life; at her decease to pass as follows:
" 2 grandsons **Thomas** and **James** (sons of **Thomas Williams** and **Katherine,** his wife) and their hrs., 300 A. "Lemster."
Test: Benjamin Young, George Pouncey, William Williams.
                                                                     19, 433.

Phillips, Phillip, planter, Dorchester Co.,
14th April, 1728; 2nd July, 1728.

To dau. **Mary,** personalty.
" wife **Alice,** extx., personal estate during widowhood; to pass to 2 sons **Thomas** and **James.**
" son **Thomas** and hrs., "Phillips Adventure," at hd. of Millingtons Br., Black Water R.
" son **James** and hrs., pt. of "Phillips Adventure," at hd. of Millington's Br., running to Hobbody.
Test: John Ford, Mary Crayer (Cryer), John Ray. 19, 433.

Roberts, Robert, Sr., Calvert Co.,
29th day, 6th mo., 1727; 16th May, 1728.

To son **Richard,** ex., and hrs., dwell. plan. ――――.
" dau. **Elizabeth Parish** (having had a child's portion), 5s.
" 7 child., viz. **Richard, Isaac, Priscilla, Kinsey, Margrett, Jane** and **Patience,** residue of estate.
Overseers: Bros.-in-law **Kinsey** and **Isaac Johns.**
Test: James Malden, John Baker, Francis Stallings. 19, 435.

Dawkins, Bennet (Benet), Calvert Co.,
10th March, 1727;
29th June, 1728.

To sisters **Elizabeth** and **Penelope,** personalty.
" bro. **William,** ex., and hrs., rights in "Smith's Purchase," where mother ——— now lives, and residue of personal estate.
Test: Thomas Brickenden, Wm. Dawkins, Joseph Dawkins.
19, 436.

Kersey, John, Talbot Co., 11th Jan., 1727;
14th May, 1728.

To son **Francis** and hrs., "Welley" and "Sarah's Neck"; sd. son dying during minority or without issue, to pass to dau. **Mary** and hrs.; and personalty, including that belonging to estate of his mother ———.
" dau. **Mary** and hrs., personalty; she dying before age of 16 or without issue, to pass to son **Francis** and hrs.
" wife **Jane,** personalty; to share residue of estate with 2 child. afsd.
Exs.: Wife ——— and son **Francis.**
Overseer: John Leeds.
Test: John Wrightson, Gemelin Pratt, Thomas Jones.
19, 437.

Smith, John, planter, Talbot Co., 20th March, 1727-8;
15th May, 1728.

To wife **Elenor,** extx., "Lamberton" and "Lamberton's Addition" over Treadheaven until Robbenist Smith comes to age, toward paying debt to Esq. Bennett.
" boy Nathan Johnson, £5.
Overseer: George Robbins.
Test: Mary Nickson, Patrick Mullikin, Edward Lee. 19, 439.

Stevens, Charles, Talbot Co., 22nd July, 1726;
22nd May, 1728.

To son **Charles** and hrs., dwell. plan. ———, pt. of 100 A. "Planter's Delight," pt. of 100 A. "Newman's Lott," 100 A. "Noble's Chance," 75 A. "Steven's his Addition," ½ of 19 A. "Charles his Lott"; sd. son dying without issue, sd. lands to pass to 3 daus. **Mary, Elizabeth** and **Katherine** and their hrs.
" dau. **Mary** and hrs., ½ of "Providence," with 20 A. adj. on Tuckahoe Ck. (for desc. see will).

To dau. Katherine and hrs., 212 A. "Llewellins Ridge," e. side Tuckahoe Ck., bou. of Esq. Loyd.

" 4 child. afsd., personal estate. Daus. of age at 16, son Charles at 21 yrs. (latter to choose own guardian at age of 16).

" dau. Elizabeth and hrs., residue of "Providence."

Dau. Mary and Roger Clayland, exs. and guardians to children.

Test: James Barweek, John Pursell, Michaell Jeromes.

19, 440.

Price, Evan, Talbot Co., 14th May, 1728; 5th June, 1728.

To son William and hrs., real estate; he dying without issue, to pass to dau. Hester and hrs.; sd. dau. dying without issue, to pass to son and dau.-in-law Robert and Margaret Booker and their hrs.; shd. son William live to enjoy lands, he is to pay to dau. Hester 3,000 lbs. tob. at her marriage; shd. wife Ann die before son and dau. afsd. are of age, they are to be in care of son-in-law John Booker, ex. with wife Ann.

Test: Thomas Hopkins, Thomas Christian, John Ray.

19, 442.

Finley (Finly), Jane, Talbot Co., 3rd Aug., 1722; 17th Aug., 1725.

To Mary, wife of Jacob Orchard; Mary, dau. of Jacob Orchard; Elizabeth, wife of Henry Price; John Sweat and his son Vertue, personalty.

Exs.: William Clayton and John Sweat instructed to sell residue of estate and transmit money to sister Jugg Watson, living at Broughton, Yorkshire, England; shd. sd. sister be dead, then to her son Batholomew Watson.

Test: Dennis Bryon, Elizabeth Bryon, Catherine Wintersell.

19, 443.

Morgin, Mary, St. Mary's Co., 12th Nov., 1726; 1st June, 1728.

To daus. Elizabeth and Elender and son William, personalty; residue of estate to 4 child. equally; son William to be in care of Thomas Plumer until 18 yrs. of age.

Ex.: Son-in-law John Sikes.

Test: Robert Ford, Ann Medley, Mary Ford. 19, 445.

Turner, John, planter, Kent Co., 25th March, 1728; 17th May, 1728.

To wife **Mary**, extx., dwell. plan. "Suffolk," bou. of James Stapeley, during life; at her decease to son **Jonathan** and hrs.; and ⅓ personal estate.
" son **John**, personalty.
" son **Jonathan**, dau. **Ann** and son **Joseph**, residue of personal estate.
Test: Harmanus Schee, John Brooke, Mary Murphy, Jonathan Hopkins. 19, 446.

Brown, Robert, Kent Co., 26th Jan., 1726-7; 5th July, 1728.

To wife **Elizabeth**, extx., entire estate.
Test: Benjamin Jones, Samuel Rigaway, Thomas Gould, Sarah Rigaway. 19, 447.

Gostwick, Joseph, planter, Baltimore Co.,
3rd March, 1722; 14th June, 1728.

To wife **Elizabeth**, dwell. plan. ——— during life; at her decease to son **Nicholas**; to divide with sons **Nicholas** and **Thomas** personal estate equally.
" Edward Sweeton, personalty when free.
Test: Jonas Bowen, Isaac Sampson, Edward Cooke. 19, 448.

Garrett, Mary, Somerset Co., 13th March, 1727-8; 18th May, 1728.

To Groves Bordman and hrs., dwell. plan. ———.
" Winneford Wats, Bridgett Gilles, Sarah Bordman, Sr., and Elenner Bordman, personalty.
" child. (unnamed) of bro. **John Gilles**, residue of estate.
Ex.: Thomas Humphris.
Test: Thos. Collier, Edmun Collens, Sr., Edmun Collens, John Collens. 19, 450.

Acworth, Richard, Stepney Parrish, Somerset Co.,
21st March, 1727-8; 15th May, 1728.

To sons **Charles** and **Thomas**, exs., 500 A. "Acworth's Delight," 200 A. "Hog Quarter," 100 A. "Acworth's Choice," sd. tracts being on s. side Baren Ck., and 18 A. "Syprus Swamp," on Gravely Br.
" son **Richard** and hrs., 100 A. "Chance," s. side Baran Ck.; sd. land not to be sold without consent of 2 bros. afsd.

To 3 sons afsd., 200 A. "Marsh Point"; "Ridges," on s. side Nanticoke R.; and personalty.
Test: Temperance Acworth, John Weall, Elizabeth Acworth, Robert Givan. 19, 451.

Mumford, Thomas, gentleman, Somerset Co.,
4th Feb., 1727-8;
17th May, 1728.

To son **James**, ex., "Venem Green" ("Vernam Dean"); and personalty.
" son **William**, ex., pt. of "Showell's Addition," on Burch Br.; residue to son **Wricksam**.
" son **Charles**, pt. of "Mumford's Lott"; residue to son **Thomas**.
" sons afsd., 100 A. "Burnt Marsh"; not to sell portions except to one another.
" dau. **Jemima**, personalty; shd. any of 3 sons, viz. **Charles, Thomas** and **Wricksam (Ricksam)**, die without issue, next survivor to inherit.
" son **Solomon**, 1s.
Test: Andrew Robertson, Richard Murrey (Muney), James Muney. 19, 452.

Evans, David, schoolmaster, Somerset Co.,
11th Sept., 1725;
———— ————.

To Capt. John Jones, his wife Elizabeth, his sons Robert, William, George, Thomas, Mitchel and Benjamin Jones, his daus. Margaret, Eliz. and Eleanor Jones, personalty.
" the public schools of Somerset Co., and to the poor of Stepney and Somerset Parishes, residue of estate.
Exs.: Chief vestryman of each parish.
Test: None. 19, 455.

King, Upshur, Somerset Co., 3rd Jan., 1727-8;
26th June, 1728.

To eldest son **Arthur** and hrs., dwell. plan. "Ox Head" with land on n. side of Traiding Branch.
" son **Zerebel** and hrs., residue of afsd. tract on s. side of afsd. br.
" son **Planner** and hrs., "King's Chase," pt. of "Gullets Advisement," 50 A. on s. side of Traiding Branch.
" son **Jesse** and hrs., residue of "Gullet's Advisement," 100 A. "Indian Bones," both tracts on n. side of afsd. branch.

Wife ———, extx.
Test: John McCormick, Daniel Monrow, Elenor King.
19, 458.

Wale, Nathaniel, Somerset Co., 23rd March, 1727-8; 5th July, 1728.

To son **William** and hrs., dwell. plan. ——— (for desc. see will); sd. son dying without issue, to pass to son **Charles** and hrs.; and personalty.
" son **Charles** and hrs., residue of land in Senepuxton Neck; and personalty at age of 16.
" **William Walton, Sr.,** and hrs., 225 A. of "Cay's Folley," originally Mount Pleasant.
" sons **Nathaniel** and **Elias** and dau. **Rachel,** personalty.
" wife **Mary** and 5 child. afsd., residue of estate.
Exs.: Wife and son **William.**
Codicil: 24th March, 1727-8. Personalty to son **Charles,** 12 yrs. 6th January last; son **Nathaniel,** 8 yrs. 25th February last; son **Elias,** 5 yrs. 22nd November last, and dau. **Rachel,** 2 yrs. 14th April next.
Test: Rodah Crapper, Margaret Wale, Richard Holland, Nath. Crapper (Craper). 19, 459.

Fleming, Lodowick, Somerset Co., 20th Jan., 1727-8; 5th July, 1728.

To dau. **Leviner** and hrs., 300 A. dwell. plan. "Killglass," 250 A. "Sand Down," on Pocomock R.; sd. dau. dying without issue, tracts afsd. to wife **Massey** during life; at her decease 300 A. afsd. to kinsman **Lodwick Walles** and hrs., and the 250 A. afsd. to Lodwick Waring and hrs.
" Rev. Mr. Stevenson, personalty.
Wife **Massey,** extx.
Overseer: Thomas Wallace.
Test: Benjamin Burton, Thomas Wallace, Sarah Walton.
19, 462.

Franklyn (Franklin), Ebenezar, gentleman, Allhallows Parish, Somerset Co., 3rd Oct., 1727; 5th July, 1728.

To 2 sons **Edward** and **Peal** and their hrs., 600 A. "Exchange"; dwell. plan. to son **Edward,** and plan. where father Cornll. John Franklin lived to son **Peal.**
" 2 sons **William** and **Charles** and their hrs., 125 A. "Long Acre," in the woods at Coys Folly, and tract on the beach that belonged to father afsd.

To John (son of William Collings) and hrs., 200 A. where Wm. Mecoy lived, being pt. of 400 A. bou. of John Freeman.
" 6 child., viz. **Edward, William, Charles, Peale, Sarah** and **Mary**, residue of personal estate. Child. to be in charge of ex.; sons of age at 18, daus. at 16 yrs.
Ex.: Son **Edward**.
Test: Benjamin Burton, Nathaniel Wale, George Wilcox.
19, 464.

Hogg, James, planter, Somerset Co., 29th Jan., 1725; 5th July, 1728.

To eldest son **James** and hrs., "Showels' Addition," on e. side Church Branch; and personalty.
" son **John** and hrs., residue of afsd. tract on n. side of Church Branch.
" dau. **Catherine**, personalty, some of which des. as owned jointly with Edward Moore.
" son **Andrew**, 100 A. of land to be taken up and pd. for out of estate; and personalty at age of 16. Testator directs that sons shall learn to read and write; shd. any die during minority, portion of dec'd divided among survivors.
" wife **Sarah**, extx., residue of estate.
Test: Wm. Robinson, Jeanet Robinsone, Rachel Williams.
19, 466.

Stevenson, William, Sr., carpenter, Somerset Co., 14th June, 1725; 29th Jan., 1727-8; 5th July, 1728.

To wife ———, Moses Goodin and Rebecka O'Brian for the remainder of their time; he by indenture and she by judgment of Court at Divideing Creeke, Ju., 1721, judged to be 6 yrs old; and personalty.
" sons **William** and **John**, dau. **Margaret**, Samuel Brain, granddau. Mary Stevenson, grandson William Hall, Moses Goodan and Rebecka O'Brian, grandchild. Margaret Braban and Hugh Braban, personalty.
" dau. **Elizabeth**, 1s.
" wife ———, son **William** and dau. **Margaret**, residue of estate.
Exs.: Wife ——— and son **William**.
Test: Wm. Robinson, Robert Stevenson.
Note: Above will not signed.
19, 468.

Taylor, George, Somerset Co., 8th Nov., 1727; 21st Aug., 1728.

To son **Samuel** and hrs., dwell. plan. ———, 400 A. "Winchester"; and personalty.
" son **Mathias** and hrs., "Friend Good-will," at head of George's Ck.; and personalty.
" dau. **Comford,** personalty.
" wife **Comford,** extx., residue of personal estate. Sons afsd. of age at 18, dau. at 16. Son **Samuel** b. 9th April, 1719; son **Mathias** b. 12th June, 1725.
Test: Joseph Taylor, John Patey (Pattey), Walter Taylor.
19, 470.

Hudson, Robert, planter, Somerset Co., 4th Feb., 1727-8; 21st Aug., 1728.

To eldest dau. **Betty Holland Hudson** and 2nd dau. **Mary,** pt. of dwell. plan. "Joneses Adventure"; dwell. house to be in portion of dau. **Betty;** and personalty.
" 3rd dau. **Peggy,** portion of afsd. tract lying above the branch; shd. dau. **Mary** die without issue, her portion to pass to dau. **Peggy,** and pt. herein bequeathed to dau. **Peggy** to revert to eldest dau. **Betty;** shd. dau. **Betty** die without issue, her portion in afsd. tract to fall to youngest dau. **Peggy;** shd. dau. **Betty** recover 130 A. "None Such," she is to confirm sd. 130 A. to dau. **Peggy** or forfeit to dau. **Peggy** her division of "Joneses Adventure"; and personalty.
" wife **Margaret,** extx., use of certain personalty during widowhood; at her marriage or death to daus. afsd.; use of "Joneses Adventure" during minority of daus., and ⅓ pt. residue of estate; remaining ⅔ to child. when of age.
Overseers: Richard and David Hudson.
Test: John Hudson, Phenix Hall, John Donaldson (Donelson). 19, 472.

Burton (Burtton), Benjamin, Somerset Co., 17th March, 1728; 21st Aug., 1728.

To son **John** and hrs., 600 A. "Divell" and 86 A. "Burtton's Chance" adj., reserving to wife **Elizabeth** ⅓ of same during her life.
" each of daus. (unnamed), personalty at age.
" wife **Elizabeth,** extx., residue of estate.
Test: Henry Turner, Edward Franklyn, John Donelson.
19, 475.

Lingoe, William, Somerset Co., 24th Dec., 1727;
28th Aug., 1728.

To son **Daniel** and hrs., 100 A. of "New Holland," where he now lives.
" son **Jacob** and hrs., 100 A. of afsd. tract; and personalty.
" son **Richard** and hrs., 100 A. at w. end of afsd. tract, adj. to Thomas Carry's.
" son **John** and hrs., 150 A. of dwell. plan. "New Holland."
" sons **Annsly** and **William** and dau. **Rebeckah Taylor,** 1s. each.
." grandson **Robertson,** personalty.
" grandson **John,** son of **Nathaniel Lingoe,** 1 yr. schooling at age of 14.
" dau. **Ann Blockson,** personalty and right to live on plan. during widowhood.
" wife **Rachel,** extx., 150 A. of "New Holland," which may be sold for payment of debts; if not sold, to revert to 4 sons, viz. **Daniel, Jacob, Richard** and **John,** and their hrs.; and personalty.
Test: Ann Blockson, Robertson Lingoe, Moses Driskell.

19, 477.

Robinson, John, Sr., planter, Calvert Co.,
9th June, 1724;
5th Sept., 1728.

To son **John,** 1s.
" wife **Mary,** extx., residue of estate.
Test: Wm. Angell, Isaac Johns. 19, 479.

Rawlings, Anthony, Jr., Dorchester Co.,
17th May, 1728;
13th Aug., 1728.

To father ———, personalty had of John Newton and David Keron.
" sister **Mary,** personalty in lieu of some sold to John Mathewe.
" 2 cousins **Mary** and **Charles Daughity** and bro. **John,** personalty.
" sister **Margaret Hail,** extx., and hrs., 50 A. ———; and residue of personal estate.
Test: Richard Smith, Mathew Jarad, Thomas Harris.

19, 481.

Makeel (Mackell), Thomas, Dorchester Co.,
23rd April, 1725;
14th Aug., 1728.

To son **John** and hrs., "Hudson's Desire," "The Addition" and "Timber Point" on Little Choptank, Dorchester Co.; sd. son dying without issue, to pass to son **Thomas** and hrs.; and personalty.
" son **Thomas** and hrs., "Fishing Creek Point," "Cod Point" and "Charles Desire" on Little Choptank R.; sd. son dying without issue, to pass to son **John** and hrs.; and personalty; to receive estate at age of 18.
" daus. **Ann** and **Eliza.**, personalty and an equal share of personal estate.
Exs.: Wife **Clare** and son **John.**
Test: Gary Powell, Thomas Eccleston, Francis Giles.
19, 482.

White, Thomas, Dorchester Co., 22nd Sept., 1727;
3rd Sept., 1728.

To wife **Eliz.**, dwell. plan. ———, 50 A. of "Anderson's Neck" during life; at her decease to son **Ebenezer** and hrs.; ⅓ of personal estate, residue to child. **Eben., Thomas, Eliz., Mary** and **Ann** equally.
" son **Eben.** and hrs., other half of "Anderson's Neck."
" son **Thomas** and hrs., 60 A. "Hogg Range," on a Beaver Dam s.e. side of Chiconomoco R.
" son **Edward** and hrs., 300 A. "The Plains," on Hunting Ck.
" sons **Eben.** and **Thomas** and their hrs., "Mill Point" equally.
Exs.: Wife and son **Eben.**
Test: Thomas Taylor, John Cook, Walter Hunter. 19, 484.

Sikes, Thomas, St. Mary's Co., 27th Feb., 1728;
7th Aug., 1728.

To dau. **Ann Hoskins,** 1s.
" wife **Mary,** extx., entire personal estate.
Test: George Carpenter, Peter Haise. 19, 486.

Jenifer, Michael, St. Mary's Co., 10th July, 1726;
2nd Sept., 1728.

To wife **Mary,** extx., 550 A. dwell. plan. ———, bou. of Coll. Thomas Sprigg, and 190 A. ———, bou. of William Hutchins, during life; at her decease to pass to son **Michael Parker Jenifer** and hrs.; he dying without issue, or during his minority, the same to pass to son **Daniel** and hrs.

To son **Michael** afsd., personalty, some of which bou. of Mr. Low.

" son **Daniel** and hrs., 202 A. "Turvey," where Christopher Orrell now lives, 350 A. "Forrest of Harvey" (both tracts bou. of Wm. Maria Farthing); and personalty, some of which bou. of Mrs. Osborn.

" godsons **George Read, Clark Read, John Mollone** and **Fran. Hutchins**, personalty, to be applied toward education.

Bro. **Daniel** to have charge of tuition of child. and of their estates, shd. wife refuse extx. Residue of estate to be divided as law directs; to be buried at the Chappell.

Test: John Read, James Smith, Ignatius Fenwick. 19, 488.

Swale, William, gent., St. Mary's Co.,
12th Aug., 1728;
23rd Sept., 1728.

To sister **Elizabeth Howson**, Lambeth Parish, County of Surry, Great Britain, £20.

" **Andrew Eaton**, St. Mary's Co., his debts conditionally.

" **Charles King**, his debts and £5.

" wife **Mary**, living at Chichester, County of Sussex, Great Britain, residue of personal estate.

Ex.: John Rousby.

Test: Wm. Miller, Jr., John Hall, Abraham Rice. 19, 490.

Holtham, John, Cecil Co., 23rd April, 1728; 26th July, 1728.

To sons **John, Joseph, William, Charles, Nicholas** and **James** and their hrs., dwell. plan. ——— equally.

" daus. **Katherine** and **Mary**, 1s. each.

" wife **Mary**, extx., ⅓ of personal estate. Empowered to sell afsd. plan. and divide proceeds between herself and sons afsd.

" sons afsd., residue of personal estate.

Test: Samuel Alexander, Martin Alexander. 19, 491.

Purnall, Richard, planter, Talbot Co.,
10th Sept., 1719;
19th June, 1728.

To son **Thomas**, ex., and hrs., real estate and ½ personal estate.

" 2 grandchild., viz. **Richard** and **Sarah Whitley** and their hrs., ¼ personal estate.

To dau. **Elinor Pratt** and hrs., ¼ personal estate with 100 A. "Dudley's Chance"; she dying without issue, her portion to revert to son **Thomas.**
Test: Paul Roux, Katherine Richardson, George Bowes.
19, 493.

Rogers, John, Talbot Co.,   8th Aug., 1726; 17th July, 1728.

To Gilbert Turner and hrs., 200 A. "Hackers Forest."
" **Ann,** wife of John Nailer, personalty.
" **William, Deborah** and **John,** child. of John Nailer, ex., residue of personal estate.
Test: John Bather, Ann Nailer, George Beswicke. 19, 495.

Sails, Elizabeth, widow, Talbot Co.,   15th Oct., 1723; 28th July, 1728.

To son **Gabriel** and hrs., 300 A. dwell. plan. "Rich Range," "Delfe" adj.; and personalty.
" **Sarah** and **Jane,** daus. of son **Clement,** personalty at age of 16.
Son **Gabriel,** ex. and residuary legatee.
Test: Samuel Pritchart (Pritchet), Richard Cooper, George Saile (Sailes). 19, 496.

Rule, Peter, St. Mary's Co.,   12th Oct., 1728; 5th Nov., 1728.

To sister **Rebecca Thomas,** "Wattses Lodge" during life; at her decease to bro. **William Wherrit** and hrs.; he failing issue, to pass in succession to bros. **John** and **Thomas Wherrit** and sister **Mary Wherrit** and their hrs.
" sisters **Rebecca Thomas** and **Mary Wherrit,** Thomas Watts, Joshua Watts and George Jenkins, personalty.
" wife **Elizabeth,** extx., dwell. plan. ———, with ⅓ of afsd. tract, and residue of personal estate.
Test: George Clarke, Daniel Watts, William Sword, Elizabeth Watts. 19, 498.

Mills, John, St. Mary's Co.,   31st Aug., 1728; 6th Nov., 1728.

To dau. **Mary,** personalty at marriage.
" son **John,** personalty at marriage or age of 21; shd. either die before that time, survivor to enjoy portion of dec'd.
" Mr. Francis Loyd, personalty.
Wife **Mary,** extx.
Test: John Greenwell, Henry Wineet, Cornelius Maning.
19, 500.

Goostree, Richard, planter, Dorchester Co.,
30th April, 1728;
12th Nov., 1728.

To wife **Rebecca,** extx., dwell. plan. "Goostree's Delight" during life; at her decease to son **George** and hrs.; he dying without issue, to pass to grandson **Robert,** son of **Robert Johnson;** and ⅛ personal estate.
" son **George,** personalty.
" 2 daus., viz. **Elizabeth,** wife of **Robert Johnson,** and **Rebecca,** wife of **Andrew Willis,** and their hrs., 100 A. "Newtown," nr. the great Beaver Dam.
" child. of son-in-law **Phillip Phillips,** 1s. each.
" son **George** and daus. **Elizabeth Johnson** and **Rebecca Willice,** residue of personal estate.
Overseers: Sons-in-law **Robert Johnson** and **Andrew Willice.**
Test: Redman Fallen, John Shenton (Shinton). 19, 501.

Falkener (Falkenor), Benjamin, planter, Queen Anne's Co., 15th Nov., 1726;
29th Aug., 1728.

To 3 sons **Benjamin, Jacob** and **Isaac** and their hrs., dwell. plan. "Marshy Creek" and 50 A. "Falkenors Lott"; and personalty.
" 2 daus. **Ann** and **Sarah,** personalty.
" wife **Elenor,** extx., residue of estate.
Test: Rebeccah Mason, Jane Manering, Edwd. Turner.
19, 503.

Jefferys, John, Queen Anne's Co., 6th Feb., 1726;
29th Aug., 1728.

To eldest dau. **Mary,** personalty at day of marriage.
" sons **John, George, Edward, Thomas** and dau. **Ann,** residue of personalty (wife's thirds being first deducted) as they become of age or marry. Sons **George** and **Edward** to live with wife **Dorothy** until age of 21. Dau. **Ann** to live with her mother until dau. **Mary** marries, and then with her until 16. Son **Thomas** to live with John Beck until of age.
Wife **Dorothy,** extx.
Test: Peter Manly, John Beck. 19, 505.

Wyatt, Thomas, Queen Anne's Co., 14th June, 1728; 29th Aug., 1728.

To wife **Ruth,** extx., ½ dwell. plan. ——— during life.
" son **Thomas** and hrs., ½ dwell. plan., and at decease of wife afsd. the other ½ thereof.
" 8 child., viz. **Thomas, Judeth, William, John, Jane, Solomon, James** and **Ruth,** residue of estate equally; sons of age at 19, daus. at 16 yrs.
Test: Humphrey Wells, James Horsley, William Lee.
19, 506.

Shaw, Richard, A. A. Co., 26th Dec., 1725; 23rd Jan., 1727.

To wife ———, extx., entire estate.
Test: Walter Phelps, Sr., Walter Phelps, Jr., John Sparks.
19, 508.

Baldwin, James, planter, A. A. Co., 7th Dec., 1727; 14th Feb., 1727.

To wife **Mary,** ⅓ personal estate.
" son **James** and hrs., 105 A. dwell. plan. ———, bequeathed testator by father **John Baldwin,** dec'd; sd. son dying without issue, to pass in succession to sons **John, Thomas** and **Tyler** and their hrs.
" son **Thomas** and hrs., 150 A. "Brushy Neck," bou. of bro. **John;** he dying without issue, to pass in succession to sons **James** and **Tyler** and their hrs.
" daus. **Susannah** and **Mary** and their hrs., 200 A. "Mother's Gift," nr. the Indian Town, Prince George's Co.
" 6 child., viz. **John, James, Thomas, Tyler, Susannah** and **Mary,** residue of personal estate.
Exs.: Wife **Mary** and Robert Tyler, gentleman, Prince George's Co.
Test: Robert Lusby, Jr., Vachel Denton, Thomas Baldwin.
19, 509.

Medcalf (Matcalf), John, Sr., 11th Jan., 1727-8; 13th March, 1727.

To 2 sons **Thomas** and **John,** "Balding's Addition," "Jonas Chance" and "Range." Wife to continue in poss. of sd. lands during her widowhood.
" son **John,** personalty.

To granddau. **Larda Holand,** certain personalty after decease of wife; shd. sd. granddau. die before marriage, sd. personalty to pass to surviving child. of dau. **Margaret Holand.**

" wife ——, residue of estate during widowhood; shd. she marry, her thirds only; after her decease all clear estate to be divided among surviving child. or their child.

Exs.: Wife —— and 2 sons afsd.

Test: John Micllbee, Thomas Shores, William Ford (Foard).
19, 511.

Chambers, Samuel, Allhallows Parish, A. A. Co., 7th Feb., 1727-8; 11th April, 1728.

To **William Chapman,** mcht. of London Town, A. A. Co., married to dau. **Rebecca,** "Pratt's Neck" and "Herring Creek Swamp," now in poss. of sd. son **William Chapman;** also lot No. 33 in London Town, deeded from Hezekiah Linthicum 31st July, 1718.

To son **Nicholas** and hrs., dwell. plan. "Bessington" and pt. of "Obligation," bou. of Thomas Stockett, deed dated 14th Sept., 1715; sd. son to pay to son **Samuel** at age of 21 yrs. £40.

" **Turner Wooten** (being married to dau. **Agnes**), dau. **Jane** and sons **Samuel** and **Nicholas,** personalty.

" wife **Ann,** extx., residue of personal estate.

Test: Rev. Mr. John Lang, Stephen Waiman, Edward Honor. 19, 513.

Pettibone, Joseph, planter, A. A. Co., 2nd Dec., 1727; 11th March, 1727.

To sons **Phillip** and **Richard** and their hrs., dwell. plan. —— and "Pyney Plaine," n. side Magothy R.; and residue of personalty; sd. sons dying without issue, sd. lands to pass to bro. **William Lewis** and hrs.; sd. sons to be for themselves at age of 18, to receive estates at age of 21.

" Robert Sping, personalty.

Test: Rev. Mr. James Cox, Robert Small, Edward Tarlow (Tharlow). 19, 517.

Chew, Nathaniel, A. A. Co., 12th Jan., 1727-8; 21st Feb., 1727-8.

Wife **Mary,** extx., empowered to sell lands in A. A. or Calvert Co. to discharge debt to Capt. John Hyde & Co., mchts. in London, and bal. due to bro. **Samuel.**
To wife **Mary** and her 3 child., viz. **Nathaniel, Joseph** and **Ann,** residue of personal estate; also to wife ¼ pt. of residue of real estate during life.
" 3 child. afsd and their hrs., residue of real estate.
Overseers: Bro. **Samuel;** Henry Darnell, of Portland, and kinsman **Samuel Chew,** of Maid Stone.
Test: Alex. Smith, Leonard Cossey, Henry Chapman.
19, 521.

Ruley, Anthony, gent., A. A. Co., 3rd Feb., 1727; 14th May, 1728.

To wife **Rebecca,** extx., "Ruley's Search" and "Edward's Neck" during life; at her decease to son **Thomas** and hrs.; and personalty; also ⅕ personal estate.
" son **Michael,** "Maiden's Head," Cecil Co., nr. Capt. Johns Creek; and personalty. Sd. land to be entailed.
" sons **Seth** and **Anthony** and dau. **Ann,** 600 A. "Senequa Point," Cecil Co. (for div. see will).
" sons **Thomas** and **Seth** and dau. **Ann,** residue of personalty.
" son **William,** £10.
" daus. **Pickett, Redle** and **Woodward,** each a gold ring.
Test: John Reeves, William Burridge, Robt. Johnson.
19, 523.

Bazzell, Ralph, cooper, A. A. Co., 27th March, 1728; 27th June, 1728.

To sons **Robert** and **John,** 10s. each.
" **Ruth,** wife of Walter Phelps, Sr., and **Mary,** wife of Walter Phelps, Jr., personalty.
" wife **Rose,** extx., entire real estate during life; at her decease to 2 sons **James** and **Joseph** and their hrs.; residue of personal estate, to be disposed of among child. as she sees fit.
Test: Walter Phelps, Rich. Phelps, William Fish. 19, 527.

Chew, Mary, A. A. Co., 23rd Aug., 1728; 26th Sept., 1728.

To dau. **Ann** (at age of 16 or marriage), personalty.
" 3 child. (unnamed), or to the survivors of them and their hrs., residue of estate; a tract called "Tuscaroro Plains" only excepted.

Testator states that her last husband **Nathaniel Chew** stood bound, jointly with Richard Blake and Thomas Howell, unto Capt. John Hyde, mcht. of London, in a certain sum of money, for £100 whereof sd. Hyde had consented to take "Tuscaroro Plains" in full satisfaction. Testator, therefore (on condition that her sisters **Susannah** and **Ann** so convey their pts. of sd. tract that her husband's estate is not chargeable with either of the said Richard Blake or Thomas Howell's pt. of the sd. £100), bequeaths to sd. John Hyde and hrs. her pt. of sd. tract; shd. sisters refuse and sd. £100 be charged against estate of sd. husband, sd. tract to pass to 3 child. ―――― and their hrs.

Exs. and guardians to child.: **Samuel Chew, Sr.,** and **Samuel Chew,** of Maidstone.

Test: Benjamin Chew, Sarah Chew, Mary Navarre. 19, 529.

Smith, Daniel, planter, Herring Bay, A. A. Co., 16th Aug., 1728; 2nd Dec., 1728.

To son **Daniel,** dau. **Elizabeth** and bro. **Isaac,** presonalty.
" wife **Sarah,** extx., ½ of estate absolutely, residue to 3 child. **Daniel, Elizabeth** and **Alice.** Son of age at 21, daus. at 16 yrs. Shd. wife die without marrying again, her bro. **Richard Purnal** to act as ex. and guardian to children.

Test: Richard Lewin, Elizabeth Ward, Richard Lewie.
19, 532.

Walter, John, A. A. Co., 20th Oct., 1728; 2nd Dec., 1728.

To wife **Catherine,** extx., grandson **Walter Gott,** granddau. **Hannah Gott** and man **William Steele,** personalty; ¼ of residue of estate to wife, and remaining ¾ to 3 grandchild., viz. **Walter, Verlinda** and **Hannah Gott.**

Test: Isaac Smith, James Mackclanan, Henry Eaden (Eadine). 19, 534.

Brown, Robert, A. A. Co., 26th July, 1727;
22nd May, 1728.

To wife **Mary,** extx., dwell. plan. "Righton" during life, and personal estate absolutety.
" 5 sons, viz. **John, Robert, Joseph, Abel** and **Benjamin** and their hrs., "Righton" after decease of wife; sd. sons to sell or dispose of their portions only to each other.

Test: Doctor Samuel Chew, of Maidstone; Mary Osborn, Thomas Owen. 19, 536.

Fowler, Joseph, Calvert Co., 26th Jan., 1727-8;
24th Oct., 1728.

To 2 sons **George** and **Joseph** and their hrs., pt. of "Tillington" not already disposed of; shd. unborn child be a son, to share equally in division of sd. tract; son **Joseph** to have first choice; and personalty.
" unborn child, personalty at age of 21 or marriage.
" wife **Catherine,** extx., personalty during life; at her decease to be divided among surviving child. "The Quarter," on Little Branch of Hunting Ck., to be sold for benefit of estate.

Test: Wm. Fowler, John Goe, Abram. Fowler. 19, 537.

Moore (Moorle), James, carpenter, St. George's Parish,
Prince George's Co., 29th Oct., 1728;
27th Nov., 1728.

To wife ———, "The Gleanings" during life; after her decease to son **Archibald** and hrs.
" son **Archibald** and hrs., "Archibald's Lott."
" sons **James** and **Robert** and their hrs., "Allisons Park" equally; shd. any afsd. sons die without issue, portion of dec'd to daus. **Euphen** and **Barbara** and their hrs.; shd. one of them die without issue, her share to survivor; shd. both daus. die without issue, to wife ———, provided always it shall be in power of each of afsd. sons to settle a joynter on any woman to whom they shall be married.

Overseers and guardians to child.: James Holmond and George Beall, planters.

Test: John Allison, Wm. Hasbon, John Johnston. 19, 539.

Pagett (Paggett), Thomas, planter, Prince George's Co.,
17th July, 1728;
26th Nov., 1728.

To wife ———, ½ of estate, real and personal, during life.
" granddau. **Elizabeth,** ½ of estate, real and personal, at age of 16 or day of marriage, and residue at decease of wife.
" **Bigger Head,** personalty.
Exs.: Wife ——— and Thomas Colman, planter.
Test: Abraham Wilson, Bigger Head, Joseph West.
19, 541.

Watson, Thomas, carpenter, Annapolis,
26th Sept., 1728;
12th Nov., 1728.

To 3 child., viz. **Mary, James** and **Lawrance,** entire estate equally; shd. personal estate be insufficient to defray debts, real estate to be sold for payment of same, and residue divided among 3 child. afsd. and their hrs.
Exs.: Capt. Robert Gorden and William Daintry, carpenter, both of Annapolis.
Test: Dr. Samuel Stringer, Johannes Ghsonsas Wolf, Thomas Morgan, Mrs. Ann Dainty. 19, 542.

Noeland (Noland), Thomas, planter, A. A. Co.,
19th Oct., 1728;
17th Dec., 1728.

To wife **Mary,** extx., her thirds.
" 4 child., viz. **Daniel, Edward, Sarah** and **Thomas,** residue of estate when of legal age.
Test: Charles Hammond, Peasley Ingram, Joshua Jones.
19, 544.

Lokey (Lakey), John, Somerset Co., 10th Feb., 1727-8;
10th Oct., 1728.

To Dormand Heath (Hath), ex., dwell. plan. "Hearn Quarter" and residue of estate, real and personal.
Test: William Brown, Wm. Abnelt (Adnelt), John Griffin.
19, 545.

Bouger (Bongor, Butcher, Boutcher), James, Somerset Co.,
10th Dec., 1727;
16th Oct., 1728.

To wife **Frances,** extx., entire estate during widowhood; shd. she marry, to child. ——— equally.
" oldest son **John,** personalty and the choice of two tracts.
" younger son **James,** tract refused by son **John.**
Test: Aaron Lynn, Abraham Ingram. 19, 547.

MARYLAND CALENDAR OF WILLS 87

Chambers, Richard, Somerset Co., 16th Sept., 1726;
26th Nov., 1728.

To dau. **Mary Brereton** and **Thomas,** her husband, and their
hrs., 250 A. ———, where they now live.
" grandson **Richard Brereton** and hrs., 100 A. of "Cock-
more."
" dau. **Sarah** and hrs., 150 A. "James Choice."
" dau. **Olive** and hrs., 100 A. "Rowle Ridge."
" granddau. **Sarah Brereton,** personalty.
" son **Richard** and dau. **Olive,** residue of personal estate.
Ex.: Son **Richard.**
Test: Barkle Fisher, Mary Lane, Alex. Hall, Jr. 19, 548.

Brown, Stephen, Charles Co., 29th Feb., 1727-8;
25th Nov., 1728.

To wife **Ann,** extx., entire estate.
Test: Daniel McDaniel (Mackdaniel, McDonnald), Patrick
Davidson. 19, 549.

Wilson (Willson), James, Jr., Kent Co.,
9th May, 1728;
5th July, 1728.

To father **James Wilson, Sr.,** ex., entire estate during life;
after his decease all lands, pt. of "Broad Oak" and pt.
"Margaret's Delight," to nephew **James,** son of **James
Wilson,** dec'd; and to **George,** son of George Wilson, Sr.,
and their hrs., to enjoy same at age of 21. Shd. father
die before nephews afsd. are of age, sd. lands to care
of bro. **George** during their minority; and personal estate
absolutely.
Test: Mary Wilson, Thomas Catlin, Domk. Kenslaugh
(Kenlagh). 19, 550.

Brooks, Catherine, widow of **Phillip Brooks,** Kent Co.,
8th Oct., 1726;
25th Nov., 1728.

To son **Philip,** entire estate, real and personal; sd. son and
his estate to care of bro. and sister, **John Turner** and
Mary, his wife, exs. until 21 yrs. of age.
Test: Abraham Redgrave, George Skirven, James Mac-
daniel. 19, 552.

Huddlestone, William, Kent Co., 25th Sept., 1728; 25th Nov., 1728.

To wife **Margaret**, extx. of entire estate, certain personalty during life, at her decease to dau. **Rachel** and hrs.; she dying without issue, to son-in-law **Francis Kinsey**.

Test: Stephen Bordley, Daniel Shawhane, John Morris.

19, 554.

Christian, Thomas, yeoman, Kent Co., 24th Nov., 1728; 3rd Jan., 1728.

To wife **Mary**, ⅓ of estate, real and personal.
" son **Thomas** and hrs., pt. of dwell. plan. ————; sd. son dying during minority or without issue, to pass to son **James** and hrs.; and personalty.
" son **James** and hrs., plan. whereon William Goodson now lives, including 200 A. of dwell. plan. afsd.; and personalty.
" son-in-law **John Yorkson** and hrs., "Round Stone," on n. side of Northeast.
" son-in-law **Hugh Terry**, daus. **Elizabeth, Rebecca** and **Ann**, personalty.
" child., viz. **Thomas, James, Rachell** and **Mary**, residue of personalty.

Exs.: Wife and Thomas Yorkson.

Test: Jacob Archer, William Goodson, Thomas Yorkson.

19, 555.

Moore, John, St. Paul's Parish, Kent Co., 4th Dec., 1724; 19th Nov., 1728.

To son **William**, ex., and hrs., dwell. plan. "Arcadai," 200 A. thereof being bou. of Arthur Miller and 100 A. of Nichs. Poore; and personalty.
" son **John** and hrs., 170 A. "Mills End," Swan Ck., bequeathed testator by Darby Cassey; and personalty.
" eldest dau. **Mary Mahone**, daus. **Eliza.** and **Ann** and eldest granddau. **Mary Mahone**, and 2 grandchild. **Eliza.** and **Thomas Mahone**, personalty.
" 4 child. **William, John, Eliza.** and **Ann**, residue of estate. Son **John** to care of son **William** until 18, to receive his estate at age of 21.

Test: John Wells, Mathew Richardson, George Debrular.

Memo. 18th Jan., 1724, states shd. either afsd. sons die without issue, surviving bro. to enjoy portion of dec'd; shd. both die without issue, lands to daus. afsd. equally. To 3 grandchild., viz. **Mary, Thomas** and **Elizabeth Manhony**, additional personalty to be paid to their father **Thomas Manhony**.

Test: James Harris, William Crow, Beniones Rickco (Ricae).
19, 557.

Parrish (Parish), William, planter, Baltimore Co.,
16th April, 1728;
28th Sept., 1728.

To bro. **John,** ex., personalty and all due testator from estate of father **John Parrish.**
" mother **Sarah Parrish,** personalty.
" bro. **Edwd.,** 40s. in Charles Ridgley's hands, and personalty in Nathaniel Davises hands.
" bro. **Richard,** personalty in poss. of Phillip Smith and William Lovel, and all that is due from sd. Smith and Lovel after two bills of exchange are paid to Edwd. Fells.

Test: Christopher Randall, Jr., Charles Wells, Edward Stocksdill (Stockdell). 19, 561.

Young, David, Queen Anne's Co., 24th Oct., 1728;
29th Nov., 1728.

To 2 daus. **Eliza.** and **Sarah,** entire estate; care and tuition of sd. daus. to sister **Christiana Barnett** until 16 yrs. of age; shd. sd. sister die during their minority, child. to care of bro. **Edward.**

Exs.: Thomas Barnett and Edward Young.

Test: Otho Coursey, George Jackson, John Smith. 19, 563.

Lowder, Charles, Queen Anne's Co., 23rd Sept., 1728;
29th Nov., 1728.

To son **Charles,** dau. **Jane Lizenbey,** daus. **Sarah** and **Ann,** and grandson **Charles Lizinbey,** personalty.
" wife **Joan,** her thirds.
" 4 child. **Jane, Sarah, Charles** and **Ann,** residue of estate.

Exs.: Wife and son **Charles.**

Test: Humphry Wells, Daniel Newnam. 19, 564.

Jackson, Thomas, planter (nunc.), Queen Anne's Co.,
2nd Jan., 1728-9.

> Bro. **Thomas Smith** to administer estate for benefit of son **Joseph Jackson**, and **Mary Ambross**, mother of **Elizabeth Ambross**.
> Test: Roger Murphey, Elizabeth Ambross. 19, 566.

Raymon, Jonathan, yeoman, Queen Anne's Co.,
29th Jan., 1727-8;
8th Jan., 1728.

> To wife **Judie**, extx., entire estate excepting following legacies.
> " son **Jonathan**, personalty.
> " sons **John** and **Priesley**, 5s. each at age of 21.
> Test: Charlton Barnes, Isaac Booth, William Barns, Richard Smith. 19, 566.

Head, Edward, Queen Anne's Co., 4th Oct., 1728;
9th Nov., 1728.

> To kinswoman **Mary Ricards**, extx., entire estate in trust for the use of her bro. **Mathew Head** during his life; after his decease all real estate to pass to afsd. **Mary Ricards** and hrs.
> Test: Ernault Hawkins, Eliza. Hawkins, Benjamin Hands.
> Note: Probate to above will taken at request of Mary Richards, of Kent Co. 19, 567.

Lenoir, Mary, widow, Charles Co., 22nd Dec., 1725;
———— ———— ————.

> To Robert Hanson, gent.; Anne, wife of Thomas Dent, gent.; Elizabeth, wife of Richard Tarvin, gent.; Dr. Daniel Jenifer and John Lawson, personalty.
> Robert Hanson afsd., ex. and residuary legatee.
> Test: John Brown, Richard Beale, Walter Dodson. 19, 569.

Goult, William, planter, Talbot Co., 16th Nov., 1728;
18th Dec., 1728.

> To Jane Arey, bros. **George** and **Thomas**, personalty.
> " **Leah Parratt**, personalty and the saddle that was her mother's. £3 to be deducted from her pt. of her father's estate.

To dau. Lydia and hrs., "Millford Might," Queen Anne's
Co.; sd. dau. dying without issue, to bro. George and hrs.,
and residue of estate; sd. dau. dying without issue, personal estate to bros. George and Thomas equally. Jane
Arey to have charge of dau. until of age at 18; shd. sd.
Jane die before sd. dau. be of age, bro. George to have
charge of her education if James Berry and Thomas
Adkison shall think fitting.

Exs.: Bro. George and Edward Nedles.
Test: Joshua Clark (Clarke), Francis Regestor, Henry
Turnor. 19, 570.

Parratt, Benjamin, Jr., planter, Talbot Co.,
10th Nov., 1728;
18th Dec., 1728.

To sisters **Mary, Hannah, Jane** and **Rebecca** and bro.
William, entire personal estate except the fourfold accruing by law to testator from George Eaton (Euton) and
William Roberts which they are acquitted from.

Ex.: Joshua Clark.
Test: Edward Nedles (Nedels), John Slaughter, William
Goult. 19, 572.

Arey, Joseph, Talbot Co., 6th Nov., 1728;
18th Dec., 1728.

To sons-in-law **Eliazor** and **William Parratt** and their hrs.,
"Sallop" after decease of wife **Jane.**
" son **Jonathan,** personalty.
Test: Edward Nedles (Nedels), George Golt, John Tomlinson, Jr. 19, 574.

Sanford (Sandford), James, gent., Talbot Co.,
9th Jan., 1728;
22nd Jan., 1728.

To Elizabeth Davis, ex., now wife of David Davis, gent.,
Talbot Co., and her hrs., entire real estate; she dying
without issue, sd. lands to Edward, son of John Oldham,
and hrs., smith of Oxford, Talbot Co.; and entire personal estate.
Test: Edward Elliott, Tamberlin Davis, Hannah Oldham,
Mary Marshaul (Mackfaal, Macfaul). 19, 575.

Wailes, Benjamin, 10th Dec., 1726;
7th April, 1729.

To son **Joseph** and hrs., 150 A. "Tossitter," 100 A. "Fortune," 50 A. "Might Have Had More" and 70 A. "Joseph's Lott"; also land bou. of John Bartley; and personalty.

" wife **Elizabeth**, extx., plan. ―――― in Patuxent during life; at her decease to son **Levin** and hrs.; also to wife and son **Levin** entire personal estate. Extx. empowered to sell, if she thinks best, land bou. of Edward Gould; to convey to Abraham Ingram tract sold him, upon payment for same; also to make over to Charles Polke tract sold him on his completing payment for same.

Test: Capell King, Hast Dashiell, James Makmorie.

19, 577.

Reviss, Thomas, millwright, Baltimore Co.,
20th Jan., 1728;
25th Jan., 1728.

To John and George Harryman, exs., personal estate.

" Thomas Sheredine and exs. afsd., "Revisis Lott" and mill for 20 years; shd. no hr. come in that time, to them and their hrs.

Test: Martin Parlett, Thomas Sutton, James Mallord (Mallard). 19, 579.

Bowen, Jonas, planter, Baltimore Co., 12th Dec., 1728;
4th Feb., 1728.

To wife **Ann**, extx., dwell. plan. ―――― and personalty during widowhood; shd. she marry, personalty to dau. **Martha Linch** and hrs.

" granddau. **Martha Linch** and hrs., personalty at decease of her mother.

" dau. **Rebecca Gray**, personalty; she dying without issue, to child. of dau. **Martha Linch**. Land to be divided equally bet. them both; son **Patrick Linch** to have his pt. on that side of the branch where he now lives and to possess the same during life; granddau. **Martha Linch** to enjoy that pt. of land belonging to **Martha Linch** after the decease of her mother. Dau. **Rebecca Gray** and hrs. to have dwell. plan. on this side of the branch; dau. **Rebecca** dying without issue, her portion to pass to granddau. **Martha Linch** and hrs. Shd. both daus. die without issue, cousin **Jonas** and hrs., son of **John Bowen**, to possess all real estate.

" son **William Reaves**, personalty.

Test: Thomas Slye (Sly), Benjamin Bowen, John Eaglestone.

Note: Widow claims her thirds. 19, 580.

Pearson, John, Calvert Co., 26th March, 1728;
11th Jan., 1728-9.
To Eliza. Pantry, personalty.
" Samuel Franklin, residue of estate, to receive same and be for himself at age of 19; shd. sd. Samuel die during minority and without wife or issue, estate bequeathed him to pass to Elizabeth Pantry afsd.
Ex.: Wm. Alnutt.
Test: Isaac Johns, Thomas Chambers. 19, 582.

Hilleary (Hillary, Hilleray), Thomas, Prince George's
Co., ——— ———, 1728;
14th Feb., 1728-9.
To 4 sons Thomas, John, William and Henry, 640 A. "The Three Sisters," to be divided at discretion of nephew Thomas Williams, who is empowered to make good their title; to receive estate at age of 21.
" daus. Sarah, Elizabeth and Elianor and sons Henry and Thomas, personalty; shd. any of sons die during minority, surviving sons to inherit portion of dec'd; shd. any of daus. die, their portion to be divided among surviving sisters.
" 6 child. John, Sarah, William, Elizabeth, Elianor and Henry, residue of estate equally. Sons of age at 18 yrs.
Wife Elianor, extx., empowered to keep each child's pt. 4 yrs. after they come of age.
Test: Jane Pavett (Pacett), I. Norton, Anne Demelion (Demilion). 19, 583.

Roberts, John, gentleman, St. John's Parish, Baltimore
Co., 9th Feb., 1728;
6th March, 1728.
To eldest dau. Mary and her hrs. (wife of William Talbot), 200 A. "Witherall's Last Addition," in the forest; sd. dau. dying without issue, to dau. Ann and hrs.; and personalty.
" 2 sons John and Stephen and their hrs., 2 lots in the town of Joppa, cont. ½ A. each; 1 taken up, the other bou. of Richard Hewet; also dwell. plan. "Forsters Neck" and "Woolfs Harbour"; and personalty.
" 3 daus. Ann, Frances and Lucina and their hrs., 400 A. in the forest where John Sumner now dwells.
" 5 child., viz. John, Stephen, Ann, Frances and Lucina, residue of estate, exclusive of wife's thirds.

Exs.: Wife **Mary** and **John Crockett.**
Test: Robert Cutchin, Hugh Copeland (Copland), Edmond Edwards. 19, 585.

Wheeler, William, Somerset Co., 29th Aug., 1728; 10th Dec., 1728.

To **William** (son of bro. **Isaac**), personalty.
" **Margaret** (dau. of bro. **John**, dec'd), £10 at age of 16 yrs.
" bro. **Isaac**, ex., residue of estate.
Test: Thomas English, Mathew Shippard (Shipard), Henry Fisher. 19, 588.

Kenady (Keneday), Timothy, Somerset Co., 5th Jan., 1728; 6th Feb., 1728.

To son **John** and hrs., 200 A. dwell. plan. ———.
" son **Timothy** and hrs., 200 A. adj. dwell. plan. ———.
" 3 daus., viz. **Margaret, Cathern** and **Ann,** £5 each.
" wife **Margaret,** 1s., she having received full satisfaction by articles of agreement.
" 2 sons and 3 daus. afsd., residue of estate; sons to receive their estates at age of 18; exs. to bind son **John** to Michall Dasheron as blacksmith, and son **Timothy** to John Dasheroon.
Exs.: Ebenezer Handy and Thomas Humphiris.
Test: Benjamin Handy, John Carr, Henry Toadvine, Thomas Hill. 19, 589.

Manardo, Peter, Cecil Co., 11th Sept., 1728; 13th Nov., 1728.

To dau. **Elizabeth Philips**, dwell. plan. ——— during life; at her decease ½ thereof to her son **Manardo Phillips** and ½ to her dau. **Ann Brooks** and their hrs.; sd. **Manardo Philips,** at age of 22 yrs., to pay £2 10s. to his sister **Elizabeth Phillips;** sd. **Ann Brooks** to pay to same **Elizabeth Phillips** £2 10s. one yr. after marriage of sd. **Ann Brooks** if she live, or her hrs. to pay same if she inherits the land.
" **Peternallo Broocks** and hrs., dau. of **Elizabeth Philips,** tract ———, now in poss. of James Fursters.
Ex.: Samuel Philips.
Test: John Tillton, Elizabeth Numbers (Numberson), Peter Picott (Picot). 19, 591.

Dowdall, John, Back Ck., Cecil Co., 29th Dec., 1728; 1st Jan., 1728.

To Dowdall and hrs., son of Augusteen Thompson and Sarah, his wife (maiden name Sarah Salter, dau. of John Saulter and Sarah, his wife, of Kent Co., both dec'd), "Woolver Hampton," at head of Dowble Ck., bou. from Capt. William Hackett, Queen Anne's Co., dec'd.

" Christian Tute, personalty. Exs. empowered to furnish sd. Christian with a home during her life either at "None So Good," in Fin-land, where testator lives, or "Sheffields" or "Ward Oak," n. side Chester R., Kent Co.

" 2 nephews **Richard Dowdall** and **John McManus**, exs., residue of estate.

Overseer: Domk. Carroll.

Test: Edward Bourk, Wm. Murphy (Murphey), Andw. Dowdall. 19, 592.

Carr, William, planter, Talbot Co., 20th Feb., 1728-9; 17th March, 1728-9.

To son **John** and hrs., dwell. plan. "Miller Purchase" after his mother's decease.

" daus. Martha Anderson, Mary and Ann, personalty.

" wife **Mary**, son **John** and daus. Mary and Ann, residue of estate equally.

Exs.: Wife and son **John**.

Test: John Feaston, Edward Vearing, John Vaine. 19, 595.

Kerby (Kirby), John, Talbot Co., 18th Nov., 1728; 26th March, 1729.

To son **Lemmon** and hrs., dwell. plan. ———— at age of 21; to be for himself at age of 18 yrs.

" 2 daus. **Elizabeth** and **Rebecca** and their hrs., 50 A. "Wolfpitt Ridge" and 30 A. adj., bou. of Edward Turner, to be divided equally at day of marriage; daus. to be for themselves at age of 16.

" wife ————, ⅓ personal estate. 3 child. to receive residue when of age; shd. their mother die during their minority, they are left to care of bro. **David**.

Test: Edward Ricketts, Richard Kerby, Mary Thornlee.

19, 597.

Mallooney (Mollooney, Moloney), Mathew, planter, Talbot Co., 23rd Jan., 1723; 16th Jan., 1728.

To wife **Martha**, extx., entire estate.

Test: David Hughs, Thomas Harryman, Thomas Smith.

19, 598.

Arey, Easther, Talbot Co., 3rd Nov., 1728; 18th Dec., 1728.

To bro.-in-law **Benjamin Parratt (Barrutt)** and hrs., 500 A. "Parker's Park."
" cousin **Jonathan** and hrs., 300 A. "Morgan's Resarve."
" cousin **David** and hrs., 125 A. "David's Ridge"; sd. **David** dying without issue, or without disposing of sd. land, to pass to cousin **Mary Arey** and hrs.
Exs.: Uncle **Joseph Arey** and bro.-in-law **Benjamine Parratt.**
Test: Edward Nedles (Nedels), George Golt, Precello Bradbury. 19, 600.

Fowler, Patrick, Dorchester Co., 12th Oct., 1728; 27th Nov., 1728.

To dau. **Sarah Stack,** 1s.
" dau. **Ann,** residue of estate.
Ex.: **William Perey.**
Test: James Kidder, Robert Jones (Gones), Sr., Robert Jones, Jr. 19, 602.

Urey (Urney), William, planter, Dorchester Co., 8th Sept., 1728; 1st Jan., 1728-9.

To wife **Honer,** extx., dwell. plan. "Hazard" during life; at her decease to youngest dau. **Margitt** and hrs.
" dau. **Mary** and hrs., "Addition to Hazard."
" 2 daus. afsd., personal estate equally.
Test: Patrick Mackalester (Mackcleston), John Mackalester (Mackcallister), David Mackalester (Mackcaleter).
19, 603.

Vickers, Thomas, Dorchester Co., 10th day, 11th mo., 1725-6; 13th Jan., 1728.

To son **Thomas,** dwell. plan. "Redding."
" son **John,** 50 A. "Morgin's Choice," "The Burned Marsh" and personalty.
" daus. **Elizabeth** and **Ann,** personalty.
Exs.: Wife ―― and son **Thomas.**
Test: Joshua Kennerly (Kenarly), David Robson, Benjamin Brunsdon. 19, 605.

Sherridine (Sheredine), Martha, Calvert Co.,
1st March, 1728-9;
19th May, 1728.

To sons **John Booth** and **Thomas Artobarey,** dau. **Elizabeth Brome,** grandson **Basell Booth** and grandson **Sherridine Brome,** personalty; that bequeathed son **Thomas** not to be sold without consent of son-in-law **Henry Brooms.**
" son **Henry Brome,** ex., personal estate.
Test: John Brome (Broome), Jr., Thomas Brome (Broome), Simon Gray. 19,606.

Hatch, Thomas, Charles Co., 16th Nov., 1728;
24th Jan., 1728.

To wife **Mary,** extx., "Thomas his Purchase" during life; after her decease to eldest son **John** and hrs.; he dying without issue, to younger son **Thomas;** shd. both die without issue, to dau. **Sarah** and hrs.; she dying without issue, to wife's dau. **Elizabeth Marles;** and personalty.
" sons **John** and **Thomas,** dau. **Sarah,** dau.-in-law **Elizabeth Marles** and **Thomas Standish,** personalty. Residue of estate to wife, to be divided among child. after her decease. Shd. wife die before child. are of age, John Butts to act as guardian.
Test: Daniel Donohoe, William Windsor, Eliza. Donohoe.
19,607.

Wight (Wightt, White), John, Prince George's Co.,
17th June, 1728-9;
12th April, 1729.

To son **John** and hrs., 456 A. on eastern br. Potomack.
" son **Jonathan** and hrs., 444 A. "Stepmother's Folly," 225 A. "Hopson's Choice."
" son ——— and hrs., 500 A. "Wights Forrest."
" son **Richard** and hrs., 530 A. "Mair and Colt," and ⅓ of land adj. to Nottingham town.
" Thomas Winsor, 100 A. of "Mair and Colt."
" hr. of John Bowin, dec'd, 100 A. of last named tract conditionally.
" dau. **Mary** and hrs., 100 A. "Taylorton."
" daus. **Innosense** and **Ann** and their hrs., "Cumpass Hills," "Anchovis Hills," "Pasqueum," in all 500 A.
" wife **Ann,** extx., dwell. plan. "The Goare" during life. Son **John** to receive a certain portion at age of 21, and after wife's decease the residue.
Test: Roger John Sasser (Sawser), Samuel Tayler (Taylar), Martha Greenfield. 19,609.

Franch (French), Henry,   12th Feb., 1727-8; 12th April, 1729.

To son **William**, personalty.
" wife **Mary**, a living with 2 daus. **Elizabeth** and **Mary** during widowhood.
" eldest dau. **Elizabeth** and hrs., ½ land bou. of George Jones; sd. land to be neither sold nor mortgaged; and personalty.
" dau. **Mary** and hrs., other ½ of sd. tract.
Test: Thomas Hodgkin deposes that above will is in handwriting of Henry French.   19, 611.

Mason, Mathew, gent., St. Mary's Co.,   12th Feb., 1722; 27th March, 1729.

To wife **Mary**, extx., personalty; to divide personal estate with 4 child. testator has by her, viz. **John, Elizabeth, Susannah** and **Mary**.
" son **Robert** and hrs., ½ of 490 A. "Paradise," Swan Ck., Baltimore Co.; sd. son to accept same in lieu of a tract in Virginia sold to William Perrie and Thomas Stanford; sd. son dying without issue or not accepting this devise in lieu of land sold as afsd., then above land in Baltimore Co. to son **John** and hrs.; and personalty.
" son **John** and hrs., other ½ of "Paradise," pt. of "Christian Temple Mannor," nr. mouth of Mattawoman, Charles Co., land in Bedlam Neck; and personalty; sd. son dying during his minority, his share of personalty to daus. **Elizabeth, Susanna** and **Mary**.
" daus. **Elizabeth, Susanna** and **Mary**, personalty, provided they live to age of 16 yrs., or day of marriage. Shd. any of them become members of the Church of Rome, or marry any one of that faith, the estate of child so doing to be divided among rest of children. Daus. to remain with their mother until 16, or day of marriage; son **John** until 18 yrs. of age.
Test: John Blackiston, Ann Blackiston, Susanna Blackiston, Philip Key.   19, 612.

Mills, Nicholas, St. Mary's Co.,   11th Nov., 1728; 18th March, 1728-9.

To grandson **John** and hrs., dwell. plan. ———; he dying without issue, to pass to granddau. **Mary** and hrs.; she dying without issue, to son **Nicholas** and hrs.
" son **Nicholas** and hrs., 309 A. "Strife" and "Strife's Addition."

To daus. **Mary Millard** and **Susanna** and their hrs., 400 A. "Neals Lott"; either dau. dying without issue, portion of dec'd to survivor; shd., both die without issue, to son **Nicholas** and hrs.
" dau.-in-law **Mary Mills**, use of lands where she now lives during widowhood.
" dau. **Susanna** and the clergy at New Town, personalty.
" wife **Elizabeth**, use of dwell. plan. from path leading from house of dau.-in-law **Mary Mills** to hd. of Floods Ck., where Charles Daft now lives, during her life; residue of estate.
Exs.: Wife and son **Nicholas**.
Test: Cornelius Maning, Mathew Dafft, James Thompson.
19, 616.

Stapelton (Stapleton), John, St. Mary's Co.,
6th March, 1728-9;
17th March, 1728-9.

To sons **Henry** and **John** and their hrs., 100 A. "Bacon Point" and personalty; sd. sons to be free at 18 yrs.
" godson **Andrew Foy**, personalty in hands of Philip Evans.
" wife **Margaret**, extx., and sons afsd., residue of estate.
Overseers: John White and Thomas Plumber.
Test: James Granan, John Conaly, Richard Vaughans.
19, 619.

Radford, John, carpenter, Sinnicar Landing, Prince George's Co.,
16th Jan., 1728;
10th March, 1728.

To wife **Sarah**, extx., "Sinnicar (Sinnacor) Landing," "Ocbrook," 727 A. "Radford's Chance," 100 A. "Newton," "Darby Island" and "Melborne"; wife empowered to sell 4 last-named tracts for benefit of estate; and personalty.
" son **Henry** and hrs., 400 A. ———, Stafford Co., Va.; lower pt. of "Three Islands United," and 100 A. "The Henry."
" son **John** and hrs., "Long Acre," 150 A. of "Samariea" and upper pt. of "Three Islands United."
" son **Thomas** and hrs., 2 first-named tracts at decease of wife, residue of "Samariea" and 300 A. "Olbias(?) Choyce." Sons to enjoy estates at age of 18, or decease of their mother; shd. any die without issue, survivors to inherit portion of dec'd.
Test: Jonathan Simmons, Joseph Brown, Jr., John Hemingway.
19, 621.

Forster, Francis, Cecil Co., 14th Dec., 1728; 8th April, 1729.

To wife Margarett, extx., and 3 child. **Thomas, Mary** and **Sarah,** entire estate; shd. wife marry within 6 yrs. of testator's decease, to have her thirds only.
Overseer: Bro. **James.**
Test: John Hamm, Lawrence Lawrenson, Anthony Whitely.
19, 623.

Baker, Nathan, Cecil Co. (bound on a voyage to Barbadoes), 12th April, 1722; 5th April, 1729.

To 3 sons **Henry, Jeremiah** and **Nathan,** £5 each at age of 21.
" dau. **Mary,** personalty at age of 16 or day of marriage.
" wife Sarah, extx., residue of estate.
Test: Francis Mauldin, Edward Jackson. 19, 624.

Van Burkeloo (Vanburkeloe), Harmen, brewer, Cecil Co., 2nd Dec., 1728; 15th March, 1728.

Testator states that dwell. plan. ——— has been already granted by himself and wife Margaret to grandson **Harmen.**
To grandson **William** and granddaus. **Catherine** and **Margaret,** personalty.
" sd. grandchild., residue of estate.
Exs.: Dau.-in-law **Catherine Vanburkeloo** and grandson **Harmen.**
Overseer: Son **Abell.**
Test: Henry Roe, James Crongelton, Mary Crongelton.
19, 625.

Butterworth, Isaac, Baltimore Co., 17th May, 1728; 1st April, 1729.

To wife Esther, 80 A. "John and Isaac's Lott" and 100 A. "The Addition" during life; after her decease to dau. **Sarah** and hrs.; and ⅛ personal estate.
" son **Isaac** and hrs., 400 A. "Isaac's Inheritance."
" dau. **Esther,** £30.
" dau. **Mary** and hrs., 400 A. "Isaac's Enlargement" and "The Addition."

To dau. **Hannah** and hrs., 300 A. "Maiden's Bower."
" dau. **Sarah** and hrs., 130 A. "Roses Green."
" 5 child. afsd., residue of personal estate; shd. any of child. die during minority or without issue, survivors to divide portion of dec'd.
Exs.: Wife and son **Isaac**.
Overseers: Bro.-in-law **Robert Clark**, 2 nephews **Michael** and **Isaac Webster** and **Thomas Shay** (Shy).
Test: Samuel Deaver, Hannah Deaver, Thomas Shay, Mary Collier, Michael Webster. 19, 627.

White, William, Sr., Kent Island, Queen Anne's Co.,
20th Feb., 1728-9;
13th March, 1728-9.

To wife **Mary**, extx., ⅓ personal estate absolutely; ⅓ real estate during life, with use of lands and residue of personal estate during widowhood.
" son **William** and hrs., after decease or marriage of wife, entire real estate, viz. 150 A. "Workmans Hazard," 50 A. "Spark's Poynt"; sd. son dying without issue, to pass to second son **Samuel** and hrs.; he failing issue, to third son **James** and hrs.; he failing issue, to 2 daus. **Letteshey** and **Alce** and their hrs.
Test: William Elliott, John Willson (Wilson). 19, 630.

Woollehan (Woolehan), Morris (Maurice), planter,
Kent Island, 3rd March, 1728-9;
13th March, 1728-9.

To wife **Ealse**, extx., dwell. plan. ——— during life; at her decease to unborn child, if a son; sd. son dying without issue, to dau. **Elizabeth** and hrs.; and ⅓ personal estate absolutely.
" daus. **Elizabeth, Susannah** and **Ann**, residue of estate. Shd. unborn child be a dau., to have an equal share in estate with daus. **Susannah** and **Ann**; dau. **Elizabeth** to have dwell. plan. ——— only.
Test: Francis White, William White, Sarah Williams.
19, 632.

Wright, Solomon, Jr., Queen Anne's Co.,
28th Jan., 1728;
28th March, 1729.

To son **Solomon** and hrs., dwell. plan. ———; he dying without issue, to hr. at law; 100 A. "Hog Harbour."·
" 3 child. **Nathaniel, Solomon** and **Sarah**, entire personal estate. Sons of age at 21, daus. at 18 yrs. or marriage.

To dau. Sarah and hrs., 250 A. "Narbrough," nr. w. br. Tuckahoe Ck.; she dying without issue, to son **Solomon** and hrs.; shd. unborn child be a son, dau. Sarah to enjoy but 125 A. of sd. land, the other 125 A., with dwell. plan. ——— and "Hog Harbour," to be divided equally bet. son **Solomon** and sd. son; shd. unborn child be a dau., to enjoy "Narbrough" with dau. Sarah, and have an equal share of personal estate with other 3 child.

" wife **Mary**, extx., use of dwell. plan. ——— during widowhood, care of child. and their estates until of ages afsd.; shd. wife not be willing to keep them, son **Nathaniel** and dau. **Sarah** to care of bro. **Edward**.

Test: Robert Norrest Wright, William Bryley, Eliza (Mary) Bryley. 19, 634.

Lockhart, John (nunc.), 22nd March, 1729; 28th March, 1729.

To Robert German, entire personal estate and the charge of son-in-law **Wm. Gregory**.
Test: Aaron Saunders (18 yrs.). 19, 637.

Jones, Frances, widow, Queen Anne's Co., 25th Feb., 1728-9; 24th March, 1728-9.

To Rachel Mathews, entire estate.
Extx.: Mary Cole, widow.
Test: Edward Spurway, Mary Earle, Sarah Sillwood.
19, 637.

Denny, Christopher, Queen Anne's Co., 3rd March, 1727; 26th March, 1729.

To wife **Ann**, extx., dwelling house with ½ the land belonging thereto during life, except ½ the orchard, which is bequeathed to son **John Earle Denny**, and the house and 1 A. where dau. **Mary Dyor** now lives; sd. dau. to have use of same during her widowhood; and residue of personal estate after legacies are distributed.

" son **John** afsd., entire real estate after decease of wife; and personalty, including silver cup marked J. E. D.

" dau. **Rachel**, personalty.

" daus. **Rhoda Sulivan**, **Mary Dyor** and **Anne Thomas**, 5s. each.

Test: Charles Downes, Richard Hynson, Robert Jones.
19, 638.

MARYLAND CALENDAR OF WILLS 103

Chaires (Chears), Nathaniel, planter, Queen Anne's Co., 14th Jan., 1728; 26th March, 1729.

To wife Elizabeth, extx., entire estate during life; at her decease to bro. **Benjamin** and hrs.
Test: John Chaires (Chears), Catherine Collins, John Hartshorne.
26th March, 1729. Elizabeth Forman, the within legatee, claims what law allows. 19, 640.

Ford, Thomas, Queen Anne's Co., 8th Jan., 1728-9; 28th March, 1729.

To wife **Rebecca**, extx., "Barton," s. side Hambleton's Br.; the profit of homestead plan. until eldest son **Isaac** comes to age of 21; and personalty, excepting legacies to following:
" son **Isaac** and other child. (unnamed) at age of 16 yrs., personalty.
Test: Jonas Edingfeild, Robert Maxwell (Maxfield), Nathaniel Fitzrandolph. 19, 642.

Helborn (Hellburn), John, Queen Anne's Co., 18th Jan., 1728-9; 28th March, 1729.

Sons **William** and **John** to remain with wife **Frances** until of age at 21 yrs. Dau. **Elizabeth** to care of Mark Hargedon (Hargedine) and Jane, his wife, until of age at 18 yrs.
To wife **Frances**, personalty.
Test: John Boulton, Edward More, Wm. Gough. 19, 643.

Coursey, Elizabeth, widow, Queen Anne's Co., 27th Nov., 1727; 29th March, 1729.

To sons **Otho** and **William** and dau. **Arraminta**, personalty.
" daus. **Elizabeth Cummins, Juliana** and **Mary**, 20s. each.
" son **Henry**, ex., residue of estate, either in Maryland, Ireland or Gr. Britain; and £160 bequeathed by mother Mrs. Elizabeth Desmyniers, late of Dublin, dec'd, with 1 moyety of residue of her estate; sd. bequests testator has ordered to be remitted to Philip Smith, mcht., London.
Test: John Emory, Robert Hassitt, John Fling. 19, 644.

MARYLAND CALENDAR OF WILLS

Chaires (Chears), John, Queen Anne's Co.,
                                           20th Jan., 1728;
                                           10th April, 1729.

To son **Thomas** and hrs., dwell. plan. ———, pt. of "Lently," on branch of Courseca (Corsica) Ck.
" son **James** and hrs., pt. of afsd. tract; shd. either of sd. sons die during minority or without issue, portion of dec'd to eldest son **John** and hrs.
" bro. **Thomas** and hrs., 150 A. "Batchelars Adventure," where he now lives.
" bro. **James** and hrs., 100 A. "Reerguards Addition."
" wife **Mary**, extx., use of personal estate during life; at her decease to 3 child., viz. **John, Thomas** and **James.**
Test: Mathew Mason, Patrick O'Bryon, Thomas O'Bryon, Robert Norrest Wright.
10th April, 1729. Widow claims her thirds.   **19, 646.**

Blangy (Blangey), Jacob,   28th Feb., 1728-9;
                                      24th April, 1729.

To bro. **John Wells Blangey** and sister **Sarah** and their hrs., dwell. plan. "Cilly," Kent Island, equally at age of 21; shd. they die during minority, to pass as follows:
" half-bro. **Nicholas Clouds** and hrs., 100 A. thereof at age of 21.
" mother ———, other pt. of sd. tract.
Ex.: Father-in-law **Benjamin Clouds.**
Test: Peter Davis, Sarah Lewis, Robert Hassitt (Hassett).
                                                                         19, 648.

Simson, Thomas, gentleman, Cecil Co., late of Jamaica, eldest son of Thomas Simson and residuary legatee of sd. **Thos. Simson** and of Edward James, both merchants of sd. island. 22nd Aug., 1728;
                                                                    14th May, 1729.

To bros. **John, William, James** and **Love** and sister **Mary**, £10 each.
" late divorced wife **Ann** (dau. of **Mary**, widow of **Jeremiah Pearce**, dec'd, mcht., of Bristol, Gr. Britain) and mother **Ann** (present wife of Peter Vallete, of Jamaica), £405 each.
" **Joseph William, George, John** and **Vallentine Douglas**, all of Cecil Co., £200 each.
" **William Ponteny**, gentleman, Cecil Co., and hrs., £1,000.
" **Musgrave Yeamans** and **Daniel Curtis**, exs. with Wm. Ponteny afsd. of estate in Jamaica, £80 each.

Exs. in Maryland: Joseph William and Valentine Douglas.
To the poor of Maryland (not receiving alms), residue of estate.
Test: Denis Nowland, Ann Ponteny, Mary Douglas, Cornelius Augustine Savin. 19, 649.

Price, William, planter, St. Mary's Co.,
20th Feb., 1728-9;
29th April, 1729.

To wife **Johana,** real estate during life; at her decease to son **William** and hrs., except the old plan. adj. William Jenkin's, which is bequeathed to son **Henry** and hrs.
" sons afsd. and dau. **Frances,** personalty.
" dau. **Susana Hook,** 1s.
Exs.: Wife and son **William.**
Test: Martha Dillon, Clare Price, James Walkden. 19, 654.

Baggley, Ralph, planter, St. Mary's Co.,
27th March, 1729;
7th May, 1729.

To son **Samuel** and hrs., entire estate; he dying without issue, to pass to bro. **William Willson** and hrs.
Bro. **William** afsd., ex. and guardian to son until 21 yrs.
Test: Thomas Alsten, Edmond Boulling (Boullin), Martin Smithson. 19, 655.

Richardson, Ruth, Talbot Co., 6th Oct., 1727;
3rd July, 1728.

To 2 sons **Daniel** and **Benjamin** and their hrs., entire estate; shd. either of sd. sons die during minority or without issue, survivor to inherit portion of dec'd; shd. both die as afsd., one portion of estate to son **John Leeds** and hrs. and other portion to 3 child.-in-law, viz. **William Richardson, Elizabeth,** wife of **William Harrison,** and **Sophia,** wife of **Charles Dickinson,** and their hrs.
Overseer: Bro. **Benjamin Ball.**
Exs.: 2 sons **John Leeds** and **Daniel Richardson.**
Test: Jane Kersey, Mary Wrightson, Mary Follard.
19, 657.

Bodfeild, John, tailor, Talbot Co., 21st Nov., 1728; 23rd Dec., 1728.

To wife Lizse (Elizabeth), dwell. plan. ―――― during life; child. to remain under her charge until they arrive at 21 yrs.; shd. wife marry, child. to receive estates as they come of age.
" son **Begnegoe** and hrs., 100 A. "Faulkners Square," adj. Phile Banning's plan.
" son **Zadock** and hrs., 100 A. "Dudley's Beginning," in Tuckahoe; shd. either of sd. sons die without issue, portion of dec'd to son **Levi** and hrs.
" sd. child., personal estate at decease of wife.
" dau. **Ellinor** and hrs., dwell. plan. afsd. at decease of her mother.
" sons **Shedrach** and **Meshach** and dau. **Mary**, 1s. each.
Exs.: Wife and Dennis Hopkins.
Test: Alexander Ray, Mary Floyd, Frances Holmes.
19, 658.

Golt (Goult), George (nunc.), Talbot Co., 18th Dec., 1728.

To Hannah Parrott (dau. of Jane Arey) and David Harrington, personalty, some of which at John Rathells.
" sister **Elizabeth Jadwin** and afsd. Hannah, residue of estate.
Test: Jane Arey (aged about 41 yrs.), Rachell Stagg.
19, 661.

Hopkins, Joseph, Talbot Co., 6th Dec., 1726; 5th Feb., 1728.

To eldest son **Joseph** and hrs., pt. of "Hopkin's Point" as far as Schoolhouse Marsh, adj. land of Dennis Hopkins; and personalty.
" son **Benjamin** and hrs., pt. of afsd. tract at hd. of Compones Cove, at age of 21; and personalty.
" wife **Susannah**, extx., residue of real estate during life; at her decease to son **Benjamin**; he dying without issue, portion bequeathed wife to pass to youngest child then living; neither son to dispose of sd. land except to one another.
" all daus. (unnamed), personalty.
Test: Dennis (Denis) Hopkins, Sr., John Robson, Sarah Hopkins.
19, 661.

Dudley, Thomas, planter, Talbot Co., 1st June, 1727; 12th March, 1728.

To son **Samuel** and hrs., 100 A. "Beaver Neck," where he now lives (for desc. see will); and personalty.

" son **Thomas** and hrs., 100 A. "Broad Lane," 27 A. "Dudley Incloser."

" dau. **Sarah Fisher,** personalty.

" 3 child., viz. **Thomas, Ellinor** and **Rebecah,** residue of estate.

Exs.: Sons afsd.

Test: William Dudley, Peter May. 19, 664.

Robinson, John, Talbot Co., 26th Feb., 1728; 21st March, 1728.

To son **John,** 20 A. "Goaldsboroughs Addition," on condition that he pays to dau. **Margarite** 2,000 lbs. tobacco when he comes to age of 21; sd. son to be in care of bro. **Solomon;** shd. sd. bro. die before son **John** is of age, to care of bro. **David.** Dau. **Margaret** to remain with sister **Mary Cox;** shd. sd. sister die before dau. is 18 yrs. of age, to care of sister **Margaret Barker.**

Ex.: Bro. **David.**

Test: Rev. Daniel Maynadier, Daniel Powell, Rowland Floyd. 19, 666.

Colston, James, corker, St. Michaels Parish, Talbot Co., ———— ———— ————;
9th April, 1729.

To eldest son **James,** 100 A. "Clays Hope," including pt. of the Manner plantation, lying on n. side Thread-haven Ck., after decease of wife.

" son **Henry,** 70 A. of afsd. tract.

" son **Jeremiah,** 30 A. afsd. tract.

" dau. **Rose,** personalty. Son **William** to be pd. 2,000 lbs. tobacco by his mother (if living) and his bro. **James.**

" wife **Elizabeth,** extx., entire plantation and personal estate during life; at her decease to 3 sons as afsd.

Son **James,** ex. with his mother when of age.

Test: Elinor Bradshaw, John Brady, Francis Cook. 19, 668.

Brocust, Samuel, Sr., Talbot Co., 23rd Feb., 1728; 9th April, 1729.

To wife **Jane,** entire estate during life; at her decease to pass to **Samuel,** son of **Samuel Brocust.**
" son **Samuel** and granddau. **Mary Ann Barran,** personalty.
Exs.: Wife and son **Samuel.**
Test: James Millard, Denis Barutt (Brutt), William Marer.
19, 670.

Grace, William, planter, Talbot Co., 3rd Feb., 1728-9; 26th April, 1729.

To youngest dau. **Susannah,** personalty for her maintenance in infancy, and full share of personal estate; to be in care of her bro. or some of her sisters.
" child., viz. **Nathaniel, Elizabeth, Sarah, Rachel, Mabell, Mary** and **Susannah,** residue of estate; daus. to receive portion at age of 16 or day of marriage.
Exs.: Father **Nathaniel** and son **Nathaniel.**
Test: William Landin, Jr., Henry Aldcock, Peter Mallard, Tho. Smith. 19, 671.

Cork (Corke), Peter, Sr., Talbot Co., 19th Nov., 1726; 9th April, 1729.

To wife **Sarah,** dwell. plan. "Lewis," St. Michael's R., during life; at her decease to 3 sons **James, Francis** and **Charles Cartwright Cork,** to be divided as wife sees fit; son **James** to have dwelling house in his portion; and personal estate during widowhood; to be divided amongst testator's own sons and daus. except her thirds.
" son **Peter** and hrs., plantation on Broad Ck.; sd. son to pay to son **John** 1,500 lbs. tob., and to son **Larance** 1,000 lbs. and give him 1 yr. schooling (wife to have her thirds of sd. land). Son **Larance** to live with his mother-in-law until 18 yrs. of age.
Test: Thomas Ashcroft, Frances Cemperson, Sarah Poorter.
19, 674.

Peck, Benjamin, Talbot Co., 18th April, 1729; 7th May, 1729.

To mother **Mary Bennett,** extx., dwell. plan. ——— during life; at her decease to pass to bros. **Daniel** and **John Peck** (for div. see will); and personal estate excepting legacies to following:
" bro. **Daniel,** bro.-in-law **George Townely** and bro. **John,** personalty.
Test: Richard Hopkins, Edward Rimner (Rimmors), Benjamin Drewitt. 19, 675.

Bennett (Benett), Peter, planter, Talbot Co.,
15th Nov., 1728;
14th May, 1729.
To wife **Mary,** extx., entire estate.
Overseer: Son-in-law **Benjamin Peck.**
Test: Elizabeth Gorden (Gordin), Mary Stoker, John Sutton. 19, 677.

Fisher, Frances, Dorchester Co., 29th Feb., 1723-4;
7th May, 1729.
To son **Richard Willis** and hrs., ½ dwell. plan. ———, on Nanticoke R.
" dau. **Frances Newton,** personalty.
" grandson **Richard Willis** and hrs., other ½ afsd. plan., pursuant to an agreement lately made with son **John Willis**; and personalty at age of 21. Son **Richard Willis** to have charge of estate during minority of sd. grandson **Richard.**
" granddaus. **Frances** and **Mary** (daus. of **Edward Newton**), personalty.
" **Elizabeth** (dau. of **Joseph Thompson**), personalty, to be delivered to her by her uncle **Edward Newton** when 18 yrs. of age.
" **Obediah, Anthony** and **Elizabeth** (child. of Richard Dawson), personalty.
" sons **Richard Willis** and **Edward Newton,** exs., residue of personal estate.
Test: Thomas Griffith, Samuel Long, William Burn (dec'd at date of probate).
Codicil: 14th April, 1729. To granddau. **Elizabeth Thomson,** son **Richard** and his sister **Mary Willis,** personalty.
Test: Thomas Thompson, Jr., William Thornell, Margaret Edwards.
Note: For deposition by Elizabeth Thompson see will.
19, 679.

Legrant, Charles, Dorchester Co., 10th May, 1729;
12th May, 1729.
To **Edward Suthell,** ex., entire estate.
Test: John Ross. 19, 684.

Smothers, James, Sr., planter, Kent Co.,
                                    9th Jan., 1723;
                                    25th April, 1729.

To dau. **Mary Iyds** and sons **William, John** and **Thomas,** 1s. each.

" wife **Elizabeth,** extx., and hrs., residue of estate.

Test: Benjamin Jones, James Bronard, Joseph Butler.
                                                    19, 684.

Ridgaway, Samuel, planter, Kent Co., 23rd Nov., 1728;
                                    1st Feb., 1728.

To wife **Sarah,** extx., entire estate during widowhood; shd. she marry, son **William** to have real estate and proper portion of personal estate; shd. sd. son die during minority, entire estate to revert to wife **Sarah** and hrs.

Test: Thomas Gould, John Cock, Alice Redgrave (Readgrave), Weniface Vandesant.   19, 686.

Mulikin, Ann, Kent Co.,   5th Feb., 1728-9;
                                    25th April, 1729.

To Mary Barber, Mary Withington and Sarah Perkins, personalty.

" **Thomas Mosell,** ex., and hrs., residue of estate; he to pay to afsd. Mary Barber portion left her by her father James Barber, dec'd, as per acct. made up.

Test: James Brouard, John Macdaniell (Macdanel), Sarah Perkins, Wm. Comegys, Sr.   19, 688.

Guibert, Thomas, St. Mary's Co., 17th March, 1728-9;
                                    7th May, 1729.

To daus. **Elizabeth** and **Anne,** personalty.

" wife **Sarah,** extx., plantation and land in the neck by Ralph Bagleys during life; at her decease to two daus. afsd. equally; and residue of personalty; to bring up daus. afsd. at her own charge.

Overseers: Bro. **Joshua** and Justinian Jordan.

Test: William Coode, James Thompson, Ann Blackiston.
                                                    19, 690.

Langly, John, Sr., St. Mary's Co., 29th Feb., 1723;
                                    26th May, 1729.

To wife **Susannah,** extx., entire estate during life; at her decease to child., viz. **John, Abraham** and **Susnanah** and their hrs.

Test: Henry Janson, William King, David Hickey. 19, 692.

Hall, Daniel, St. Mary's Co., 30th April, 1729; 26th May, 1729.

To son **John** and hrs., dwell. plan. ——— and personalty.
" sons **William** and **Daniel** and their hrs., "Coursey Point," to be divided bet. them when son **Daniel** is 21 yrs. of age; and personalty. Shd. son **John** die without issue, plan. bequeathed him to pass to son **William** and hrs., son **William** to yield his right in "Courseys" to son **Daniel**; shd. son **Daniel** die without issue, his portion to pass to his bro. **William**; shd. all 3 sons die without issue, plans. afsd. to pass to dau. **Ann** and hrs.
" dau. **Ann,** personalty.
" wife **Margaret,** extx., residue of estate.
Test: Jane (Jeane) Dunbar, William Dunbar, Thomas Underwood. 19, 693.

Coghill, William, Prince George's Co., 24th April, 1729; 4th June, 1729.

To son **Smallwood** and hrs., 70 A. "Athys Folly," nr. Broad Ck., and personalty at age of 16 yrs.
" daus. **Mary** and **Lidia,** personalty at age of 16 or day of marriage.
" wife **Ann,** extx., residue of personalty; in event of her death care of child. to Mrs. Mary Smallwood.
Test: John Abington, Philip Evans, Francis Tolson. 19, 695.

Hanley (Handley), Hugh, Dorchester Co., 29th Aug., 1726; 4th June, 1729.

To son **Hugh** and hrs., 300 A. dwell. plan. "Hanley's Regulation."
" son **Marmaduke** and hrs., 88 A. "Hanley's Adventure," 25 A. "Levin's Chance."
" dau. **Elizabeth** and hrs., 40 A. "Point Look-out," on n.w. fork of Nanticoak R.
" 3 child. afsd. (wife's thirds being first deducted), personal estate equally.
Exs.: Wife **Elinor** and sons afsd.
Test: Francis Jelly, Rodger Mackemee, John Summers, Samuel Long. 19, 697.

Robinson, Sarah, Dorchester Co., 11th Feb., 1728-9; 11th June, 1729.

To son **Solomon,** ⅓ of estate; to be in charge of dec'd husband's bro. **Solomon** until 21 yrs. of age. Shd. bro.-in-law **Solomon** die before son **Solomon** is 18 yrs. of age, he and his estate to care of **William Barke.**
" sons **William** and **Richard,** remaining ⅔ of estate; they and their estates to care of uncle **William Barke** until 21 yrs. of age.
Exs.: **Solomon Robinson** and uncle **William Barke.**
Test: Thomas Barnett (Barnitt), John Abbitt. 19,700.

Powell, Gary, Dorchester Co., 11th April, 1729; 11th June, 1729.

To bro. **Charles,** ex., and hrs., real estate left by father ———; he dying without issue, to pass to **Charles,** son of **John** and **Blanch Lecompte;** sd. **Charles** dying without issue, to pass to his bro. **Anthony Lecompte** and hrs.
Test: John Lecompte, Charles Beckwith, Thomas Mackeele. 19,701.

Hurly (Hurley), Mary, widow, Dorchester Co., 13th May, 1728; 12th June, 1729.

To **Mary Hurly** (widow), dau. **Margaret Quaturmas** and her son **Patrick Quaturmus,** personalty.
" sons **John** and **Roger,** 1s. each.
" 2 daus. **Mary** and **Elizabeth,** ⅛ of personal estate.
" son **Darby,** ex., residue of estate.
Test: Edward Elliott, Richard Hart, Grace Woodcock. 19,702.

Nelson, Ambrose, Baltimore Co., 15th Aug., 1717; 12th March, 1728.

To wife **Martha,** 200 A. dwell. plan. "Smith's Range" during life, 50 A. excepted.
" grandson **Ambros Johnson** and hrs., 50 A. of afsd. tract; he dying without issue, to granddau. **Ruth Johnson** and hrs.; and personalty at age of 21.
" 5 child., viz. **Ambrose, Richard** and **John** and daus. **Martha Pinkston** and **Sarah Frissel,** dwell. plan. afsd. at decease of wife (for div. see will).
" dau. **Sarah Johnson,** 10s.

Wife extx. and residuary legatee.
Test: Timothy White, Phillip Tennerly, Richard Young, Jr.
Note: Vide further probate, Lib. 20, page 118, anno. 1730.
19, 704.

Nickolls (Nicholls, Nicols), Henry, St. Mary's Co.,
——— ——— ———;
18th March, 1728-9.

To sister **Mary,** goddau. Susannah Nickolls, godson Henry Nickolls and Thomas and Elizabeth Nickolls, personalty.
" wife ———, residue of estate.
Test: Elizabeth Nickolls (Nicols), Thomas Nickolls (Nicols), Elizabeth Nickolls. 19, 706.

Lowe, Nicholas, gent., St. Mary's Co., ——— ——— ———;
22nd May, 1729.

To sister **Susannah Diggs** and hrs., "Bennetts Lowe," Kent Co., "Green Oak," in sd. co., and "Spries Hills," Cecil Co., on condition that her husband **Charles Diggs** will make over to sister **Mary Neale** and hrs. all rights and interests in lands in Prince George's Co., where his dwelling now stands; shd. he refuse, 2 tracts last named to revert to sd. sister **Mary** and hrs.
" sister **Mary Neale** and hrs., 1,500 A. "Barbados," Charles Co., exchanged with Mr. John Diggs.
" sister **Elizabeth Darnall** and hrs., dwell. plan. pt. of "Delabrook Manor"; 3 tracts nr. St. Mary's C. H., which Maria Farthing formerly had, and tract adjoining.
" sister **Dorothy** and hrs., "Golden Grove," Dorchester Co.
" Mrs. **Mary Young,** St. Mary's Co., "Workinton" during life; after her decease to revert to sister **Elizabeth** afsd.; and personalty.
" sisters afsd., residue of personal estate.
Exs.: **Charles Diggs** and **Henry Darnall.**
Note: Above will not signed or witnessed, proven by depositions of Robert Elliott, gent., St. Mary's Co.; Christian Geist, gent., Annapolis (30 yrs.); Philip Key, St. Mary's Co. (32 yrs.), and Edward Cole, gent., St. Mary's Co. 19, 707.

Lane, George, planter, Talbot Co., 5th May, 1729;
31st May, 1729.

To Mary Day, of Talbot Co., entire estate.
Ex.: Richard Porter, Esq.
Test: Ann Mattison, Charles Markland. 19, 709.

Wharton, Henry, Broad Ck., Talbot Co.,
2nd April, 1729;
26th June, 1729.

To wife Anstes, ½ plan. ——— during widowhood; shd. she marry, her portion to son **Henry** and hrs.
" son **Henry** and hrs., residue of plan.
" daus. **Mary Wharton** and **Margaret Murdy**, personal estate equally.

Test: Richard Aldern, Alice Roberts, Martha Smith.
19, 710.

Browne, William, cordwinder, Talbot Co.,
10th March, 1728;
24th April, 1729.

To son-in-law **Thomas Vickors** and hrs., 50 A. of "Charlwell" and personalty.
" dau.-in-law **Anne Nailer** and hrs., 100 A. of "Dunns Ranges."
" **David** and hrs. (son of dau.-in-law **Elizabeth Kerby**), 100 A. "Dunns Range."
" **Sarah** and hrs., dau. of son-in-law **William Vickors**, 50 A. of "Dunns Range," adj. land of sd. son-in-law, on condition her father gives her tract adj.; otherwise to pass to **David Kerby** afsd.
" **William Browne Vickors** and hrs., son of son-in-law **John Vickors**, dwell. plan. ——— at decease of wife **Mary**; shd. he die during minority or without issue, sd. plan. to be divided among other child. of sd. **John Vickors**; and personalty.
" **William**, son of dau.-in-law **Sarah Broadaway**, £10 when of age or day of marriage.
" **Sarah Broadaway** afsd., £6.
" **William** and **Mary Nailer**, £6 each at day of marriage, or when of age.
" **William Parlett**, apprentice, personalty, at freedom.
" wife **Mary**, residue of personal estate during life; at her decease to be divided among living child. of **John Vickors** and of **Michael Kerby**.

Exs.: Wife **Mary**, son-in-law **John Vickors** and **Michael Kerby**.

Test: Mathew Skillitt, William Parlett, Thomas Parlett, Edward Turner.
19, 711.

Smart, Capt. Richard, mariner, Dorchester Co.,
1st Aug., 1727;
21st June, 1729.

To wife Elizabeth, extx., ⅓ personal estate.
" dau. **Mary Lecompt,** 1s.
" son **Richard** and hrs., entire real estate, except tract where John Hendricks dwells; wife to have use of dwell. plan. during life; and personalty at age of 21; sd. son dying during minority or without issue, personalty bequeathed him to pass to his 3 sisters **Elizabeth, Jane** and **Smart Rebecca,** or the survivor. Shd. son Richard die without issue, lands to pass as follows: To **Smart Rebecca** and hrs., "Dorsey's Chance," "Moxam" and ⅓ of "Smart's Folly"; residue of lands to daus. **Elizabeth** and **Jane** and their hrs.; shd. daus. die without issue, sd. lands to survivor and hrs.
" daus. **Jane, Smart Rebecca** and son **Richard,** personalty.
" granddau. **Sarah** and hrs. (dau. of **William** and **Mary Lecompt**), tract where John Hendricks now dwells. Her grandmother **Elizabeth Smart** to enjoy profits of sd. land until sd. Sarah arrives at age of 18.
" child., viz. **Richard, Elizabeth, Jane** and **Smart Rebecca,** residue of estate. Wife to enjoy all estate during widowhood, or until child. are of age to choose guardians.

Overseers: Bros. **Thomas Hayward,** Somerset Co.; **William Hayward,** Dorchester Co., and **William Murray,** of same county.

Test: John Hodson 2nd, Hugh Handly, John Summers, James Farrer. 19, 714.

Crockett, Richard, Somerset Co., 28th Feb., 1726-7;
26th April, 1728.

To son **John** and hrs., pt. of tract beginning at Ceader Landing, Shileses Ck. (for desc. see will).
" 2 sons **Robert** and **Richard** and their hrs., residue of land lying in the neck; son **Richard** to have dwell. plan. ———; and personalty.
" wife **Alice,** extx., personal estate during life; at her decease to be divided among 6 child. (unnamed) now living with testator.

Test: John Evans, Jr., Robert Crockett, Jno. Crockett, Richard Crockett. 19, 716.

Pennewell (Penewell), Richard, 13th July, 1728; 22nd April, 1729.

To wife **Anne,** estate during widowhood; plan. to pass to son **George** and hrs.
" sons **Thomas, Charles, William, Richard** and **John,** personalty.

Test: Stanton Atkins (Attkins), Jonathan Williams, William Davis. 19, 718.

Gray, Westcot (Wescot, Wescoott), planter, Somerset Co., 5th March, 1729; 22nd April, 1729.

To wife **Mary,** dwell. plan. during widowhood and personalty.
" dau. **Sarah,** personalty; she dying without issue, to pass to dau. **Rebecca.**
" son **Joseph,** "Mound Hope" (Wm. Freemon to alienate sd. tract), and £10 at age of 20; shd. sd. son leave his mother, to live with Angelo Atkinson.
" son **William** and hrs., pt. of "Greens Chance," bet. Mr. Allen's and dwelling.
" Francis Allen and hrs., residue of afsd. land.
" **Rebecca, Mary** and **William,** residue of personalty.
Overseers: John Scott and Robert Mitchell.
Test: Robert Mitchell, John Atkinson, Cor. Dickeson. 19, 719.

Collins, Andrew, Somerset Co., 13th April, 1728; 4th June, 1729.

To wife **Mary,** dwell. plan. ———— during life; at her decease plan. to pass to sons **Thomas** and **Levin** and their hrs. Sons **Andrew** and **John** to have certain privileges during minority of their young bros.; and ⅓ personalty during widowhood to pass to all child. equally.
" dau. **Mary,** personalty at decease of wife.
" son **William,** ½ of "Isaac Folly," other half of sd. tract to Thomas Davis; and personalty.
" sons **Andrew** and **John** and to 3 daus. and youngest sons, personalty. Sons to serve until 21 yrs.; shd. their mother die, to be free at 18 yrs.
Test: William Davis, George Parker, Thomas Truitt. 19, 720.

Benton, Peter, planter, Somerset Co.,
3rd March, 1728-9;
13th June, 1729.

To Benton Coston and hrs., 50 A. "Saplen Ridge" and personalty.
" Mathias Coston and hrs., 50 A. "Bare Hole." Afsd. tracts to be possessed at decease of their grandmother Comfort Benton; and personalty.
" wife Comfort, extx., and hrs., entire personal estate.
Test: William Handy, William Mills, John Harris. 19, 722.

Hugg, Thomas, Stepney Parish, Somerset Co.,
17th Feb., 1726-7;
11th May, 1729.

To wife Johana, extx., dwell. plan. ——— during widowhood; shd. she marry, her thirds; and ⅓ personal estate absolutely.
" eldest dau. Jane and hrs., dwell. plan. ——— at decease or marriage of wife and ⅓ personal estate; sd. dau. to pay to youngest dau. Mary £5 to buy land.
" dau. Mary, ⅓ personal estate.
" son William (by former wife), 1s.
Test: John Wootton, John Read, Edward Wootton. 19, 723.

Jenifer, Daniel, chyrurgeon, Charles Co.,
22nd Aug., 1728;
4th June, 1729.

To son Daniel of St. Thomas Jenifer and hrs., pt. of "Durham," bou. of John Beale; pt. of "St. Edmond's," bou. of Robert Wade, and land bou. of Richard Lemaister called "Betty's Delight," "Lemaister's (Leinaster's) Delight" and "Coates Retirement."
" child. (unnamed), personal estate equally; to be in care of Rev. William Maconokie, ex., until of age.
Test: Esther (Easter) Parran, James Smith, Josias Jeffery.
19, 724.

Burch, Oliver, King and Queen Parish, Charles Co.,
15th Feb., 1726-7;
27th May, 1729.

To son Benjamin and hrs., 75 A. of "Bowling's Plains."
" son Edward, personalty.
" son Jonathan and hrs., "Lumley" ("Lombey") and "Penrick" ("Penray").

To sons **Thomas, John, Justinian** and daus. **Katherine Swan, Anne Swan, Barbary Allison, Elinor Burch** and **Elizabeth Cade,** 5s. each.
" wife **Barbary,** extx., dwell. plan. ——— during life; at her decease to son **Jonathan** and hrs.
Test: George Brett, James Phillips and Anne Phillips, his wife. 19, 725.

Dement, George, Charles Co., 2nd March, 1728-9; 31st May, 1729.

To son **George** and hrs., "Crabbtree" and 1s.
" dau. **Mary Jonson,** 1s.
" son **William** and hrs., pt. of "Miles End" that was formerly John Broockes.
" son **John** and hrs., pt. of "Miles End" that was formerly Giles Willsons.
" 6 youngest child. (undesignated), residue of personal estate.
" wife **Elizabeth,** £15 out of estate of Benjamin Word.
Ex.: **William Dement.**
Test: Edward Turner, William Ward, Edward Davis, Jr.
19, 726.

Boarman, William, Charles Co., 26th Feb., 1728-9; 30th June, 1729.

To son **William** and hrs., "St. Dorrothys," Clement's Bay, St. Mary's Co.; pt. of tract had from father, beginning at branch bet. plan. where mother-in-law ——— now dwells and Elizabeth Procters; and personalty.
" son **James** and hrs., pt. of tract had from father, including dwell. plan. and plan. where mother-in-law now lives (for desc. see will); 50 A. "Coventry"; and personalty.
" dau. **Elizabeth,** personalty. Tract nr. uncle **Benjamin's** to be sold and proceeds invested for sd. dau.
" cousin **Raphael Neal, Jr.,** personalty.
" 3 child. ———, int. in any other lands, and residue of personalty.
Exs.: Sons afsd.
Test: Rev. George Thorold, Raphael Neale, Theophilus Grew.
19, 727.

MARYLAND CALENDAR OF WILLS 119

Gardiner, Hugh (nunc.), Charles Co., 15th June, 1729.
To bros. Douglas Gifford Gardiner and Bullet, personalty.
Test: Patrick Mullen, Mathew Cheshire. Dep. show testator declared will at house of William Cheshire. 19, 729.

Cooper, Nathaniel, planter, St. Mary's Co.,
1st April, 1729;
3rd June, 1729.
To son Henry, 150 A. "Part of Scotland," Clements Bay, after death of wife.
" wife Heneritta, extx., personal estate; she dying before son comes to age of 21, Peter Jarboe to have charge of him until 18 yrs. of age.
Test: Richard Thompson, Richard Farthing, Mark Lampton.
19, 729.

Litell (Little, Littell), John, St. Mary's Co.,
31st March, 1729;
3rd June, 1729.
To godson Robert Thomas, personalty.
" wife Mary, extx., residue of estate.
Test: Robert Ford, Francis Hopewell, Robert Jackson.
19, 730.

Russel (Russell), Luke, St. Mary's Co.,
15th March, 1728-9;
3rd June, 1729.
To son Luke and hrs., 50 A. ———.
" wife Mary, to possess ½ of sd. 50 A. called "Brough," on Cooks race, during life; at her decease to revert to son Luke.
" sons, viz. Thomas and Robert Russell and Joseph Watkins and their hrs., "Golden Springs" equally; they to lay out to Elias Hannington his pt. of sd. lands.
Exs.: Wife and son Thomas.
Test: Samuel Hurst, Hudson Wathen, Marmaduke Simmes.
19, 731.

Emerson, Mary, widow, Talbot Co., 7th May, 1729;
16th July, 1729.
To grandson Aldren Williams, ½ estate.
" grandchild. William, Thomas and Mary Williams, residue of estate.
Exs.: Son Anthony Williams and his son Aldren.
Test: William Edmondson, Eliza. Baker, William Harper.
19, 732.

Maxwell, Asael, Baltimore Co., 2nd April, 1729; 16th May, 1729.

To wife **Hannah,** extx., and hrs., dwell. plan. "Taylors Choice" and lands adj. devised testator by dec'd father _____.

" sister **Anne** and hrs., "Majors Choice at the Land of Nodd"; but shd. a child be born being lawful issue of testator, then afsd. lands devised to wife and sister to pass to sd. child after decease of wife; and £15.

" bro. **James,** the younger, £24; residue of personalty to wife **Hannah.**

Test: Roger Mathews, Elizabeth Mathews, Anne Lester.

19, 733.

James, Isaac, farmer, Cecil Co., 18th March, 1728-9; 27th May, 1729.

To son and only hr. **Evan** and hrs., entire real estate, and certain personalty at age of 21. To be maintained and educated by extx. until 14 yrs. of age; shd. sd. son die before age of 21, "Elk Plaines" to be poss. by wife **Rachel** and hrs.

" wife **Rachel,** extx., entire personal estate and use of dwell. plan. afsd. during widowhood.

Overseer: Thomas Jacobs, Joseph Thomas, New Castle Co.
Test: John William, Thomas Thomas, Thomas Evans.

19, 733.

Harvey, Thomas, Calvert Co., 2nd April, 1729; 8th May, 1729.

To 3 grandchild. (unnamed), personalty.

" son **John,** pt. of real estate, and personalty; he dying without issue, to remain to **Samuel Harvey.**

" **James Harvey,** pt. of real estate; and personalty.

" **Newman Harvey,** pt. of real estate; and personalty; he dying without issue, to fall to **Samuel Harvey.**

" **Mary Stalling, Sarah Harvey** and **Samuel Harvey,** personalty.

" wife **Jane,** extx., residue of personal estate.

Test: Henry Austin, Elizabeth Bowin, Anne Somnor.

19, 735.

Harvey, Thomas, Jr., Calvert Co.,
19th March, 1728-9;
8th May, 1729.

To son **Thomas,** pt. of the land and personalty after death of his mother; to be free at age of 16.
" daus. **Elizabeth** and **Jane,** pt. of the land, and personalty; shd. the 2 child. die without issue, the land to remain for **Samuel Harvey.**
" wife **Mary,** extx., residue of personal estate.
Test: Thomas Harvey, Robert Lyle (Lyles), Priscilla Lyle (Lyles). 19, 736.

Hailes (Hails), Roger, planter, Kent Co.,
15th Jan., 1728;
30th May, 1729.

To dau. **Jane Rickits** and hrs., and to her husband **Philip Rickits** during his life, 50 A. "Green Meddow," at hd. of Farlo.
" son **Roger** and hrs., 50 A. of "The Grange." If son **Edward** will pay his bro. **Roger** 6,000 lbs. when he comes of age, the land shall be his and his hrs.
" wife **Anne,** extx., £10 and ⅓ personal estate.
" all child. ———, residue of personalty.
Test: John Williams, George Read, Richard Davis. 19, 737.

Dunn, William, Kent Co., 21st Feb., 1728-9;
14th June, 1729.

To wife **Martha,** entire personal estate during widowhood, and then to 3 child. ———; they and their estate to care of their grandfather ——— **Dunn;** he dying, to their uncle **Robert.**
Exs.: Wife and father **Robert Dunn.**
Test: Nicholas Joce, Wm. Copper, Thomas Unick. 19, 739.

Wiatt (Wyatt), James, planter, Kent Co.,
10th June, 1728;
27th Sept., 1728.

To wife **Mary,** ½ dwell. plan. ——— during widowhood; shd. she marry, her thirds and ⅓ of personal estate.
Exs. to deliver to their mother estates of the 3 child., viz. **William, Joseph** and **Elizabeth,** same to be used for their support and education. Sons to receive their estates at age of 21, daus. at 16 or day of marriage.

To dau. **Mary** (wife of **Solomon Parsons**) and dau. **Elizabeth,** personalty.
" son **James,** pts. of "Wiatt's Chance," "Wiatt's Addition" and "Charles' Lott."
" son **John,** "Harmonton," Double Ck., Q. A. Co.
" son **William,** "James Addition," w. side Ward's Branch; "Ward's Hope" and the pt. of "Wiatt's Chance" lying on lower side of sd. ck.
" son **Joseph,** residue of "Charles' Lott," pt. of "Ryhall," Q. A. Co., upper side Roistern's Ck.
" son **Thomas,** ex., residue of "Wiatt's Chance" with dwell. plan. after marriage of wife (except pt. herein bequeathed to sons **James** and **William**), and ½ "Wiatt's Addition"; sd. son to have care of sons **James** and **John** and render them their estates at age of 21.
" 6 child., viz. **Thomas, James, John, William, Joseph** and **Elizabeth,** personal estate equally.
Test: Wm. Beck, John Hitchcock, Joseph Thomas, John Withington. 19, 740.

Pearce, Isabella, Kent Co.,   21st Feb., 1728; 22nd April, 1729.

To dau. **Sarah Rogers,** grandson **Benjamin Hopkins,** grand-daus. **Anne,** wife of **Thomas Bowers; Isabella,** wife of **William Beck,** and **Elizabeth,** wife of **Augustine Terry,** and son-in-law **John Roger's** 4 child. (unnamed), personalty.
" 2 sons **Gideon** and **Benjamin** and dau. **Sarah,** wife of **John Rogers,** residue of estate, both here and in England.
Exs.: Sons **Gideon** and **Benjamin** and son-in-law **John Rogers.**
Test: Joseph Dowding, George Williamson. 19, 742.

Sanders, George, planter, Kent Co.,   18th Nov., 1728; 21st April, 1729.

To wife **Selanah,** extx., dwell. plan. ⸺ with ½ the land adj. (after dau. **Margaret Bostick** has 50 A. adj. to James Bostick's plan., being pt. of "Pryer's") during life; at decease of sd. wife to son **William** and hrs.; entire personal estate.
" son **Thomas** and hrs., plan. where William Rosser now lives, with ½ the land adj.
Test: John Rogers, William Rosser, Eliza. Rosser. 19, 743.

Murphy, James, Kent Co., 18th Jan., 1718; 21st April, 1729.

To wife **Margaret,** extx., 50 A. "Deane's Choice" (or Chance), bou. of John Cleaver, and by sd. Cleaver of William Deane, adj. "Hailstone," now in poss. of William Worrel, formerly belonging to Edward Swetnam, dec'd, with 200 A. "Churnell's Neck," s. side Chester R., bou. of John Sennott and taken up by one Churnell (Charnell); sd. lands to wife during widowhood; shd she marry, to be possessed by dau. **Prysilla;** and personal estate during widowhood.

" dau. **Pryscilla** and hrs., all afsd. lands at death or marriage of her mother; sd. dau. dying without issue, sd. lands to fall to son-in-law **William Hynson** and Simon Wilmore, Jr. (son of Simon Wilmer, now sheriff of Kent Co.), equally; shd. sd. dau. die before she comes under guardianship of Simon Wilmer, Sr., then sd. lands to pass to **Wm. Hynson;** shd. wife marry, sd. dau. to have her share of personal estate, subject to afsd. conditions.
Overseer: Simon Wilmore, Sr.
Test: Michael Miller, Jacob Glen, Thomas Hynson.

19, 745.

Brissett, John, planter, Kent Co., 9th Jan., 1728-9; 22nd April, 1729.

To son **William** and dau. **Mary,** personalty.
" 3 child. **William, Mary** and **Sarah,** residue of personal estate; to be in care of bro. **George Davis,** ex.
Test: George Skirven, Francis Barney, Robert Foreman.

19, 747.

Spearman, William, planter, Kent Co., 13th Feb., 1728-9; 16th May, 1729.

To wife **Charity,** ½ estate during widowhood, the other ½ to son **Francis;** shd. wife marry, to have her thirds, and residue of estate to sd. son, who is left to care of Friends of Kent and Cecil Meeting, who are to endeavor to bind him apprentice to Michael Corse.
Exs.: Wife and bro. **Philip.**
Test: John Williams, Thomas Bowers, Joseph Kellee.

19, 747.

Piner, Thomas, Kent Co., 4th Dec., 1728; 16th May, 1729.

To 3 sons **Thomas, John** and **Matthew,** entire real estate equally, division to be made by Simon Wilmer, Francis Lewis and James Smith, or any two of them. Son Thomas to have first choice; sd. lands not to be sold nor leased by any of sd. sons until they arrive at age of 25, and then only to one another.

" wife **Rachel,** use of dwelling house during widowhood; shd. she marry, her thirds.

" child. (unnamed), personal estate (wife's thirds excepted) when youngest child comes to age of 16, and in case that shd. die before, then when the next youngest comes to age.

Exs.: Wife and son **Thomas.**
Test: Samuel Thomas, Roger Murphey, Mary Murphey.
19, 749.

Davis, George, planter, Kent Co., 21st Jan., 1728-9; 11th July, 1729.

To wife **Elizabeth,** extx., an equal pt. with dau. **Mary** of entire estate.
Test: Berbary Robertson (Robbertson), Joseph Sill, Joseph Kellee. 19, 750.

Browne, John, Collector of Customs for distr. of Pocomoke, Somerset Co., 20th June, 1727; 21st April, 1729.

To wife **Rachel,** extx., entire estate, including that expected at death of mother, **Mrs. Margaret Browne,** of England, widow.
Test: Phillip Kennard, Jr., George Wilson, Joseph Warner.
19, 751.

Tibbot (Tibbet), James, planter, Kent Co.,
6th day, 10th mo., 1728; 21st April, 1729.

To eldest son **Samuel** and hrs., mill and land bou. of Peter Allaby; sd. son dying during minority or without issue, to pass to youngest son **Richard** and hrs., who in this event is to make over to his bro. **James** all rights and titles in lands herein bequeathed him; and personalty ordered from Robert Crookshankes, of London.

To sons **James** and **Richard** and their hrs., lands bou. of Isaac England's exs., "Tibbet's Venture," adj.; and residue of personal estate; land to be divided when son **James** comes of age. All sons, viz. **Samuel, James** and **Richard**, and sons-in-law **Thomas** and **James Mostin** to care of Monthly Meeting of afsd. co. Mill bou. of Peter Allaby to be put in poss. of Lambert Wilmore and William Simcockes until son to whom mill may fall is of age.
Exs.: Henry Evans and William Bayer, Jr.
Test: Jacob Caulk, Oliver Caulk, Samuel Smith. 19, 752.

Scott, Edward, Kent Co., 7th Feb., 1728-9; 25th April, 1729.

To son **Edward** and hrs., dwell. plan. ———.
" son **John** and hrs., other lands; and personalty.
" wife **Hannah**, extx., over and above her thirds until 2 sons are of age, all profits of estate; also a house to be built in Chester Town by Wm. Brown during her life; and personalty. Shd. wife die during minority of 2 sons, father-in-law **James Smith** and John Gresham to act as exs.
" bro. **William**, personalty; he dying during minority, to pass to bro. **Charles**, and he dying during minority, to son **Edward**.
Test: Nathaniel Rogers, John Godfrey, James Ringgold.
19, 755.

Wilkinson, Christopher, cler., St. Paul's Parish, Queen Anne's Co., 2nd April, 1729; 6th May, 1729.

To son **Christopher** and male hrs., "Royston's Creek"; he failing male hrs., to pass to son **Thomas** and his male hrs. Shd. the male line discontinue in both sd. sons, then sd. plan. to the female issue of sd. 2 sons equally.
" son **Thomas** and male hrs., dwell. plan. "Barbados Hall"; he failing male hrs., to pass to son **Christopher** and his male hrs. Shd. the male line discontinue in both sd. sons, sd. plan. to Dr. Michael Hutchinson, Rector of Hammer Smith, during life of dau. Anne Coward, in trust for use of sd. dau. with authority to sd. dau., shd. she die childless, to bequeath the same to whom she may think fit; and servant John Moore during remainder of his time, conditionally.

To wife **Sibella**, over and above settlements made on her in marriage, and her dower interests, certain personalty.

" dau. **Anne Coward**, personalty.

Exs.: Wife and son **Thomas**.

Test: William Scandret, William Nevitt, John Dawson, William Killiowe. 19, 756.

Denny (Denney), John Earle, Queen Anne's Co., 5th Jan., 1728; 16th April, 1729.

To unborn child, real estate, including dwell. plan. ———; if a son, to be of age at 21, if a dau. at 18; and personalty. Sd. child dying during minority, real estate to pass to sisters **Mary Dyre** and **Rachel Denney** and their hrs.; dwell. plan. ——— to sister **Mary**, and plan. where mother now lives to sister **Rachel**; personalty to pass to wife **Susannah** and sisters afsd.

" wife **Susannah**, extx., residue of personalty.

Test: Vincent Vanderford, Thomas Macclannahan, Robert Jones. 19, 759.

Alvey, Joseph, St. Mary's Co., ——— ——— ———; 25th July, 1729.

To eldest son **Leonard** and hrs., 200 A. "Greens Inheritance"; and personalty.

" son **Joseph** and hrs., 100 A. "Noting."

" wife ———, residue of land during life; at her decease to pass to youngest son **Arthur**.

" eldest dau. **Elinor** and dau. **Margaret**, personalty.

Test: George Knott, Richard Power, Jonathan Spencer. 19, 761.

Wheeler, Mary, Dorchester Co., 8th July, 1729; 4th Aug., 1729.

To James Rawley, ex., and hrs., entire estate.

Test: Robert Dixon, William Rawley, James Jones. 19, 762.

Reede, William, Dorchester Co., 21st Feb., 1728; 13th Aug., 1729.

(Son of **William Reede**, of Chip in Candin, Glostershire.)

To wife **Rosanna** and hrs., entire estate, including house and farms in Chip in Candin; a legacy to granddau. **Rosanna Harber** excepted.

Test: Thomas Travers, William Travers, Roger Hooper.

19, 763.

Dod, William, Dorchester Co., ——— ——— ———;
27th Aug., 1729.

To son **John** and hrs., 100 A. "Hogg Quarter," "Dod's Choice"; and personalty.
" daus. **Mary** and **Sarah**, personalty.
" wife **Sarah**, extx., residue of estate. Son to be free at 16, daus. at 15.

Test: William Jones, William Bradly, Joseph Dod.
Note: Above will not signed. 19, 764.

Jones, William, planter, Dorchester Co.,
10th May, 1729;
5th Sept., 1729.

To son **William** and hrs., 100 A. on n. side Cabbin Ck. (being pt. of tract bou. of Jacob Gray); he dying without issue, to 2 daus. **Sarah** and **Elizabeth** and their hrs.; and personalty.
" 2 daus. **Sarah** and **Elizabeth** and their hrs., 50 A. of afsd. tract; they dying without issue, to son **William** and hrs.; 100 A. dwell. plan. ———, bou. of Thomas Gray; and personalty.
" dau. **Rebecca Vearing**, personalty.
" 4 grandchild. (issue of dau. Jennet Willis, dec'd), 1s. each.
" wife **Jennet**, extx., use of dwell. plan. ———, and residue of personalty during life; at her decease personalty to pass to son **William** and daus. **Sarah** and **Elizabeth**.

Test: Capt. Henry Hooper, Frances Thomas, Mary West.
19, 765.

Benny, James, planter, Talbot Co., 23rd March, 1723;
16th July, 1729.

To 3 sons, **John, William** and **James,** real estate (220 A.) equally. Son **James** to live on dwell. plan.
" wife **Katherine**, extx., use of dwell. plan. during life; entire personal estate absolutely.

Overseer: John Morgain.
Test: Walter Riddle (Riddell), Nicholas Brown, Isaac Hall.
19, 767.

Marlow, William, planter, Charles Co.,
13th Dec., 1728;
12th Aug., 1729.

To son **Joseph** and hrs., 100 A. dwell. plan. pt. of "Aberdeene" after decease of wife.
" daus. **Anne** and **Mary**, personalty at age of 16.
" wife **Elinor**, extx., personalty and ⅓ personal estate.
" sons **Edward, William, Richard** and **James,** residue of personal estate. Sons to be for themselves at 20.
Test: John Critswell, Mary Paggitt, Henry Acton, Sr.
19, 768.

Erickson, Gunder, Prince George's Co.,
7th March, 1728-9;
22nd Aug., 1729.

To wife **Mary,** extx., and hrs., ½ of 927 A. "Erickson's Hazard"; and ½ personal estate.
" dau. **Martha** and hrs., other half afsd. tract; and ½ personal estate at age of 21 or day of marriage. Testator directs that 630 A. "Norway," on Rock Ck., 200 A. "Gunder's Delight," 2 houses and lots in Nottingham Town, Prince George's Co., and house and lot in Queen Ann Town be sold for benefit of estate.
" William Middleton, Thomas Hodgkin and Richard Deacon, personalty.
Overseer: Thomas Hodgkin.
Test: Thomas Dorsett (Dorsitt), John Anderson, Darby Rine, Thomas Hodgkin. 19, 769.

Johns, Kensey, Calvert Co.,
31st day, 1st mo. (March), 1729;
16th July, 1729.

To son **Richard** and hrs., 200 A. dwell. plan. "Mears," 200 A. of "Angellica," adj., and 1 lot in Prince Frederick Town, west of Court House.
" son **Benjamin** and hrs., 76 A. of "Whittles Rest," formerly in poss. of Spicanell and Thompson; 50 A. of same tract, formerly in poss. of Robert Woodin; also 157 A. same tract, formerly in poss. of James Beacham; 200 A. "Darby," 50 A. "Chance," 115 A. "Ball," 50 A. "Addition to Ball," and 1 lot in town afsd., east of Court House.
" son **Samuel** and hrs., 367 A. "Gunterton," bou. of William Warring; 50 A. "Hardisty," adj., bou. of Fielder Parker.
" son **Kensey** and hrs., 180 A. of "Truman's Chance," bou. of Alphonso Cosden; 500 A. "Christopher's Camp," Baltimore Co.

To daus. Eliza, Rachel and Mary, personalty at 16 or marriage.
" the Quakers, £6.
" 7 child. afsd., residue of estate; sons to receive portions at age of 18. Cargo of goods in hand and debts due in tobacco to be disposed of for benefit of estate.
Exs.: Sons Richard and Benjamin.
Overseers: Bros. Isaac Johns and Samuel Chew, of Maid Stone; George Harris and Benjamin Hance.
Test: Constance Young, George Beck, Josiah Burton.
19, 771.

Davis, John, Calvert Co., 15th Sept. 1725;
8th March, 1728-9.

To grandson **John Scarf** and hrs., 50 A. woodland; and personalty. To receive estate at age of 21.
" grandson **Henry Scarf,** personalty.
" wife ———, extx., residue of estate.
Test: James Dossey, James Ayres, James Scarth (Scarffe), John Strickland. 19, 774.

Touchstone, Richard, Sr., planter, Cecil Co.,
16th Dec., 1726;
13th Aug., 1729.

To wife **Christian,** extx., entire estate during life; at her decease to pass to son **Andrew** and hrs.; shd. wife survive sd. son, to poss. entire estate absolutely.
Test: John Williams, Godfrey Hartsfield, Richard Arindill (Arrindell). 19, 775.

Vanderheydon, Matthias, gent., Cecil Co.,
27th Aug., 1724;
10th June, 1729.

To wife **Anna Margaretta,** extx., use of entire estate during life.
" 3 daus., viz. **Francina Shippin, Aug. Harris, Ariana Bordley,** and grandson **Mathias Harris,** entire estate at decease of wife; daus. **Francina** and **Ariana** to allow estate what is due from them. Shd. sd. grandson die before he comes to age to enjoy estate, his portion to be divided amongst sd. daus.
Overseers: Sons-in-law **B.** and **J. H.**
Test: Richard Thompson, Josiah Sutton. 19, 776.

Jones, Lewis, yeoman, Cecil Co., 15th Aug., 1727;
14th Oct., 1729.

To wife **Elinor,** £5 and ⅛ of estate.
" eldest son **John** and dau. **Mary,** £31 each.
" The Church of Christ, meeting at Christiana Ck., nr. Iron Hills, £30.
" youngest son **Samuel,** ex., and hrs., entire real estate.
Test: Sarah James, Elizabeth Thomas, Elisha Thomas.

19, 777.

Preston, James, planter, Baltimore Co., 5th Nov., 1728;
5th Nov., 1729.

To 2 eldest sons **James** and **Daniel** and their hrs., 300 A. dwell. plan. "Denises Choice."
" youngest son **Barnard** and hrs., 100 A. "Preston's Chance."
" wife **Sarah** and child. (unnamed), personal estate; £6 to be deducted from share of dau. **Grace,** wife of **Charles Anderson.**
Test: Daniel Scott, George Rigdon, John Kearsey. 19, 778.

Grover, George, planter, Baltimore Co.,
29th Sept., 1729;
8th Nov., 1729.

To son **George** and hrs., pt. of land bet. river and road to William Denton's.
" son **John** (son of wife **Magdolin**) and hrs., residue of sd. land; he dying without issue, to pass to next in blood of the Grovers; and personalty.
" wife **Magdalen,** extx., residue of estate.
Test: William Wood, Anthony Asher, Ann Jones. 19, 779.

Taylor, Richard, Baltimore Co., —— ——, 1726;
18th May, 1729.

To dau. **Frances** and hrs., 275 A. of "Taylor's Discovery"; and personalty; sd. dau. dying without issue, land to pass to son **Joseph** and hrs.; he dying without issue, to son **Thomas** and hrs.
" son **Thomas** and hrs., 300 A. "Taylor's String," 125 A. "Addition to Taylor's String" and 80 A. of "Taylor's Discovery"; sd. son dying without issue, to pass to son **Joseph** and hrs.

To son **Joseph** and hrs., 860 A. dwell. plan. "Taylor's Range," 70 A. "Addition to Taylor's Range," 99 A. "Addition to Shoomaker's Hall"; sd. son dying without issue, to pass to son Thomas and hrs.; both sons failing issue, to pass to dau. **Frances** and hrs.
" granddau. **Margaret Sing** and hrs., 150 A. of "Taylor's Discovery"; she dying without issue, to son **Thomas** and hrs.; he failing issue, to son **Joseph** and hrs.
" son **Richard**, 5s.
" son **Joseph**, 1 A. bou. of John Ensor for a Meeting House and burying place for Friends.
" wife **Ann**, use of dwell. plan. ——— during life and ⅓ personal estate.
" sons **Thomas** and **Joseph,** dau. **Frances** and granddau. **Margaret Sing,** residue of personal estate equally.
Exs.: Sons **Thomas** and **Joseph.** Son **Joseph** empowered to convey a tract mentioned in bond given John Hillen, dated 1725.
Test: John Cross, Benjamin Price, Edward Fell, George Hitchcock. 19, 781.

Murphy (Murfey), John, Baltimore Co.,
30th March, 1729;
5th Aug., 1729.

To son **John,** ½ (50 A.) of plan. ———.
" son **Edward,** other half of sd. plan. "Murfey's Hazard." Sons to be of age at 21; when son **John** arrives at age the Vestry of St. George's Parish to appoint 2 men to divide sd. land. Shd. either son die without issue, sd. pt. or whole to fall to next hr., and so from hr. to hr., without sale, forever.
" wife **Mary,** extx., ⅓ personal estate, residue to child. equally.
Test: Mary Burchfeld, Ann Curtis, Ann Swelvan, Owen Swelvan (Swillivant). 19, 783.

Burnell, Jane, spinster, Annapolis, 3rd March, 1728;
11th March, 1728.

To Caleb Dorsey, ex., and hrs., lot, dwelling and household goods in afsd. city.
" The Church, £5 toward repairs.
" Thomas Hinton, £15.
" Thomas Clark, 3 pistoles.
" Mrs. Beckingham and Mrs. Ann Gough, £5 each.
" Edward, son of Edward Smith, dec'd, £3.

To Sarah (dau. of John Smith, carpenter), personalty.
" widow Cainswell(?), Abigl. Rind, Elinor Meek, Susan Pain, Mary Toby, Eliza. Lawley and Eliza Beesly, 20s. each.
Test: Charles Cole, Dr. Samuel Stringer, John Smith, Isabell Smith. 19, 784.

Carter, Edward, A. A. Co., 30th Jan., 1728; 14th March, 1728.

To 3 sons of bro. **Sparrow**, viz. **William, Edward** and **Solomon**, £40, or in lieu thereof 50 A. of "Loyd's Triangle," pt. adj. Capt. Cowman and Capt. Larkin's line; sd. 50 A. may be sold to pay sd. sum of money.
" Eliza. Lewis, extx., residue of afsd. tract during life; at her decease to dau. **Tomeson** and the 2 child. of the sd. Eliza., viz. Kely and Elinor Lewis.
" Marjory Green, 1 A. with house rent free during life.
Test: William Hood, Richard Briant, John Roberts. 19, 785.

Attwood, Henry, A. A. Co., 20th Feb., 1729; 31st March, 1729.

To dau. **Jane**, dwell. plan. ———, in Baltimore Co., and 100 A. bou. of Jonathan Tipton; sd. dau. dying during minority, sd. lands to wife ——— and hrs.
" wife ———, extx., use of ⅓ dwell. plan. ——— during life and ⅓ of estate; residue to dau. afsd.
Test: William Ford (Foard), Joseph Pratt, Robt. Kendall.
19, 787.

Watson, Mark, butcher, Annapolis, 18th May, 1726; 12th April, 1729.

To George Johnson, of sd. city, personalty.
" Elizabeth, wife of George Johnson, extx., and hrs., entire real and personal estate.
Test: William Cullen, Michael Kelly, John Michiell.
19, 787.

Holliday (Holloday), William, planter, A. A. Co., 7th Nov., 1720; 9th April, 1729.

To 6 child., viz. sons **Benoni** and **William**, daus. **Rachell**, Eliz., Sarah and Catherine, entire estate equally as they come of age or marry. Son **William** to be free at 16.
Ex.: Son **Benoni**.

Overseers: Samuel Harrison and Samuel Chew, of Maidstone, to see that child. are educated as Quakers.
Test: Wm. Ludwigg, Charles Steward, Tobias Lawrence, Mary Mayhew. 19, 789.

Carroll (Caroll), James. "Fingaul," Allhallows Parish, A. A. Co., 12th Feb., 1728; 27th June, 1729.

To 40 mendicants of and in the parishes of Eglish and Lorrah, in Lower Ormond, Co. of Tipperary, Ireland, each 10s., Irish money.
" 20 poor people in this parish, and the parish where quarters are in Prince George's Co., personalty, to be delivered if applied for at dwelling place or at "Carrolburgh." Exs. instructed to sell lands in Baltimore, Somerset and Calvert Counties, also all mortgages, bills of sale, etc., and 2 lots in Annapolis, at hd. of ck., bou. of John Hammond. After payment of debts £1,000 of proceeds to be applied toward education of nephew and hr. apparent **Anthony** (only son of bro. **Daniel**); shd. sd. nephew die or prove incorrigible, want application or prove vicious before he attains age of 21, sd. money to be applied to education of nephew **James** (son of bro. **Michael**) if he shall not exceed 16 yrs. at death of testator, otherwise to be used for such one of his bros. as shall not be 16 yrs. at sd. time, decision to be made by exs.; residue of proceeds to be used for education of 2 sons of bro. **Michael** nearest 15 yrs. of age at death of testator. Exs. empowered to make over to George Ijams and Francis Day land sold to them, also 200 A. of "Pork Hall" to George Roberts.
" cousins **Domnick, Anthony** and **Daniel** (sons of bro. **Michael**) and their hrs., 500 A. each of "Pork Hall," at Pipe Ck.
" sister **Johanna Croxell** and cousin **Mary Higgins** and their hrs., 980 A. of afsd. tract.
" cousin **Michael Taylor** and hrs., 700 A. "Bin."
" cousins **Edward Tully** and **Michael Tully's** 2 sons (unnamed) and their hrs., "Hopyard."
" cousin **Anthony** and sister **Johanna**, personalty.
" cousin **Charles** and hrs., lot given testator by him and his mother ———, lot adj. thereto, ½ lot bou. of Benj. Tasker, all adj. in the city of Annapolis; dwelling place cont. 260 A., residue unsold of "Bright Seat" and "Ayno," nr. Patuxent, above hd. of South R.; "Carrols Burgh," "Cheney's Plantation," 60 A. "Ridgely and Tylors

Chance," in all about 200 A., Prince George's Co.; 2 lots Queen Anne Town, and 2 tracts nr. sd. town bou. of Thomas Lancaster and Turner Wootton; personalty and personal estate not otherwise disposed of.

To nephew **James**, £100 for education, and for expenses in London to be paid out of money due in England.

Cousin **Anthony**, residuary legatee and ex. with cousin **James** afsd.; during their minority and absence kinsmen **Charles Carrol, John Diggs, Francis Hall** and cousin **Dr. Charles Carroll**, of Annapolis, to act as exs.

Test: Dr. Samuel Chew, of Maidstone; William Richardson, Dr. Richard Hill, Andrew Taile.

Codicil: 12th Feb., 1728. Bequest to cousin **Charles** of a certain pt. of estate revoked and sd. lands bequeathed to George Thorold and hrs., Portobacco, Charles Co. Shd. sd. Thorold die before testator, sd. lands to Peter Attwood and hrs., of Portobacco afsd.; and in case of both their deaths as afsd., sd. lands, etc., to pass to Joseph Greaton and hrs.

Test: John Welsh (Walch), Anthony Carroll, John Galloker.
19, 791.

Stinchcombe. Nathaniel, planter, A. A. Co.,
15th March, 1728-9;
25th June, 1729.

To wife **Anne**, extx., and child. ———, entire estate divided as law directs; child. to be of age at 18.

Test: John Merriken, Frances Smith, George Venum.
19, 799.

Jordan, John, innholder, Annapolis,   6th Sept., 1729;
20th Sept., 1729.

To dau. **Mary** and hrs., all real estate in Province, except such as hereafter excepted; and personalty, including white servants named Timothy Collahone, Jacob Merrifield and Mary Hungerford (portion of personalty desc. as in poss. of Wm. Beckingham).

" wife **Margaret**, extx., ½ of afsd. real estate during widowhood; shd. she marry, use of ⅓ thereof during life, and use of house wherein Ralph Smith now lives until dau. afsd. arrives at age of 16 (provided sd. house is not sold for payment of debts). Shd. dau. die during minority, sd. house to wife and hrs. absolutely, and ½ of sd. lands and personalty to pass to **Edmond** and **Walter** and their hrs. (sons of bro. **William**, Athlone,

Ireland) at such time as they arrive in Maryland. Exs. instructed to sell a lot in pt. of city called "Newtown," bounded at one end by Scotch St. and at other by Severn R.; also house in city called Kentish House, and land bet. it and water; and if necessary, house where Ralph Smith now lives for benefit of estate.

Overseers: Daniel Dulany, Charles Carroll, chirurgeon; Robert Gordon and John Galloway. Shd. wife die during minority of dau., or marry, overseers are instructed to care for education of sd. dau.

Test: William Cumming, Robert Alexander, John Beale, Robert Gordon.

1st Nov., 1729. Widow claims her thirds, f. 807.   19, 800.

Conaway (Conoway), John, planter, A. A. Co.,
29th March, 1728;
12th Aug., 1729.

To son **John** and hrs., dwell. plan. "Low Neck" and personalty.
" son **Charles** and hrs., "Luckey Hole."
" daus. **Jane** and **Sarah** and cousin **Joseph**, personalty.
" 4 child. afsd., residue of personal estate after wife's thirds are deducted.

Extx.: Wife **Catherine**.

Test: Mordecai Hammond, William Houchin, Sebastian Oley.   19, 805.

Randal (Randall), Catherine, A. A. Co.,
8th Nov., 1728;
14th March, 1728-9.

To grandson **James Lewis** and hrs., dwell. plan. "Town Hill"; he dying without issue, to grandson **Robert Welsh, Jr.**, and hrs.; son-in-law **Robert Welsh** to have use of sd. plan. until **James Lewis** afsd. arrives at age of 25.
" son **Robert Welsh** and hrs., "Diligent Search," A. A. Co., on condition that sd. tract is not needed for payment of debts.

Test: Samuel Smith, Margery Green, James Welsh.
    19, 808.

Faudry (Faudrie) Moses, planter, Herring Ck., St. James Parish, A. A. Co., 31st Aug., 1728;
22nd April, 1729.

To wife **Elizabeth**, extx., entire estate.

Test: John Elliot Brown, William Vernon.   19, 809.

Jubb, Robert, planter, A. A. Co., 5th April, 1723;
17th Oct., 1729.

To dau.-in-law **Helen** (dau. of Daniel Brigdell), personalty at age of 16 or marriage.
" **Robert Crabtree,** £5.
" sister **Mary Jackson,** now living in Great Britain, and her child., £15.
" wife **Helen,** extx., and hrs., residue of estate, real and personal.
Test: Edw. Griffith, Sarah Griffith, Sebastian Oley. 19, 811.

Magee, John, planter, Somerset Co., 20th April, 1728;
28th July, 1729.

To wife **Elizabeth,** extx., ⅓ of estate; if she remains unmarried, 4 sons, viz. **Peter, Samuel, Moses** and **David,** to remain with her until they are 21; if she marries, to be free at 18.
" 3 sons **George, John** and **Peter** and their hrs., 300 A. "Coxes Choice" equally, the eldest to have first choice and **John** next; if either of 3 shd. die without issue, his pt. to fall to next eldest bro. that has no land.
" 7 child. ———, residue of estate equally.
Test: John Shockley, Margery Ruak, John Reddish.
19, 813.

Laws, William, planter, Somerset Co.,
21st May, 1729;
20th Aug., 1729.

To wife **Sarah,** dwell. plan. ——— and personal estate during widowhood.
" son **William** and hrs., dwell. plan. ——— and 50 A. adj. "Law's his Last Choice," after his mother's widowhood or decease; and personalty.
" son **John** and hrs., 150 A. "Cumber Land" and 50 A. adj. at day of his mother's marriage or death; and personalty.
" sons **Elijah** and **Bolitha** and daus. **Esther** and **Rachael,** personalty.
" sons **William, Elijah** and **Bolitha** and dau. **Esther,** cash on hand and money due from John Atkinson.
" child. **Rachel, William, Esther, John, Elijah** and **Bolitha,** residue of personal estate.
Exs.: Wife Sarah and John Beavans.
Test: Samuel Taylor, Elizabeth Johnson, James Noble.
20th Aug., 1729. Widow renounces above will. Test: William Marchment, John Sheldon.
20th Aug., 1729. John Beavans renounces as ex. Test: Francis Allen, John Sheldon. 19, 814.

Nutter, Christopher, Stepney Parish, Somerset Co.,
13th Feb., 1728;
23rd Aug., 1729.

To sons Christopher and William, exs., and their hrs., real estate (reserving to wife her dowry during life), division to begin at marked tree on line formerly made bet. lands of bro. Matthew, to run to a ridge nr. William Austin's (for desc. see will); dwell. plan. upon Monumpco and sd. div. of land adj. to son Christopher and hrs., other div. on Quantico side to younger son William.

" son Christopher, £60 and personalty. Wife Margaret not to be disturbed on dwell. plan. during life.

" wife Margaret and sons afsd., residue of personal estate.
Test: Anna Makmorie, Sarah Austin, John Jones, James Makmorie. 19, 818.

Wilson, Thomas, Sr., planter, Somerset Co.,
30th March, 1722;
16th Aug., 1729.

To son John, ex., and hrs., entire estate, real and personal; sd. son to give to granddau. Mary (dau. to son Thomas, dec'd) either 100 A. or money to purchase 100 A., to be pd. her at day of marriage.
Test: Thomas Wood, Edward Wheatly, Rachell Wood.
19, 821.

Johnston (Johnson, Joneston), Samuel, St. Mary's Co.,
4th Aug., 1729;
24th Nov., 1729.

To dau. Susanah and hrs., choice of dwell. plan. ——— or "Redman's Hardship"; the other plan. to son Samuel and hrs.

" son and dau. afsd., exs., residue of estate.
Test: Paul Grugen, Ann Foye, Geo. Craghill. 19, 823.

Whislor, Thomas, St. Mary's Co., 23rd Nov., 1729;
8th Dec., 1729.

To Catherine Welsh (an orphan girl desc. as living with testator), entire estate at age of 16 or day of marriage.
Ex.: James Conen.
Test: William Keating, Martha Warrin. 19, 824.

Kemp, William, joyner, St. Michael's Parish, Talbot Co.,
10th March, 1728;
14th Nov., 1729.

To son **William** and hrs., 223 A. "Mable (Mabel) Enlarged" and pt. of "Kemp's Lot"; sd. son dying without issue, sd. tracts to pass to 3 eldest daus. **Elizabeth, Rachel** and **Martha** and their hrs.; sd. daus. to pay to their 2 youngest sisters **Jane** and **Constant** 3,000 lbs. each at age or marriage.

" all child. ———, personal estate.

Exs.: Wife **Martha** and son **William.**
Test: John Blackitt (Blacki), William Suel, Elizabeth Hughes (Hughs).   19, 825.

Woolman (Wollman, Wolman), Sarah, Talbot Co.,
29th Feb., 1728;
26th Nov., 1729.

To **Sarah** (dau. of John Emerson) and hrs., plan. ———, where John Huet lives, with land adj.; and personalty; sd. Sarah dying without issue, to pass to her bro. **Vincent Emerson** and hrs.; he dying without issue, to **Robert** (son of John Hewet).

" **Robert Hewet** afsd., dwell. plan. ———; and personalty.

" **Sophia Sutton, Elice Hewet, Sophia Start, Sarah Emerson,** sister **Alice,** cousin **Rachel Gibson, Barbara Gibson,** Sarah (dau. of John Sutton) and her sister Elice Sutton, kinsman **Vincent Emerson,** cousin **Ephraim Start** and John Hewet, personalty. Exs. to give **Vincent Emerson** 1 year's schooling.

" **Richard Gibson,** Elice Hewet and Sophia Sutton, residue of estate.

Exs.: Cousin **Richard Gibson** and John Hewet.
Test: Richard Hews, Chrisopher Hews, William Harper.
19, 827.

Leeds, John, planter, Talbot Co.,   3rd Nov., 1729;
3rd Dec., 1729.

To wife **Esther,** extx., entire real estate, including land had from father ———, "Long Delay"; and personal estate.
Test: William Hambleton, Solomon Horney, Philemon Hambleton (Hamilton).   19, 831.

Clarke, Edward, cordwinder, Talbot Co.,
12th day, 5th mo., 1723;
13th Nov., 1729.

To grandson **Edward Kane Clarke,** at age of 21, portion intended for his father **Henry.**
" son **Caleb** and hrs., 100 A. "Delaroy"; and personalty.
" son **Joshua,** dau. **Jane** (after decease of wife) and dau. **Hannah,** personalty.
" wife **Jane,** use of dwell. plan. ——— during life; and personalty.
" son **Edward,** residue of estate.
Exs.: Wife and son **Edward.** Testator directs that he be buried at Tuckahoe Meeting.
Test: Joseph Arey (dec'd at date of probate, signature sworn to by Jane Arey, his wife, and John Loveday), Benjamin Laurence (dec'd at date of probate, sig. sworn to by Edward Clarke, Jr.), W. Goult, Thomas Turner.
19, 833.

Oldham, John, gent., Talbot Co., 14th Oct., 1729;
9th Dec., 1729.

To wife **Mary,** ⅓ estate, real and personal, during life.
" dau. **Mary,** 2 yrs. after decease of testator, and dau. **Martha,** at age of 21, personalty.
" son **Edward** and hrs., residue of real and personal estate.
Exs.: Wife and son **Edward.**
Test: Benja. Pemberton, William Skinner, Jr., Sarah Skinner.
19, 834.

Jenkins, Ann, Charles Co., 25th June, 1729;
3rd Dec., 1729.

To Elizabeth Windsor (Windzer), personalty, some of which desc. as in poss. of Robert Deyne.
" dau. **Mary Narris,** personalty.
" sons **Edward** and **William,** exs., residue of estate.
Test: Mathew Stone, Martha Walley. 19, 836.

Rich, Stephen, Queen Anne's Co., 25th May, 1722;
26th June, 1729.

To son **Stephen** and hrs., dwell. plan. ———.
" dau. **Anne Eyter,** personalty.
" child. ———, residue of estate (wife to have her equal part therein).

Ex.: Solomon Clayton.
Test: Thomas Butler, Harry Williams, Henry Oldson, Andrew Helsen.
19, 838.

Benham, Benjamin, Queen Anne's Co., 10th July, 1729; 11th Sept., 1729.

To 4 sons, viz. **John, Mathew, Benjamin** and **Thomas**, entire estate. Son **Mathew** to care of John White until 18 yrs. of age; sons **Benjamin** and **Thomas** to care of son **John Boussell** until of sd. age.
Exs.: John Bussell and John White.
Test: John Harris, Thomas Jackson, Robert Offley.

19, 839.

Davis, Simon, Queen Anne's Co., 6th Sept., 1729; 27th Nov., 1729.

To wife Katherine, extx., personal estate during life; at her decease to pass to Nathan and hrs., son of Charles Wright, and for want of such hrs., to Sarah, dau. of Richard Powel.
Test: John Tillotson, Nath. Cleve (Cleaves), W. Harper.

19, 841.

Elliot, George, Queen Anne's Co., 8th Nov., 1729; 18th Dec., 1729.

To son **George** and hrs., dwell. plan. "Rawlin's Chance"; and personalty, some of which des. as bou. of Simon Wilmer and Capt. Vincent.
" son **John** and hrs., "Elliot's Addition," adj. to afsd. tract; and personalty.
" son **William** and hrs., 50 A. "Mount Hope," bou. of Henry Wilcocks; sd. land to be sold only to bros. afsd. Shd. son **William** die without issue and in poss. of sd. land, to pass to son **John** afsd.; shd. son **John** die without issue, land bequeathed him to pass to son **William**; and personalty.
" daus. **Mary Carpenter, Anna** and **Mary Anna**, granddau. **Mary Anna** and **John Carpenter**, personalty. Testator des. himself as a Quaker.
Exs.: 3 sons afsd.
Test: Thomas Trickey, Daniel Wilcocks, Ann Hamer,

19, 842.

Clayton (Claytan), Rachel, Queen Anne's Co.,
25th April, 1729;
28th Aug., 1729.

To dau. **Mary** and hrs., 300 A. of "Smith's Ridge," where John Swallowe lived.
" son **Edward** and hrs., dwell. plan. ———, pt. of "Chesterfield."
" dau. **Rachel** and hrs., 100 A. of "Sheppard Forrest."
Note: Above will with consent of husband **Solomon Clayton**.
Test: Thomas Butler, Esther Banbury, Walter Carmichall.
19, 848.

Perry, Daniel, planter, Queen Anne's Co.,
13th July, 1729;
28th Aug., 1729.

To Elizabeth, wife of Benjamin Ridgway, personalty.
" wife **Mary**, dwell. plan. ——— during life, to pass at her decease to son **John**; and personal estate divided equally with son **John** and dau. **Margaret**.
Ex.: Son **John**.
Test: William Ridgway (Ridgers), James Scotten, Jonathan Jolley.
19, 849.

Hutson (Hudson), Richard, planter, Kent Island,
6th Nov., 1729;
18th Dec., 1729.

To son **John** and daus. **Mary** and **Frances**, personalty.
" wife **Catharine**, extx., residue of estate.
Test: Robert Walters, Francis White, John Blaides (Blades).
19, 852.

Hemsley, Vincent, Talbot Co., 4th Jan., 1728;
16th Jan., 1729-30.

To cousin **Ann Hemsley** and hrs., 40 A. "Long Point," adj. to a tract formerly called "Wilkinson's Choice," now called "Carter's Inheritance."
Test: William Gough (Gought), Lazarus Cox, Edward Downes.
19, 853

Whips, Elizabeth, widow, Calvert Co., 11th Nov., 1729;
5th Dec., 1729.

To younger bro. and sister **William** and **Jane Madcaff,** living in Yorkshear, nr. Askrig, entire estate except legacies to following: Thomas Vernon, Rachell Griffith and Eliza. Foudry.

Ex.: Roger Crudgenton, of A. A. Co., to sell estate and send proceeds to Phill. Smith, mcht. in London, who is to pay same to bro. and sister afsd.

Test: William Phillips, Eliza. Fadry, Rachel Griffith.

19, 855.

Williamson, Samuel, gent., St. Mary's Co.,
19th June, 1713.

(Articles of agreement with **Judith Swann,** widow.)
In consideration of marriage to be consummated bet. sd. parties, the sd. **Samuel** agrees as follows:

1st. Denies for himself and hrs. any rights or interest to any pt. of personal estate of sd. **Judith,** and gives his free consent for sd. **Judith** to dispose of personal estate poss. by her before marriage to her child. as to her shall seem fit.

2nd. Should sd. **Judith** survive him, the sd. **Samuel** agrees that she shall poss. his entire personal estate during her lifetime, relinquishing for herself and hrs. all interest in his real estate, excepting a certain rent to be pd. to her annually during her widowhood. The afsd. **Wilkinson** gives bond for £500, dated 19th June, 1713, to Thomas Swan, carpenter, of Charles Co., trustee of **Judith Swann,** of Saint Mary's Co., widow of Capt. James Swann, of sd. co., dec'd.

Test: Philip Briscoe, Edward Lorde. 19, 857.

Cooke, Thomas (nunc.), St. Mary's Co.,
13th Nov., 1729.

To dau. **Dianna,** personalty, some of which des. as having belonged to proper mother of sd. **Dianna.**

" unborn child of wife **Johannah,** personalty.

Test: John Jones, planter; Catherine, wife of Walter Sykes, Poplar Hill Hundred. 19, 860.

Haliewell (Holliwell, Holloway), William, St. Mary's Co.,
2nd Feb., 1729;
13th Feb., 1729.

To Thomas Scott, entire estate after legacies are pd.; shd. any of bros. in England come into this country and make demand for estate, sd. ex. is to yield same to them, names of which are as follows: Lawrence, John and Richard Holloway, William Ward, Thomas Asmuth and George Ashworth.

" Hannah Phillips (wife's goddau.), Jane, dau. of Phillip Tippet; Butler, son of Dennis Tippet; John and Alexander, sons of Robert Cook, dec'd, and James Baily, personalty.

Thomas Scott, ex. and resid. legatee.
Test: Philip Dorey, Samuel Hurst, John Monocks. 19, 862.

Robson, William, Dorchester Co., 3rd July, 1728;
4th Feb., 1729.

To son-in-law John Woolland and dau. Jane Kersey, personalty.

" wife Jane, extx., 100 A. "Robson's Outlett"; sd. wife to allow Henry Keene and Eliz. Martin certain privileges therein. Deeds of gift to Mary Keene and dau. Eliz. Martin confirmed. Wife empowered to make over land sold to John Robson on e. side St. John's Ck. Residue of personal estate absolutely.

Test: John Meekins, Sr., John Meekins, Jr., William Gadd.
19, 865.

Pinder (Pindar), Edward, Dorchester Co.,
26th Jan., 1729;
13th Feb., 1729.

To sister Dorothy Stableford and hrs., "Surveyor's Forrest," s. side Ingram's Ck.
" bros. Charles Stableford and Thomas Stableford and their hrs., dwell. plan. "Horne."
" aunt Eliz. Taylor, extx., entire personal estate.
Test: Walter Campbell, John Lecompte, Charles Powell.
19, 866.

Smith, Arthur, Dorchester Co., 28th July, 1721;
12th March, 1729.

To wife **Margret,** extx., entire estate.
Test: Mark Fisher, Elinor Fallen (Falen), Alce Kirke.
Codicil: 19th Jan., 1729. Confirms above will.
Test: John Briscoe, Thomas Parker (Parks). 19, 867.

Mace, Josias, planter, Dorchester Co., 13th Jan., 1729;
12th March, 1729.

To father ———, ex., and hrs., entire estate.
Test: John Brannock, Jr., Robert Still, Catherine Ross.
19, 869.

Lambdin, William, Sr., planter, Talbot Co.,
28th Nov., 1729;
14th Jan., 1729.

To son **William, Jr.,** and male hrs., dwell. plan. "Summerton."
" son **Daniel** and male hrs., "Winterton."
" son **John** and male hrs., "William and Maries Addition," bounded according to lines mentioned in deed from John Lowe; sd. tract escheated out of "Grafton's Mannor"; and personalty.
" son **George** and dau. **Ann Roberts,** daus. **Elizabeth** and **Sarah,** certain personalty above their share of personal estate. Wife **Sarah,** after her former husband's legacies are pd., to have privilege of making her choice in her thirds of estate. Tobacco due from Richard Richardson's store in Oxford to be pd. to clothe child., viz. **Elizabeth, John** and **Sarah;** son **John** to make no bargain without consent of his 2 bros. afsd. until of age.
" all child., viz. **William, George, Daniel** and **John, Anne Roberts** and **Elizabeth** and **Sarah,** residue of personal estate; dau. **Sarah** to receive her portion at age of 16.
Exs.: Sons **William** and **Daniel.**
Test: George Collison, Edward Auld, Andrew Orem, Thomas Smitz. 19, 870.

Blake, Peter, Talbot Co., 16th Nov., 1729;
14th Jan., 1729.

To eldest son **John,** second son **Peter** and dau. **Elinor Wrightson,** personalty.
" son-in-law **Nathaniel Santee,** personalty, in lieu of his portion of his own father's estate.
" wife **Elizabeth** and 3 child., residue of estate.

Exs.: Wife and son-in-law **Francis Wrightson**.
Test: Francis Perkins, John Davis, John Parr.   19, 874.
28th Jan., 1729. Widow claims her thirds.

Bennet (Benett, Benet), Mary, widow, Talbot Co.,
                                11th Jan., 1729;
                                4th March, 1729.
To dau. **Elizabeth Towing**, personalty, with condition that sd. dau. give certain personalty to Sarah Feck.
" son **John Peck**, ex., personalty.
Test: Nicholas Goldsborough, Jr., Samuel Small.   19, 876.

Dunn, Robert, Kent Co.,   30th Dec., 1710;
                                28th Nov., 1729.
To wife **Mary**, extx., estate which was hers at marriage, she paying debts and legacies she was obligated for in full of her thirds or any other claim to estate; shd. she object, to have ⅛ of estate as law directs, with privilege of living on dwell. plan. ——— and keep testator's 2 daus. and all children's estates in her hands during widowhood; to give security for payment of same to each as they come to age.
" son **Robert** and hrs., dwell. plan. "Broadnox"; he dying without issue, to pass to dau. **Jane** and hrs.; and personalty.
" son **William** and hrs., "Hawkins" and "The Adventure," bou. of Anthony Workman, dec'd; sd. son dying without issue, to pass to dau. **Mary** and hrs.; and personalty.
" daus. **Jane** and **Mary**, personalty.
" 4 child., residue of estate equally.
Ex.: Bro. **James Harris**.
Test: Peter Read, George Hills, Wat Harris, Charles Neale.
                                                            19, 877.

Wetherell (Weathrill), George, blacksmith, Kent Co.,
                                  14th Jan., 1729-30;
                                  13th Feb., 1729.
To eldest son **George** and hrs., his choice bet. dwell. plan. ———, nr. Steal Pone Ck., or "Weatherill's Hope," the other plan. to son **John** and hrs.; shd. either die without issue, their portions to fall to son **Samuel** and hrs.; 3 sons to be of age at 20 yrs.
" wife ———, extx., use of dwell. plans. during widowhood.
" 3 child., personal estate; son **Samuel** to have £16 out of same before division.
Test: Griffith Jones, Mary Jones, George Foxson.   19, 879.

Brown, William, carpenter, Kent Co.,
                                   28th Jan., 1729-30;
                                   16th Feb., 1729.

To son **William,** dau. **Mary,** wife of **James Dill,** and dau. **Naomy,** 5s. each.

" wife **Jean,** extx., entire estate during life; at her decease to son **Calup** and hrs.

Test: William Crackan, David Dowlen, Anthony Murrett.
                                                    19, 880.

Leonard, Charles, planter, Kent Co., 29th Jan., 1728-9;
                                   19th Sept., 1729.

To wife **Eleanor,** use of estate for benefit of children. Sons to remain with their mother until 21 yrs. of age; shd. wife marry, to have her thirds only, and child. to care of exs.

" child. **Henry, James, John, Winefrid, Katherine** and **Patrick,** equal share of estate as they come of age; boys of age at 21, girls at 16. 2 daus. **Mary Pell** and **Elizabeth** to have their equal share, to be pd. them by wife or exs. 10 yrs. after decease of testator.

Exs.: Robert Mansfield, David Perkins.

Test: Joseph Bazenbe (Bazenbie), James McDaniel, James Weeding.   19, 882.

Sheehe, David, Somerset Co., 29th April, 1626 (sic.);
                                   27th Jan., 1729.

To wife **Sarah,** her son **David** and dau. **Margery,** entire estate; shd. one of these 2 child. die without issue, survivor to inherit portion of dec'd.

" Pottr. **Sheehe, Elizab. Paromer** and **Mary Word,** 1s. each, and no other pt. of estate.

Test: Christopher Nutter, Sr., Christopher Nutter, Jr.
                                                    19, 884.

Baily, Stephen,   13th Feb., 1729;
                                   7th March, 1729.

To 2 sons **Elias** and **William** and their hrs., dwell. plan. ———, plan. at other side of branch; and personalty.

" wife **Sarah,** extx., personalty; residue of estate divided according to law; sons to be free at 18 yrs. if their mother marries, otherwise at 21.

Test: John Christopher, Clement Christopher, Christopher Dowdall.   19, 885.

Hangline (Hongline), William, planter, Somerset Co.,
                                                         3rd Sept., 1720;
                                                         24th March, 1729.

    To wife **Izabel**, extx., and hrs., entire estate, real and personal, including "Evan's Purchase," s. side Nanticoake R.
    Test: Neal McClester, Thomas Laramur, Izabell Samuell, Elizabeth Samuell, Williabe James.   19, 886.

Wordie, Alexander, Somerset Co.,   20th Feb., 1729;
                                                         24th March, 1729.

    To wife **Susannah**, extx., ⅓ real estate during life; at her decease to pass to son **John** and hrs.; to divide residue of estate equally with 2 child. **John** and **Hannah**.
    Test: Levin Gale, Archibald Stirling, Patrick Stewart.
                                                                              19, 887.

Fenwick, Cuthburt, St. Mary's Co., ——— ——— ———;
                                                                     23rd March, 1729.

    To 2 eldest daus. ———, 10s. each; gifts to them confirmed.
    " dau. **Elizabeth**, wife ——— and son **Bennet**, personalty.
    " son **Cuthbert** and hrs., dwell. plan. ———; and personalty.
    " son **Robert** and hrs., tract at Hervy Town bou. of James King; shd. either son die without issue, land to pass to son **Bennet**.
    " 5 youngest or last child., personalty; and to 2 grandchild. **Robert** and **Mary Brooke**, personalty left to 2 child. by their grandmother ———.
    Exs.: Wife ——— and son **Cuthbert**.
    Test: Adam Head, Phillip Clarke, Cuthbert Fenwick.
    Note: Widow claims her thirds.   19, 888.

Booth, John, St. Mary's Co.,   18th Feb., 1729;
                                                           5th March, 1729-30.

    To only child **Basil** and hrs., ⅔ of entire estate, to remain under care of wife ——— until of age; shd. wife die during his minority, to care of Randolph Morris; shd. son die during minority, entire estate to pass to wife **Mary**, extx., and hrs.
    Test: Elizabeth Adler, Coll. Thomas Truman Greenfield, Thomas Brooke.   19, 890.

Boarman, Joseph, Charles Co., 26th Dec., ———;
13th April, 1730.

To bro. **Thomas James Boarman** and hrs., entire real estate.
" **Thomas Bucknan** and **Peter Attwood,** personalty.
" mother **Mary Boarman,** extx., residue of personal estate.
Test: Luke Gardiner, Jane Neale, Mary Gardiner. 19, 891.

Sanders, John, Charles Co., 22nd Oct., 1724;
15th April, 1730.

Ex. instructed as to payt. of debts, especially debt to estate of Wm. Hutchison, dec'd.
To priest attendant at death, 500 lbs. tob.
" wife **Mary** and hrs., in lieu of dowry, certain designated personalty absolutely (not to include altar or church furniture); and certain personalty for life, to pass to dau. **Mary Power** for her life, and then to grandson **John Power** and hrs.
" daus. **Mary Power** and **Jane Doyne,** 20s. each.
" son **John** and hrs., 100 A. of "Cane's Purchase" at Porttobacco (for desc. see will); and personalty.
" son **Edward** and hrs., pt. of last named tract adj. to land of bro. ———.
" dau. **Ann,** personalty.
" son **William** and hrs., residue of land at "Port-tobacco," being plan. where Thomas Osborn lived; and personalty; to receive estate at death of testator.
" eldest son **Thomas,** ex., and hrs., residue of estate, real and personal (except land in Virginia sold by father **Edward Sanders** to Nicholas Russell, whose rights therein is hereby acknowledged).
Test: Thomas Mudd, Robert Thompson, Joseph Gardner, Benjamin Gardner, Charles Clements.
Codicil: 6th July, 1729. Testator states that estate of **Ethelbert Doyne,** dec'd, with 3 small child. being in his hands, is to be distributed as follows: Grandson **Ethelbert Doyne,** to care of Clement Gardiner until of age to receive his estate, real and personal, as designated; 2 granddaus. **Mary** and **Jane Doyne,** with personalty, to care of Thomas Thompson, Port-tobacco.
Test: James Whitgreave, Edward Neale, Edward Magatee.
19, 892.

Wheeler, John, planter, Dorchester Co.,
11th Nov., 1727;
25th March, 1730.

To eldest son **Henry** and hrs., 10 A. "Ennallses Ridges," adj. land now poss. by sd. son.

" 3 sons **James, John** and **Solomon** and their hrs., 140 A. afsd. tract. Son **Solomon** to have dwell. plan. ——— after his mother's decease; shd. either of sd. sons die without issue, portion of dec'd to surviving bros.

" wife **Sarah,** extx., personal estate during life, to pass as she thinks fit.

Test: Alexander Strahans, Henry Hayward, Anthony Dawson. 19, 898.

Hodson, John, gent., Dorchester Co., 11th Dec., 1727;
21st April, 1730.

To eldest son **John** and hrs., pt. of "Hodsons Adventure," n. side Chickinanocomoco R. (for des. see will), and personalty; residue of real estate not herein bequeathed.

" youngest son **John,** ex., and hrs., residue of specified tract; "Pounds second Addition," n. side afsd. R., and 150 A. of "Holbourn," n. side Ingram's Ck.; and residue of personal estate.

Test: Patrick Broughan, James Hayes (dec'd at date of probate), Elizabeth Hayes. 19, 899.

Edgar, James, Dorchester Co., 11th April, 1730;
1st May, 1730.

To sons **William, Henry, James,** daus. **Isabel Gray, Triphany Edger, Rebecca Fisher, Anne Edger** and son-in-law **Anthony Sharter,** personalty.

" wife **Susannah** and daus. **Triphana, Rebecca** and **Anne,** personalty.

Ex.: Son-in-law **Jacob Gray.**

Test: Ezekiel Keene, Lewis Griffin (Griffith), Jr., Peter Bramble. 19, 902.

Hewet (Hewett, Huett), Richard, Baltimore Co.,
3rd Nov., 1729;
28th Feb., 1729.

To dau. **Mary,** entire estate excepting legacies to following:

" wife **Elizabeth,** Charles Ridgely, John Flaman, son-in-law **John Frazer,** dau.-in-law **Elizabeth Frazer,** goddau. **Eleanor Powel,** godson and goddau. **John Ridgely** and his sister **Pleasance,** Henry Butler's son ——— and

mother **Elizabeth Huett.** Shd. dau. **Mary** die without issue, estate to be divided among following: **John Ridgely** and his sister **Pleasance, John Frazer** and his sister **Elizabeth.**
Exs.: Wife **Elizabeth** and **Charles Ridgely.**
Test: Christopher Gardiner, Jonathan Hanson, Francis Hinckley.
Note: Widow claims her thirds. 19,904.

Calvert, Edward Henry, Annapolis, A. A. Co.,
24th April, 1730;
15th May, 1730.

To wife **Margarett,** extx., entire estate absolutely.
Test: Gov. Benedict Leonard Calvert, Hon. Charles Calvert, Dr. Samuel Stringer. 19,906.

Brewer, John, A. A. Co., 5th April, 1730;
13th May, 1730.

To son **John** and hrs., 300 A. "Larkinton"; and personalty.
" sons **Joseph** and **Ferdinando** and their hrs., "Brewerton" equally.
" son **Joseph** and hrs., 152 A. "Brewer's Chance"; and personalty.
" son **Nicholas** and hrs., 100 A. "Jacob's Hope," formerly pt. of "Cheney's Adventure," Prince George's Co.; and personalty.
" dau. **Sarah,** 150 A. dwell. plan. "Collierby" during life; at her decease to pass to son **Henry** and hrs.; also personalty on condition sd. dau. pay to son **Henry** at age of 21 £27.
" dau. **Elizabeth Sanders,** son **Ferdinando,** daus. **Dinah** and **Deborah,** personalty.
" child. afsd., personal estate equally.
Exs.: James Movat and dau. **Sarah.**
Test: John Wilmott, Steven Stewart, Thomas Gassaway, Jr.
Note: F. 910-915. Interrogatories to above will show that John Wilmott wrote sd. will, and that Anna Wilmott, his wife, was present. 19,908.

Mackdaniell, Edward, Talbot Co., 3rd Nov., 1729;
1st April, 1730.

To bros. **Laughlin** and **Daniel** and sister **Mary** and their hrs., entire estate.
Ex.: Bro. **Laughlin.**
Test: Risden Bozman, John Wrightson, John Kemp, Jr.
19,915.

Abbott, John, Talbot Co., 18th Aug., 1729; 23rd Nov., 1729.

To wife Elizabeth, entire real estate during life, and personal estate absolutely.
Test: Mathew Jenkins, Thomas Dillehay, Catrin Shahan.
19, 916.

Fisher, Sarah, widow, Talbot Co., 18th Aug., 1729; 28th Jan., 1729.

To dau. Mary, personalty.
Son Edward Brayning, ex. and residuary legatee.
Test: W. White, Charles Harbert, William Robinson.
19, 917.

Howgill, James, Talbot Co., 27th March, 1729; 24th March, 1729.

To son James, personalty.
" wife Elenor, extx., personal estate.
Test: Joseph Hague, Thomas Bradshaw, William Combs, Daniel Thomson.
19, 918.

Newman, Walter, farmer, Cecil Co., 20th Nov., 1725; 9th Feb., 1729.

To wife Mary, extx., plan. —— and personalty during life.
" 2 sons Samuel and Jonathan, plantation and personalty equally at age of 21. Not to disturb their mother in poss. thereof. Shd. either of two youngest sons die without issue, portion of dec'd to eldest son Walter and hrs. Residue of estate divided among child. at discretion of extx.
Test: Thomas Ward, Thomas More (Moor), William More (Moor).
19, 919.

Holmes, William, merchant tailor, Baltimore Co.,
1st Feb., 1729-30; 17th Feb., 1729.

To Zarah Anderson, personalty.
Exs.: Samuel Sorrency and John Thomas, farmers, Cecil Co.
Test: Jacob Johnson, Zebulon Hollingsworth.
17th Feb., 1729-30. Samuel Sorrency renounces as ex. of above will.
Test: James Roberts, David Ricketts.
19, 921.

Rutter, Ralph, boat-wright, Cecil Co., 4th Aug., 1725;
12th March, 1729.

To son **Ralph,** 1s.
" son **Richard,** ex., entire estate.
Test: Joshua Latham (Lathum), Mathias Kemp, John Thackary. 19, 922.

Mankin, Josiah (nunc.), Charles Co., 6th March, 1730;
20th April, 1730.

3 sons **John, Stephen** and **William** to remain with bro. **Stephen;** son **John** to be of age at 18. Son **Joseph** and dau. **Eliza.** and son **John** to remain with bro.-in-law **John Chapman.** Entire estate to be in hands of bro. **Stephen Mankin** and **John Chapman** afsd., and divided among child. as they come of age.
Test: John Howison. 19, 923.

Crowly (Crowley), David, Kent Co., 24th June, 1729;
15th Sept., 1729.

To wife **Sarah,** dwell. plan. "Chedle" during life; at her decease to dau. **Mary** and hrs.; and ½ personal estate.
" daus. **Rebecca** and **Mary,** ½ personal estate at age of 16 yrs.
Exs.: Vencen Hatchison and wife **Sarah.**
Test: John Hailes, Isabella Mackey, William Blakston (Blakyston). 19, 924.

Withington (Whittington), John, schoolmaster, Kent Co., 9th April, 1724;
19th Nov., 1729.

To **Mary Withington,** 10s.
" dau. **Ann Covington,** entire estate; extx. with sister **Ann Mollikin.**
Test: Richard Nordrik, Jacob Perkins, Isabella Lanahan, James Wiatt. 20, 1.

Gilbert, John, planter, Kent Co., 27th April, 1725;
19th Dec., 1729.

To wife **Phebe,** extx., dwell. plan. ——— to be divided with son **John** at age of 19; at her decease entire plan. to pass to sd. son, excepting plan. and house where mother ——— now dwells, who is not to be disturbed in poss. thereof, after her decease to pass to sd. son.
" son **John** and dau. **Mary,** personal estate.
Test: David Pearkins (also written David Jenkins), Edward Hollyday (Holyday), James Wiatt. 20, 2.

Cooly (Cooley), Daniel, Kent Co., 30th Aug., 1729;
6th Feb., 1729.

To 6 child. (unnamed), personal estate; wife ——— to have her thirds.
" son **Benjamin** and hrs., 80 A. "Bristow."
Wife ———, extx.
Test: Edward Worrell, James Willcocks, Thomas Stalker.
20, 3.

Kellee, Joseph, schoolmaster, Kent Co.,
4th day, 12th mo., 1729-30;
19th March, 1729.

To bro. **Francis,** son of **William Spearman,** Kent Co., dec'd, 130 A. of "Angels Lott," taken up by Bryan O'Neale, escheated by Edward Harris and bou. of sd. Harris. Shd. sd. **Francis** die during minority or without issue, sd. land to **Benjamin** and hrs. (son of Benjamin Kellee).
Test: George Read, Thomas Rasin (Regin), Joseph Warner, David Hull.
20, 5.

Blackledge, Benjamin, Kent Co., 10th Nov., 1729;
10th Jan., 1729.

To Rebecca and Judith Skidmore, personalty.
" dau. **Hannah** and hrs., "Orchard's Neck" and "Gallaway's Fancy," cont. c. 300 A. being land where father-in-law ——— and mother ——— now dwell, lying at hd. of Farloe Ck.; sd. dau. dying without issue, to pass to sister **Rebecca** and hrs.; she dying without issue, to Blackledge Woodland and hrs.; he dying without issue, ½ thereof to use of parish and ½ for use of a free school; and residue of personal estate. Sd. dau. to be in care of father-in-law **John Clove** and mother, wife of sd. **John Clove,** ex., until 16 yrs. of age.
Test: Rev. Alexander Williamson, James Smith, William Munk.
20, 6.

Cock, John, tailor, Kent Co., 5th March, 1729-30;
3rd April, 1730.

To George Humberstone, entire estate; he to deliver certain personalty to John, son of George Vansant, at age of 7 yrs.
Ex.: John Rogers.
Test: Jacob Caulk, Abel Stevens.
20, 7.

Watson (Wattson), Thomas, Kent Co.,
17th March, 1729;
11th April, 1730.

(Serv. to Jane, widow of George Hanson, dec'd, planter.)
To John Stevenson, ex., shipmate, serv. to Mr. Frederick
  Hanson, personalty, and 46s. lent to afsd. George Hanson
  before his decease.
Test: Fred. Hanson, Hance Hanson, Richard Pullman.

20, 9.

Cock, John, Kent Co.,
27th March, 1730;
11th April, 1730.

To Abel Stephens and John, son of George Vansant, personalty.
Ex.: George Humberstone (Umberstone).
Test: John Hankins, Edward Mitchell, Jr.

20, 10.

Griffen (Griffin), William, St. Mary's Co.,
24th March, 1729-30;
25th April, 1730.

To William (son by first wife Mary), personalty; shd. sd.
  son die without issue, to pass to son Ezekiel (son of last
  wife Pathena).
" son Ezekiel and hrs., personal estate, wife's thirds excepted.
Wife Pathena, extx.
Test: Mark Cooper, Theophilus R. Miller.
Note: To William Jaction, son of other wife Mary, personalty.

20, 11.

Beall, Benjamin, Prince George's Co.,
18th March, 1729-30;
21st May, 1730.

To father Thomas Beall, personalty received from him by
  deed of gift, dated 24th July, 1719, during his life; at
  his death to pass to bros. Thomas and William and sister
  Dryden.
" bro. Ninian, ex., residue of estate.
Test: John Orme, Caleb Norris, William Smith.

20, 12.

MARYLAND CALENDAR OF WILLS 155

Cogghill, Anne, Charles Co., 24th Nov., 1729;
18th March, 1730.

To son **Smallwood,** personalty at age of 16, but not to make sale thereof without consent of mother **Mary Smallwood** or his uncle **Mathew Smallwood** until of age at 21; daus. **Mary** and **Lidia,** personalty at 16 or marriage.

" 3 child. afsd., residue of estate.

Ex.: Mother **Mary Smallwood;** shd. mother die before child. are of age, bro. **Mathew Smallwood** to act.

Test: Henry Acton, Sr., Henry Acton, Jr. 20, 13.

Culver, Henry, planter, Prince George's Co.,
27th Feb., 1729;
26th March, 1730.

To son **Henry,** personalty; sd. son having bound himself (13th Nov., 1729) to make over 2 tracts, viz. 350 A. "The Addition to Culvert's Chance" and 50 A. lower end of Culver's Chance"; sd. 2 tracts are bequeathed to son **William** and hrs.; he dying without issue, to be divided between daus. **Mary, Sarah, Margaret, Monica, Catherine** and **Elinor** and their hrs.; sd. **William** not to sell, mortgage or encumber any pt. thereof.

" dau. **Elinor Brooke,** 40s.

" dau. **Mary** and hrs., "Littleworth," adj. tract now in poss. of Thomas Blanford; she dying without issue, to be divided bet. son **William** and daus. **Sarah, Margaret, Monica, Catherine** and **Elinor** or the survivors.

" son **William** at age of 21 and daus. **Mary, Sarah, Margaret, Monica, Ann** and **Elinor** at age of 16 or marriage, personalty.

" wife **Catherine,** extx., use of "Woodbridge" and testator's share of "Pitchcroft" during widowhood; shd. she marry, ⅓ interest in sd. tracts during life; and to divide with all her child. residue of estate; shd. wife die during minority of child. or marry a Protestant, child. with their estate to care of son **Henry** and trustees.

Overseers: John Boon, Charles Bevan.

Test: John Adams, James Hall, Henry Smith. 20, 14.

Jenifer, Daniel of St. Thomas, gent., St. Mary's Co.,
7th Sept., 1722;
2nd July, 1730.

To wife **Elizabeth,** extx., entire estate, real and personal, in Maryland, Virginia, England or elsewhere.

Test: Richard Sparkling, Dan. Jenifer, Jos. Wilson, John Andrew. 20, 17.

Camperson, Stephen, Kent Island, Queen Anne's Co.,
       1st Nov., 1729;
       25th March, 1730.

 To dau. Mary and son **Leonard,** entire estate equally.
 Wife Sarah, extx.
 Test: William Rabbitts (Rabbetts), John Thawloe (Thawlow).   20, 18.

Floyd, Richard,   9th March, 1729-30;
       16th April, 1730.

 To George Jackson, ex., Queen Anne's Co., planter, entire personal estate and care of son **Moses** (aged 2 at date of will) until Thomas, son of sd. George Jackson, arrives at age, then to have sd. son **Moses** until of age at 21.
 Test: Eliza. Dobson, Barbara Grimes, Robt. Hassitt.
             20, 19.

Sutton, John, Queen Anne's Co., 5th March, 1729-30;
       25th March, 1730.

 To wife Sarah, extx., dwell. plan. ——— during life; at her decease to pass to son **James** and hrs.
 " son **James,** dau. **Ann** and son **Ellicksander,** certain personalty above their share of estate.
 Test: Andrew Finley (Finly), Sr., Thomas Jones, Andrew Finley (Finly), Jr. 20, 20.

Knowles, James, gent., Queen Anne's Co.,
       2nd Feb., 1729;
       26th March, 1730.

 To bro. and sister **Risdon** and **Frances Bozman** and their hrs., "Watson," Talbot Co., and "Partnership," Queen Anne's Co.
 " sister **Mabell Hall** and hrs., "Folly," Talbot Co.
 Bros. **Risdon Bozman** and **Thomas Bullen,** exs. and residuary legatees.
 Test: Richard Dawson, James Dawson, Jr., John Hall.
             20, 21.

Sheaffield, Samuel, planter, Queen Anne's Co.,
       5th May, 1727;
       20th April, 1730.

 To wife **Mary,** extx., entire estate except legacy to kinsman **James Cockett.**
 Test: Samuel Beck, Vincent Hinds, William Phanton (Fanton).   20, 22.

Clayton, Joan, widow, Queen Anne's Co.,
23rd March, 1730;
30th April, 1730.

To grandson **John Gough**, at age of 21, and son **Joseph's** wife ———, personalty.
" son **William Gough**, ex., entire estate.
Test: James Towers, Mark Hargedon, Hannah Marlow.
20, 23.

Phillips, James, Baltimore Co., 27th March, 1689;
4th June, 1689.

To son **James**, ex., "Phillip's Island," in Gunpowder R.
" sons **James** afsd. and **Anthony**, residue of real estate, excepting 400 A. to daus. **Mary** and **Martha** at age or marriage.
" all child. ———, personal estate equally.
Test: Thomas Heath, John Rawlings (Rallings), Nicholas Rogers. 20, 25.

Griffin (Grifin), John, Dorchester Co., 21st Oct., 1728;
8th June, 1730.

To wife **Hannah**, extx., dwell. plan. ———, n.w. side World's End Ck., during widowhood; and personalty.
" son **George** and hrs., "Orphan's Increase," "World's End," s.e. side of sd. ck., and "Hogg Range," w. side Blackwater R.
" son **Lewis** and hrs., dwell. plan. ———, bet. hd. of World's End Ck. and hd. Staplesford's Ck., at decease or marriage of wife; and "Cold Comfort," Blackwater R.
" son **Joseph** and hrs., pt. of "World's End," formerly called "Turkey Ridge"; "Turkey Range," "Barbadoes," w. side Blackwater R.; and personalty.
" son **Robert** and hrs., "Galloway," "Duck Swamp," "Addition to Duck Swamp"; and personalty. Personal estate to remain on plan. for maintenance of wife during widowhood. Shd. wife marry, ⅔ of personal estate to child., viz. **George, Joseph, Lewis** and **Robert Griffin** and dau. **Elizabeth Baker.**
Test: John Meekins, Lewis Griffin, Sr., Grace Gadd, Mary Meekins. 20, 26.

Beckwith, Nehemiah, Dorchester Co.,
21st Jan., 1729-30;
10th June, 1730.

To wife **Frances,** extx., dwell. plan. ——— during widowhood (adj. to tract formerly belonging to Stephen Gary); after her marriage or decease to eldest dau. **Elizabeth** and hrs.; she failing issue, to dau. **Dorothy** and hrs.; and personal estate during widowhood, to pass to 2 daus. **Eliza.** and **Dorothy.**
" dau. **Dorothy** and hrs., 860 A. s. side Ingram's Ck., in freshes of Great Choptank.
Test: Elizabeth Taylor, Charles Powell, William Irons.
20, 28.

Anderton, James, Dorchester Co.,   17th May, 1730;
10th June, 1730.

To 2 sisters **Sarah Anderton** and **Mary Brown,** residue that remains from sale of 250 A. "Widdow's Purchase" (nr. n.w. fork Nanticoke) and from personal estate after payment of debts.
Ex.: Bro. **John.**
Test: John Eccleston, Fran. Anderton, Eliz. Taylor. 20, 29.

Travers, William, planter, Dorchester Co.,
1st March, 1728;
15th June, 1730.

To son **William** and hrs., dwell. plan. ———; shd. unborn child be a son and live to age of 18, to have ½ thereof.
" son **Mathew** and hrs., "Taylor's Folly," on Taylor's Island; sd. sons to receive estate at age of 18.
" child., viz. **William, Mathew,** dau. **Rebecca Ferguson,** dau. **Mary** and unborn child, personal estate equally. Dau. **Mary** of age at 16 or marriage.
Wife **Eliza.,** extx.
Test: Mathew Travers, Roger Hooker, Mathew Travers, Jr.
20, 30.

Newton, Edward, Sr., Dorchester Co., 30th Jan., 1729;
17th June, 1730.

To son **John** and hrs., 130 A. "Newton's Purchase" (formerly "Addition to the Partnership"), where David Coarson now lives, lying on w. side of branch of Transquaking R., about ½ mile above Kennerly's Mill; and personalty.

To son **Richard** and hrs., "Fork Neck," where John Williams now lives, adj. to afsd. tract.
" son **William** and hrs., 300 A. ———, including dwell. plan.
" son **Edward** and hrs., residue of real estate.
" dau. **Frances Caimon (Cannon)**, personalty.
" wife ——— and 5 child., viz. **Edward, Richard, William, Mary** and **Sarah**, personal estate equally.
Exs.: Wife ——— and son **Edward**.
Test: Sarah Person (Pearson), Sarah Perey, John Williams, Fran. Jelly, David Courson.
16th July, 1730. **Frances Newton**, one of exs. of afsd. will, claims her thirds.
Codicil: 15th May, 1730. Shd. son **Richard** die during minority without issue, "Fork Neck" to pass to son **Edward** and hrs.; shd. son **William** die during minority without issue, land bequeathed him to pass to sons **Richard** and **Edward**.
Test: David Poole, John Edwards, Henry Cannon, William Murray.   20, 32.

Spicer, John, carpenter, Dorchester Co.,
                                        11th Aug., 1724;
                                        14th July, 1730.

To child., viz. **Thomas, William, Phillip, Elizabeth Bright** and **Mary**, 1s. each.
" son **James** and hrs., 50 A. dwell. plan. "Crab Island"; sd. son dying without issue, to pass to his bro. **John** and hrs. Wife **Elinor**, extx., to have use of sd. plan. during widowhood; shd. she marry, her thirds.
" son-in-law **Bartholomew Gibbs** at age of 16, son **John** at age of 15 and dau. **Rachel** at age of 8, personalty.
Test: Timothy Rewark, John Muse, Henry Wingate. 20, 35.

Cole, Rachel, widow, Dorchester Co.,
                                        23rd Jan., 1729-30;
                                        20th June, 1730.

To father **Morgan Addams**, ex., mother **Elinor Addams**, sister **Johannah Lewis** and godson **Thomas Lewis**, personalty.
" son **John** and hrs., residue of estate; he dying during minority, sd. estate to remain in custody of parents afsd. during their life, to be equally divided bet. bro. **Summer Addams** and sister **Johannah Lewis**.
Test: Michael Todd, Sr., Summer Addams (Addoms), Elizabeth Addams (Addoms).   20, 36.

Boyer, Thomas, yeoman, Kent Co., 23rd Jan., 1728-9;
27th April, 1730.

To wife **Ann,** ⅓ of estate, real and personal.
" son **Nathaniel** and hrs., dwell. plan. ———; he dying during minority or without issue, sd. land to pass to his sister **Hannah.**
" dau. **Hannah** and hrs., tract lying on North East.
Exs.: Wife **Ann** and bro. **William.**
Test: William Goodson, Philip Christfeild (Chrisfeild), Thomas Yorkson. 20, 37.

Thomas, Samuel, Kent Co., 2nd April, 1730;
23rd June, 1730.

To eldest son **Edward** and hrs., dwell. plan. "The Venture."
" son **William** and hrs., "Chance," bou. of Thomas Talley.
" wife **Mary,** extx., afsd. land during widowhood, and personal estate for maintenance and education of children. Sons to be of age at 18.
Test: Elias Ringold, William Slipper, Hugh Frasher.
20, 39.

Smith, Simon (nunc.), Charles Co., ——— ——— ———;
30th June, 1730.

To son **Simon** and dau. **Sarah,** entire estate equally; son **John** and son-in-law **Richard Wilson** (who married dau. ———) to have no part therein, having received their full shares.
Test: John Stokes (aged about 23). 20, 40.

Gilpen, Isaac, planter, Portobacco Parish, Charles Co.,
4th May, 1730;
24th June, 1730.

To son **Edward** and hrs., 100 A. of "Thompson's Town."
" son **Thomas** and hrs., 170 A. of afsd. tract after decease of wife **Charity.**
" son **Isaac** and hrs., 140 A. "Pyes Chance."
" wife **Charity,** certain personalty besides ⅛ of estate.
" 4 child. **Henry, William, Mary Ann** and **Jane,** residue of estate.
Exs.: Son **Edward** and **Thomas.**
Test: Thomas Reeves, William Whitter (Witter), John Jones. 20, 41.

Reynolds, William, Calvert Co.,   2nd Aug., 1729;
16th June, 1730.
John Crichard, ex.
Test: John Johnson, John Simpson.   20, 42.

Fogg, Thomas, marriner, of London, 29th June, 1727;
11th June, 1730.
(Des. as in Province and bound on voyage to Great Britain.)
To wife **Ann,** extx., entire estate.
Test: Coll. John Smith, William Holland, Jr., Robert Wheller.   20, 42.

Higgins, John, planter, Talbot Co., 20th March, 1729;
24th June, 1730.
To son **William** (by former wife **Mary**), personalty. Son **John** to remain with Benjamin Bullock, ex., until 21 yrs. of age.
Test: Daniel Boyer, William Kerry, Stephen Stichbury.
    20, 43.

Ward, Thomas, Durham Parish, Charles Co.,
2nd May, 1730;
7th Aug., 1730.
To dau. **Catherine Lemaster,** grandson **Thomas Lemaster** and daus. **Christian Pickum, Mary Goldring, Sary** and **Ann,** personalty.
" son **Thomas,** ex., residue of personal estate and 250 A. dwell. plan. ———.
Test: John Franklin, Richard Davis.   20, 45.

Coffer, John, Charles Co.,   11th Oct., 1724;
9th July, 1730.
To wife **Elizabeth,** extx., ⅓ of estate during life.
" son **John,** 2s. 6d.
" son **Gerrard** and hrs., 100 A. "Coffer's Chance," at Portobacco.
" son **Richard** and hrs., "St. Michals"; afsd. lands not to be sold or mortgaged out of the name of Coffer. Shd. sd. son die without issue, to pass to son **Henry** and hrs.; and personalty. Sons **Gerrard** and **Richard** to be free at age of 18.
" sons **Mathew** and **Henry,** personalty.
Overseers: Godshall Barns, Joseph Thomas.
Test: Joseph Thomas, James Simpson, Edward Lawn.
    20, 46.

Barton, Thomas, planter, Baltimore Co.,
6th Jan., 1730;
22nd May, 1730.

To wife **Abigal**, 100 A. ——— during life; at her decease to be equally divided bet. **Thomas** and **John Barton**.
" son **James**, 50 A. ———, adj. John Norris.
" **Elizabeth** and **Ann Barton**, personalty at marriage.
Test: John Norris, Peter Carroll.   20, 47.

Cottrell, John, planter, Baltimore Co., 22nd Jan., 1721;
8th April, 1730.

To wife **Elizabeth**, extx., and dau. **Isabella**, 100 A. "Cottrell's Purchase," divided equally; wife to have her first choice, after her decease to pass to dau. **Sarah** and hrs.
" dau. **Isabella** and hrs., 50 A. dwell. plan. ——— afsd. at age of 16 yrs., after wife has made her choice.
" daus. **Elizabeth,** wife of **William Perkins,** and **Margaret,** wife of **Joseph England,** 20s. each.
" daus. **Isabella** and **Sarah,** personal estate at age of 16, wife's thirds excepted.
Test: George Wood, Richard Jenkins, William Robinson.
Memo.: To wife **Elizabeth,** dau. **Isabella** and grandchild. **Mary,** dau. of **William Perkins,** personalty.   20, 49.

Baker, John, marriner, Dover, Kent Co.,
8th Oct., 1722;
Lond., 7th Jan., 1729.

(Des. as bound on voyage to Leghorn.)
To John Peele, of London, Founder, amount of debt.
" wife **Mary,** residue of estate.
Exs.: Wife afsd. and John Peele.
Test: John Hatfeild, Joseph Fitch.
Note: Above will recorded at request of Thomas Gassaway, gent., A. A. Co.   20, 51.

Haile, Nicholas, Baltimore Co.,   27th Feb., 1729-30;
18th April, 1730.

To eldest son **Nicholas** and hrs., ½ of "Haile's Fellowship," where he now lives; son **George** to have upper end next to George Hitchcock's; sd. sons dying without issue, their portions to pass to hr. at law.

MARYLAND CALENDAR OF WILLS 163

To wife **Frances,** extx., dwell. plan. "Part of Merryman's Lott" and "Hails Addition" during life; at her decease to son **Neale** and eldest dau. **Mary** (for div. see will); and personalty.
" daus. **Hannah** and **Ann** and their hrs., 150 A. "Mount Pleasant"; shd. either or both die without issue, to pass to hr. at law.
" 2 daus. **Millisant** and **Sabbiner** and their hrs., 100 A. "Hailes Folly," on Stony Run; and personalty, with equal share in personal estate.
" son **George,** personalty.
" all child. ———, residue of personal estate.
Test: John Merryman, Sr., Johannah Merryman, Francis Hinckley. 20, 54.

Vandever, Jane (Jean), Baltimore Co., 2nd July, 1730; 25th July, 1730.

To kinswoman **Sarah Gambrell,** extx., entire estate.
Test: Thomas Taylor, William Rayman, Charles Wells.
20, 56.

Harris, William, Prince George's Co., 12th April, 1730; 23rd June, 1730.

To wife **Ann,** extx., and son **Joseph,** personal estate, legacies herein bequeathed excepted; shd. they decease without issue, to be divided among rest of children.
" son **William** and hrs., real estate (excepting that where widow Elizabeth Lomas now lives); and personalty; shd. sd. son die without issue, sd. personalty to pass to dau. **Amy** and hrs.
" son **Joseph** and hrs., tract where widow Lomas lives, on condition that John Lomas be pd. £15 in 3 yearly payments.
" dau. **Amy,** personalty at 16 or marriage, and rent of plantation where Edward Thursby now lives during sd. Thursby's term.
" son-in-law **Thomas Webster,** personalty at age of 21 or marriage.
Test: Richard Read, Sr., Thomas Hodgkin, Richard Read, Jr. 20, 58.

Truitt, Job, Somerset Co.,   10th May, 1730;
1st April, 1730.

    To dau.-in-law **Partheny Truitt,** 50 A. where she now lives during her widowhood, and to granddau. **Leninah** during life.
    " son **George** and hrs., afsd. plan. and dwell. plan. "Truitt's Choyce."
    " son **Nehemiah** and hrs., 250 A. "Belfast"; he dying without issue, sd. land to pass to son **George** and hrs.; and personalty.
    " grandson **Job** (son of **Job**) and hrs., 50 A. "Job's Fishing Hole," adj. to John Bradford's.
    " daus. **Alice, Cassiah** and **Rebecca,** personalty.
    " daus. **Sarah** and **Rebecca Timmans,** 1s. each.
    " wife **Mary,** 2 sons **George** and **Nehemiah** and 3 daus. **Alice, Cassiah** and **Rebecca,** residue of estate equally, div. to be made by William Richards and Warren Hadder.
    Exs.: Wife and son **George.**
    Test: Robert Hodge, William Richards, Benjamin Truitt.
                                                    20, 60.

Heatch, William, Somerset Co.,   ——— ——— ———;
10th April, 1730.

    To 4 sons, **William, Thomas, John** and **Nehemiah,** real estate, eldest to have first choice.
    " wife ———, ex., and dau. **Rachel,** personalty.
    " son **Ezekiel,** £10 at age of 18; all sons to be free at that age.
    " child. ———, residue of personal estate after wife's thirds are deducted.
    Overseers: Father ———, Thomas Humphries and bro. **Solomon Heatch.**
    Test: John Heatch, Samuel Heatch, Cornelius Linch.
                                                    20, 63.

Price, Crispin, Somerset Co.,   ——— ——— ———;
10th April, 1730.

    To eldest son **Alex.,** dwell. plan. ——— as divided, remaining pt. to son **Solomon.**
    " child. **Alexander, Rachel, Ann, Solomon** and **Eve,** personal estate after wife's thirds are deducted.
    Ex.: Wife ———.
    Test: Adam Heatch, Thomas Humphris (Humphrys), Finch Jones, Samuel Hitch.   20, 64.

Mercer, Francis, mcht., Somerset Co., 6th Nov., 1729;
10th April, 1730.

To cousin **John Stewart (Steward)**, ex., and hrs., dwell. plan.
"Cork," bou. of Thomas Robins (bou. by him of Thomas
Layfeild and John McKnight); sd. **John Stewart** to deliver to wife ———, in lieu of her dower rights, certain
personalty; also to sd. cousin all debts due testator.

Test: Isabella Allen (Allin), John Allen (Allin), Hannah
Turpin, Francis Allen (Allin). 20, 65.

Bushaw (Bashaw), Thomas, Somerset Co.,
16th Jan., 1729-30;
20th April, 1730.

To 2 eldest sons **Garret** and **William**, 100 A. "Hoggs Down,"
bou. of Giles Bushaw; and personalty; sd. sons dying
without issue, sd. land to pass to 2 younger sons. Daniel
Corbitt to live on sd. land for 5 yrs.
" son **Thomas** and hrs., 100 A. dwell. plan. ———; sd. son
dying without issue, to pass to youngest son **William**;
and personalty.
" youngest son **William** and hrs., 70 A. adj. to plan. bou.
of Graves Jarrett; sd. son dying without issue, to pass
to son **Thomas.**
" wife **Ann**, extx., personalty.
" 4 youngest child., viz. **Thomas, William, Anne** and **Elinor**,
residue of estate after wife's thirds are deducted.

Test: Daniel Corbitt, John Collins (Collince), Thomas
Goslee. 20, 67.

Tull, John, planter, Manokin, Somerset Co.,
13th Dec., 1729;
28th Jan., 1729.

To wife **Esther**, use of certain personalty during life and ⅓
of real estate.
" son **John** and hrs., land bou. of John Harris; and personalty.
" son **Joshua** and hrs., dwell. plan. ———, being pt. of
"Desart"; also rest of lands and marshes lying in Annamessex and Mannoking, on condition he pay to 2 sons
Richard and **Stephen** each £10 at age of 21 yrs.; and
personalty.
" daus. **Mary** and **Esther** and sons **Richard** and **Stephen**,
personalty.
" 6 child., viz. **John, Joshua, Mary, Richard, Stephen** and
Esther, residue of estate after wife's thirds are deducted.

Ex.: Son **John**, provided he surrenders children's estate to his mother until they come of age.
Overseers: Booz Walston, Charles Hall.
Appraisers: Jeoffrey Long, John Benson.
Test: Richard Hall, Joy Walstone, John Benson. 20, 69.

Dashiell (Dasheill), Hast, Somerset Co., 12th March, 1729; 8th May, 1730.

To bro. **James** and hrs., "Johnson Lott," on condition that sd. James makes over the land he holds at Wetipkin to his bro. **Mathias** and hrs., otherwise sd. **Mathias** to possess "Johnston's Lott," where mother ——— now lives; and personalty.
" Sarah King Stewart, personalty, to be pd. her at marriage by Alex. Stuart or his wife.
" **Mathias** and **William Dasheil**, personalty.
Alex. Stuart, ex. and residuary legatee.
Test: George Dashiell, Capell King, Joseph Wailes.
Codicil: 14th March, 1729. Godson Benjamin, son of Eben. Handy; Daniel and John, sons of Joseph Wales, and Ann, dau. of Michael Dashiel, each to have 1 year's schooling if they live to age of 12 yrs.
Test: Same as above. 20, 71.

Bruff, Richard, Talbot Co., 27th May, 1730; 6th Aug., 1730.

To wife **Susanna**, the brick house to live in and ⅓ real estate during life.
" son **Thomas**, ex., and hrs., 125 A. dwell. plan. ———, adj. William and Charles Walker's on the cove side, and "Daniel's Addition," bou. of Robert Hall; sd. son dying without issue, sd. lands to pass to son **Richard**.
" son **Richard** and hrs., 150 A. "Charles Walker's Land"; he dying without issue, to pass to son **James**.
" son **James** and hrs., 126 A. of afsd. land had of Richard Bennett, Esq.; sd. son dying without issue, to pass to dau. **Rachel Benson** and hrs.
" dau. **Rachel Benson** and hrs., 200 A. "Ramsey's Folley," Queen's Co., and personalty. Sons not to sell any of land unless to each other; son **Thomas** to whitewash the Brick House for his mother-in-law.
Test: Robert Goldsborough, Jr., Elinor Higgs, Joseph Rashfield. 20, 73.

Chandler, William, Charles Co., 19th Aug., 1725; 17th Sept., 1730.

To nephew **William** and hrs. (son of bro. **Henry Brent,** dec'd), dwell. plan. ———, 900 A. "Goose Creek," with 100 A. "Chandler's Addition," at age of 21 yrs.; and certain personalty at age of 18.

" nephew **William** and hrs. (son of sister **Mary Neale,** dec'd), 1,000 A. "Chandler's Hope" at age of 21 yrs.; and certain personalty at age of 18.

" nephew **Henry** and hrs. (2nd son of sister **Mary Neale**), 600 A. "Green Spring," 200 A. "Chandler's Hills," where Patrick Conneley now lives, at age of 21; and certain personalty at age of 18. Shd. any of nephews afsd. die during minority or without issue, survivors to divide portion of dec'd; shd. all 3 die during minority and without issue, afsd. lands and personalty to be divided among uncle **Nicho. Sewall,** aunt **Eliz. Digges,** aunt **Rozers** and Alice Pyes children; sister **Jane,** relict of bro. **Henry Brent,** to have her living on dwell. plan. during her widowhood.

" George Thorold, money in hands of Capt. John Hyde & Co.

" goddau. Kathrine Rozer, niece Mrs. Ann Rozer, goddau. Mrs. Jane Pye, George Thorold and his successor, personalty.

" the poor Roman Catholics of this and St. Mary's Counties, certain personalty, to be at disposal of Mr. Geo. Thorold or his successors.

" 2 nephews **Edward** and **Charles Neale,** money in hands of Richard Howton.

Exs.: 3 nephews **William Brent, William Neale** and **Henry Neale.**

Test: Jesse Doyne, John Hington (Hinkson), James Gauff, Jr. (Goffe).

Codicil: 15th Jan., 1726-7. John Parnham having bou. 2 lots in Port Tobacco in Chandler Town of John Speake, one of which was not made over to sd. Speake, and the sd. Parnham having built a stone house on land adj. to sd. lots, testator bequeaths to sd. Parnham land on which stone house stands, as also that lot not made over to Speake.

Test: John Chalmers (Chatmere), John Parnham, Jr., Samuel Adams. 20, 75.

Bodien, Francis Ludolph, Kent Co., *11th July, 1730; 2nd Oct., 1730.

To wife Hannah, extx., dwell. plan. ———, to pass to one of 5 child. as she sees fit.
" son **Henry Augustus** and hrs., "Good Hope," ½ of "Seward's Hope," "Wolf's Hook" and "Addition to Good Hope," all lying in Kent Co., at hd. of Morgan's Ck.
" 4 daus. **Anne Elizabeth, Sophia Sidonia, Hannah, Frances Lucia,** £30 each at marriage or age of 16; residue of personal estate divided bet. wife and 5 child. afsd.; shd. sd. 5 child. be debarred from instruction in principles of the Church of England, then Mr. Phillip Kennard is left their trustee and is to spend a certain sum in personalty for their benefit.
Test: Edward Willer, Theophelet Bleckhynden, John Coleman.   20, 80.

---

*According to computation of the Lutheran Church.

Higginbothom (Higgenbothom), Oliver, carpenter, Kent Co.,   1st Jan., 1728-9; 24th Nov., 1729.

To 4 child. (unnamed), £14 divided when they are of age.
" wife ———, residue of estate during widowhood; shd. she marry, ⅔ of estate to be divided amongst sd. 4 child., and the 3 boys to be bound apprentices to George More, joyner (if so bound to be free at 18 yrs.).
Test: Thomas Hynson, Sr., Stephen Thomas, Alex. Crabin.   20, 83.

Godman, Thomas, Kent Island,   1st March, 1728-9; 15th May, 1730.

To James Ringold, ex., personalty.
Testator directs that a tombstone be sent for from England; that £10 be expended for a pulpit cloth and cushion for the church, and a large Common Prayer-book be purchased for church use. Ten mourning rings, at 15s. each, to be distributed as follows: One to James Ringgold, one to Mary Wright (his sister), one to Samuel Wright, one to bro. ———; one to sister ——— if living, and if dec'd to his wife and her husband; one to Susannah Wright, one to minister who shall preach the funeral sermon, one to Isaac Barnes, and the other two to wife ———.
" wife ———, her thirds; residue of estate to sisters sons ———, the eldest having no pt. therein.
Test: Isaac Barnes, Thomas Atchison, Henry Carrew.   20, 85.

Tollet, John, Dorchester Co., 21st Aug., 1730;
12th Sept., 1730.

Exs.: Thomas Brannock, James Jarrard and Charles Dean.
Test: John Kirke, Capt. James Woollford, Dr. Wm. Murray.
20, 87.

Walker, Charles, Sr., planter, Prince George's Co.,
28th May, 1730;
30th Oct., 1730.

To wife **Rebecca,** extx., dwell. plan. ———, being pt. of "Bacon Hall," and tract s. of a line marked by testator and bro.-in-law **Richard Isaac** (for desc. see will), and 50 A. adj. on the eastern branch during life; at her decease afsd. lands to pass to son **Joseph** and hrs.; sd. son dying without issue, to pass to son **Charles** and hrs.; and use of personal estate.
" eldest son **Charles** and hrs., residue of "Bacon Hall."
" sons afsd. and their hrs., "Cut Short," on Collington Branch.
" 7 daus., viz. **Elizabeth, Rebecca, Mary, Ruth, Ann, Creecy** and **Rachel,** residue of personal estate of wife.
Test: Joseph Peach, Mathew Robson, Elizabeth Parsons.
20, 87.

Wainwright, Thomas, gent., A. A. Co., 9th Nov., 1729;
13th Dec., 1729.

To cousin **Priscilla** (dau. of uncle **Hayford Wainwright,** dec'd), £10.
" wife **Pleasance,** ⅓ of personal estate in lieu of dower.
" cousin **Ellen Noble,** ⅔ of residue of personal estate and ⅔ of real estate.
" cousin **John Noble** (bro. of **Ellen Noble** afsd.), residue of real and personal estate.
Exs.: Cousins **Ellen** and **John Noble,** and Christopher Randall, of Baltimore Co.
Test: Hyde Hoxton, Basill Poole, Thomas Goof. 20, 90.

Brown, James, Calvert Co., 7th May, 1730;
6th Oct., 1730.

To George Tomson and son-in-law **William Jones,** personalty.
" wife **Mary,** extx., residue of estate.
Test: William Skinner, Jr., John Horsman, Benj. Hance.
20, 92.

Coot, Mary, Prince George's Co., 6th Nov., 1730; 25th Nov., 1730.

To husband **Robert** and hrs., dwell. plan. "Lundee," had by will of former husband **John Cozen,** dec'd.
Test: Joseph Belt, Jr., Henry Durnford, Garratt Fizgerald, Benjamin Belt, Jr. 20, 93.

Wood, Robert, A. A. Co., 8th Feb., 1727; 12th Dec., 1729.

To Priscilla and hrs. (dau. of Stephen West by Elizabeth, his wife), dwell. plan. ———; she paying her 2 sisters £10 each at age, or else plan. to be disposed of and proceeds divided among the three—Priscilla, Elizabeth and Elinor.
" Stephen West, George and Thomas Henderson, Katherine Mary Griffin (wife of Samuel Griffin, on the Clifts), each a gold ring.
" Priscilla, Elizabeth and Elinor West, residue of personal estate.
Ex.: Cousin **Stephen West.**
Overseers: Stephen West and George Henderson.
Test: John Mardrain, John Griffin, Samuel Gover. 20, 94.

Barber, John, planter, A. A. Co., 9th Jan., 1729; 4th March, 1729.

To son **John,** "Pinkstones Fancy" and 10 A. of "Barber's Addition."
" son **Samuel,** residue of last-named tract.
" wife **Sarah,** extx., and 3 daus. **Elizabeth, Macdillion** and **Mary Barber,** entire personal estate.
Test: Orlando Griffith, William Cooly (Culle), John Jeames. 20, 95.

Broxon (Brockson), William, Cecil Co., 28th July, 1730; 27th Aug., 1730.

To Thomas Terry, Jr., son **William** and daus. **Mary** and **Ann,** personalty; child. to be in care of bro. **Thomas** and his eldest son **John** until of age; boys of age at 18 and girls at 16.
Exs.: Bro. **Thomas** and nephew **John.**
Test: Thomas Terry, Jr., Ann Terry (Tery), Alphonso Cosden. 20, 97.

Hodgkins, Charles, planter, St. Mary's Co.,
5th Feb., 1729;
5th Nov., 1730.

To sons **Charles** and **Daniel** and their hrs., "Middle Ground" equally; sd. sons to provide for wife **Jane** during her life; and personalty.

" **Thomas Tolley** and godson **John** (son of **John Rigby**), personalty.

Exs.: Wife **Jane** and son **Charles**.

Test: John Miles, Charles Ganyatt, Joseph Patshall. 20, 98.

Herbertt (Harbert), Charles, Talbot Co.,
3rd Sept., 1730;
14th Oct., 1730.

To son **James** and male hrs., entire real estate; wife **Margrett** to have a living on dwell. plan. —— during her life; and personalty.

" daus. **Sarah, Elizabeth** and **Rachel,** son **Edward** and wife **Margrett** and her 2 child., personalty.

" granddau. **Mary Ann** (dau. of son **John**, dec'd), 1s.

" wife and 4 child., viz. **James, Sarah, Elizabeth** and **Rachel,** residue of personal estate; shd. either **Elizabeth** or **Rachel** die before age of 16 or unmarried, their pt. to fall to survivor.

Test: William White, Nicholas Higgens, William Robinson.
20, 100.

Framton, Robert, planter, Talbot Co., 18th Oct., 1729;
21st July, 1730.

To eldest son **John**, 1s. and 16 A. of dwell. plan. "Collin's Pasture," bou. of Benj. Parrott, Sr., dec'd, to be laid out to include dwelling house and all other improvements made by sd. son since his marriage; sd. son to possess same during life, at his decease to revert to the then possessor of residue of lands.

" wife **Sarah**, extx., residue of estate during life; at her decease to son **Thomas** and hrs.; sd. son dying without issue, to son **Robert** and hrs.

" sons **William** and **Robert**, 1s. each.

" dau. **Sarah Booth**, personalty.

Test: Roger Hunter, Robert Hunter, Joseph Turner.
20, 103.

Giles, Nathaniel, Baltimore Co.,   12th Aug., 1730;
                                                          27th Oct., 1730.

    To 2 sons **Nathaniel** and **John** and their hrs., entire real estate.
    " 4 child., viz. **Elizabeth Webster, Mary, Nathaniel** and **John,** residue of personal estate equally.
    Ex.: Son-in-law **Michael Webster.**
    Test: Nicholas Haile, John Long, Anne Maria Giles.
                                                                                           20, 105.

Smith, Edward,   13th Aug., 1729;
                                                  6th Nov., 1730.

    To son-in-law **Charles Symonds,** ex., entire estate.
    Test: William Jackson, James Stanford (Standford), James Presbury.
    3rd Oct., 1730. Charles Simmons renounces as ex. to John Crockett of Baltimore Co.
    Test: Edward Polly, Thos. Coale.   20, 106.

Long, Samuel, Dorchester Co.,   9th Sept., 1730;
                                                         19th Oct., 1730.

    To bro. **John** and to his son **Thomas,** personalty.
    " wife **Elizabeth,** extx., residue of estate.
    Test: John Hodson, Edward Trippe, William Dohaney.
                                                                                          20, 107.

Loockerman, Coll. Jacob, Dorchester Co.,
                                                                           21st July, 1729;
                                                                           27th Oct., 1730.

    To son **Jacob,** ex., and hrs., dwell. plan. "Regulation," on condition sd. son and hrs. make over to youngest son **Thomas** (now a minor) and his hrs. 400 A. on Cabbin Ck., formerly given to son **Jacob;** shd. son **Thomas** die during minority, sd. land to be made over as afsd. to son **Nicholas** and hrs.; son **Jacob** failing to do so, sd. dwell. plan. to son **Thomas** and hrs.
    " sons **Nicholas** and **Jacob** and their hrs., 500 A. of "Taylor's Promise," at hd. of Hunting Ck.; and personalty.
    " grandson **Jacob** (son of son **John**), personalty at age of 21.
    " son **John,** 5s., and to his youngest son now living by this wife, personalty.
    " dau. **Mary** (wife of **Francis Allen**), 5s.

To grandson Govertt and granddau. Elizabeth (son and dau. of son Govertt, dec'd), personalty.
" wife Dorothy and hrs., ⅓ personal estate.
" sons John, Nicholas and Thomas and Govert (son of Govert, dec'd), residue of personal estate equally.
Testator revokes other wills, especially one made by Thomas Taylor, witnessed by Coll. Rider and Coll. Ennalls.
Test: Coll. Roger Woollford, John Woollford, Elizabeth Woollford. 20, 109.

Jelly, Francis, gent., Dorchester Co., 3rd Nov., 1730; 26th Nov., 1730.

To dau. Elizabeth and hrs., entire estate excepting legacies to following:
" Margaret Edwards, Thomas Kannerly, James Hughes when free, father **Richard Willis** and his wife ———, personalty.
" Patrick Leonard, 12 days of his time.
Ex.: Father **Richard Willis.**
Test: Isaac Nicholls (Nichols), David Poole, Frances Newton.
Codicil: Dau. **Elizabeth** left to care of father afsd. until of age. 20, 112.

Lyle (Lyles), Samuel, Calvert Co., 15th Oct., 1726; 13th March, 1726-7.

To son Samuel, ex. and hrs., dwell. plan. ———.
Test: Sal. Sollers, Richard Blake, John Robinson. 20, 114.

Smith, Philip, Calvert Co., 31st July, 1725; 22nd Jan., 1725.

To bro. **Joseph,** ex., all interest in estate of father ———; testator stating he (testator) has not arrived at age to possess same.
Test: Samuel Chew, of Maidstone; Michall Askew, James Harvey. 20, 115.

Brown, Daniel, Calvert Co., 10th Feb., 1726-7; 24th July, 1727.

To son **John Richard,** ex., and hrs., north pt. of "Hambleton's Park," adj. Richard Hall's land (for desc. see will).
" son **Benjamin** and hrs., south pt. of afsd. tract.
" son **John Brown** and dau. **Dinah Buce,** 1s. each, to be pd. by ex.
Test: John Bickerton, James Simpson, Thomas Boram.
20, 116.

Fowler, Samuel, Sr., Calvert Co., 7th Nov., 1728;
24th Jan., 1728.

    To dau. Margaret and her child. (unnamed), son **Abraham** and dau. **Rebecca**, personalty.
    Wife **Elinor**, ex.
    Test: William Yoe, John Arnill (Arnoll).   20, 117.

Woollford, Roger, Dorchester Co., 7th Oct., 1730;
8th Dec., 1730.

    To son **John** and hrs., pt. of "Woollfords," cont. 900 A. on n. side Monokin R., Somerset Co.; 200 A. "Happy Addition," adj. afsd. tract; 300 A. "Chance" (except 30 A. thereof sold to John Jones); 50 A. "Adventure," at Dam Quarter; and personalty.
    " dau. **Roseannah** and hrs., 75 A. "Charles Delight," lying in Blackwater; and personalty.
    " dau. **Sarah** (now wife of **John Jones**), pt. of "John's Desire," pt. of "Garies Choice," "Persimon Point," "Persimon Point Addition," pt. of "Middleland," pt. of "Woollford's Foresight" during life; at her decease to pass to her male hrs., in default of such sd. lands to revert to hrs. of testator.
    " dau. **Mary** (wife of **John Pitts**) and dau. **Elizabeth** (wife of **Thomas Hicks**), 20s. each.
    " grandchild. **Mary** and **Roger Pitts**, personalty.
    " son **Thomas** and hrs., residue of "Woollford's Foresight" and land on the White Marsh to include James Island.
    " wife **Elizabeth**, dwell. plan. ———, with following tracts belonging thereto: "John's Point," "Addition to John's Point," "Woollford's Meadows," "Woollford's Outlet," "Woollford's Pasture" during life; after her decease to **Roger** and hrs. (son of son **Thomas**, who is to have right to live thereon); and certain personalty during widowhood; shd. she marry, to have right to dispose of ⅓ thereof; also tract called "Sandwich" during life.
    " sons **Thomas** and **John** and their male hrs., 500 A. "Thompson Islands," bou. of James Bowles. Testator directs that 200 A. "Woollford's Inheritance" and 100 A. "Heart's Content," bou. of John Tucker, be sold for benefit of estate.
    Exs.: Wife and **Thomas** and **John Woollford**.
    Test: John Day, Hugh Procter, William Keys.   20, 119.

Demiliane, Ann, Queen Ann Parish, Prince George's Co.,
13th Oct., 1730;
5th Feb., 1730.

    To 2 daus. **Elizabeth** and **Ann**, extxs., entire estate.
    Test: Dr. George Steuart, Rev. James Macgill, Rev. Jacob Henderson.   20, 124.

Brooke, Thomas, Prince George's Co.,
16th Nov., 1730;
25th Jan., 1730-31.

To son-in-law **Dr. Patrick Sim** and hrs., 1½ A. at Nottingham; residue of "Prospect" to 2 youngest sons **Baker** and **Thomas** and their hrs.; sd. sons to be brought up in Church of England under care of their mother; shd. wife die or marry, sd. sons to care of sons-in-law **Thomas Gantt** and **Alexander Contee.**

" son **Baker,** son **Thomas** (son by present wife) and dau. **Lucy,** personalty.

" grandson **Benjamin** and hrs., pt. of "Vineyard."

" 2 youngest sons **Baker** and **Thomas** and 2 grandsons **Walter** and **Richard** (sons of eldest son **Thomas**) and their hrs., 100 A. of "Delabrooke Mannour," commonly called "Quantico," Patuxent R., St. Mary's Co. (having been at law about right to sd. land with Edward Cole).

" dau. **Elenor** (wife of **Charles Sewall**), 130 A. of "Brooke Chance," where Derby Rhine lately lived, during life; at her decease to her eldest son **Thomas Tasker** and hrs.

" 3 youngest child. **Lucy, Baker** and **Thomas,** residue of personal estate after wife's thirds are deducted. Testator directs that following tracts, "The Wedge," "Cross Cloth" and "Brookfield," lying s. of land sold to Daniel Dulany, Esq., and 100 A. of "Brookfield," adj. on n.e. to land of Philip Lee, Esq. (last parcel settled by John Rabeling), be sold by eldest son **Thomas** and sons-in-law **John Howard** and **Alexander Contee** to discharge debt due to Capt. John Hyde & Co., and land to w. of run where water mill stands be sold to discharge debt due Mr. Charles Carroll.

Exs.: Eldest son **Thomas** and son-in-law **Thomas Gantt.**
Test: Philip Lee, Jr., Thomas Withers, Mary Delihunt (Dellihunt).
Note: Widow claims her thirds. 20, 125.

Berry, John, cooper, Talbot Co.,
27th day, 2nd month, 1713;
5th Aug., 1730.

To wife **Ann,** plan. bou. of uncle **Thomas** during life; at her decease to dau. **Elizabeth;** shd. sd. dau. die before wife, sd. plan. to wife absolutely.

To dau. Elizabeth and hrs., all lands had from father ———
or grandfather ———; shd. sd. dau. die before the age
of 18, or without issue, sd. lands both in this Province
and in Pensilvania to pass to wife Ann and hrs.; shd.
wife marry without consent of George Bowes and the
rest of the Friends of Tuckahow Meeting, to have her
thirds only during life, and uncle Thomas afsd. to have
entire real estate.

Exs.: George Bowes and wife Ann.
Test: William Wheeler (Wheler), Margaret Wheler, William
Michall. 20, 129.

Howard, William, Sr., planter, St. Mary's Co.,
16th Aug., 1729;
24th Nov., 1730.

To sons William and Thomas and daus. Rachel Ford, Anne
Dartt and Margaret Shanks, 1s. each.
" son Peter and hr., dwell. plan. "Twittnam"; sd. son dying
without issue, sd. plan. to son James and hrs.; and personalty.
" sons James and John, personalty.
Wife Mary, extx.
Test: Robert Lang, John Shurtliff, Peter Shurtliff. 20, 130.

Jowles, Sybill (Sibill), St. Mary's Co., 30th Aug., 1730;
22nd Dec., 1730.

To bro. Richard Groome, £30 due from exs. of Tobias Bowles,
of London, mcht., dec'd.
" Rand. Morris, personalty.
" Capt. John Southorne, Knellum Greenfield Jowles and
Mrs. Rebecca Jowles, residue of personal estate.
Ex.: Mr. John Southorne.
Test: Marg. Crabb, Jonathan Wilson, Robert Magruder.
20, 132.

Farr, Edmund (Edman), St. Mary's Co.,
8th Dec., 1730;
5th Jan., 1730.

To son Clement (in 15th year) and hrs., dwell. plan. ———;
and personalty.
" 2 daus. Mary and Sarah, residue of estate equally.
Thomas Reeves, ex., to have care of 3 child. during
minority.
Test: Richard Cooper, Thomas Brown, Thomas Olfent.
20, 133.

Keech, Elizabeth, St. Mary's Co., 30th Oct., 1718;
24th Nov., 1730.

To son **Courts,** ex., land ——— given by father **John Courts** to testatrix and her dec'd husband ———.
Test: James Keech, Mary Keech, Ann Daine. 20, 134.

Salisbury (Saulsbury, Saulesbury), John, Queen Anne's Co., 24th Jan., 1728-9;
7th Sept., ———.

To bro. **James** and hrs., dwell. plan. ———; and personalty.
" niece **Sarah** at marriage or age of 21, sister **Mary,** niece **Mary** at marriage or age of 21, cousin **William Yarde** and George Yarde, personalty.
" bro. **James,** ex., and sister **Mary,** residue of estate equally.
Test: William Ratcliffe, John Merideth, Jr. (Merrideth), Hannah Ratcliffe. 20, 135.

Coursey, Thomas, Queen Anne's Co., 12th Nov., 1729;
24th Nov., ———.

To nephew **Solomon Coursey Wright,** personal estate at age of 21; he dying during minority, to pass to nephew **Solomon Wright** at age of 21.
Test: Thomas Hynson Wright, William Norman, John Murray.
Probate to above will taken at request of Mary Wright.
20, 137.

Hamilton, Alexander, planter, Charles Co.,
14th Jan., 1730-31;
20th Feb., 1730.

To wife ———, extx., dwell. plan. ——— during life, and personal estate absolutely; sd. wife to give certain personalty to dau. **Mary** at marriage.
" 4 sons, viz. **John, William, James** and **Patrick,** real estate equally; **John,** the eldest, to have his choice and to be for himself 1st Dec. next, son **William** the following Dec., and rest as they come of age; sd. 4 sons to pay to youngest son **Samuel** certain personalty after age of 21.
Test: Richard Combes, Tecla Green (Gren), Gilbert Canty.
20, 138.

Chapman, Edward, Charles Co., 19th Oct., 1730;
23rd Feb., 1730.

    To mother ———, a servt. boy, George Flanikin.
    " nephew **Thomas Goley,** nieces **Ann Goley** and **Elizabeth Warner,** personalty.
    " nephew **Thomas Goley** and nieces **Susanna** and **Ann Goley,** residue of estate; they all dying during minority or without issue, entire estate to **Elizabeth Warner.**
    Ex.: Father **Richard Chapman.**
    Test: John Craxson (Craxon), James Ross, John Chapman.
    20, 139.

Smith, Dorothy, widow, Calvert Co.,
18th Aug., 1730;
13th Feb., 1730-31.

    To dau. **Mary Sawell** and sons **Basill** and **Roger,** personalty.
    " all child. ———, residue of estate equally, except certain personalty to son **Thomas Taney** and £42 to son **John,** on condition son **John** make over to son **Basill** "Letchworth," now in poss. of sd. son **John.**
    Exs.: Sons **John** and **Bazill.**
    Test: Patrick Owen, James Owen.
    Codicil: 10th Nov., 1730. To son **John,** £3 additional for making over afsd. land to his bro. **Basill**; to both sd. sons interest in crops, cattle, etc.
    Test: Ann Clenten, Susana Lucus.
    20, 141.

Pritchard (Pritchit, Prichit), Richard, Dorchester Co.,
28th Dec., 1730;
16th Jan., 1730.

    To son **William** and hrs., 100 A. ———.
    " 2 sons **James** and **John,** "Hap-at-a-venture," Transquaking R., and household goods carried by their grandmother ——— to John White's.
    " son **William,** dau. **Ann,** sons **James** and **John,** son-in-law **Samuel Stanford** and **Mary Donaway,** personalty.
    " 4 child. ———, personal estate. John White to have the bringing up of 3 sons **William, John** and **James** until 18 yrs. of age.
    Test: James Sloan (Slone), Jane Sloane (Slone), Elizabeth Helsby, Mark Fisher.
    20, 143.

Chezum, William, Dorchester Co., 24th Dec., 1730; 20th Jan., 1730.

To son **Samuel** and hrs., dwell. plan. ———, pt. of "Poplar Ridge," pt. of "Willing Borrow" ("Willenbrough"), left testator by Richard Bowdidg, and 50 A. "Bitt-by-Chance."
" wife **Ann** and unborn child, "Chezum (Chezom's) Prevention" and personalty.
" niece **Ann,** dau. Judith and dau. Mary Carter, personalty.
Son **Samuel,** ex. and residuary legatee.
Test: William Chipley, Peter Newell (Nawel), James Kidder. 20, 145.

Taylor, William, Dorchester Co., 27th Nov., 1730; 3rd March, 1730.

To wife **Elizabeth,** all land lying bet. the Beverdam and Second Branch, with dwell. plan. ——— during life; and personalty.
" dau. **Mary** and hrs., afsd. lands at decease of wife and residue of real estate; she dying without issue, to pass to cousin **Thomas Taylor Price** and hrs.; he failing issue, to pass to Charles and Thomas, child. of George Staplefort, and their hrs.; and personalty.
" Henry Trippe, "Tripps Horse Range" and personalty, to discharge a bond to Shadreck Feddeman; shd. bond not be recovered, sd. lands to wife **Elizabeth** and hrs.
Wife **Elizabeth,** extx. and, with dau. **Mary,** residuary legatee.
Test: John Eccleston, James Slone, Jane Slone. 20, 147.

Hambrook, Mary, Dorchester Co., 14th Sept., 1727; 10th March, 1730.

To son **Henry Hayward,** 40s.
" 2 granddaus. **Mary** and **Ann Hayward,** personalty.
" 2 sons **John** and **Thomas Stuart,** exs., residue of estate, real and personal.
Test: Richard Webster, Ann Webster, Peter Sermon.
 20, 149.

Hill, Agathia, Dorchester Co., 10th Oct., 1717; 11th March, 1730.

To eldest dau. **Hannah,** **John,** son of John Hill, Sr., son **William,** and **Mary,** dau. of Robert Mills, personalty.
Bequest to son **William** to be performed by exs. Richard and Amy (Hill).
Test: Joshua Kennerly, Peter Stoakes (Stoaks), Mary Cryer (Crayer). 20, 150.

Rice (Reece), William, blacksmith, Cecil Co.,
2nd Aug., 1729;
24th Feb., 1730.

To wife **Mary** and son **Thomas**, exs., entire estate; to be poss. by sd. son after wife's decease, he to pay to his elder bro. **David** and his sisters **Catharine** and **Mary** 1s. each.
Test: Nicholas Hyland, Edward Johnson, Joseph More.
20, 151.

Ward, Edward, Baltimore Co., 21st April, 1730;
5th Nov., 1730.

To wife **Ann**, extx., and dau. **Camilla** and their hrs., entire estate.
Test: Edward Dorsey, Jr., Benja. Jones, Joshua Dorsey, Jr., William Lowe (Low). 20, 152.

Wilbourne (Willbourne), Edward, Baltimore Co.,
23rd Jan., 1730-31;
3rd March, 1730.

To wife **Elizabeth**, extx., 50 A. dwell. plan. ——— during life; at her decease to dau. **Ann** and hrs.; and ⅓ personal estate.
" son **William** and hrs., residue of real estate.
" son **Thomas**, personalty.
" 3 child., viz. **Eliza. Wood, William** and **Ann**, residue of personal estate equally.
Test: John Coale (Cole), John Dawley, Michael Webster.
20, 154.

Steel, John, St. John's Parish, Baltimore Co.,
21st Dec., 1730;
3rd March, 1730.

To wife **Sarah**, extx., entire estate.
Test: John Butters, Jacob Bull (Ball), Robert Powell.
20, 155.

Edgar, Johanna, Prince George's Co.,
——— ——— ———;
3rd March, 1730-31.

To son **John**, ex., daus. **Johanna Barnes, Margerett, Sarah Eilbeck** and **Elizabeth Wade**, personalty.
" child. afsd., residue of estate equally.
Test: John Stoddert, Alex. Adair, Stephen Gordon. 20, 156.

Tolson, Francis, Prince George's Co.,
23rd April, 1730;
11th March, 1730-31.

To wife **Ann**, personalty (exclusive of her thirds).
" eldest son **Henry**, personalty, some of which formerly belonged to late wife ———, his mother, and some to **Henry Fuller**.
" dau. **Frances** and son **John**, personalty; son **John** to be in care of his mother until 18 yrs.; in case of her decease under care of his bro. **Henry** until 16 yrs. of age.
" dau.-in-law **Alice Lindsay**, certain personalty, some of which for use of her son **Samuel** when of age; her husband **Anthony Lindsay** to be discharged of all debts due testator.
" wife, son **Henry** and dau. **Frances**, residue of estate equally.
Exs.: Son **Henry** and John Abington.
Test: William Clarkson, James Kendall.
8th March, 1730-1. John Abington renounces as ex. Test: Robert Wade. 20, 158.

Neale, James, Charles Co., 7th Jan., 1730-31;
8th March, 1730.

To son **James** and hrs., entire real estate, including "Woollestan Mannor," ½ thereof to be reserved for use of wife **Jane** during her life; and personalty at age of 21; he dying during minority or without issue, all lands to pass to 2 daus. **Jane** and **Mary Ann** and their hrs.
" dau. **Eliza.** and hrs., land in St. Mary's Co. had with former wife ———, her mother; and personalty at age of 16 or marriage.
" daus. **Jane** and **Mary Ann**, personalty at age of 16 or marriage.
" wife **Jane**, extx., residue of personal estate.
Test: Raphael Neale, John Lancaster, Bennett Hoskins.
20, 160.

Parandeor (Parandyer, Parrandyer), James, Charles Co., 20th Feb., 1730-31;
6th April, 1731.

To bro. **John** and hrs., "Saint Thomas."
" goddau. **Elliner Haththorne White** and hrs., "Parrandyer (Parenders') Lott" and "Archibald's Desert"; and personalty.
" **Henry Blansett, Mathew Breding** and sister ———, personalty, some of which des. as in poss. of Richard White.

Exs.: Bro. **John** and **Charles Musgrave.**
Test: William Williams, Edmond Bury Godfrey Paine, Ann
Williams. 20, 162.

Galwith, James, planter, Charles Co.,
8th March, 1730-31;
21st April, 1731.

To daus. **Mary, Elizabeth** and **Sarah** and son **Jonas,** personalty. Dau. **Mary** to give to dau. **Tamer** certain personalty. Son **Jonas** to care of William Lawson, ex.; if sd. Lawson dies in his minority, to care of Thomas Lawson.
" child. ———, residue of estate equally.
Test: James Davies, Thomas Lawson, John Strange.
20, 164.

Winser (Winsor), Garvis, Charles Co.,
——— ———, 1727;
10th March, 1730.

To son **William** and hrs., ½ dwell. plan. ———; he dying during minority or without issue, to pass to son **Joseph** and hrs.
" dau. **Elizabeth** and hrs., ½ afsd. plan.; she dying without issue, to pass to dau. **Ann** and hrs.
" sons **Thomas** and **John,** 12d. each.
" wife **Elizabeth,** extx., entire personal estate.
Testator directs that he be buried beside first wife ——— on dwell. plan.
Test: Richard Chidley (dec'd at date of probate), Edward (Eadman) Grainnan, Giancet Crecian (test. mentions Jennat Club, lately called Jennet Bryan). 20, 165.

Roberts, Richard, Talbot Co.,
19th Aug., 1730;
31st March, 1731.

To son **Bartholomew** and hrs., dwell. plan. ———; sd. son dying without issue, to pass to son **William** and hrs.; son **Bartholomew** to make over to son **Nicholas** and hrs. pt. of "James Progress," on St. Michael's R., nr. the church, or pay sd. Nicholas 1,000 lbs. tobacco at age of 21.
" dau. **Mary Edgar** and hrs., tract (for desc. see will).
" dau. **Elizabeth Jones** and son **William** at age of 21, personalty.
Son **Bartholomew,** ex. and resid. legatee.
Test: John Wrightson, Henry Sorden, Elizabeth Tomson.
20, 166.

Anderton, Francis (Frances), Dorchester Co.,
24th March, 1730;
8th April, 1731.

To sister Sarah and hrs., 200 A. "York" and 50 A. of "Westward."
" sister Sarah afsd. and bro.-in-law John Brown, exs., residue of estate equally.
Test: John Briggs, Thomas Smith, Henry Murray. 20, 168.

Mace, Nicholas, planter, Dorchester Co.,
15th June, 1730;
5th May, 1731.

To 2 sons Thomas and John and their hrs., "Head Range" and "Cornwall." Son John's portion to be on side of cove next to James Busick's.
" son John and daus. Elizabeth and Anne, personalty.
Exs.: Wife Ann and sons Thomas and John.
Test: John Brannock, Jr., Isaac Meekins, Thomas Shehawn, Catherine Ross. 20, 169.

Walls, John, Kent Co., 12th Sept., 1730;
28th Jan., 1730.

To wife Elizabeth, entire personal estate.
" sons William and John and their hrs., 100 A. of "Britain."
" son William and hrs., dwell. plan. ———; wife to have her pt. therein during her widowhood.
" dau. Martha, personalty.
Exs.: Wife and son William.
Test: John Morris, Anne Hallady. 20, 171.

Warner, Joseph, planter, Kent Co.,
22nd day, 1st mo., 1729;
25th Jan., 1730.

To Walter Waters, sister Mary Rasin and Mary Theckstone, shd. she survive her husband Thomas Theckstone, personalty.
" use of Friends of Cecil Meeting, £20.
" dau. Mary and hrs., dwell. plan. ———, "Warner's Levell" and plan. whereon the widow Winn now lives; shd. sd. dau. die during minority or without issue, sd. lands to pass to cousin Joseph, son of George Warner, dec'd; shd. sd. Joseph die as afsd., sd. lands to pass to his bro. George and hrs.; shd. sd. George die during minority or without issue, lands to pass to sister Mary Raisin's youngest son ———.

To wife Ann, ⅓ of estate, real and personal; residue of personalty to dau. Mary afsd.; she dying during minority, entire personal estate to be divided among sister Mary Rasin's children. Monthly Meeting to have oversight of education of child during her minority.
Test: George Dunkin (aged 58), Thomas Rasin, David Hull (aged 33).
Note: Above will not signed, testimony of witnesses shows that Joseph Warner at time of death had another dau. (unnamed). 20, 173.

Smothers, Richard, Kent Co., 23rd Dec., 1730; 18th May, 1731.

To wife Mary and hrs., lands, goods, etc., which she had a right to as the relict of John Carvile, or by any other way. Testator ratifies a deed made by testator and sd. wife to Mrs. Martha Paca, 17th Aug., 1723; sd. deed being made in trust to sd. Paca for payment of sd. Carvill's debts, as well as the several portions of his children.
" dau. Blanch, all things brought over the bay; sd. dau. to care of wife.
" John Carville, bro. James, Parker Hall, Peter Leaster and son John, personalty.
Test: William Graves, Phebe Carvill, Anthony Noleman.
31st Dec., 1730. To wife Mary, extx., residue of estate.
Test: William Graves, Thomas Bordley, Phebe Carvill.
20, 177.

Tunhill (Turnhill), Robert, St. Mary's Co., 15th Feb., 1730-31; 25th Feb., 1730.

To wife Elizabeth, 5 child. (unnamed), sons John and William, and William Cook, personalty; son William to be free at age of 18.
Exs.: Wife and son John.
Test: Joseph Sikes, Stephen Chilton (Chillton), George Craghill. 20, 179.

Shierclieff, Peter, St. Mary's Co., 4th May, 1730; 25th Feb., 1730.

To bros. John, ex., and Thomas and their hrs., entire real estate, they paying certain personalty to bro. William.
Test: Edward Knott, Leonard Green, James Thompson.
20, 180.

Searson, Alice (nunc.), St. Mary's Co., 4th April, 1731.
Justinian Jordan to take grandson **Thomas Jordan** and entire estate for use of sd. grandson.
Test: Mrs. Mary Jordan, Mrs. Ann Dorey. 20, 182.

Deal (Deale), William, planter, Calvert Co.,
13th Dec., 1718;
10th April, 1731.

To son **Richard** and 4 child., viz. **Jacob, Alexander, Sarah** and **John**, as they come to age of 16 yrs., and son **James**, personalty.
" all child., viz. **Richard, Elizabeth Wells, William, James, Jacob, Alexander, Sarah** and **John**, residue of estate equally.
Son **Richard**, ex. and guardian to children.
Test: Richard Stallinges, Jacob Stallinges.
22nd April, 1731. Richard Deale renounces ex. to James Deale. 20, 182.

Harris, Sarah, Calvert Co., 19th Sept., 1730;
19th April, 1731.

To 2 daus. and 2 sisters, viz. **Ann Roberts, Hannah Clare, Mary Howell** and **Rebecca Young**, personalty.
" 2 sons **Robert Roberts** and **John Clare**, exs., each £80.
" 3 sons, viz. **Robert Roberts, John Clare** and **Benjamin Harris**, residue of estate; ⅓ thereof to son **Robert**, he paying his dau. **Mary** £5; ⅓ to son **John**, he paying to each of his sons now living £5, and ⅓ to son **Benjamin** and hrs. at age of 21; shd. son **Benjamin** die during minority or without issue, his portion to 2 sons afsd.
Test: Dr. James Somervell, William Skinner, William Oulds.
27th May, 1731. John Clare renounces as ex. 20, 184.

Parlot, William (nunc.), 3rd April, 1731.
To Joseph Attwell, all personalty at sd. Attwells, except small legacy to Edward Carslake.
Test: Edward Carslake. 20, 186.

Baker, Thomas, carpenter, Pocomoke R., Somerset Co.,
18th Oct., 1730;
16th Jan., 1730.

To eldest son **William,** second son **James,** third son **Henderson** and godson **Benjamin Benston,** personalty.
" dau. **Mary,** personalty and £30 now in hands of her uncle **John Merrill.**
" wife **Mary,** residue of personal estate during life; at her decease to 4 child. afsd.
Ex.: Son **James.**
Test: Joseph Marrill (Merrill), Thomas Layfield, George Layfield.
20, 186.

Heatch, Adam, Somerset Co., 22nd Jan., 1730;
15th Feb., 1730.

To wife **Mary,** ⅓ dwell. plan. ——— during life, ⅓ personal estate and an equal interest with child. in water-mill during her widowhood.
" son **Elgatt** and hrs., plan. included bet. Samuel Heatches land and the mill branch, pt. of "Come by Chance" and pt. of "High Suffolk."
" grandson **John Price** and hrs., 90 A. where John Price now lives, after decease of his mother.
" all child., viz. **Solloman,** ex., **John, Samuel, Elgatt, Elizabeth, Catherine, Mary Price** and **Eve Smith,** personal estate equally; **William Heatches** child. having an equal pt. thereof.
Overseer: John Handy.
Test: John Handy, George Langake, John Crouch.
20, 188.

Parker, John, Sr., Somerset Co., 1st Dec., 1730;
1st April, 1731.

To son **George** and hrs., 400 A. "Wicconies Neck"; and personalty. Testator states that having sold 350 A. in Accomac Co., Va., to Henry Scarbrough (given to testator by father **George Parker**) shd. sd. son **George** insist on an interest in sd. 350 A., then sd. **George** to be utterly debarred from any benefit by this will, and portion bequeathed him shall be divided among 8 child., viz. **John, Tabitha, Philip, Charles, Samuel, Elinor, Sarah** and **Leah.**
" dau. **Tabitha Nicholas** and hrs., 175 A. "Dumfreeze" and "Brotherhood," lying at hd. of sound; and personalty.
" 2 sons **Philip** and **Charles** and their hrs., 300 A. "Castle Green"; and personalty.

To grandson **John Turner** and hrs., 150 A. "Parker's Adventure," residue thereof (50 A.) to son **George**.
" wife ———, 400 A. "Parker's Adventure" during life; at her decease to son **Samuel** and hrs.; ⅓ personal estate, residue of personal estate to 9 child. afsd.
Exs. Wife **Tabitha** and son **Samuel**.
Test: Isaac Morris, Henry Tarman, James Nicholson.
20, 190.

Taylor, James, planter, Coventry Parish, Somerset Co., 4th April, 1730-31; 1st April, 1731.

To son **William** and hrs., dwell. plan. ———.
" son **James** and hrs., "Hogg Quarter"; wife ——— to have use thereof during widowhood.
" 2 sons **Mathias** and **Gilbert** and their hrs., tract nr. William Whittington's quarter; shd. either die without issue, survivor to have portion of dec'd. If wife ——— abides by this will she is to receive certain personalty, also son **John** to receive certain personalty, and both of them to receive a proportionate pt. of estate with rest of child., otherwise both to be debarred from any interest therein.
Ex.: John Bevins.
Overseers: Edmund Hough, John Murray.
Test: Edmund Hough, Joseph Houston, Caleb Beavans.
Note: **Margaret Taylor** accepts above will, same test.
20, 192.

West, Randall, Somerset Co., 22nd Jan., 1730; 27th April, 1731.

To dau. **Ann** and hrs., dwell. plan. ———, had from mother ———, and ½ tract of land bou. of William West.
" dau. **Catherine** and hrs., £15 at age of 16, and 324 A. "Brothers United," lying in a neck called "Double Purchase."
" bro. **William**, personalty.
" bro. **Anthony** and hrs., ½ of tract bou. of Wm. West.
" 2 daus. afsd., residue of personal estate; shd. either die without issue, survivor to enjoy portion of dec'd.
Bro. **Randell Revill**, ex., to have care of children.
Overseers: Coll. Levin Gale, Ephraim Wilson.
Test: William Turpin, Edward Adams, Sarah Wilson.
20, 194.

Watson (Wattson), Peter, Somerset Co.,
5th Oct., 1728;
20th Aug., 1730.

To 3 sons, viz. **Peter, James** and **Urias,** and their hrs., 150 A. dwell. plan. "Black Ridge" and 50 A. on w. side of land where Rowland Hodgson now lives; if son **Peter** be willing to pay to his 2 younger bros. (viz. **James** and **Urias**) at age of 21 certain personalty, then sd. **Peter** and hrs. to possess entire 200 A.

" dau. **Elizabeth,** sons **James** and **Urias,** personalty.

" daus. **Sarah** and **Frances** and son **Luke,** 1s. each.

" wife **Comfort,** extx., residue of estate.

Test: John Walker, Edward Chapman, Bushap Henderson.
20, 195.

Haddock, James, gent., Prince George's Co.,
16th Sept., 1726;
2nd May, 1731.

To nephew **John Gibson** and hrs., ½ of "Weston," lying on Collington, now in poss. of John Green, after decease of wife **Sarah;** and personalty.

" grandson **James Haddock Waring** and hrs., other half afsd. tract.

" son **Marsham Waring, Basil Waring, John Murdock** and **Samuel Perrie,** and to each of their wives, one mourning ring; also to godson **James Wilson,** Coll. **Thomas Addison** and to each of his 2 sons **Thomas** and **Henry Addison** a mourning ring.

" 3 sisters **Elizabeth Gibson, Sarah Newland** and **Mary Reynolds,** 20s. each.

" wife **Sarah,** extx., and hrs., lot and house in Marlborough Town bou. from John Middleton, also use of "Weston" during life; residue of estate absolutely.

Test: Winnefred Simmons, Henry Keene, Edward Owen, John Barton.
20, 197.

Gardiner (Gardner), Joseph, planter, Kent Island, Queen Anne's Co., 12th Dec., 1730;
23rd March, 1730.

To **Geo. Vinscent** and **Ann Harper,** personalty, some of which des. as at John Rawles, Jr.

" Mrs. **Mary Browne,** residue of estate.

Ex.: Marmaduke Goodhand.

Test: Thomas Williams, Matthew Browne, John Wells.
20, 200.

London, James, Queen Anne's Co., 4th Dec., 1729;
8th April, 1731.

To son **Richard,** 60 A. of dwell. plan. ——— adj. to James Bells.
" son **James,** wife **Eleanor** and dau. **Rebecca,** personalty.
" wife **Eleanor,** residue of real estate with dwell. plan. during life, and then to son **James.**
" child. afsd., personal estate after wife's thirds are deducted; shd. wife die before son **James** comes of age he is left to care of his godfather Philemon Blake.
Exs.: Wife and Thomas Baynard.
Test: Timothy Lane, William Banning (Baning), Thomas Bullen. 20, 201.

Busey, Paul, Prince George's Co., 29th May, 1731;
23rd June, 1731.

To mother ———, bro. **John** and sister **Sarah,** personal estate equally.
Test: John Mawdesly, Samuel Busey, Joshoa Busey.
20, 202.

Evans, Walter, planter, Prince George's Co.,
18th Jan., 1730-31;
22nd June, 1731.

To son **Thomas,** personalty during life; at his decease to pass to his dau. **Elizabeth.**
" son **Walter** and hrs., 300 A. formerly laid out for him and ½ the island lying west of Butler Evans' tract by Potomack; shd. sd. son die without hrs., to pass to his son **Charles** and his hrs.
" son **Butler** and hrs., "Dunghill," the other pt. of the island, the tract lying bet. James Harbut and Walter Evans, upon Potomack; and personalty.
" dau. **Elizabeth Locker** and her son **Walter,** residue of "Dunghill," adj. to James Harbut; shd. her sd. son die before he comes of age, to sd. dau. absolutely.
" dau. **Elinor Harbut,** personalty.
" son **Philip,** ex., "Stony Hill," "Littleworth"; and personalty.
" **Elizabeth** and **Ann** (daus. of son **Philip**), grandsons **Philip** and **Thomas** (sons of son **Philip**), personalty.
Test: William Hughes, George Wilson (Willson), Agnes Wilson (Willson). 20, 203.

Pecker, Hannah, Dorchester Co., 28th March, 1731;
24th June, 1731.

To dau. **Mary Beck,** personalty.
" dau. **Cornealy Jones,** residue of personalty.
Test: John Lecompt, John North, Elenor Pulling (Pullin).
20, 205.

Tanner, Henry, Charles Co., —— —— ——;
8th June, 1731.

To son **Joseph** and hrs., ½ of real estate; he dying without issue, to pass to son **John** and hrs.
" son **John** and hrs., ½ of real estate after decease of wife **Ann.**
" son **Henry** and daus. **Ann** and **Elizabeth,** personalty; shd. sons **Joseph** and **John** die without issue, land to daus. afsd. equally; sd. daus. dying without issue, to pass to son **Henry** and hrs.
Exs.: William Williams and Joseph Chambers.
Test: Joseph Chambers, Henry Taylor (Tayler) (dec'd at date of probate), William Clarke.
9th June, 1731. Widow Anne Tanner claims her thirds.
20, 206.

Steward, Eleanor, Charles Co., 12th Oct., 1725;
9th June, 1731.

To dau. **Katherine Mosgrove,** granddau. **Eleanor** and granddau. **Katherine Mosgrove,** personalty.
" son **John Parandier** and granddau. **Eleanor Criger,** 1s. each.
Son **James Parandier,** ex. and resid. legatee.
Test: William Nelson (Nellson), Sarah Nelson (Nellson), Honnere Blanchet. 20, 207.

Walker, John, Dorchester Co., 5th Dec., 1730;
12th July, 1731.

To bro. **James** and hrs., land in Dorchester Co.
Ex.: Thomas Stewart.
Test: John Woollford, George Staplefort, Catherine Kees (Keese). 20, 209.

Loockerman, Jacob, Talbot Co., 28th June, 1731;
27th July, 1731.

To wife **Magdalen,** certain personalty during widowhood, to pass at her marriage or death as follows: To bro. **John** during his life, then to his son **Jacob;** to **Sarah** and

Elizabeth, daus. of bro. Govert, dec'd; to nephew Jacob Hindman (son of sister Mary Allin) and to son-in-law John Edmondson.

To John Edmondson afsd., personalty, including debts due on condition he discharge estate from all demands.

" wife Magdalen, half remaining personal estate in Talbot Co. absolutely, and half remaining pt. in sd. co. during her widowhood, to pass to following relations: Jacob (son of bro. John), Jacob Hindman (son of sister Mary Allen) and William and Joseph (sons of Thomas and Mary Haskins) equally, provided sd. wife shall accept bequests in lieu of her dower, and also pay to James Edmondson and Sarah, wife of Howel Powel, £5 each.

" bro. John and Francis Allen and sister Mary, his wife, all debts due, on condition they discharge estate of debt due them.

" nephew Govert (son of bro. Govert) and his male hrs., "Rochester," Dorchester Co., and failing such issue to pass in surname of Loockerman forever; also personalty on sd. plantation, same to remain in hands of his bro. Jacob during his minority; sd. Jacob to pay out of profits £3 yearly to his sisters Sarah and Elizabeth while unmarried.

" nephew Jacob Hindman (son of sister Mary Allen) and male hrs., "Popler Neck," Dorchester Co., bou. of John Kirke, and failing such issue to the male hrs. of the surname of Loockerman forever.

" nephew Jacob (son of bro. Govert) and hrs., lot in town of Islenton, Dorchester Co.; also all debt book of accounts relating to Sheriff's office, Dorchester Co., and all profits accruing therefrom; shd. he refuse, sureties for same, to have same power as is given sd. nephew, overplus to remain to sd. nephew Jacob, he paying out of same to bro. John personalty, and deliver to bro. John and Mary his wife, to bro. Nicholas and his wife ———, to bro.-in-law Francis Allen and Mary his wife, to cousin Thomas Haskins and Mary his wife and to Coll. William Holland and Elizabeth his wife each a ring; and residue of personalty in Dorchester Co. or elsewhere (excepting Talbot Co.); he paying to bro. Thomas £10 toward his education, and also to indemnify the securities given for due administration of estate of father Jacob Loockerman. Son-in-law Howell Powell to be discharged from all debts due estate, provided he discharge estate from all claims that may be due him.

Exs.: Wife **Magdalen** for personalty in Talbot Co., nephew
Jacob (son of bro. **Govert**) in Dorchester Co. and elsewhere.
Test: William Holland, Elizabeth Holland, Thomas Holland,
John Berry. 20, 210.

Medley, George, St. Mary's Co., 1st April, 1731; 1st June, 1731.

To son **Clemant** and hrs., dwell. plan. ——— after decease of his mother; shd. sd. son die during minority or without issue, sd. land to pass to son **Often** and hrs.
" son **Bennet** and hrs., all land that falls to testator's share when divided bet. wife ——— and Mary Tant; sd. son dying during minority or without issue, to pass to son **George** and hrs.
" 4 sons afsd., personalty at age of 21, or day of marriage, and residue of personal estate.
Wife **Ann**, extx.
Test: Enoch Combs (Combes), Thomas Thompson, Ignatius Ford, Robert Ford (Foord).
Note: Widow claims her thirds. 20, 214.

Johnson, Joseph, Baltimore Co., 15th March, 1730; 28th July, 1731.

To bro.-in-law **Josias Middlemore**, ex., mcht., "Spry's Inheritance," Rumny Ck.; to sell or dispose of sd. tract and apply proceeds toward payment of all debts, etc., which sd. **Josias** has against estate, either on his own acct. or on acct. of the company whereof Capt. Edward Hankin, of London, dec'd, was one, and to apply any surplus to payment of other debts.
Test: John Maccarthy, Ann Maccarthy (Mecerthy) and Frances Dunawin. 20, 215.

Todd, Michael, cordwainer, Dorchester Co., 17th Oct., 1730; 6th Aug., 1731.

To son **Michael** and hrs., pt. of "Andrews Fortune" (for desc. see will); and personalty.
" son **Benjamin** and hrs., pt. of "Westmoreland," pt. of "Stanaway's Forrest" (for desc. see will); and personalty.
" son **James** and hrs., residue of last-named tract, pt. of "Scotland"; and personalty; sd. son to live with his bro. **Michael** until 18 yrs. of age.

To sons **Benjamin** and **James** and their hrs., residue of
"Westmoreland," "Scotland" and "Todds Horse Pasture"
equally; shd. either die without issue, survivor to inherit
portion of dec'd.
" daus. **Elizabeth Dean, Dorothy Coal** and **Ruth**, personalty.
" all child., personalty equally.
Exs.: Sons **Michael** and **Benjamin**.
Test: Robert Ross, Summer Adams (Addoms), William
Dean. 20, 217.

Stone, William, Charles Co., 17th April, 1730;
12th Aug., 1731.

To eldest son **Thomas** and hrs., plan. beginning at mouth
of Could Spring Branch (for desc. see will) and plan.
where William Mansell lives, adj. land of cousin **David
Stone** and Gerd. Fowke; and personalty.
" dau. **Mary** and hrs., plan. where she and her husband
Thomas Matthews now live, adj. lands of cousin **Matthew
Stone** and Robert Doyne; and ½ of "O'Neales Dezearts,"
bou. of James Tyer; and personalty.
" youngest son **Richard** and hrs., residue of dwell. plan.
"Poynton Manner," his mother to have use of house and
portion of plan. during life; and personalty, including
that on plan. where John Bannister is overseer.
" dau. **Verlinda Harrison** and hrs., 100 A. "Dover's Clifts,"
tract bou. of Martin Campbell and Mary, his wife; 39 A.
adj. "Dover Clifts," and money due from her.
" dau. **Theodosia** and hrs., other half of "O'Neales Dezearts"
and pt. of "Market Overton," at Pomankka, now leased
to Robert Gording; and personalty.
" dau. **Pretious (Precious) Jones** and hrs., 300 A. "Millner,"
bou. of John Dickeson, and 113 A. "Langham's Rest,"
Prince George's Co., made over by George Langham; and
personalty.
" youngest dau. **Bethia Barnes** and hrs., 143 A. "Stone's
Rest," adj. to land of Thomas Jenkins, dec'd, and ½
"Market Overton," the pt. where John Queen now lives;
and personalty.
" wife **Theodosia**, certain personalty during life, to be
divided among child.; sd. wife being obligated to make
over "Market Overton" to her 2 daus. **Theodosia** and
Bethia before her death or marriage; shd. son **Thomas**
interfere and not make over sd. land, then the plantations
where his bro. **William** lived and Daniel McDaniell now
lives shall pass to the sd. **Theodosia** and **Bethia** and
their hrs.

Exs.: Wife and sons **Thomas** and **Richard**.
Test: William Mansell, John Boye, James Murdock.
Codicil: Shd. **Thomas Matthew** bring any account against estate, to have no share therein. To dau. **Theodosia**, personalty to remain in poss. of her mother during life.
Test: Same.   20, 221.

Pile, Richard, physician, Prince George's Co., 24th May, 1731; 10th July, 1731.

To wife **Mary**, 130 A. dwell. plan. ———, formerly bou. of Solomon Rothery first and afterward of Leonard Holliday; also "Joices Plantation," being pt. of "Major's Lott," cont. 50 A.; 50 A. "Bells Purchase," 40 A. "Copes Hill" (in all, about 270 A.) during life; to be sold after her decease, proceeds to 2 grandsons **Richard** and **William** (sons of son **William**).

" grandson **Richard** (son of Edward Sprigg) and hrs., "Expedition," on Eastern br. of Potomack R.; "Rantom," on Jones Western br.; "Mistake," lying on both afsd. branches; 200 A. "Piles Gift"; in all, about 600 A., to be for use of wife until sd. **Richard** comes to age of 21; also to sd. grandson all rights and interest in warrant for 1,650 A.

" grandsons **Richard** and **William** afsd., £500 divided equally at age of 21 yrs.; shd. either die during minority, survivor to inherit portion of dec'd; shd. both die during minority, sd. sum to fall to the next hr. of son **William**, and failing such hr. to sd. son **William**.

" son **William**, £20 and personalty.

" dau. **Elizabeth** and her husband **Edward Sprigg**, £20 each.

" wife **Mary** and grandsons **Richard** and **William**, residue of estate equally.

Ex.: Wife and son-in-law **Edward Sprigg**.
Test: Richard Duckett, John Perre, Sr., William Sescell, John Perry (Perre), Jr.   20, 227.

Currant, Elizabeth, Calvert Co., 6th Jan., 1730; 17th March, 1730.

To dau. **Hannah** (aged 5, 5th Dec., 1730), entire estate at age of 16; sd. dau. and her estate to care of Thomas Littell, ex., and his wife Assilla.
Test: John Braben, Mary Collings, Jone Roiston, Eliza. Shehon (Sheehon).   20, 230.

Wilson, Josiah, planter, Calvert Co.,
18th Jan., 1730-31;
10th April, 1731.

To dau. Ann and hrs., 150 A. in Prince George's Co., nr. Rock Ck., bou. of Joseph West, at age of 16 or day of marriage; also pt. of "Newington" left testator by father, being pt. whereon mother now dwells, after decease of wife Susanah; shd. sd. dau. die during minority, afsd. tracts to pass to bro. **John** and hrs.

" wife **Susanah**, extx., use of last-named tract during life, and personal estate divided equally with dau. afsd.

Test: William Hickman, Thomas Ireland, Jr., Sarah Everest.
20, 231.

Sinclar, William, planter, Cecil Co., 24th Jan., 1730; 30th April, 1731.

To dau. **Rachell** and hrs., dwelling tenement held by lease from Col. Eph. Aug. Herman; also pt. of tenement of land assigned to testator by Capt. Thomas Handrey (having transferred to Obadiah Holt pt. of sd. tenement 23rd Jan. inst.); wife **Rachel** to enjoy profits of sd. 2 tenements until sd. dau. arrives at age of 16 or marries; shd. wife marry, to have her interest in ⅓ thereof.

" Benjamin Lancaster and bro. **Phillip Barrett**, personalty.

" Abraham (son of Martin Nicholason, dec'd), £5 at age of 21. James (son of Charles Fitzpatrick, dec'd) to be kept at school 18 mos.; ⅔ residue of estate to dau. afsd. and remainder to wife and her hrs.; in case of daus. death sd. ⅔ to be disposed of as exs. see fit.

Exs.: Wife and Peter Bouchelle and Robert Veazey.

Test: Eph. Aug. Herman, Anthony Whitley, Lawrence Lawrenson, Anne Hughes. 20, 233.

Alexander, Joseph, tanner, New Munster, Cecil Co.,
13th Dec., 1726;
9th March, 1730.

To son-in-law **Elias Alexander**, bond, dated 19th Aug., 1718, assigned to testator by Sarah Steven, except so much as is already pd., and 40s. to dau. **Sophiah**.

" son **Francis**, 20s.

" daus. **Jane Muley** and **Abigail Clapan**, 10s. each.

" son **James**, ex., residue of estate.

Test: Owen O'Donnell, Anne Taylor, John Dail, John McKnight (Macknite). 20, 235.

Weatherlee (Weatherley), James, Sr., Stepney Parish, Somerset Co., 29th April, 1731; 1st June, 1731.

To son **James** and hrs., dwell. plan. —— and land on Rewastico Ck. below watermill.
" son **John** and hrs., lands above sd. mill.
" 2 sons afsd. and their hrs., "Weatherleys Marshes," "Sankes Island," on afsd. ck.; and certain personalty; sd. sons to be of age at 19.
" son **John** and hrs., residue of land.
" wife ——, extx., and child., personalty equally.
Test: William Piper, William Weatherlee, Robert Twillee.

20, 236.

Sanders, William, planter, Charles Co.,
25th Aug., 1731; 14th Oct., 1731.

To dau. **Frances** (wife of **Charles Sample**) and hrs., ½ of "Hazard"; sd. land not to be sold or mortgaged.
" dau. **Elizabeth** (wife of **Benjamin Stennett**) and hrs., residue of "Hazard," same conditions.
" dau. **Ann** and hrs., land where mother **Eleanor Sanders** now lives; sd. dau. dying without issue, to pass to dau. **Rachel** and hrs.; if both die without issue, to hr. at law; and personalty.
" dau. **Rachel** and hrs., after her mother's decease, dwell. plan. ——; she dying without issue, to pass to dau. **Anne** after decease of her mother-in-law **Catherine**; and personalty.
" wife **Katherine**, extx., dwell. plan. —— during life and residue of personalty; to keep dau. **Anne** until of age or marriage; shd. sd. **Catherine** die during minority of dau. **Ann**, to be in care of her sister **Frances Sample**.
Test: William Ross, Eliza. Elder, T. Thompson. 20, 239.

Comings, Michael, Talbot Co., 3rd Feb., 1730-31; 1st Sept., 1731.

To son **William** and hrs., 25 A. "Thomas Haddawayes Lott," adj. to dwell. plan.; and personalty.
" 2 sons **Thomas** and **Nicholas** and their hrs., 100 A. "Knave Keep Out"; shd. either die without issue, survivor to inherit portion of dec'd; shd. both die without issue, sd. land to 2 daus. **Sarrah** and **Dianah** and their hrs.
" son **Nicholas** and daus. **Sarrah** and **Dianah**, personalty.
" wife **Mary**, residue of personalty during widowhood; shd. she marry, to be divided bet. 7 child., viz. **William, Thomas, Nicholas, Mary, Elizabeth, Sarah** and **Dianah**.

Exs.: Wife and son **William**.
Test: Joseph Cox, John Leeds, Daniel Lambdon (Lambdin).
Note: Widow claims her thirds. 20, 241.

Watson, Elizabeth, Queen Anne's Co., 4th May, 1731; 24th June, 1731.

To son **Francis** and hrs., 150 A. "Brits (Bretts) Hope," Dorchester Co., and personalty.
" son **Benoni** and hrs., "Widow's Folly" and "Watson's Swine Range," at hd. of Red Lion Branch; sd. son dying without issue, to pass to son **Francis** and hrs.; he dying without issue, sd. lands to pass to **Mary Ann**, dau. of William Watson and her hrs.; and personalty.
" son **William**, 1s.
" granddau. **Mary Ann** (dau. of William Watson), personalty at marriage.
" **Elizabeth Lewis** (orphan child), personalty; sd. child to be brought up by son **Benoni** as specified in her indenture.
" **Mary** (dau. of William Mackoy), personalty.
" 2 sons **Francis** and **Benoni**, exs., residue of estate.
Test: James Horsely, Lewis Clothier (Clother), William Swift, Jr. 20, 243.

Hogdston, Alexander, planter, Kent Island, Queen Anne's Co., 21st May, 1731; 25th June, 1731.

To son **Samuel**, £10 at age of 18.
" wife **Katherine**, extx., residue of estate.
Test: William Coughlan, Grace Cooper, John White.
20, 245.

Barkhust, James, Sr., Queen Anne's Co., 30th Aug., 1729; 21st Oct., 1731.

To wife **Elizabeth**, entire estate during widowhood; shd. she marry, her thirds, residue to be divided among 11 child. **James, Ann, Mary, Rachell, Rebeckah, Sarah, John, Elizabeth, Charles, Suanah** and **Jane**; shd. any die without issue, survivors to divide portion of dec'd.
Test: William Burroughs, Sr., Ebinezer Blackston. 20, 247.

Jackson, William, planter, Queen Anne's Co., 8th Jan., 1728; 6th May, 1731.

To Elizabeth Danin, extx., entire estate.
Test: Barbary Grimes, Mary Jackson, George Jackson.
20, 248.

Hatton, Mary, Prince George's Co., 6th Sept., 1730; 13th Oct., 1731.

To grandson **Hatton Middleton**, 100 A. left testatrix by husband ——— (now rented to Humphry Whitmore) during life; at his decease to be divided bet. his dau. **Penelope Hatton Middleton** and granddau. **Susana Middleton** and their hrs.
" grandchild **Elizabeth Middleton**, her sister **Sarah**, her 3 younger sisters (unnamed) and her sister **Susana**, personalty.
" sister **Sarah Copping**, of St. Mary's Parish, Norwich; cousin **Abraham Alloy**, of St. Lawrence Parish, 30s. each, if found in a year and a half.
" **William Sympson**, in Virginia, 20s.
" **Barbary Frazier** and grandsons **Hatton** and **Thomas Middleton**, personalty.
" dau. **Penelope Middleton's** 4 youngest child., ½ of residue of estate divided as follows: To **Sarah, Elizabeth, Elenar** 1 pt., and to their sister **Susana** 2 pts., to be pd. at marriage or in case of their father's decease and their need, at age of 16; shd. one die during minority, surviving three to divide portion of dec'd.
" son **Joseph**, the other ½ of residue of estate; shd. he die before his wife ———, his pt. to be equally divided among his sons ———.
Exs.: Son **Joseph** and grandson **Hatton Middleton**.
Testatrix directs she be buried in vault with husband and dau., and that a brick wall be built around vault.
Test: Humphry Whitmore (Whitimore), Mary Whitmore, Margret Whitmore.
20, 249.

West, Joseph, planter, Prince George's Co., 25th Aug., 1731; 23rd Nov., 1731.

To eldest son **William** and hrs., 300 A. of "Two Brothers," where he now lives; 100 A. of "The Joseph," on n.w. side Muddy Branch.

To son **John** and hrs., 200 A. of first-named tract, on n. side Watt's Branch; 200 A. of "The Joseph," on s. side Muddy Branch.
" dau. **Mary Kelly** and hrs., 100 A. of "The Two Brothers," where she now lives.
" son **Benjamin** and hrs., dwell. plan. "Blakeburn," on w. br. Patuxent R., after decease of wife ———; and personalty.
" wife **Rebeccah**, extx., use of any of afsd. tracts, and all personal estate, except as otherwise bequeathed, during life; at her decease personal estate to be divided among 4 child. afsd.
" grandson **Joseph Kelley**, personalty at decease of wife.
Test: James Beck, John Hallam, Nicholas Rhodes.
20, 252.

Coole (Coale), John, Dorchester Co., 21st Sept., 1731; 30th Oct., 1731.

To daus. **Mary Foxwell**, **Margret**, sons **John** and **Joseph**, **Eliza. Paul**, dau. **Rosamund** and James Hoxon, personalty.
" wife **Sarah**, extx., residue of personalty.
Test: John Stanton, Jacob Jones, Ruth Todd.   20, 254.

Glover, Thomas, planter, St. Mary's Co., 2nd June, 1731; 3rd Nov., 1731.

To sons **Thomas** and **Richard**, 12d. each.
" unborn child, personalty; sd. child if a boy to be of age at 18, if a girl at 16; shd. sd. child die during minority, pt. of afsd. legacy to unborn child of son **Richard**.
" wife **Weneford**, extx., residue of personalty either in Maryland or Virginia.
Test: Patrick Brady, Rebecca Williams, Ubgatt Reeves.
20, 256.

Pain, Thomas, St. Mary's Co., 31st May, 1731; 16th Nov., 1731.

To 3 sons **Henry**, **Thomas** and **James**, lands leased for 61 yrs. of John Baptist Carbery; ⅓ pt. next Deap Spring br. and Thomas Thomas' br. to son **Henry**, ⅓ next to Bryery's br. and Mr. Carbery's n. line to son **Thomas**, and ⅓ being dwell. plan. to son **James** (after decease of wife **Tecla**, extx.).
Test: Robert Drury, James Thompson, Leonard Pain.
20, 258.

Tayman, Benjamin, planter, St. John's Parish, Baltimore Co., 6th June, 1731; 2nd Nov., 1731.

To Quiller and William, sons of Fillis Cammell, John Tayman and Elizabeth Davis, personalty.
" Fillis Cammell, extx., residue of estate.
Test: Nicholas Day, Gilbert Crockett, Peter Malane (Mallane).
Note: Extx. within mentioned being dead, and none to represent her, administration granted to testator's widow ———. 20, 259.

Talbott, Edmund, Baltimore Co., 3rd Nov., 1731; 24th Nov., 1731.

To 4 child., viz. sons **Edmund, William** and **John** and dau. **Elizabeth Elinor,** 200 A. each; sons **Edmund** and **William** the plantations where they now live, son **John** dwell. plan., and dau. **Elizabeth Elinor** the remaining pt.; child. not to dispose of lands until 30 yrs of age; 2 eldest sons empowered to make over land bargained with John Crockett.
" wife **Mary,** personality during widowhood; shd. she marry, her thirds. **John** and **Elizabeth** to stay with their mother until of age, except she shd. marry, in which case son **John** to be free at 18, dau. at 14.
Exs.: Wife and eldest son **Edmund.**
Test: John Powell, John Taylor, John May. 20, 261.

Gallion, John, Baltimore Co., ——— ———, 1730; 10th June, 1731.

To son **John,** 1s.; sd. son having rec'd pt. of personal estate and having removed himself and family from his dwell. plan. is to have no share in real or personal estate.
" son **James** and hrs., 100 A. of "The Agreement"; sd. son dying without issue, to pass to dau. **Sarah** and hrs.
" son **Thomas** and hrs., 100 A. "Gallion's Addition," e. side Humphries Run; sd. son dying without issue, to pass to son **Solomon** and hrs.; and personalty.
" son **Solomon** and hrs., 120 A. of "Gallion's Hazard"; he dying without issue, to pass to his bro. **Thomas** and hrs.; and personalty immediately after decease of testator.
" son **Samuel** and hrs., pt. of "Whiteacres Ridge," bou. of Samuel Hughs; sd. son dying without issue, to pass to his bro. **Henry** and hrs.; and personalty at age of 25.

To son **Henry** and hrs., pt. of "Whiteacres Ridge," on n. side of Little Run; sd. son dying without issue, to pass to his bro. **Samuel** and hrs.; and personalty at age of 25.

" son **Joseph** and hrs., lower pt. of "The Agreement," including dwelling house; sd. son dying without issue, to pass to hrs. of son **John**; and personalty at age of 20.

" dau. **Ann** (wife of **John Phibble**) and hrs., upper pt. of "Gallion's Hazard."

" son **James**, ex., residue of estate for maintenance of youngest child.; sd. son to live on dwell. plan. with his young bros. and sister until bros. attain age of 21, or sister the age of 16, without impediment or claim on behalf of son **Joseph**, or on behalf of the hrs. of son **John** after decease of sd. **Joseph**.

Test: James Fowler, Samuel Fowler, Sarah Fowler, William Hunter. 20, 263.

Geist, Christian, A. A. Co., 22nd Oct., 1731; 22nd Dec., 1731.

To wife **Sarah**, extx., and son **Samuel** and their hrs., entire estate equally; shd. sd. son die during his minority, his portion to pass to wife **Sarah** and hrs.

Test: Dr. Samuel Stringer, Richard Hill, Eleanor Farrell, Joseph Large. 20, 267.

Franklyn, Robert, A. A. Co., 8th Nov., 1730; 27th March, 1731.

To 3 sons **Richard, John** and **Jacob** and their hrs., 570 A., viz. "Collier," "Robert's Luck," "Gordon" and "Beverdam," divided equally.

" son **Richard**, dau. **Sarah Steward**, sons **John** and **Jacob** and dau. **Artridge**, personalty.

" wife **Artridge**, extx., ⅓ of residue of personal estate, remainder to children.

Test: Deborah Balleston, William Fisher, William Fish.
20, 268.

Stuart, Alexander, tanner, Annapolis, A. A. Co.,
2nd Jan., 1730; 22nd March, 1730.

To son **James**, £60, to be expended by advice of Robert Gordon, Robert Alexander and William Cumming, of city afsd., gents.; remainder if any to be pd. sd. son at age of 21.

To dau. **Mary**, extx., and hrs., piece of ground within the city gate lying bet. Docwra's Tann Yard and the hd. of the ck.; pt. of Common, adj. to the city, bou. of Abraham Childs; and residue of estate.

Test: William Cumming, William Williamson, Charles Lewis, John Michiell. 20, 270.

Boice, Mary, A. A. Co., 23rd July, 1726; 6th April, 1731.

To child., viz. **John Meek, James Meek, Christopher Meek, Susanah Phelps** and **Ruth Meek**, personalty.

" servt. **James Daceus**, his freedom.

Exs.: Son **John Meek** and **David Ross**.

Test: David Ross, Ann Grimes, Mary Harris. 20, 271.

Larkin, Thomas (aged about 58 yrs.), A. A. Co., 10th April, 1731; 19th May, 1731.

To wife **Elizabeth** and dau. **Elizabeth**, exs., personal estate equally. Exs. empowered to offer for sale lands mortgaged by Mrs. Mary Woodward and Mrs. Elizabeth Ginn, co-heirs of Amos Garrett, of Annapolis, dec'd. Testator desires that wife and dau. afsd. shall live together in dwelling until one of them marries a man who hath a better freehold, then to remove and leave the other in poss.

" dau. **Elizabeth** and hrs., 855 A. "Larkin's Hills" and certain personalty in lieu of gifts made unto sd. dau. by Madm. Mary Hemsly and Mrs. Wotton. John Gresham having in his hands an assignment of warrant for tract called "Ferry Point," having rec'd £12 for same, wife **Elizabeth** is empowered to demand return thereof, and when recovered to enjoy same during her life.

Test: Stephen Warman, John Watkins, Capt. Joseph Cowman. 20, 274.

Slade, William, Baltimore Co., 2nd April, 1726; 19th May, 1731.

To son **Josias** and hrs., 300 A. "Courtice (Curtis') Neck"; he dying without issue, to son **William** and hrs.; and personalty.

" son **William** and hrs., 200 A. "Winslows Range"; shd. both afsd. sons die without issue, sd. tracts to pass to hr. at law; and personalty. Extx. enjoined to see that no tenant of "Winslow's Range," during minority of son **William**, be permitted to clear beyond main road.

To son Thomas and hrs., 238 A. "Slades Camp"; he dying without issue, to pass to hr. at law.
" son Ezekiell, £30 to purchase land.
" daus. Elizabeth Cockey and Mary Buckinham, 10s. each.
" all sons and dau. by present wife Elizabeth, extx., personalty.
" Barzealey Foster, personalty.
Overseer: John Cromwell.
Test: John Brooks, William Houchin, Nicholas Beston.
20, 276.

Hobbs, John, A. A. Co., 12th July, 1731; 3rd Aug., 1731.

To wife Dorothy, extx., dwell. plan. —— during life; at her decease to son William and hrs.; sd. son dying during his minority sd. lands to pass to dau. Margaret and hrs.; and ⅓ personal estate absolutely.
" 3 sons Samuel, John and Joseph and their hrs., residue of real estate equally; shd. either die during minority and without issue, survivors to divide portion of dec'd.
" 3 sons and 1 dau. former wife Susannah had by William Powel, viz. Henry, James, Josias and Elizabeth, 1s. each when they come of age.
" sons Samuel, John, Joseph and William and dau. Margret, residue of personal estate.
Test: Robert Browne, William Cornwall, Benjamin Cox, Thos. Whitaker, John Ozborn. 20, 279.

Coyle, Edward, A. A. Co., 1st Feb., 1730; 14th April, 1731.

To wife Elizabeth, extx., son John and dau. Ann Burton Coyle, personal estate equally.
" cousin Andrew, son of Andrew Pitts, of A. A. Co., and Joseph Greaton, personalty.
" son and dau. afsd., all real estate in A. A. and Baltimore Co., reserving to wife afsd. her dower interest in same; at her decease to revert to son and dau. afsd. or their hrs.
Test: Dr. Richard Hill, Francis Linthicum, Dr. Charles Carroll. 20, 281.

Williams, Thomas, carpenter, Annapolis, A. A. Co.,
9th Dec., 1723; 20th Oct., 1731.

To wife Katherine, extx., and hrs., dwelling house and lot in city afsd., and entire personal estate.
Test: William Williams, John Chalmers, William Cumming.
20, 282.

Foreman, William, A. A. Co.,   11th Sept., 1727;
                                                         15th Dec., 1730.

To dau. Mary Aldris and hrs., half of dwell. plan. ———.
" grandson Joseph Aldris, at age of 18, grandsons **William** and **Thomas Aldris** and **William** and **Philip Foreman** (sons of **Joseph Foreman**), at age of 16, personalty.
" wife **Elizabeth**, extx., ⅛ personal estate, residue to be divided bet. 2 child., **Joseph Foreman** and **Mary Aldris**.
Test: John Nicholson, Richard Humphreys, William Worthington.   20, 284.

Govane, Elizabeth, A. A. Co.,   3rd June, 1730;
                                                       28th April, 1731.

To son **Benjamin Hammond** and hrs., 50 A. "Forked Neck," bou. when a widow of his uncle **John Hammond**.
" husband **James**, personalty.
Exs.: Husband and son afsd.
Test: Samuel Hodgson, Mrs. Susannah Lillingston, Lawrence Hammond.
3rd May, 1731. Above will ratified by within-mentioned **James Govane**.
Test: Samuel Hodgson, William Hammond.   20, 286.

Smeaton, William, mariner, London,
                      Annapolis, 11th Jan., 1730;
                                             12th Jan., 1731.

To bro. **Thomas**, St. Margaret's, Westminster, 1s.
" Marmaduke Smeaton, or his wife, of same place, £10.
" Jeffry Pollard, or his wife, late of Barbadoes, now of Philadelphia, £8.
" Margaret Hues, when free, 20s.
" Abram Vineing, Philadelphia, £3.
" Capt. James Mullinton, Philadelphia, 30s.
" Warner Richards, New Barbadoes Neck, nr. Hackinsack, £5 currency of N. Y.
" Mordock Dowlin, 2 pistols.
Exs.: Jane Falkner, Chester R., Md., and Susannah Price.
Overseers: Gilbert Falkner, Chester R., Md., and Mordock Dowlin.
Test: Griffith Beddoe, Thomas Wildgus (Wilgus), Charles Steward.   20, 287.

Young, Henry, Calvert Co., 19th Aug., 1731;
21st Dec., 1731.

To wife Elizabeth, extx., dwell. plan. "Young's Desire" during life and certain personalty.
" son Philemon and hrs., 124 A. "Dividing Branch," in Bowen's Neck, bou. of David Bowen; "Young's Desire" after decease of wife; and personal estate; sd. son dying without issue, lands to pass to Samuel, son of bro. William, and hrs.; sd. Samuel dying without issue, to pass to William, son of afsd. William, and hrs.; and in case of his death without hrs., to pass to next of kin of same name.
Test: John Yoe, Jr., John Young, Ellis Slator.
Note: Widow claims her thirds. 20. 290.

Edmondson, James (nunc.), Talbot Co.,
29th Nov., 1731;
6th Dec., 1731.

To mother Magdalen Loockerman, entire estate.
Test: Peter Sharpe, Thomas Jones. 20, 293.

Taylor (Talor), John, ship carpenter, Kent Co.,
4th March, 1730;
26th March, 1731.

To wife Rebecca, extx., personalty.
" son John and hrs., dwell. plan. ———, pt. of "Fairly," and personalty.
" sons Philip and William, personalty, including to each son and their hrs. a seat in St. Paul's Church. After estates of Matthew Piner's child. are taken out and wife's thirds are deducted, residue of estate to 3 sons afsd. equally.
Test: George Skirven, James Strahan, Thomas Simson, William Simson.
Note: Widow claims her thirds. 20,294.

Moll, Mary, widow, Chester Town (commonly called New Town), Kent Co., 30th Dec., 1730;
19th Aug., 1731.

Testatrix states that having no child. or relation, and that David, son of late husband John Moll, being an object of pity on acct. of being an idiot and being left unprovided for by his father, she bequeaths her entire estate to Symon Wilmer, ex., and hrs. on condition that he and his hrs. will give security for maintaining the sd. **David** during his life.

Test: John Evans, Charles Hynson, James Calder. 20, 296.

Jones, Thomas, carpenter, Kent Island,
19th Feb., 1730-31;
17th March, 1730.

To son **James,** personal estate.
Ex.: Thomas Macey.
Test: Thomas Gould, Sarah Davis, Isabella Heirs. 20, 298.

Palmer, Olliver, planter, Kent Co., 20th Jan., 1722;
6th Aug., 1731.

To wife **Sarah,** extx., entire estate, real and personal.
Test: George Dunkan, George Wetherall (Wetherell), Samuel Smith. 20, 299.

Gatinbe (Gatenby), Elizabeth, 22nd Aug., 1726;
16th Nov., 1731.

To husband **William** and hrs., "Demby," Hynson's Haven, Kent Co., and "Hunting fields," Hunting Ck., Talbot Co.
Test: Thomas Tibbott (Tibbett), Robert Green, John Huff. 20, 300.

Ennalls, William, Dorchester Co., 7th Oct., 1731;
5th Dec., 1731.

To dau. **Mary** and hrs., the Great House lands (for desc. see will).
" bros. **Bartholomew, Thomas** and **Joseph** and their hrs., ½ of "Marsh Range," to be sold in common or divided.
" cousin **William,** son of **John Ennalls,** dec'd, and hrs., all lands given him by his uncle **Thomas** in his last will.
" bro. **Henry** and hrs., "Beaver Dam Range," on br. of Chickennacomico, given him by his uncle **Thomas**; the branch bet. Dunkins and Joseph Causways dividing the lands of afsd. William and Henry Ennalls; and personalty.
" bro. **Joseph** and hrs., lands lying on the neck where he now lives; he dying without issue, sd. lands to dau. **Mary** and hrs.; ½ of 500 A. "Ennall's Timber Yard," lying at mouth of neck where sd. **Joseph** lives; sd. **Joseph** dying without issue, to dau. **Ann** and hrs.

To dau. Ann and hrs., residue of last-named tract; tracts in the neck called Cook's or Pitt's Neck as conveyed from Pitts and Rawlings; also 150 A. "Ennall's Lott," one side of neck being bounded by Pitts land and other by Beaver Dam br. (above where Edward Southel lives), including "Thompson's Lott," bou. of Anthony Rawlings, and another bou. of John Cook.
" dau. Betty and hrs., 1,300 A. "Darly," on Blackwater R., and land where John Thompson lives.
" John Harper and hrs., 200 A. "Darly," he having pd. £25 on same. Richard Bradly to hold plantation where he now lives, rent free, during life.
" Thomas Thomas, 15 pounds of debt.
" the chapel at Chickennacomeco (for finishing same) and great bell at Transquaking, 5,000 pounds.
" cousin **Mary Ennalls**, personalty.
Ex.: Bro. **Joseph** to have charge of estates for child., who are to be educated and maintained according to their estates.
Overseers: Bros. **Bartholomew, Henry Hooper** and **Charles Goldsborough.**
Test: Mary Cratcher (Crotcher), Elizabeth Ball, James Hust, Elizabeth Long. 20, 301.

Harris, John, Dorchester Co., 7th Feb., 1729; 24th Dec., 1731.

To wife **Elizabeth,** extx., dwell. plan. ―――― during life; son **John** to live with his mother-in-law until 20 yrs. of age.
" son **John** and daus. **Jane** and **Elizabeth,** personalty; residue of personal estate to wife afsd.
Test: Charles Dickinson (Dickenson), Abraham Gambell, Mary Gambell.
Mem. of debts due to testator: Moses Nicolls 126 lbs. tob.
20, 305.

Nicholson, William, mcht., A. A. Co., 28th Dec., 1731; 2nd March, 1731.

Testator directs that debts due him, goods from Mr. Wm. Hunt, proceeds from sale of The Annapolis Adventure, and money in hand, be applied to payment of debts. Extx. empowered to sell "Poplar Neck," Baltimore Co., if necessary, for same purpose. Proceeds from sale of unfinished house in Annapolis to be secured to son **Beale,** sale of same to be made under advice of **John Beale, Robert Gordon, Dr. Charles Carroll, Thomas Worthington** and **Robert Alexander.** Shd. sd. house be sold and sd. son die during his minority, £240 of proceeds to bro. Samuel, residue to wife; and in case sd. house is not sold, and sd. son shd. die as afsd., sd. house to bro. **Samuel** and hrs., he paying to wife afsd. £250; in default of such payment sd. house to wife afsd. and hrs. In case sd. house shall be sold, and debts paid by ways and means above mentioned, and in case of death of sd. son without issue during his minority, "Poplar Neck" to be divided bet. bros. **Benjamin** and **Edward** and their hrs. Shd. sd. son die in minority and without issue, lots in Chester Town, Kent Co., and in London Town, A. A. Co., to bro. **Samuel** and hrs. Son at age of 10 yrs. to be sent to school at Edinburgh, then to college for 3 yrs. and to London for study of the law. £5 is bequeathed to the master who shall instruct sd. son while at school, and £10 to the one who tutors him during his study of law. Sd. son to be brought up in the faith of the Established Church of Scotland.

To wife ———, extx., 150 A. of "Norwood's Beale" during life; at her decease to son **Beale** and hrs.; he dying without issue, to rightful hrs. of **John Beale**, wife's father; and ⅓ personal estate.

" aunt **Elizabeth Nicholson**, of Berwick-on-Tweed, £50.

" **William Hunt** and **William Montague**, mcht., of London, each a ring.

" servt. **Thomas Raisin**, 40s. at expiration of time.

Test: Daniel Dulany, Dr. John Hamilton, Thomas Jennings.

Codicil: 29th Dec., 1731. Shd. afsd. house in Annapolis not be sold, and son **Beale** shd. die without issue, sd. house to wife ——— and hrs.; shd. house be sold and sd. son dying as afsd., proceeds of sale to wife ——— absolutely.

To father-in-law **John Beale**, mother-in-law **Elizabeth Beale**, bro. **Joseph**, sister-in-law **Anne Beale**, kinswomen **Mrs. Anne Norwood** and **Hannah Norwood**, personalty. In case of death of sd. son without issue and in his minority, "Poplar Neck" to bro. **Samuel** and hrs.; shd. sd. bro. die during minority and without issue, sd. lands to bros. **Benjamin** and **Edward** and their hrs. Shd. sd. bro. **Samuel** die as afsd., lots in Kent and A. A. Co. to pass to bros. **Benjamin** and **Edward** and their hrs.

Test: Edmund Jenings, William Stevenson, Thomas Jennings. 20, 306.

2nd Codicil: 14th Jan., 1731. Father-in-law **John Beale** appointed guardian to son; in case of his death, James Mouat, Thomas Worthington and John Galloway to act.

Test: Anne Norwood, Richard Dorsey, Richard Goldsmith.
20, 306.

Falconer (Falconar), Sarah, widow, Queen Anne's Co.,
7th Nov., 1730;
23rd June, 1731.

To son John, hand-mill during his life, after his decease to his son John; sd. grandson dying without male issue, sd. mill to second son of son John (shd. such son be born after decease of testatrix), otherwise sd. mill to Burton Francis Falconer during his life, and after his decease to grandson Thomas Ford Falconer; sd. mill not to be removed from dwell. plan. during life of relation Thomas Falconer, Sr.

" sons Thomas, James, William and Emmanuel, dau. Ann Rakes, son-in-law John Rakes and dau. Temperance, personalty.

" Thomas Falconer, Sr., ex., residue of personalty during life, to be divided at his decease or marriage bet. sons Francis, Thomas, James, William and Emmanuel and dau. Ann Rakes.

Test: Wm. Rakes, Eleanor Hall, Martha Goult.

Mem.: Sons William and Emmanuel to be under care of ex. Thomas Falconer, Sr., until of age at 21 yrs. Shd. sd. Thomas marry, son William to care of within named John Falconer, and son Emmanuel to care of son-in-law Burton Francis Falconer.

" Michael Penkinde, personalty.

Test: Same. 20, 314.

Thomas, Edmond, planter, Queen Anne's Co.,
9th May, 1731;
15th Nov., 1731.

To son Edmond and hrs., 150 A. where Thomas Stevens now lives; sd. son dying without issue, to pass to son James and hrs.; he dying without issue, to son Tilden and hrs., and in failure of issue afsd. to daus. Mary Ann and Martha and their hrs.

" son James and hrs., 200 A. dwell. plan. "Trustram," on n. side of Madbury's Branch, adj. John Clayland's land.

" wife Anne, extx., dwell. plan. during life, with residue of "Trustram"; after her decease all of sd. lands to son Edmond and hrs., entailed as the afsd. 150 A.; and ⅓ personal estate.

" son Tilden and hrs., 227 A. "Thomas' Addition," in Tully's Neck.

" child. ———, residue of personal estate.

Test: Trustram Thomas, Jr., George Thorne, John Beck, Charles Quick. 20, 317.

Leake, John, innholder, Leonard Town, St. Mary's Co.,
2nd Oct., 1731;
14th Jan., 1731.

To son **Richard** and hrs., 3 lots and houses in Leonard Town and land bou. of John Baptist Carberry; sd. son dying during minority, sd. land to his mother during her life, at her decease to dau. **Catherine** and son **John** and their hrs. Catherine to have the plan. in her portion; and personalty, some of which des. as bou. of Oswald Thompson and bill of exchange drawn by Mr. Parnham. Sd. son to remain with his mother, she to keep him at school until 19 yrs. of age and endeavor to bring him up in faith of the Church of England. Shd. sd. son die during minority, his portion of real and personal estate to wife **Katherine** during her life, at her decease to be divided bet. son **John** and dau. **Katherine** and their hrs.
" son **William** and hrs., 50 A. bou. of Thomas Williams; and personalty.
" dau. **Mary Brewer,** 1s.
" dau. **Katherine** and **John Tole,** personalty.
" wife **Katherine,** extx., residue of real and personal estate.
Test: William Russell, Jacob Delan (Detan), Mary Williamson. 20, 318.

Redman, John, planter, St. Mary's Co.,
20th Jan., 1731;
18th Feb., 1731.

To dau. **Elizabeth** and hrs., lands adj. to plan. of Nicholas Brown; and personalty.
" sons **Jeremiah, Thomas, Daniel, Vincent,** daus. **Anne Leake, Sarah Robinson** and **Elizabeth,** personalty (some of which des. as debt due from Peter Peake).
" sons **Soloman** and **John** and dau. **Frances Fryer,** 1s. each.
" grandson **John Lake (Leake)** and hrs., a piece of land in the pasture.
Exs.: Sons **Vincent, Jeremiah** and **Daniel.**
Test: Sons Thomas Howard, William Medcalf, Peter Mugg.
20, 321.

Booth, Jacob, St. Mary's Co., 7th Feb., 1731-2;
2nd March, 1731.

To bro. **Abraham,** personalty.
" sister **Ann,** extx.. residue of personal estate.
Test: James Granan, Edward Horn, Stephen Watts.
20, 324.

MARYLAND CALENDAR OF WILLS 211

Bratten (Brattan), Quanton, Somerset Co.,
27th March, 1731;
18th Oct., 1731.

To wife **Hannah** and son **Joshua,** personalty.
" dau. **Mary,** certain personalty des. as having been her mother's and in hands of her uncle **John Camble;** if she dies during minority, to pass to his dau. **Elizabeth Camble.**
" son **Joshua** and hrs., dwell. plan. ———; he dying without issue, to dau. **Mary** and hrs.
Exs.: Samuel Bratten, Hannah Bratten.
Test: Adam Bell, James Bratten, Samuel Bratten. 20, 325.

Wilson, William, Sr., Annamessex, Somerset Co.,
15th April, 1731;
16th Dec., 1731.

To wife **Elizabeth,** extx., dwell. plan. ——— and marsh "Persimon Point" during life; at her dceease to son **George** and hrs.
" son **John** and hrs., "Hog Ridge," adj. dwell. plan., at age of 21, not to sell same except to his bro. **George** or next hr.
" sons **George** and **John,** personalty.
" sons **William** and **Abraham** and dau. **Sarah,** 1s. each.
Test: John Colhoon (Colhone), Josina Duncarter, Joseph Eames. 20, 327.

Treger, James, Dorchester Co., 25th Oct., 1731;
17th Feb., 1731.

To dau. **Mary,** personalty.
Exs.: Wife **Elizabeth** and son **James.**
Test: Richard Stanley, Danyel (Daniel) Ryson, Thomas Trygor. 20, 328.

Clarkson, Thomas, Dorchester Co., 20th Dec., 1731;
13th March, 1731.

To son **Thomas,** 137 A. of "Brown's Meddows" (formerly known as "Clarksons Forest"), £10 for schooling expenses at age of 16 yrs.; and personalty.
" daus. **Sarah** and **Rachel,** personalty and money for schooling at ages of 10 and 13 yrs.
" bro.-in-law **Thomas Brown,** personalty.
" son **Thomas** and daus. afsd., residue of estate. Bros. **William** and **Robert** to have charge of money for schooling expenses of children.

To wife **Sarah**, extx., personalty and use of estate during widowhood, afsd. legacies excepted.

Test: Abraham Covington, James Cannon, Richard Clarkson, James Brown, Jr.

Extx. claims her thirds. 20, 329.

Hicks, Liven, Dorchester Co., 25th Feb., 1731; 16th March, 1731.

To eldest son **Liven** and hrs., pt. of dwell. plan. "Hinchman's Neck," adj. land of John Rider.
" son **Henry** and hrs., residue of sd. tract and "Crucked Ridge."
" son **John** and hrs., lands on Chickacone R.
" youngest son **Denwood** and hrs., tract by Chiconocomoco upper bridge and tract at Marsh a Hope.
" dau. **Anne Travers**, 20s.
" wife ——— and 6 child., viz. **Liven, John, Henry, Denwood, Mary** and **Sarah**, personal estate equally.

Exs.: Wife ——— and son **Liven**.

Test: John Rider, William Murray, John Brown Sloan.

20, 331.

Heath, James, mcht., Cecil Co., 6th May, 1731; 31st Jan., 1731-2.

To wife **Mary**, pt. of dwell. plan. "The Holt," and "Todes Purchase," adj. thereto, during life, provided sd. tracts are accepted in lieu of dower rights; wife empowered to sell lands in Queen Anne's Co. and proceeds to be in hands of exs. as personal estate, provided the same be sold before son **James Paul** shall attain age of 21.
" nephew **Charles**, £50.
" dau.-in-law **Mary Chetham** and son-in-law **Edward Chetham**, £10 each.

Exs.: Wife **Mary** and son **James Paul**.

Test: Joshua George. 20, 333.

Tannehill, William, Prince George's Co., 15th Sept., 1729; 28th March, 1732.

To wife ———, extx., ⅓ personal estate and dwell. plan. ——— during life.
" son **James**, real estate after death of his mother; shd. there be any residue after wife's thirds are deducted and debts paid, to be divided amongst all child. Certain personalty at death of wife to be divided bet. sons **William** and **James**.

Test: Thos. Evans, Mark Mcallom, Mary Evans.

Note: Widow claims her thirds. 20, 334.

Warner, Samuel, planter, Prince George's Co.,
21st Nov., 1731;
29th March, 1732.

To son **Samuel** and dau. **Sarah,** personalty at age of 16 yrs.
" wife **Elizabeth,** extx., residue of estate.
Test: John Henry, Richard Harrison, Sarah Bennett.
20, 335.

Robinson, William, Charles Co., 4th Dec., 1731;
18th Dec., 1731.

To the poor, certain personalty and £5.
" **Anna Maria Parnham** and **Eliza. Parnham,** residue of estate, both here and in England.
Ex.: John Parnham.
Test: Joseph Pile, William Howes. 20, 336.

Speake, John, innholder, Charles Co., 4th Dec., 1731;
1st Jan., 1731.

To wife **Mary,** extx., lot and dwelling houses in Charles Town, co. afsd., during life; at her decease to grandson **John,** son of **Thomas Speake;** and personalty, including some left her by her former husband James Semmes.
" sons **John, Richard** and **Thomas** and dau. **Jane,** wife of Edward Maddocke, personalty, and residue of estate equally.
Test: Francis Ware, Allon Hewton, Robert Hanson.
20, 337.

Sanders, John, Charles Co., 18th Nov., 1731;
7th Feb., 1731.

To son **Ignatius** and hrs., lands and dwell. plan. at Porttobacco as left testator by will of his father ———; sd. son to pay to his bro. **Richard,** at age of 18 yrs., the sum of 2,000 lbs.; and personalty.
" wife **Valinda,** extx., residue of estate to be divided bet. 3 child., viz. **Ignatious, Prudence** and **Richard;** sons to be of age at 18, dau. at 16 yrs. or day of marriage.
Test: Sarah Combs (Coombes), Thomas Sanders, William Sanders. 20, 339.

Ward, John, planter, Talbot Co., 19th Oct., 1731;
26th Nov., 1731.

To wife **Parthenia,** extx., dau. **Jane** and son **John,** personal estate equally; son **John** to receive certain personalty at age of 18.
Test: Thomas Bruff, John Christian, Sr., William Whaley.
20, 341.

Morgan, John, planter, Talbot Co.,   1st Jan., 1727;
                                                  16th Feb., 1731.

To eldest son **James**, 120 A. of dwell. plan. ———.
" sons **Charles** and **Samuel**, "Dudley's Clifts," bou. of Richard Dudley, Sr.
" wife **Mary**, ⅛ personal estate absolutely and use of all lands not yet disposed of during life; at her decease to pass to sons **Hugh** and **Robert** and their hrs.
" granddau. **Cicelia Williams,** 1s.
" 6 child., viz. **James, Charles, Samuel, Hugh, Elizabeth** and **Robert**, residue of personal estate.
Exs.: Wife and son **James.**
Test: Nicholas Brown, John Rathall (Rathell), John Karby.
                                                                      20, 342.

Davis, David, planter, Talbot Co.,   1st Oct., 1731;
                                                    4th Nov., 1731.

To wife **Elizabeth**, extx., and hrs., entire real estate absolutely, except dwell. plan. "Ashby"; shd. testator have right to devise same it is also left to wife afsd. during life; and personal estate.
Test: Tench Francis, James Hollyday, James Hurlock, Mary Hurlock.   20, 344.

Smith, William, Baltimore Co.,   11th Jan., 1731;
                                                4th March, 1731.

To son **Winstone** and hrs., "Martins Rest," "Gash's Neglect"; and personalty.
" son **William** and hrs., "Broom's Bloom"; and personalty.
" dau. **Elizabeth** and hrs., "Owens Outland Plains"; and personalty.
" mother **Elizabeth Smith**, maintenance during life.
" nephew **Richard Caswell** and son-in-law **William Dallam,** personalty.
" **John Haycock,** ½ his debt.
" wife **Elizabeth**, extx., ⅓ personal estate, residue to be divided amongst 3 child.
Test: Robert Oliver, John Haycock, Michael Webster.
                                                                     20, 345.

MARYLAND CALENDAR OF WILLS

Shepherd (Shephard), Rowland, Baltimore Co.,
13th Jan., 1731-2;
9th March, 1731.

To dau. **Ann,** 100 A. of land, chosen where she pleases, and certain personalty in addition to her pt. of personal estate.
" dau. **Mary Little,** 100 A. "Shepherd's Park."
" dau. **Sarah Brown,** her equal portion of personal estate.
" son **Christopher,** ex., all lands in Bush R. Neck except the 100 A. to be chosen by dau. afsd., and land in Somerset Co.
" 4 child., viz. **Christopher, Sarah Brown, Mary Little** and **Anna,** personal estate equally.

Test: William Reid, Abraham Cord, Jonathan Hughs.
Codicil: 11th Jan., 1731. 100 A. devised to dau. **Ann** and her hrs. to be laid out for her out of that pt. adj. James Drew's land and to include "Doggwood Ridge." Land bequeathed son afsd. and dau. **Mary** to be to them and their hrs. forever.
Test: Roger Mathews, William Ozburn, Joseph Pritchard.
20, 347.

Deaver, John, Baltimore Co., 3rd Jan., 1731-2;
8th March, 1731.

To son **Richard** and hrs., pt. of "Turkey's Hills"; sd. land to begin at land bou. of testator by Richard Ruff, to run n.w. until it intersects land bou. by Benjamin Jones, to run with sd. land until it intersects "Come by Chance." In case sd. son will not accept of above bequest in full satisfaction for tract bou. by him, afsd. land to be sold and the proceeds to be pd. to sd. **Richard** or hrs. for satisfaction for afsd. land "Broken Islands."
" son **Samuel** and hrs., all other lands, with dwell. plan.
——, at decease of his mother **Hannah**; sd. son dying without issue, sd. lands to be divided bet. daus. **Elizabeth Preston** and **Mary** and their hrs.
" sons **Richard, John** and **Antill,** 1s. each.
" wife **Hannah,** extx., residue of personal estate during life; at her decease to be divided among 3 child., **Samuel, Elizabeth Preston** and **Mary.**

Test: John Wagstafe, John Wagstaff, Ann Tredway (Treadway), Thomas Brasier (Brazer). 20, 350.

Hutchins, Thomas, planter, Baltimore Co.,
1st March, 1731-2;
4th April, 1732.

To eldest son **John** and hrs., "Boon's Delight," being pt. of "Leafs Chance," in fork of Gunpowder R. falls; pt. of "Hutchin's Neglect," on w. side of Primrose Branch; and personalty.

" sons **Thomas** and **Nicholas** and their hrs., "Hutchins Lott" and pt. of "Hutchins Neglect," on e. side of sd. branch, son **Nicholas** to have first choice.

" 3 daus. **Elizabeth, Ann** and **Susana** and their hrs., "Hutchin's Addition" equally.

" 5 youngest child., viz. **Thomas, Nicholas, Elizabeth, Ann** and **Susana,** residue of personalty and proceeds from sale of "Begining," lying in back Gunpowder. Shd. any of 3 sons afsd. die without issue, his pt. of land to be divided amongst surviving sons and their hrs.; shd. any of 3 daus. die without issue, their land to fall to son **Nicholas** and hrs.; shd. all child. die without issue, above lands to go to the poor of the parish wherein sd. land lyeth; shd. dau. **Susana** marry a certain William Deson, she is to have 1s. and no more, and her portion of land to pass to her 2 eldest sisters, and her portion of personalty to be divided among 4 child., viz. **Thomas, Nicholas, Elizabeth** and **Ann.**

Exs.: Sons **Thomas** and **Nicholas.**
Appraisers: John Elliott, Thomas Gittings.
Test: John Elliott, Robert Cutchin, John Cocken. 20, 352.

Cullen (Culling), Thomas, Baltimore Co.,
4th Oct., 1731;
3rd Nov., 1731.

To 3 godchild., viz. **John, Mary** and **Elizabeth,** child. of Robert and Ann Hawkins, 30s.

" cousin **William Jinkins,** personalty.

" **Joseph,** son of Joseph Jinkins, 30s.

" wife **Catharine,** extx., estate, real and personal, during life, with right to dispose of ½ personal estate, residue to be divided amongst 3 child. of sister Sarah, viz. **Sarah Gwin, Aves Jinkins, Thomas Jinkins. William Jinkins** to pay to his bro. **Thomas** £5 before division of estate; sd. **William Jinkins** to have tract "The New Design," and kinsman **Francis** to have Mannor plantation equally divided bet. them both.

Test: Robert Hawkins, Francis White, William Walker.
20, 354.

Ward, Samuel, St. John's Parish, Baltimore Co.,
>1st Sept., 1731;
>5th Nov., 1731.

To grandsons **Simeon Collings** and **Samuel Collings** and granddaus. **Amey Collings** and **Hanner Asbrook,** £5 each.
" 2 grandchild. of **Mary Anna Ward,** £5 each. **Ephraim Tomlinson** and **Joseph Tomlinson,** of the Co. of Gloucester, N. J., guardians to sd. grandchild., to take charge of legacies until of age; boys at 21, girls at 18 yrs. Shd. any of sd. child. die during minority, their portions to be pd. to extxs. of estate.
" dau. **Mary Anna Ward,** £30.
" 2 daus. **Hannah** and **Rosanna,** extxs., residue of estate, real and personal.
Test: Abraham Johns, Nicholas Martineaux, Nicholas Day.
>20, 356.

Johns, Abraham, chyrurgon, Baltimore Co.,
>10th Oct., 1731;
>15th Feb., 1731.

To father-in-law **Roger Mathews,** and **John Mathews,** bro. of wife, personalty.
" wife **Hannah,** extx., entire estate, above legacies excepted; shd. wife be now with child and same live to legal age, sd. child to enjoy the ½ of all real and personal estate.
Test: Nicholas Day, John Weasly (Wisely), Parker Hall.
>20, 358.

Cook, William, planter, Baltimore Co.,
>24th Sept., 1731;
>8th March, 1731.

To 2 sons **Jeremiah** and **John** and their hrs., dwell. plan. "Cook's Dubble Purches" equally at age of 21; shd. sd. sons die without issue, sd. plan. to 2 daus. **Elizabeth** and **Sarah;** they failing issue, to pass to the line of Cooks forever.
" wife **Sarah,** extx., personal estate, dower rights during life and care of child. until of age; shd. wife die, sons to be in poss. of lands at age of 19.
Test: Patrick Ruork, John Burton, Bennett Garrett.
>20, 359.

Malden, James, Calvert Co., 8th Jan., 1726; 17th Feb., 1731.

    To wife **Eleanor,** extx., dwell. plan. 200 A. "Lower Bennet" during life; after her decease 100 A. of sd. tract, next the bay, to eldest son of bro. **Francis,** 100 A. to eldest son of sister **Sarah Clagett,** and in case he dies during minority then afsd. 100 A. to pass to next hr.; personal estate absolutely.

    " son-in-law **Benj. Elle,** personalty at age of 21.

    Test: John Rigby (Ribby), Mary Morgan, Frances Stallins.
                                                                    20, 361.

Hutchins, Frances, Calvert Co., 22nd Feb., 1726; 9th March, 1731-2.

    To mother **Elizabeth Hutchins,** extx., personal estate during life; at her decease to pass with testator's share of father's personal estate to kinsman **Francis,** son of **Francis Hutchins,** and hrs.; he dying without issue, same to pass to bro. **Francis Hutchins** and hrs.

    " kinsman **Francis Hutchins** afsd. and hrs., pt. of "Stoakly," left testator by father ———; he dying without issue, to pass to bro. **Francis Hutchins** and hrs.

    " niece **Ann Brooke** and nephews **Francis Birckhead** and **Francis Hance,** personalty.

    Test: Nehemiah Birckhead, Sarah Birckhead, Ann Skinner.
                                                            20, 362.

Duke, James, planter, Calvert Co., 10th Nov., 1731; 21st Dec., 1731.

    To son **James,** ex., and hrs., tract where he now lives, being pt. of "Brook Place Manner," bou. of Robert Brooke, dec'd.

    " granddau. **Martha** and hrs., dwell. plan. "Rich Levell" during life; at her decease to pass to grandson **Benjamin** and hrs.; he dying without issue, to pass to next of kin.

    " grandson **Samuel Rowland** and hrs., tract where his father **Samuel Rowland** now lives, known as "The Shirt Come Off"; and personalty.

    " dau. **Martha Gray** and son **Andrew Duke,** 1s.

    " dau. **Catherine Beal,** 20s.

    " wife ———, ⅓ of estate as law directs.

    Test: Grace Hambleton, William Dawkins, John Dorrumple.
                                                                20, 364.

MARYLAND CALENDAR OF WILLS 219

Smith, Rachel, widow, Calvert Co., 26th Oct., 1730;
3rd Feb., 1731.
To each of sons and daus. (unnamed), a mourning ring.
" dau. **Elizabeth,** extx., residue of estate.
Test: Walter Smith, Freshes, James Smith, Francis Wilkinson. 20, 366.

Horn, Henry, 20th March, 1731;
7th April, 1732.
To mother ——— and sister **Francis Forrest,** personalty.
" wife **Patients,** extx., residue of estate.
Test: George Clarke, Abraham Smith. 20, 367.

White, William, planter, St. Mary's Co.,
3rd April, 1732;
17th April, 1732.
To John Guyther and John White, personalty.
" bro.-in-law **George Beaverlye,** ex., residue of estate.
Test: Daniel Duggens, John Thomas. 20, 368.

Peirce (Pierce, Peirse), Edward, planter, St. Mary's Co.,
31st Dec., 1720;
24th April, 1732.
To wife **Elinor,** extx., real estate in afsd. co. and personal estate during life.
" youngest son **Edward** and hrs., dwell. plan. "Chance" after decease of wife.
" sons **John** and **Robert** and their hrs., 50 A. of "Courtney's Fancy," equally, after decease of wife. Shd. son **Edward** die without issue, sd. tract to be divided bet. sons **John** and **Robert**; and if son **John** shd. die without issue, his portion of 50 A. to pass to son **Robert**; and if son **Robert** shd. die without issue, his portion to son **John**; and shd. both die without issue, their portions to son **Edward** afsd. Shd. sons **John, Robert** and **Edward** die without issue, sd. lands to fall to dau. **Mary Perry** and hrs. Sons not to rent or sell lands except to one another. After wife's decease personal estate divided bet. dau. **Mary,** eldest son **Thomas** and sons **John, Robert** and **Edward.**
Test: John Bactson, Thomas Mohoney, Pheby Harwood, John Leigh. 20, 369.

Sewall, Nicholas, Jr., St. Mary's Co., 28th Oct., 1727; 11th April, 1732.

To nephew **Nicholas Lewis Sewall**, personal estate at age of 21; shd. sd. nephew die during his minority, personalty to be divided among the bros. and sisters of testator living at decease of sd. nephew; also in event of the death of sd. nephew without issue, the reversion of tract where testator now lives, "Mattapany Sewall," will by law descend to testator, and is devised to **Charles**, second son of bro. **Charles**, and to his hrs. Shd. sd. nephew **Charles** die without issue, or during minority, sd. land and appurtenances to become right of nephew **Nicholas**, second son of **Peregrine Frisby**, gentleman. Rights to administer on estate of bro. **Henry** having been signed over to testator by **Elizabeth**, widow of sd. bro., and Philip Lee, Esq., her now husband by deed 8th Dec., 1725, testator makes over to afsd. bro. **Charles** all claims to administer on estate of bro. **Henry**, dec'd.

Ex.: Bro. **Charles**.
Test: Thomas Aisquith, Thomas Tolley, George Reade, Richard Hopewell. 20, 371.

Martin (Marting), William, planter, Charles Co., 23rd Feb., 1732(?); 20th April, 1732.

To wife **Ann**, personal estate, excepting certain personalty to son **William** and dau. ———— when of age.
Test: Adam Crump, Richard King, Robert Lee. 20, 373.

Gilpen, Charity, Portobacco Parrish, Charles Co., 5th April, 1732; 6th May, 1732.

To son **Edward**, ex., certain personalty for use of daus. **Mary Ann** and **Jane** when of age.
" sons **Isaac, Thomas** and **William**, personalty; sons **Isaac** and **William** of age at 18 yrs.
" child., viz. **Edward, Thomas, Henry, William, Isaac, Mary Ann** and **Jane**, residue of estate equally.
Test: John Jones, Thomas Burroughs. 20, 374.

Lemmon, Hickford (nunc.), 22nd May, 1732;
To John Hawkins, Sr., entire estate.
Test: Rev. John Fraser, Joseph Noble. 20, 375.

Read, Richard, mariner, Deptford, County of Kent,
14th May, 1711;
23rd May, 1732.
To wife Mary, extx., entire estate.
Test (in England): Frederick Collyer, Jo. Scobie, R. Sanders, John Kenny, Jerome Collins.
Test (in Maryland, 18th June, 1723): John Chesley, William Harris, William Barnes. 20, 376.

Powell, Daniel, planter, Talbot Co.,
26th day, 8th mo. (Oct.), 1710;
29th April, 1732.
To Henry Troth, pt. of "Boston Clift."
" son John and hrs., upper pt. of afsd. tract, on condition that sd. son, when of age, make over to his bro. Joseph the pt. of "Cold Rain" left sd. son John by his grandfather John Pitt; shd. son John refuse to do so, son Joseph to have all that pt. of sd. "Boston Clift" bequeathed son John, the division of sd. land to be made by bro. Howell and cousin William Harrison.
" son Howell and hrs., lower pt. of "Boston Clift" after decease of wife ———.
" wife Susannah, ⅓ personal estate, remaining ⅔ to be divided among 9 child. ———; boys to receive portions at 21, girls at day of marriage; shd. any child die during minority, their portion to be divided among survivors.
Exs.: Wife Susannah and son John, the monthly meeting in Talbot empowered to settle any differences that may arise bet. exs. and children.
Test: Howell Powell, William Harrison, William Edmondson, George Robins, John Bush. 20, 377.

Edmondson, James, Talbot Co.,   11th Feb., 1728-9;
24th May, 1732.
To bro. John, ex., his son John at age of 18, his dau. Elizabeth, and Sarah and Elizabeth Powell, daus. of sister ———, personalty.
" bro. William, personalty, pt. to be used to pay Samuel Dickenson.
Test: Dennis Hopkins, William Bush, Jr., Edward Higginson.
Note: Memo. of debts due testator annexed. 20, 380.

222   MARYLAND CALENDAR OF WILLS

Esgate, Caleb, planter, Talbot Co.,   3rd May, 1732;
26th May, 1732.

To son **Caleb,** ex., and hrs., dwell. plan. ———, being pt. of "Hopkins Point"; sd. son not to sell to Mathew Kirby or any others except some of the Hopkins, or Thomas Spry or John Weamoth.
" **James** and **Benjamin Hopkins** and their hrs., all rights, interest, etc., in sd. "Hopkins Point" except as above mentioned.
" child. of sons **Caleb** and **Stephen,** residue of estate.
Test: Samuel Small, Thomas Dukes, John Lenan.   20, 382.

Slater (Slator), John, planter, Kings Creek, Talbot Co.,
30th Sept., 1725;
19th May, 1732.

To Benjamin Silvester, Aaron Parrott and Henry Buckingham, personalty.
" wife **Susannah,** extx., residue of personalty.
Test: Robert Walker, Jonathan Tyler, Rebekah Buckingham.   20, 384.

Hill, John, planter, Cecil Co.,   17th Jan., 1731-2;
1st March, 1731.

To bro.-in-law **Augustine Terry,** personalty.
" wife **Mary,** extx., entire estate during life; at her decease to be divided among child. by sd. wife or to the survivors; bro.-in-law **Hugh Terry** to act as ex. in event of wife's death.
Test: Alexander McCarter, Ann Wharton, Thomas Noxon.
20, 385.

Oates, John, Cecil Co.,   18th March, 1732;
18th May, 1732.

John Pennington and James Wroth appointed exs. to look after estate until such time as hrs. shall come to receive it out of their possession.
Test: John Roberts, Sr., Judith Roberts, John Roberts, Jr.
20, 386.

Foster, Richard, Cecil Co.,   2nd April, 1732;
13th June, 1732.

To son **James** and hrs., dwell. plan. ——— and land belonging thereto; if the survey of Mr. Henry Ward shd. take any land from son **James,** then dwell. plan. afsd. with remaining land is given to son **William** and hrs.

To sons **Richard** and **James** and their hrs., 200 A. "Brittan," w. side of Elk R., son **Richard** to have first choice. Shd. sd. Henry Ward not take plantation, so that son **James** possesses it as first intended, entire 200 A. "Brittan" to son **Richard**; sd. son to pay to son **John**, he having no land, 2,000 lbs. tob. Sons **Isaac**, **Thomas** and **Jeremiah** to be for themselves at age of 18.

" 8 child. ———, personal estate.

Test: John Penington, Andrew Price, John Caldcleugh (Caldclugh). 20, 387.

Young, Joseph, planter, Cecil Co., 10th April, 1727; 13th June, 1732.

To sons **Samuel** and **William** and their hrs., dwell. plan. ——— after death or marriage of extx.

" sons **Jacob** and **John** and their hrs., "Poplar Neck."
" son **Joseph** and hrs., "Hanley's" and personalty.
" each dau. ——— living at the dividing of personal estate, £5 over and above their equal shares.
" wife **Katherine**, extx., residue of estate during life or widowhood; after her decease or marriage to remain to use of all child. then living. Sons not to sell or any wise dispose of afsd. lands except to each other or their children.

Test: James Campbell, Charles Thomas, Patrick Conner, Thomas Hopkins. 20, 390.

Terry, Thomas, planter, Cecil Co., 9th April, 1730; 9th Nov., 1731.

To dau. **Ann**, Thomas Savin, son **Augustine**, dau. **Mary Hill**, sons **Thomas** and **Hugh** and grandson **Augustine**, personalty; sd. legacies to be pd. after decease of wife **Rosamond**.
" 3 sons **Thomas**, **Hugh** and **Augustine**, 1s. each.
" 3 daus. **Mary**, **Ann** and **Elizabeth**, 1s. each.
" wife **Rosamond**, extx., dwell. plan. "The Bank" during life, and residue of personal estate absolutely.

Test: John Ryland, John Keys. 20, 391.

Green, Thomas, yeoman, Cecil Co., 4th May, 1730; 11th Nov., 1731.

To wife **Rachel**, extx., house and land in Huntly, Gloucestershire, England, absolutely; also dwell. plan. 250 A. "Coxes Prevention," on Susquehanna R., and 150 A. of "Coxes Fancy" during life; sd. tracts being bou. of Wm. Cox, mcht., of Cecil Co.

To daus. **Catherine** and **Elizabeth** and their hrs., 125 A. each, of "Coxes Prevention" after decease of wife afsd.
" dau. **Rachel**, 5s.
" grandson **John Mannery** and hrs., 100 A. given in her lifetime to dau. **Hannah**, wife of **John Mannery, Sr.**, dec'd, by deed of gift dated 28th May, 1725, and 25 A. adj. to that of his mother **Hannah Mannery**, dec'd.
" grandson **Thomas Mannery** and hrs. after decease of wife **Rachel**, 125 A. adj. to land of his bro. **John**, being ½ of "Coxes Fancy" afsd.
" son-in-law **John Mannery**, 5s.
Test: Francis Bradley, John Maynard, Francis Bradley, Jr., James Bradley. 20, 393.

Archer, Jacob, yeoman, Cecil Co., 10th Oct., 1731; 20th March, 1731.

To dau. **Mary**, at day of marriage, and bros. **John** and **Thomas Yorkson**, ex., personalty.
Test: Edward Rumsey, John Ryland, Jr., Rebecca Ryland.
20, 396.

Howell (Howall), William, Cecil Co., 30th April, 1730; 13th June, 1732.

To wife **Ann**, extx., and hrs., entire estate.
Test: John Smith, Andrew Brown. 20, 397.

Dawson, Edward, Sr., planter, Prince George's Co., 15th Dec., 1729; 28th June, 1732.

To son **Edward** and hrs., 214 A. "Mill-land," where he now lives, except 50 A. thereof which is bequeathed to grandson **John**, son of **John Cash**, dec'd, and hrs., to be laid out of afsd. tract by son **Edward**, and after decease of wife sd. son **Edward** to enjoy all land left to her; and personalty.
" granddau. **Mary**, wife of **William Harr**, and hrs.; grandson **Edward**, son of **John Perry**; **Mary**, wife of **Alexander Traqueer**, and grandson **John Cash** afsd., personalty.
" wife **Mary**, extx., dwell. plan. —— during life or widowhood; shd. she marry, ⅓ thereof; residue of personal estate during life and remainder to son **Edward** afsd. and hrs.
Test: Richard Daintry, Nathan Ward, Richard Duckett.
20, 398.

Winsor, John, Somerset Co., 20th March, 1730-31; 20th March, 1731.

To son **John,** 250 A. where he now lives, at hd. of Broad Creek, being pt. of "Coxes Preformance," during life and afterwards to his 2 sons **John** and **James.**
" **John,** son of son **James,** and hrs., 250 A. out of afsd. tract.
" son **Lazarus** and hrs., 150 A. "Wollidge," on Devil's Island.
" **John,** son of son **Lazarus,** and hrs., 150 A. out of "Coxes Preformance"; residue of estate to be divided equally bet. all children.
Overseers: John Laws, Thomas Laws.
Exs.: Sons **John** and **Lazarus.**
Test: Thomas Lawes, Thomas Roe (Row), Sarah Row.
20, 400.

Long, Jeoffry, Somerset Co., 1st July, 1731; 17th June, 1732.

To son **Samuel,** ex., and hrs., dwell. plan. ———; also 68 A. bou. of David Wilson; and personalty, provided he gives son **David** 2 and son **Sewell** 1 and dau. **Mary** 1½ yrs. schooling, and also pay to son **David** at age of 21, and to dau. **Mary** at age of 18, or day of marriage, £5 each.
" son **Jeoffry,** all land at Morrumscoe and personalty, he to pay to son **David** at age of 21 and to dau. **Mary** at age of 18 each £5.
" sons **Sewell** and **David** and daus. **Jane** and **Mary,** personalty; shd. any of child. die during minority, their portion of estate to be divided among survivors. Son **Sewell** to be for himself, son **David** and dau. **Mary** to live with son **Samuel** until of age.
" 6 child., viz. **Samuel, Jeoffry, Sewell, David, Jane** and **Mary,** residue of personal estate.
Test: Samuel Long, Edward Stockdell (Stogdell), John Benson. 20, 402.

Gray, John, Sr., Somerset Co., 6th Jan., 1730-31; 18th June, 1732.

To son **John** and hrs., "Come by Chance"; and personalty.
" son **William,** ex., and hrs., dwell. plan. "Killmenum" and "Derrey."
" dau. **Margarett** and hrs., "Patrick's Folly."
" wife ———, certain fields during life.
" son **William** and 3 daus. **Sarah, Margaret** and **Rebecca,** residue of personalty.
Test: William Steward, Kathrine Steward. 20, 404.

Hill, Robert, planter, Somerset Co.,
6th March, 1731-32;
21st June, 1732.

To son **Johnson**, personalty, des. as brought from Newport.
" youngest son **William Stevens Hill** and son-in-law **Samuel Taylor**, personalty at age of 18.
" dau. **Neomy**, personalty.
" wife **Comfort**, extx., residue of personalty.

Test: William Fassitt (Fossett), Jr., Walter Tayler, William Kennett.   20, 406.

Truett, Eleanor, relict of George Truett, Somerset Co.,
20th April, 1732;
21st June, 1732.

To sons **George** and **Samuel**, dau. **Susanna Nicholson**, granddau. **Sarah Nicholson** (dau. of Susanna afsd.), dau. **Sarah Mumford** and dau. **Tabitha Parker**, personalty.

Exs.: Sons **George** and **Samuel**.
Test: Samuel Hopkins, Sr., Henry Jarman, James Martin.   20, 408.

Collins (Colins), Charles, Somerset Co.,
8th April, 1732;
22nd June, 1732.

To son **Thomas**, dwell. plan. ——— and personalty; to be in care of John Tingle, ex., until 18 yrs. of age.
" dau. **Esther**, personalty that was her mother's; to be in care of Mary Lockwood or Margaret Hudson.
" son **Elijah**, personalty; to be in care of Richard Beherd.
" youngest son ———, bro. **Thomas** and to his sons ———, personalty.
" wife ——— and 3 eldest child., residue of personalty.

Test: Paul Alexander, Daniel Conner.   20, 410.

Ellis, Merick (Merrick), Somerset Co., 2nd Dec., 1728;
23rd June, 1732.

To wife **Alice**, entire estate.
Test: Levin Gale, John Stewart, Thomas Lawes, William Stoughton, David Murray.   20, 411.

MARYLAND CALENDAR OF WILLS 227

Countess (Countiss), James, planter, Queen Anne's Co., 29th Dec., 1731; 4th May, 1732.

To son **Peter,** dwell. plan. ———, being pt. of "Recsom Planes."
" **Rebekah Vanderford,** 20s.
" sons **James** and **William,** 300 A. "Dublin," lying in sd. co. bet. hd. of Choptank R. and "Old Town"; and personalty.
" daus. **Catharine, Rachel, Hannah** and **Sarah,** residue of estate equally.
" wife ———, extx., dwell. plan. ——— during life.
Test: James McCleane (Mackcleane), John Williams, William Boyd. 20, 412.

Wright, John, Queen Anne's Co., 10th Jan., 1731; 29th March, 1732.

To son **John** and hrs., 100 A. "Narbrough Addition."
" dau. **Mary** and hrs., 50 A. "Littleworth," lying at hd. of Colonel's Quarter Branch; and personalty.
" son **John** and dau. **Mary,** residue of personal estate after wife's thirds are deducted. Tuition and bringing up of sd. child. to be in care of exs., viz. bro. **Thomas Hynson Wright** and **John Tillotson,** who are to see that they are bro. up in Faith of the Church of England; shd. they think needful, to take them from their mother ———.
Test: Nathaniel Cleaves, Solomon Wright, Robert Reynolds. 20, 414.

Flinn, Laughlin, innholder, Kent Co., 10th April, 1729; 3rd March, 1731.

To wife **Margaret,** extx., and hrs., entire estate, both real and personal, with power to sell plantation "Ruerdon," Langford's Bay, for benefit of estate.
" **John Griffith,** who has served his time, 700 lbs. tobacco.
Test: John Evans, John Hollinsworth, Abraham Milton. 20, 415.

Wickes, Samuel, Sr., Kent Co., 5th Sept., 1729; 14th April, 1732.

To wife **Francis,** certain personalty over and above her third pt. of personal estate.
" son **Samuel** and hrs., dwell. plan. 370 A. "Wicklief," on Eastern Neck Island; sd. son dying without issue, sd. lands to next of blood.

To son Benjamin and hrs., 300 A. "Bath"; sd. son dying without issue, to pass to next male hr.
" son Simon and hrs., 300 A. "Buckingham," on e. side Morgan's Ck.; sd. son dying without issue, to pass to next male hr.
" son Joseph and hrs., 200 A. "Wickes Marsh," on Eastern Neck Island; sd. son dying without issue, to pass to next male hr.
" son Lambeth and hrs., 200 A. "Chester Point"; sd. son dying without issue, to pass to next male hr.
" 8 child., 5 sons and 3 daus., viz. Samuel, Benjamin, Simon, Lambeth, Joseph, Martha, Rebecca and Ann, personal estate equally; sons to be of age at 18, daus. at 16 or day of marriage.
Exs.: Wife Francis and eldest son Samuel.
Test: Samuel Tovey, James Ringgold, William Pearce.
20, 417.

Kennard, Philip, mcht., Kent Co., 28th Nov., 1731; 17th Aug., 1732.

To John, eldest son of Philip Kennard, Jr., and hrs., dwell. plan. ———; sd. John dying without issue, to pass to next son of sd. Philip.
" Philip, son of Philip Kennard afsd., and hrs., lands adj. to plantation where sd. Philip Kennard now lives.
" Joseph, son of Philip Kennard afsd., "Lynn," on n. side Steelpone Ck. Shd. Philip Kennard afsd. die without male hrs., lands bequeathed his sons to descend to daus. of sd. Philip Kennard and their hrs.; shd. all child. of sd. Philip Kennard die during his lifetime, leaving no issue, the real and personal estate herein devised shall be vested in Philip Kennard, the father of the afsd. children.
" Ruth Barney, personalty.
" Philip Kennard afsd., ex., share of personal estate during his life; at his decease to be divided among his children.
" child. of Philip Kennard afsd., residue of personal estate.
Test: Aaron Alford, Robert Meekes, Vyvian Beck. 20, 421.

Wilson, James, mcht., Kent Co., 23rd July, 1732; 18th Aug., 1732.

To wife Catherine, dwell. plan. ——— and half the orchard during widowhood; shd. she marry, her thirds.
" grandson James and hrs., 30 A. adj. land formerly given to son John.

To son **George** and hrs., dwell. plan. ———, with remaining pt. of "Verina," except the graveyard, 30 foot sq., which shall be kept in repair by any of hrs. who possess the plantation; remainder of orchard during wife's widowhood and residue of "Broad Oak."
" grandson **John**, son of son **John**, and hrs., 120 A. of "Margrett's Delight" when of age.
" grandson **Wilson Woodland** and hrs., residue of last-named tract, including pt. where Christopher Ry lives.
" granddau. ———, dau. of son **John**, at day of marriage, and grandsons **James** and **John**, when of age, £10 each.
" son-in-law **Thomas Jones**, £5.
" son **George** and dau. **Mary Woodland**, residue of personal estate after above legacies and wife's dowry are paid.
Exs.: Wife **Catherine**, son **George** and son-in-law **William Woodland**.
Test: Thomas Gould, Isaac Freeman, Ann Trulock.
20, 423.

Rasin, Thomas, Kent Co.,   18th day, 10th mo., 1731;
3rd March, 1731.

To wife **Mary**, extx., dwell. plan. ——— during widowhood, being the first purchase from Thomas Thackstone, land where sd. Thackstone now lives, after his decease and his wife's; certain personalty and ⅓ personal estate absolutely. Shd. wife **Mary** marry before eldest son **George** arrives at age of 21, then sd. son shall have ½ the afsd. tract for his own use.
" son **George** and hrs., afsd. tracts after his mother's decease.
" son **William** and hrs., 300 A. "Forrester's Delight," bou. of Thomas Thackstone, with pt. of "Hillen's Adventure."
" son **Abraham**, 150 A. of "Fair Promise," bou. of George Warner; land bou. of Andrew Riddle, with 100 A. adj. thereto, being pt. of "Friendship."
" 4 sons **George, William, Abraham** and **Joseph**, residue of personal estate when they arrive at age of 21. Shd. any child die during minority, survivors to divide portion of dec'd; shd. wife die during minority of child., they are to be under care of the Friends of Chester and Cecil Meetings. Sister **Elizabeth Kirby** not to be pressed by extx. for money due testator.
Test: George Dunkan, Bastion Tyschow, Thomas Bowers.
20, 426.

Theckstone, Thomas, planter, Kent Co.,
28th April, 1730;
10th March, 1731.

To Ann Kenley, personalty.
" wife Mary, extx., and hrs., "Webb," bou. by father ——— of Edward Webb, to be sold by her for benefit of estate, Richard Bennett, Esq., to have offer of the same; and residue of estate, real and personal.

Test: Sarah England, Eliza. Greenwood, Joseph Warner.
20, 429.

Elmes, William, Kent Co.,
31st Jan., 1731-2;
28th April, 1732.

To godson James Harris and William Graves, 20s. each for a ring.
" servt. woman Mary Sheppard, £5 at expiration of her time; her son Ezecale to have 1 year's schooling.
" Loveday Turner, personalty.
" wife Sarah, extx., and hrs., residue of estate.

Test: Robert Kay (Key), James Kendrick, Hannah Jones, William Vivian.
20, 430.

Johnson, John, attorney-at-law, Kent Co.,
21st Nov., 1731;
24th Dec., 1731.

To son Richard and hrs., 400 A. "Johnson's Forrest," 200 A. "Party Chance."
" dau. Mary and hrs., 200 A. "Gleave's Adventure."
" son and dau. afsd. "Outrange" equally.
" son John, personalty.
" wife Susannah and child. ———, residue of estate equally.

Exs.: Wife Susannah and son John, who are to live together on dwell. plan. "Thornton and Bateman's farm"; shd. sd. son die without issue, his share of sd. farm to pass to son Richard.

Test: Gilbert Falconer, John Johnson, Jr., Mary Perraro, Rachel Browne, Rebekah Sehee.

24th Dec., 1731. **Susannah Johnson** claims her thirds.
20, 432.

Johnson, John, Kent Co., 19th Oct., 1730.

To eldest son **John** and hrs., dwell. plan. ———, mortgage on tract in Queen Anne's Co.
" son **Richard** and hrs., "The Forrest," bou. of Mr. Miller, and "Ambrosia," adj.
" dau. (intended to be called **Mary**), "Outrange" and "Chance," hd. of Chester R.
" wife **Susannah** and hrs., "The Adventure," at hd. of Chester R.; personal estate divided with 3 child. after a legacy to sister **Phillips** in England is paid.
Above will recorded at request of John Johnson, eldest son of testator. 20, 435.

Brooke, Clement, Jr., gentleman, Prince George's Co., des. as of London, mariner, bound on voyage for City of London. 31st Aug., 1731; 28th Nov., 1732.

To wife **Mary**, extx., also bound for voyage to London, and dau. **Rachel** and their hrs., entire real and personal estate divided equally, division to be made by father **Clement Brooke**; shd. wife die before her return to Maryland, entire estate to dau. afsd. and her hrs.
Test: Mary Brooke, Jr., Ann Brooke, Walter Brooke, John Orchard. 20, 436.

White, James, Sr., St. Mary's Co., 27th May, 1732; 24th June, 1732.

To wife **Sarah**, entire personal estate during life; at her decease to be divided among children ———.
" 2 sons **James** and **William**, real estate, equally, after decease of wife.
Test: Patrick Forest, Nicholas Richardson. 20, 438.

Hill, Richard, Dorchester Co., 29th March, 1732; 10th July, 1732.

To sister **Amy** and cousin **John Madkins**, "Hill's Platt" equally, **John Madkins** to have pt. next John Granger's.
" sister **Amy** afsd., entire personal estate.
Test: Thomas Bright (Brite), Thomas Mace, Sarah Hill.
20, 439.

Chattell, William, planter, Dorchester Co.,
19th May, 1732;
22nd July, 1732.

To William Harper and hrs., dwell. plan. ———.
" William Harper and James Vinson, exs., and their hrs., residue of estate equally.
Test: William Fountain, Joseph Blackwell, Margaret Harper. 20, 440.

Christopher (Cristerfer), John, Dorchester Co.,
2nd July, 1732;
28th Aug., 1732.

To sons Thomas, Samuel and William, personalty.
" wife Sarah, extx., residue of personalty.
Test: Charles Powell, Dennis Kelly, Cathrine Kelly. 20, 442.

Noble, William, Baltimore Co., 14th March, 1731-2;
8th April, 1732.

To Samuel Durham, personalty.
" wife Ann, extx., and hrs., pt. of "Turkey Range" and of "Noble Desire"; entire personal estate.
Test: Daniel Scott, William Rose, Christopher Durbin Shaw.
20, 443.

Stokes, John, Baltimore Co., 2nd March, 1727;
5th Sept., 1732.

To son George and hrs., pt. of "Montserada," bou. of Edward Parrish, who had bou. it of Henry Ward, Cecil Co.; 200 A. "Ebenezar's Lott," Deare Ck.; also "Harman's Towne," or commonly called "The Ferry," excepting 100 A. bou. of Wm. Simpson; and personalty.
" son John and hrs., 100 A. afsd.; 400 A. "Bourne," tract bou. of Joseph Johnson; 220 A. "Johnson's Delay," 100 A. "Simpson's Hazard"; and personalty.
" son Humphry and hrs., land in Maryland or elsewhere not otherwise bequeathed; also house and lot at Joppa, on Gunpowder R.; and personalty.
" dau. Frances, now wife of Aquilla Paca, 10s., she having received a portion at marriage.
" 3 sons afsd., personal estate after their mother's portion is deducted.
" kinsman Philip Key, of Charles Co., and Thomas White, overseers, £5 each.
Exs.: Wife ——— and 3 sons afsd.
Test: Erick Erickson, John Erickson, Zacharias Spencer, Casparum Erickson. 20, 444.

Tolley, Thomas, gentleman, Baltimore Co.,
12th Sept., 1732;
9th Oct., 1732.

To wife Mary, extx., use of lot and house in town of Joppa during life; at her decease rents and profits therefrom to be divided among 3 sons until Michael, son of Michael and Elizabeth Miller, arrives at age of 21, from thence to him and his hrs. forever.

" son **Walter** and hrs., 1 moiety of "Cullins's Lott"; "Tracey's Level" and pt. of "Long Point."
" son **James** and hrs., other pt. of "Cullin's Lott"; pt. of dwell. plan. ———, n. of Spring Branch and adj. to line of the county school, including "Fall Hill."
" son **Thomas** and hrs., that pt. of "Richardson's Outlet" s. of afsd. branch.
" the parson of St. John's Parish in county afsd., Garett Garettson, and John Scott, personalty; residue of personal estate to 3 sons afsd.

Test: Edward Day, Elizabeth Goodwin (Goodin), Joseph Perry.

Note: Widow claims her thirds.   20, 447.

Tibbs, William, clk., Baltimore Co.,   25th Sept., 1732;
13th Oct., 1732.

To sister Ann, extx., and hrs., dwell. plan. ——— and personal estate.

Test: Mary Mead, John Oakley, John Scott.   20, 449.

Waring, Marsham, gent., Prince George's Co.,
12th March, 1730;
20th Oct., 1732.

To wife Eleanor, certain personalty and use of dwell. plan. ——— for one year, at expiration of that time to live at "Mount Pleasant" and to have use of ½ the land during widowhood, with the 48 A. bou. of William Smith, bequest not to be taken for her right of dower; and ⅓ pt. of household stuff.

" daus. Sarah and Ann, certain personalty, and each ⅓ of personal estate after certain legacies are deducted; portion of dau. Ann to be in care of Clement Hill until she arrives at age of 16.

" son **Basil** and hrs., 300 A. of "Hearts Delight," on w. branch of Patuxent, bou. of Thomas Brooke; also 38 A. "Brooke Land," adj. to afsd. tract; 300 A. "Indian Field," nr. Zachia Swamp, Charles Co.; 96 A. "Bryan Dayley," adj. to same; certain personalty and ⅓ of personal estate.

To son **Richard Marsham**, ex., and hrs., 48 A. bou. of William Smith, after decease of his mother; and certain personalty.
" Peter Davis, £5.
" slave Sarah at Mt. Pleasant, £10 and her freedom.
Overseers: Clement Hill, Charles Sewell.
Test: Ann Watton, James Haddock, Clement Hill, Jr., James Haddock Waring. 20, 450.

Fraser, Alexander, chyrurgeon and apothecary,
Annapolis, 25th June, 1729; 23rd Oct., 1732.

To son **Stephen Samuel Alexander** and hrs., all real estate in that pt. of Scotland called "Frewehie," being in the parish of Faulkland, sheriffdome of Fyfe; and personalty.
" dau. **Anne** and hrs., dwelling house and grounds lying in "Newtown," in the city of Annapolis, furnishings of sd. house and wearing apparel formerly belonging to her late mother **Elizabeth Fraser**.
" son and dau. afsd., all debts due testator; shd. present wife by a claim of any pt. of estate occasion any difficulty bet. sd. child., sd. wife may have no more than is required by law.
Exs.: John Beale and William Stoughton in Somerset Co.
Test: Sarah Frisby, Ann Turner, Phillis Wilgus, John Pasmore. 20, 455.

Holland, William, A. A. Co., 17th Aug., 1724; 25th Oct., 1732.

To son **Francis** and hrs., lands now in poss. of testator, formerly the right and inheritance of his grandfather and uncle **Francis Holland**, dec'd, except what is already disposed of by deed of gift to grandson **Francis**, son of sd. Francis; also 135 A. "Herring Creek" and "Conants Chance," bou. of Wm. Russell and John Dikes; and 1,100 A. nr. Bush R., Baltimore Co., bou. of Bennett Creed and William Wilson; and personalty; exs. instructed to pay £130 to Richard Bennett and £140 to Daniel Dulany, testator being security for payment on acct. of sd. son.
" sons **Francis**, **William** and **Thomas** and hrs., 200 A. "Minor's Adventure."
" son **William** and hrs., 960 A. "Dowsdale" and "Abington's Mannour," bou. of hrs. of John Abington, dec'd; 335 A. "Biggs Purchase," bou. of hrs. of Seth Biggs, dec'd;

MARYLAND CALENDAR OF WILLS 235

950 A. "Batchelours Good Luck," on Deer Ck., Baltimore Co., and 50 A. adj., bou. of Cadwallader Jones, of sd. co.; and personalty.
To son **Thomas** and hrs., "St. James Enlarged," Calvert Co., 37½ A., pt. of "Alexander's Hope," adj. thereto; 425 A., pt. of "His Lordshipp's Favour," bou. of John and Aron Cobreath; 25 A. bou. of Hercules Humes, 50 A. bou. of John Dodson and 110 A., "The Neglect," adj. thereto.
" kinsman **Thomas Haskins** and hrs., 300 A. "Hunt's Chance," bou. of William Russell.
" wife **Elizabeth**, personalty possessed by her at time of marriage, use of dwell. plan. ——— and "Bennetts Island" and "Holland's Addition" during minority of grandson **Francis**; shd. wife die, son **Thomas** to have poss. thereof during minority of sd. grandson.
" grandsons **Utie** and **Francis** and granddau. **Mary**, personalty; last named to receive portion at age of 16 or day of marriage, the boys at age of 21, or to the survivor of them. Whatever personalty has been made over for security of a debt due from son **Francis** to be equally divided among afsd. 3 grandchild. **Utie, Francis** and **Mary.**
" grandson **William Thomas** at age of 21, nephew **Thomas Haskins** and sister **Mary Haskins** and to each of her child. living, personalty.
" sons **William** and **Thomas**, residue of estate, reserving to wife her third pt. thereof.
Exs.: Wife **Elizabeth** and sons **William** and **Thomas.**
Overseers: Coll. John Smith, Doctor William Lock.
Test: Samuel Harrison, William Phillips, George Taylor, Mary Loockerman (formerly Mary Haskins). 20, 458.

Note: F. 462, 3rd Nov., 1732. Additional probates to will of **James Makey** (**Macky**) taken at request of Thomas Annis, who intermarried with **Elizabeth**, relict and extx. of **James Makey**, vide will Lib. 14, f. 335, Abstract Md. Cal. of Wills, v. 4, p. 97.

Fottrell, Ann, Talbot Co., 6th Oct., 1731;
17th April, 1732.

To husband **Edward Fottrell**, ex., and hrs. (in consideration of great expense he has incurred in lawsuits for benefit of the orphans of late husband), entire estate; sd. husband recommended to pay to **Ann Lloyd**, youngest dau. of testatrix, £30 at age of 18, or day of marriage, if sd. marriage be with consent of her bro. **Robert Lloyd**

(Loyd). Testatrix desires to be buried by body of **James Lloyd**, her late dec'd husband, and instructs that none be asked to interment but her sister, her child. and the Rector of the Parish, and states that she revokes a will deposited in hands of dau. **Henrietta Maria Chamberlain.**
Test: Mrs. Margaret Lloyd, Margaret Cohune (at date of probate des. as Margaret Barrow), Eliza. Lewen.

20, 463.

Sealy (Seelye), Joseph, farmer, Bohemia Mannor, Cecil Co., 25th March, 1730; 4th Oct., 1732.

To wife **Mary**, extx., dwell. plan. "Bohemia Mannor" during life; at her decease to grandson **Ephram**, son of son **Ephram**; and ½ personal estate.
" sons **Joseph** and **Henry** and dau. **Martha**, other ½ of personal estate.
Test: John Chick, Samuel Craford, Howell James. 20, 465.

Aikins, James, Talbot Co., 3rd Nov., 1732; 8th Nov., 1732.

To son **James** and dau. **Mariam** and their hrs., entire estate.
Ex. in Maryland, Capt. Thos. Gasaway; ex. in London, William Black.
Test: Nicholas Lowe, William Sharp, Sarah Kinner.

20, 467.

Hedges, Joseph, Manaquicy, Prince George's Co., 6th Sept., 1732; 29th Nov., 1732.

To son **Solomon** and hrs., 258 A. on Manaquicy Ck.
" 2 sons **Charles** and **Joshua** and their hrs., each 200 A. at Opeckan.
" sons **Jonas** and **Joseph** and their hrs., 400 A. to be bou. by exs. at Opecken divided equally.
" son **Samuel** and hrs., 100 A. to be bou. by exs. at "Manaquicy."
" daus. **Ruth**, **Cathren** and **Dorcas** and sons **Joseph** and **Samuel**, personalty.
" wife ―― and child., residue of estate.
Exs.: Sons **Solomon** and **Charles**.
Test: Chidly Mathews, Thomas Hillard, John Hillard.

20, 468.

Facer, Thomas, shoemaker, A. A. Co., 15th Nov., 1731;
16th Dec., 1731.

To Achsa, wife of Amos Woodward, and hrs., entire estate.
Ex.: William Cumming.
Test: Amos Bickardike, William Dowdle, John Lomas.

20, 470.

Rutland, Thomas, South River, A. A. Co.,
18th Nov., 1731;
24th Dec., 1731.

To son **Thomas,** ex., and hrs., 67 A. "Rutland's Discovery," n. side South R.; 400 A. of "Rutland's Purchase Inlarged" (for des. see will), dwell. plan. —— and tract bou. of Hezekiah Linthicum. Sd. son to pay £25 to dau. Elizabeth Stuard; shd. he refuse to do so, afsd. 2 tracts to be equally divided bet. sd. son and 2 daus. Ann Wayman and Elizabeth Stuard; and personalty.
" dau. **Elizabeth Stuard** and hrs., 200 A. of "Rutland's Purchase Inlarged"; and personalty.
" grandson **Thomas Sappington** and hrs., 100 A. of last-named tract; and personalty, at age of 21.
" dau. **Ann Wayman** and hrs., 200 A. of last-named tract; and personalty.
" granddau. **Jeane Wayman,** personalty.
" son **Thomas,** ½ residue of personal estate, other ½ to 2 daus. afsd.
Overseer: Richard Snowden.
Test: Robert Sanders, James Mouat, William Sanders.

20, 471.

Galloway, Richard, "Cumberstone," A. A. Co.,
6th day of 12th mo., 1730-31;
16th Feb., 1731.

To wife **Mary,** extx., and hrs., ⅓ of personal estate absolutely; dwell. plan. ——, being pt. of "Cumberstone," bou. of bro. **John;** another tract called "Cumberton," and all tracts bou. of Elizabeth Waters, during widowhood.
" dau. **Susannah,** residue of personal estate at age of 16 or day of marriage; shd. sd. dau. die during minority, her portion of personal estate to be divided into 6 equal pts. and pass as follows: ⅙ to bro. **John,** ⅙ to bro. **Peter,** ⅙ to bro. **Joseph,** ⅙ to child. of late sister **Ann Johns,** ⅙ to child. of sister **Mary Chew** and ⅙ to child. of sister **Sarah Cowman;** entire real estate. Shd. sd. dau. die during minority and without issue, real estate to pass as

follows: to bro. **John** and hrs., the pt. of "Cumberstone" bou. of him, also ⅕ pt. of lands bou. of Elizabeth **Waters**; to bro. **Peter** and hrs., pt. of "White Hall," nr. South R.; to bro. **Joseph** and hrs., ⅘ of land bou. of Elizabeth **Waters**.

Overseers: 3 bros. afsd.

Test: Jonathan Munn, Thomas Hobbs, Elizabeth **Watson**.

Codicil: 8th day, 12 mo., 1730. Shd. dau. afsd. die during minority, £10 from her pt. of personal estate to sister Hannah **Ford**.

Test: Elizabeth Watson.

16th Feb., 1731. Mary **Galloway** claims her thirds. Test: Richard Galloway, Jr., Joseph Cowman.

18 March, 1731. Mary **Galloway** accepts above will. Test: Charles Hammond, Margaret Lomas. 20, 474.

Smith, Ralph, taylor, Annapolis, 30th Dec., 1731; 4th March, 1731.

To wife **Frances**, extx., and hrs., dwelling house and lot and personal estate. Godson John Pitts (9 yrs.), apprenticed to testator until 21 yrs. of age, to be sent to Philadelphia and apprenticed to Daniel Jones, taylor of sd. city; care of unborn child to wife afsd.

Test: Michael Macnemara, John Samuel Minskie, Humphry Meredith. 20, 479.

Lock, William, physician, A. A. Co., 29th Aug., 1729; 8th June, 1732.

To son **William** and hrs., dwell. plan. ———, being pt. of "Dinah's Beverdams," bou. of Robert Brown and wife, other pt. of sd. tract bou. of Thomas Foord and Robert Frankline; "Halloway's Increase," 200 A. of "Padget"; shd. sd. son die during minority or without issue, afsd. lands to be equally divided bet. cousins David **Weems** and his bro. James **Weems**.

" dau. **Sarah** and hrs., youngest dau. of wife ———, residue of "Paget," 85 A. bou. of John Gioles; sd. dau. dying without issue, to pass to son **William** and hrs.; he failing issue, to cousins afsd. and hrs.

" cousin David **Weems**, the pt. of "Brewsly Hall" where he now lives, bou. of his wife and of Richard Lane; "Gott's Plantation," bou. of James McIntosh; and personalty.

" cousin James **Weems** and hrs., plantation in Virginia bou. of Edward Williams, right of land escheated of Jonas Jordan; and personalty.

To cousin **Williamina Moore**, £50.
" St. James Parish, £10 for plate.
" child. of wife by Samuel Lane, and to cousins and their child., personalty; ⅔ of residue of personal estate after wife's thirds are deducted to son **William** afsd. and ⅓ to dau. **Sarah** afsd.

Exs.: Wife ——— and cousin **David Weems**; child. to be brought up in faith of the Church of England.

Test: Robert Franklin, William Fisher, James Newson.
20, 480.

Greeme, James, labourer (nunc.), Annapolis,
27th Aug., 1732;
23rd Oct., 1732.

To Frances Shorter, of sd. city, entire estate.
Test: Dr. George Steuart, Charles Brown, mcht. 20, 483.

Barclay (Barkley), John, mcht., Annapolis, late of Edenburgh, North Britain. 13th Oct., 1732;
28th Nov., 1732.

Testator having made a will and appointed his wife **Grace Hay** extx. thereof directs that his countrymen Robert Gordon and William Tweedie, of Annapolis, gent., exs., shall collect and receive all debts, money, etc., and transmit same to wife afsd. so sd. money may be applied as directed in sd. will.

Test: William Cumming, Dr. George Steuart, Burgis Copner.
20, 484.

Lusby, John, A. A. Co., 28th July, 1730;
7th Dec., 1732.

To wife **Ellenor,** extx., "Little Harness" during widowhood, to pass at her decease or marriage to son **Jacob** and hrs.
" sons **Jacob, John, Aaron, Thomas** and **Samuel** and daus. **Rachell, Mary** and **Ellenor,** personalty.
" child. afsd., residue of estate at death or marriage of wife afsd.

Test: William Ruley, Elizabeth Ruley (dec'd at date of probate), Moses Adney. 20, 485.

Williams, Benjamin, planter, A. A. Co.,
30th March, 1730;
16th Nov., 1732.

To son **Benjamin,** 5s.
" son **Joseph** and hrs., 200 A. of "Williams Range," Prince George's Co., where he now lives; £5.
" dau. **Mary,** wife of John Cheny, £5.

To dau. Margaret, £50 at age of 16 or day of marriage.
" wife Margaret, extx., and hrs., dwell. plan. "Foldland," pt. of "Williams Range"; and residue of estate, real and personal.
Test: Richard Poole, Walter Phelps (Philps), Sr., Elizabeth Clerk (Clarke). 20, 487.

Stockett, Thomas, planter, A. A. Co., 13th Oct., 1732; 8th Dec., 1732.

To son Benjamin and hrs., ½ dwell. plan. "The Obligation"; and personalty.
" youngest son Lewis and hrs., other half sd. tract; and personalty.
" son Thomas, 5s.
" dau Elleanor, wife of Richard Williams, personalty, inc. silver tankard and spoons, which were her mother's.
" wife Damaris, extx., ⅛ of residue of estate, remaining ⅔ to her daus. (unnamed), which are now unmarried.
Test: Daniel Carroll, Sarah Stockett, William Fish. 20, 490.

Harvey, Samuel, A. A. Co., 21st Oct., 1732; 28th Oct., 1732.

To wife Elizabeth, extx., entire estate during life; at her decease to dau. Ann; sd. dau. dying without issue, to revert to wife afsd. and her hrs.
Test: Dr. Samuel Stringer, William Roberts, John Reynolds. 20, 492.

Duckworth, Ann, widow, St. Mary's Co. 9th May, 1731; 27th Nov., 1732.

To son Richard Hopewell, money due from estate of George Muschamp, dec'd.
" son Joseph Hopewell, ex., certain personalty during life, to pass at his death to grandchild. Hugh, John, Ann and Elizabeth Hopewell; ½ stock on plantation to pass to grandson William Hopewell, to whom sd. son is desired to leave his plantation.
" grandsons Hugh, John, Richard (at age of 21) and Thomas Francis Hopewell, dau. Ann Aisquith, granddaus. Ann and Elizabeth Hopewell, personalty.
" dau. Susannah King, 1s.
" grandchild. Richard, William, Joseph, Hugh, John, Thomas Francis, Ann and Elizabeth, produce from sale of ½ stock, etc.
Test: John Seager, William Hopewell, Elizabeth Herbert (Harbert). 20, 493.

Calvert, Benedict Leonard, late of the Co. of Surrey, Great Britain, 22nd April, 1732; 10th Nov., 1732.

To the Free-school, called "King William School," Annapolis, ⅛ of personal estate; shd. there be no master for sd. school for space of one year, the trustees of sd. school are directed to pay to the vestry of St. Ann's Parish, Annapolis, the money unapplied to sd. school, which money is to be expended in purchase of a farm for a glebe in the name of sd. vestry.
" sisters **Charlotte Brerewood** and **Jane Hyde,** £50.
" Mrs. **Theodosia Lawrence,** £40 per annum for so long as she may have been in employ of testator.
" servts. **Robert Young** and **Margaret Hands,** £10 each, if living with testator at time of death.
" the Poor of Annapolis, £10.
" goddau. **Elizabeth,** dau. of **Charles Calvert,** commissary general of Province, personalty.
" sister **The Lady Baltimore** and to bro. **Charles, Lord Baltimore,** each a mourning ring. Charges pd. on acct. funeral of late bro. **Edward Henry Calvert** not to be charged to or pd. by sister-in-law **Margaret Calvert.** Shd. bro. **Hon. Cecilius Calvert** at time of testator's death not have right and title to an immediate poss. of £10,000, residue of personal estate is bequeathed to sd. bro.; otherwise residue of personal estate is to be divided among all child. born at or after the date hereof of bro.-in-law **John Hyde,** of Kingston Lisle, in the Co. of Berks, and sister **Jane** (except the eldest son) which shall be living at time of testator's death.
" exs., bro. **Cecilius** and **Edmund Jennings,** of Annapolis, £150.
Test: George Plater, John Ross, Thomas Doughty. 20, 496.

Sharp, Peter, Talbot Co.,
12th day, 4th mo. (June), 1730; 25th Oct., 1732.

To child., viz. **William, Soloman, Henry, Samuel** and **Isaac** and their hrs., entire estate, divided equally; shd. any of sd. sons die during minority, without issue, or intestate, survivors to divide portion of dec'd. Division to be made by bro.-in-law **Samuel Dickenson,** cousins **William** and **Solomon Edmondson, William Harrison,** bro.-in-law **Jonathan Taylor** and **John Leeds.**
Exs.: Sons **William** and **Solomon.**
Test: Douglas Chase, John Edmondson, Elinor Chase.
20, 501.

Larranc (Larrance, Laranc), Daniel, turner, Dorchester Co.,   23rd May, 1718;
23rd Oct., 1732.

    To granddau. **Susanah Plasstid,** extx., and hrs., 3 tracts on Taylords (Taylor's) Island, viz. "Barrell Green," "Davis' Chance" and "Pillgrome's (Pilgrim's) Rest"; and personal estate.
    Test: Tobias Pollard, John Barnes, Charles Barnes. 20, 503.

Wheyland, William, Dorchester Co.,   13th Nov., 1732;
23rd Dec., 1732.

    To wife **Sarah** and hrs., ⅓ personal estate.
    " 2 daus. **Elizabeth** and **Lurana,** certain personalty that had belonged to their dec'd mother.
    " son **William,** before division of estate, a sum of tobacco toward the purchase of a piece of land.
    " 4 child. and their hrs., residue of estate, divided equally when son **William** arrives at age of 18. Child. to be kept at school and educated from interest of estate.
    Ex.: Son **Benjamin.**
    Test: J. Eccleston, Thomas Young, James Melowny (Melowney).   20, 504.

Valliant (Valiant), James, carpenter, Talbot Co.,
25th Oct., 1732;
8th Nov., 1732.

    To sister **Elizabeth Spry,** personalty during life; at her decease to pass to cousin **Elizabeth Spry;** shd. sd. cousin die without issue, to pass to cousin **Tho. Sprye,** joiner.
    " sister **Mary Wainoth** and cousin **John Hopking,** personalty.
    " bros. **John** and **Joseph,** sister **Dorety Esgate** and **Susaney Clift** and their hrs., residue of estate, real and personal.
    Exs.: Bros. **John** and **Joseph.**
    Test: Edward Hopkins, Edward Hall, Susannah Ashcroft.
                                                                           20, 506.

Cooley, George,   29th Nov., 1732;
17th Jan., 1732.

    To **Peter** and **Rowland Haddaway,** personalty.
    " **Elinor Lowry,** residue of estate after wife's thirds are deducted.
    Ex.: Robert Lowry.
    Test: John Ecklees (Ackels, Ackeles), Francis Cook.
                                                                     20, 507.

Nairne (Neairn), Robert, Sr., gentleman, Somerset Co.,
2nd Sept., 1732;
6th Aug., 1732.

To eldest son **Robert**, grandson **John**, granddau. **Mary**, personalty, des. as in poss. of son **Robert**.
" son **Jeames** (**James**), ex., residue of personalty.
Test: William Wood, Henry Schoolfield. 20, 508.

McCallagan (Colligan), Hugh, Coventry Parish, Somerset Co.,
9th Feb., 1731;
14th Oct., 1732.

To Aaron Jordan and hrs., parcel of land sold out of dwell. plan. ———.
" son **Hugh** and hrs., residue of afsd. tract; shd. sd. son die without issue and without disposing of sd. land, to pass to son **Moses** and hrs.
" dau. **Brigett**, personalty that was her mother's.
Wife **Ann**, extx.
Test: James Cain (Cane), Alexander Monrow, Nehemiah King. 20, 510.

Robins, Thomas, Somerset Co., 15th Feb., 1730;
22nd March, 1731.

To son **John** and hrs., plantation where Samuel Hudson lived, with land bet. line of Nehemiah Hollon and William Cord; sd. line to pass through Little Swamp to Coll. Litleton's line.
" son **James** and hrs., tract bou. of Markus Andrews, on Blackwater R., Dorchester Co.
" son **Thomas** and hrs., tract bou. of John Justice and Mary, his wife, it being the land formerly of John Dod, Sarah's Ck., Gloucester Co., Yorke R., Va.; shd. son **Thomas** come into poss. of his bro. Bowdin's land, by his death or for want of issue, then sd. land on York R. to pass to son **James** and hrs.
" son **Bowden** and hrs., residue of dwell. plan. "Gingeteague."
" 4 sons afsd., land and marsh on Gingoteague I., Accomack Co.; sd. sons not to sell except to each other or to any of the other Robinses who hold other pt. of afsd. Island. Son **Bowdin** to confirm the gift of land already made to son **John**.
" daus. **Mary, Elizabeth, Easther** and **Susannah**, personalty.

To wife ———, certain personalty during life; at her decease to daus. **Ester** and **Susanah**; shd. either dau. die before marriage or during minority, survivor to receive portion of dec'd; ⅓ of personal estate, residue to 8 child. afsd.

Exs.: Wife ——— and sons **Bowdin** and **Thomas**.
Overseer: Kinsman **John Robins**.
Test: John Purnell (Purnall), Cuthbert Russell, Jonas Joie(?), John Patrick. 20, 512.

Larrimore (Larimur, Larimer), Thomas, Sr., planter, Somerset Co., 7th Feb., 1731-2; 4th April, 1732.

To eldest son **John**, ex., and hrs., 100 A. "Cooper's Mistake," and pt. of "Ticknel" ("Ticknell"), bou. of Leonard Jones, adj. afsd. land.

" boy **John Larimur** and hrs. (which boy son **John** got from Indians and thinks to be his son which was lost), 75 A. of "Turnstile," on condition that sd. boy will live with testator during his life; shd. he refuse, afsd. 75 A. to **William**, son of **Thomas Larimore, Jr.**, and hrs.

" wife **Wenefret**, ⅓ personal estate, residue to child. equally.
Test: James Dashiell, William More, Alice Hopkins. 20, 515.

Godman, George, Somerset Co., 6th May, 1732; 13th July, 1732.

To Elizabeth Aikman and her son Thomas, personalty.
" **George**, son of Elizabeth Aikman afsd., residue of estate, to be kept in hands of Patrick Stewart, chirurgeon, ex., till he arrives at age of 21; his schooling to be paid for, providing those to whom he is bound will allow him the time while in servitude.
Test: Archbald Simpson, John Cameron. 20, 517.

Lidster, William, planter, Somerset Co., 20th July, 1732; 12th Aug., 1732.

To wife **Jane**, extx., use of dwell. plan. ——— during widowhood, to pass to son **Thomas** and hrs.; and use of personal estate, the pt. remaining at her marriage or death to be divided amongst 4 children.

MARYLAND CALENDAR OF WILLS 245

To daus. **Abigail** and **Leah** and sons **Thomas** and **Jesse**, personalty. Son **Jesse** to have 2 and dau. **Leah** 1½ yrs. schooling.
Test: Edward Stockdell, Jeffery Long, John Benson (Benston). 20, 518.

Nicholson, Roger, planter, Somerset Co.,
9th June, 1729;
24th Aug., 1732.

To son **John**, bro. **James**, ex., dau. **Jean Hopkins**, dau. **Sarah Passons**, child. of son **Nehemiah**, child of dau. **Margrit White** and child. of son **Roger**, personalty, some of which des. as having belonged to John Bacon.
" 3 child., viz. son **John** and daus. **Jean Hopkins** and **Sarah Passons**, residue of estate equally.
Test: Jacob Mezick, Michael Sullivan, John Reed (Read).
20, 520.

Noble, Isaac, Somerset Co., 12th Jan., 1731;
21st Nov., 1732.

To (son) **Isaac**, 50 A. "Isacs Addition," 50 A. of "Friggs Adventure," adj. afsd. tract, and personalty.
" (son) **John**, residue of "Friggs Adventure," and other Additions adj. to sd. tract, except as herein bequeathed.
" wife **Susannah**, extx., personalty.
" daus. **Grace** and **Jane**, personalty.
" 4 child. **Mary**, wife of Peter Surman, **John**, **Grace** and **Jane**, personal estate equally.
Test: Brent Nuthall, Joseph McClellun (McClalan), Thomas Caldwell. 20, 522.

Porter, Hugh, gent., Somerset Co., 15th Dec., 1731;
22nd Nov., 1732.

To wife **Mary**, extx., dwell. plan. ——— during widowhood; and personalty.
" son **James** and hrs., dwell. plan. afsd. at decease or marriage of wife ———, as well as all other lands, on condition that he pay to his bro. **Nehemiah**, within 3 yrs. after sd. bro. arrives at age of 21 yrs., £30; shd. he fail to do so, afsd. land shall be divided bet. the sd. **James** and **Nehemiah**.
" bros. **Francis, William, Joshua, Jonathan** and **McKemie**, personalty. Residue of estate to be divided into fifths; ⅕ to wife, and residue to 4 child., viz. **James, Nehemiah, Leah** and **Mary**.
Test: John Fleming (Flemming), John Dennis, Jr., Francis Allen (Allin), John Sheldon. 20, 524.

Wilson (Willson), Ephraim, Back Ck., Manoken, Somerset Co., 5th Jan., 1732; 26th Nov., 1732.

To wife **Frances,** certain personalty, as well as what she was possessed of at time of marriage.
" **John Irving** (son of wife afsd.) and hrs., all interest in 216 A. of "Hab-Nab," and 48 A. at head of Jeangaukin Neck. Wife to pay all portions due her child. from their father's estate out of what testator releases to her, and is to make no demand for dower interest in his estate.
" son **Samuel** and hrs., dwell. plan. ———, lying bet. land of John Turpin and William Furnis; and personalty.
" son **David,** grandson **Ephraim King** and **Briget Irving,** personalty.
" grandson **Ephraim Wilson** and hrs., 165 A. "Great Hope," bou. of Randell West.
" Mr. **William Stewart,** provided he continues to preach at Manoken, personalty.
" sons **David** and **Samuel,** exs., and their hrs., land and marsh in Broad Ck. Neck had by bond from **Thomas Brown** or any other way; residue of personal estate. Testator directs that should sons or grandsons follow any other way of worship than the Presbyterian Religion, bequests herein made to them shall revert to the rest who follow the afsd. way of worship.
Test: Richard Swift, John Cairns, Robert King. 20, 526.

Samuells, Richard, Sr., Stepney Parish, Somerset Co., 17th Sept., 1732; 8th Nov., 1732.

To son **Peter,** 140 A. of "Samuels Lott" during life; at his decease to his son **Robert** by his first wife; (other pt. of sd. tract having been conveyed to **Steven Hopkins** and dau. **Elizabeth,** his wife); and £4 out of personal estate.
" dau. **Martha** and hrs., dwell. plan. ——— and £6 out of personal estate.
" wife **Ann,** use of sd. dwell. plan. during life, and certain personalty above her third pt. of personal estate.
" daus. **Elizabeth,** wife of **Stephen Hopkins; Ann,** wife of **John Phipps; Mary,** wife of **John Neale,** and **Sarah,** wife of **Daniel Wallter,** 40s. each out of personal estate. Residue of personalty to be divided bet. wife **Ann,** extx., son **Richard** and dau. **Martha.**
Test: John McClester, William Hickman, William McClester, George McClester. 20, 530.

Kennerly (Kenarly), Joshua, planter, Dorchester Co.,
12th day, 7th mo. (Sept.), 1731;
10th Jan., 1732.

To son **William** and hrs., dwell. plan. "Caverton," on condition that one room be reserved as a Meeting House for Quakers, and one for use of dau. **Sarah** while she remains unmarried; shd. sd. son not comply with above conditions, afsd. land to pass to dau. **Sarah** and hrs.

" dau. **Sarah** and hrs., 17 A. "End of Contraversey," bou. of William Dawsey, and 83 A. of same tract bou. of John Dawsey; sd. dau. dying without issue, afsd. tracts to pass to grandson **Joshua** and hrs.; and personalty left to her by Father Everdons will.

" son **Joshua** and hrs., 2 tracts bou. of John Loockerman lying on Fishing Ck., known as "Kennerly's Addition"; sd. son dying without issue, to pass to grandson **William Edmondson**; also mark (for stock) bou. of Edward Harden.

" dau. **Martha,** now called Right, 1s.

" grandson **Joshua Edmondson** and hrs., lot and house at Viana, lot being No. 22, bou. from William Rounds and John Hampton; sd. grandson dying without issue, to pass to granddau. **Mary Edmondson** and hrs.

" child. **William, Hester Edmondson** and **Sarah,** residue of personal estate. Certain personalty to be appraised and included in personal estate. Two accounts of goods delivered to William Kennerly and Solomon Edmondson are inclosed in will, so sd. accounts may be equalized and dau. **Sarah** have to the same value.

Overseers: Peter Sharp, William Edmondson, Thomas Brannock and Daniel Cox.
Exs.: Son **William** and Solomon Edmondson.
Test: David Peterkin, Thomas Shehawn, Peter Stokes (Stoakes), David Shehawn. 20, 532.

Ralleigh, Morries (Morris), planter, Dorchester Co.,
3rd Jan., 1732-3;
16th Jan., 1732.

To wife **Frances** and dau. **Mary,** entire estate divided equally. Dau. **Mary,** her estate and tuition to be in charge of Adam Muir, merch. of sd. co., ex.
Test: William Ralleigh, Jr., Thomas Thomson. 20, 536.

Summers, John, Dorchester Co., 28th Dec., 1732; 27th Jan., 1732.
To wife Susannah and daus. Anne and Sarah, estate equally; shd. wife die, estate to daus. afsd.
Exs.: Wife and Owen Ward; shd. wife die, Owen Ward to act as ex. and give daus. sufficient schooling.
Test: Henry Ennalls, Elizabeth Carr, Michael Collins.
20, 537.

Clifton, Jonathan, Dorchester Co., 11th Jan., 1728-9; 15th Feb., 1732.
To eldest son **William** and hrs., 15 A. "Clifton's Chance," 40 A. "White Marsh."
" son **Thomas** and hrs., 100 A. "Boyce's Adventure."
" son **Daniel** and hrs., 40 A. "Evinses Adventure."
" young. son **Jonathan** and hrs., 100 A. in 2 tracts, "Becksley's" and "Linkhorn"; sd. son to be instructed to read the Bible through perfectly, to be for himself at age of 16, and until that age to be under conduct of his mother-in-law during her widowhood; at her decease to his godfather John Boyin. Daus. to be at liberty at day of testator's decease. Residue of estate to all children.
Exs.: 2 eldest sons **William** and **Thomas.**
Test: Thomas Hickman, Daniel Morris, James Hickman, Elizabeth Hickman.
50, 538.

Pain, Mary (nunc.), Charles Co., 10th Nov., 1732; 30th Dec., 1732.
To Thomas Douglas, debt due him.
" Ann Shaw, Margery Lomax, Jane Walker and John Fearson, personalty.
George Sympson, ex. and resid. legatee.
Test: Atwicks Fearson, Eliza. Hamilton.
20, 541.

Furnis (Furnes), William, Somerset Co., 28th Dec., 1732; 12th Feb., 1732.
To son **James** and hrs., 245 A. "Middle Plantation."
" son **William** and hrs., land where Patrick Mathews now lives, and a small parcel that lies bet. bro. **James'** and Sollomon Long's.
" son **George** and hrs., pt. of dwell. plan. from Ephraim Wilson's line to the marked Great Poplar.

To son Nehemiah and hrs., land lying bet. the Great Poplar and John Tillman's line. When child. come to age mill to be valued and taken by one of them, who shall pay to others their equal pt. If agreement made with Solomon Long stands, dau. Esther to have £20 of price of sd. land. Personal estate to be divided amongst wife and children.
Wife Ann, extx.
Test: John Dear (O'Dear), James Furnis, James Strawbridge. 20, 541.

Nutter, Margerett, Stepney Parish, Somerset Co.,
6th Dec., 1732;
13th Feb., 1732.

To sisters, viz. Ann and Elizabeth, personalty.
" son William, 20s. gift to him confirmed; and personalty.
" niece Margerett, now wife of John Jones, personalty, and gift made unto sd. Margaret under name of Margaret Makmorie confirmed.
" son Christopher, ex., 20s.
" grandson Christopher, personalty and half residue of estate; his share to be in hands of his father (son Christopher) during his minority.
" first child born to son William, personalty.
Test: Matthew Nutter, David Johnson, James Duncan.
20, 543.

Hopewell, Richard, son of Richard Hopewell, gent. (nunc.), St. Mary's Co., 25th Nov., 1732.

To bro. Joseph, personalty; sd. bro. dying during minority, sd. legacy to bro. John.
" sisters Ann and Elizabeth, personalty; in case of death of either of them, sister Mary to inherit portion of dec'd.
" sister Mary, personalty.
Ex.: Father afsd.
Test: Thomas McWilliams, Thomas Kirby (Kearby).
20, 545.

Heard, William, St. Mary's Co., 18th April, 1732;
3rd Jan., 1732.

To dau. Mary and her husband Francis Hopewell, 150 A. of "Thirds," as already divided to them, during life; 40 A. thereof, being where sd. Hopewell has built, is bequeathed to granddau. Susannah Hopewell and hrs.; she dying without issue, sd. 40 A. with the other to return to son Marke and hrs.

To son **Marke** and hrs., 275 A. of "Thirds"; he dying without issue, sd. land to fall with that of **Mr. Francis Hopewell's** after their decease to son **Mathew** and hrs.; and personalty.

" son **Mathew** and hrs., 115 A. "William Heard's Purchase" and 150 A. of dwell. plan. to be laid out bet. bro. **John's** and **John Norris'** land; sd. son dying without issue, to fall to son **Luke** and hrs.; and personalty.

" son **Luke** and hrs., residue of real estate after decease of wife; and personalty.

" daus. **Susannah, Prisilla, Elioner, Elizabeth Wiseman** and **Mary Hopewell**, personalty.

" wife **Elizabeth**, extx., certain personalty during life, at her decease to be divided among 3 sons and their hrs.; also produce of 3 hhds. Tobacco in England, and ½ residue of personalty, the other ½ to be equally divided bet. 3 sons afsd. and 3 daus. **Susanna, Prisilla** and **Elioner** and their hrs., to be pd. them at marriage or when they go to housekeeping.

Overseer: Bro. **Edward Cole**.

Test: John Heard, Ignatius Heard, James Thompson.

20, 546.

Allaby, Anne, Kent Co.,   21st Jan., 1731-2; 10th March, 1731.

To **William Gudson**, ex., entire estate.
Test: John Bennett, Johannah Ballew, Susannah Kew.

20, 549.

Rogers, Sarah, Kent Co.,   25th Nov., 1731; 21st March, 1731.

To son **John** and hrs., one pt. of "Hangman's Folly," sd. pt. to include dwelling house.

" son **Nathaniel** and hrs., other pt. of afsd. tract; shd. either son die without issue, survivor to inherit portion of dec'd; shd. both sd. sons die without issue, sd. tract to youngest son **Joseph** and hrs.

" daus. **Sarah** and **Isabella** and son **Benjamin Hopkins**, personalty.

Test: Sarah England, Ann Pearce (Pers), William Barneby.

Above will also signed by **John Rogers**, ex., husband of testatrix.   20, 551.

Wilmer, Lambert, Kent Co., 26th Jan., 1729;
25th Sept., 1732.

To wife **Ann,** extx., certain personalty and ⅓ personal estate not otherwise disposed of.
" son **Simon** and hrs., pt. of dwell. plan. "Rich Levell," nr. Duck Ck. Road (for desc. see will), and northernmost 150 A. of "Wilmer's Arcadia"; sd. son dying without issue, lands to pass to son **Lambert** and hrs.; and personalty.
" son **Lambert** and hrs., residue of "Wilmer's Arcadia," including plantation where William Jones now lives, and remaining pt. of real estate not herein disposed of; and personalty.
" dau. **Rebecca Tilden,** 100 A. of "Rich Levell," being pt. bou. of Philip Holeger, during her widowhood, and after to return to son **Lambert** and hrs.
" wife and child. **Ann, Francis, Simon, Martha** and **Lambert,** residue of personal estate as law directs.
Test: Richard Hawton, Francis Bonner, Simon Wilmer.
20, 553.

Jones, Elizabeth, Kent Co., 31st May, 1732;
30th Sept., 1732.

To William Strickland, of Duck Ck., Pennsilvania, and hrs., 100 A. at hd. of Steelpone Ck., Kent Co., on s. side of Cabbin Branch, adj. land of Nicholas Jones and adj. tract called "Hillen's Adventure."
Ex.: Nephew **William Strickland.**
Test: Henry Knock, Sr., Henry Knock, Jr., Thomas Burn.
Above will signed by **William Jones,** husband of testatrix.
20, 555.

Rasin (Rason), Philip, Kent Co., 9th Nov., 1732;
22nd Nov., 1732.

To eldest son **Joseph** and hrs., dwell. plan. ———.
" son **Benjamin** and hrs., 1 A. and dwelling house in Chester Town, and £20 above his third pt. of personal estate.
" wife **Mary,** extx., personalty.
Test: Thomas Rasin, Griffith Jones. 20, 557.

McGachan, Alexander, mcht., Chester Town, Kent Co.,
19th Aug., 1732;
27th Nov., 1732.

    To wife Sarah, extx., 2 lots and houses in Chester Town during life, at her decease to dau. Sarah and hrs.; shd. wife decide to sell sd. lots, she is hereby empowered to do so, money from same to be divided with dau. afsd. as well as personal estate. Dau. not to receive her portion of plate and household goods until after death of her mother. Shd. wife die before dau., sd. wife is empowered to dispose of £200 of her own pt. of personal estate as she shall think fit.

    Test: James Cruickshank, John Nelson, James Calder.

    Codicil: Dau. Sarah to receive only £200 as her share of personal estate when she arrives at age of 16, or marriage, and residue of her portion to be pd. at death of wife. Same test. 20, 558.

Beck, Vivian, Kent Co., —— —— ——;
19th Jan., 1732.

    To wife ————, daus. Ann Beck and Mary Foreman, personal estate equally.

    Ex.: John Foreman.

    Test: Humpry Younger, John Rasin, Thomas Bowers.
20, 561.

Rolph, Thomas, Kent Co., 8th Nov., 1732;
25th Jan., 1732.

    To wife Margrett, extx., entire estate and care of all children.

    Test: Elias Ringgold, Mary Ringgold, Elizabeth Holadgr (Hollager). 20, 562.

Wilson, John, Kent Co., —— ——, 1732;
19th Jan., 1732.

    To wife Mary, extx., 2 lots in Chester Town, Nos. 41 and 49, and entire personal estate; also care of all child. until of age.

    " sons **James** and **John** and their hrs. at age of 21, lot No. 53.

    " son **George Augusta** and hrs. at age of 21, 50 A. purchased from Wm. Dicas.

    Test: Walter Dougherty, James McClean, Christian Cully.
20, 563.

Holland, John Frances, planter, Baltimore Co.,
23rd Feb., 1731;
28th Oct., 1732.
To John Copper, John Eaglestone and Edward Sweeting, personalty.
" Frances Holland Watts, dau. of Edward and Mary Watts, entire estate, real and personal, to be possessed by her when she comes of age. Her mother Mary Watts to be allowed £4 yearly for her clothes and schooling and to have use of plantation until sd. Frances comes of age; shd. sd. Frances die during minority, real estate to be divided bet. exs., and personal estate to be for use of St. Paul's Church. Testator directs that exs. shall wall in graveyard.
Exs.: John Eaglestone and Robert North.
Test: Thomas Sligh, Benjamen Bowen, Jr., Bowen Stansbury. 20, 565.

Lee, James, planter, Baltimore Co., 29th Jan., 1732;
7th March, 1732.
To son James and hrs., 150 A. adj. Isaac Bolch's land; and personalty.
" dau. Margaret Webster, personalty.
" Isaac Webster, Jr., son of Isaac Webster, Sr., and hrs., dwell. plan. ———; and personalty.
" dau. Mary Linch, certain personalty during life, and after her decease to granddau. Mary, dau. of **James Linch;** and if sd. Mary Linch shd. die before son James Lee, sd. personalty to belong to son James Lee, and James Lynch to have no pt. in estate.
Exs.: James Lee and Isaac Webster, Sr., to sell personal estate for payment of debts; any residue to be divided bet. sd. exs.
Test: Henry Cole, James Cobb, Francis White. 20, 567.

Smithson, Thomas, Baltimore Co., 11th Aug., 1731;
8th March, 1732.
To wife Ann, extx., entire estate during life; at her decease real estate to be divided bet. 2 sons **Thomas** and **Daniel** and their hrs., personal estate to sons afsd. and 2 youngest daus., viz. Sarah and Avarilla, after their mother's decease. Four married daus., viz. **Elianor,** wife of Samuel Durham; Rebecca, wife of Samuel Wilson; **Rachel,** wife of Henry Donahue, and Elizabeth, wife of **Robert Clark,** having already received their portions, to have no further share in estate.
Test: Daniel Scott, Daniel Scott, Jr., Richard Rhoads, Richard Rhoads, Jr. 20, 568.

Smith, Richard, mcht., Lower Marlborough, Calvert Co., 23rd Oct., 1732; 29th Dec., 1732.

To wife **Elinor,** extx., dwelling house on 15 A. of "Hardisty's Choice"; "Bell," adj. thereto; "Howards"; 2 pts. of "Hardisty's Choice," bou. of Caleb Hardisty and Richard Hall, with marsh adj. called "Black Wall," and pt. of "Hall's Craft" given testator by his father; sd. tracts in lieu of her third interest of real estate during life, after which to son **Walter** and hrs.

" son **Walter** and hrs., 400 A. of "Park Hall," on w. branch Patuxon R., Prince George's Co., to be laid out at end of land where the tree called "Brooke tree" stands.

" son **Richard** and hrs., residue of "Park Hall."

" son **John Addison Smith** and hrs., testator's pt. of lands lying on Swan Ck., Prince George's Co., after division made bet. George Plater, Esq., and testator; shd. sd. son die during minority, son **Richard** and hrs. to have 400 A. of sd. lands, and other pt. to be divided equally bet. two daus. **Rebecca** and **Rachel** and their hrs.

" dau. **Rebecca** and hrs., 250 A. of "Bare Neck," Baltimore Co.

" dau. **Rachel** and hrs., 250 A. of "Tasker's Camp," Baltimore Co.

Test: Walter Smith, Freshes, Elizabeth Smith, Jr., Elizabeth Smith. 20, 570.

Leach, Samuel, Calvert Co., 3rd Nov., 1732; 8th Jan., 1732.

To **Samuel,** son of Arthur Jones, and hrs., all lands at Hunting Ck., being ½ of "Rattle Snake," and all that other tract now in poss. of William Kid.

" **James,** son of Ann Heighe, personalty.

Ex.: Bro.-in-law **Arthur Jones.**

Test: Thomas Shephard, John Washington (Washinton), Jane Corkett. 20, 572.

Byrn, John, planter, Calvert Co., 24th Dec., 1732; 24th Feb., 1732.

To wife **Jane,** extx., dwell. plan. ———, being pt. of "Burks Purchase," bou. of Thomas Kinghart, during life; after her decease to son **Thomas** and hrs.; after all child., viz. **Thomas, Ann, Martha, Jane, Mary** and **Elizabeth,** are paid 12d. each, wife afsd. to enjoy all remaining pt. of personal estate.

Test: Robert Lee, Mary Rix, Henry Lee. 20, 573.

INDEX

A

	PAGE
Abbitt, John	112
Abbott, Elizabeth	151
Abbott, John	151
"Aberdeene"	128
Abington (Abengton), John	56, 111, 181, 234
"Abington's Mannour"	234
Abnelt (Adnelt), William	86
Ackels (Ackeles, Ecklees), John	242
Acton, Henry	28, 128, 155
Acworth, Charles	71
Acworth, Elizabeth	72
Acworth, Richard	71
Acworth, Temperance	72
Acworth, Thomas	71
"Acworth's Choice"	71
"Acworth's Delight"	71
Adair, Alex.	180
Adams, Alexander	35
Adams, Edward	187
Adams, Francis	29
Adams, Henry	28
Adams (Addams), Jacob	8
Adams, John	155
Adams, Samuel	167
Addams, Elinor	159
Addams (Addoms), Elizabeth	159
Addams, Morgan	159
Addams (Adams, Addoms), Summer	159
Addams, Thomas	45
Addison, Ann	30
Addison, Anthony	29
Addison, Eleanor	30
Addison, Henry	29, 188
Addison, John	29
Addison, Thomas	29, 36, 188
"Addison's Choice"	30
"Addition, The"	10, 15, 29, 54, 55, 77, 100
"Addition to Ball"	128
"Addition to Culver's Chance"	155
"Addition to Duck Swamp"	157
"Addition to Good Hope"	168
"Addition to Hazard"	96

	PAGE
"Addition to Island Neck"	13
"Addition to John's Point"	174
"Addition to Shoemaker's Hall"	131
"Addition to Taylor's Range"	131
"Addition to Taylor's String"	130
"Addition to the Golden Road"	60
"Addition to the Partnership"	158
Addoms, Summer	159
Adkison, Thomas	91
Adler, Elizabeth	147
"Admariothoria"	36
Adney, Moses	239
"Adventure, The"	15, 145, 174, 231
"Agreement, The"	200
Aikins, James	236
Aikins, Mariam	236
Aikman, Elizabeth	244
Aikman, George	244
Aikman, Thomas	244
Aing, John	13
Aisquith, Ann	240
Aisquith, Thomas	220
Aldcock, Henry	108
Aldern, Richard	114
Aldris, Joseph	204
Aldris, Mary	204
Aldris, Thomas	204
Aldris, William	204
Alebone, Edward	49
"Alebone's Addition"	49
Alexander, Elias	195
Alexander, Francis	195
Alexander, James	195
Alexander, Joseph	195
Alexander, Martin	78
Alexander, Paul	226
Alexander, Robert	135, 201, 207
Alexander, Samuel	78
Alexander, Sophiah	195
Alexander, Thomas	62
"Alexander's Hope"	235
Alford, Aaron	228

INDEX

Name	Page
Alford, Ambrose	52
Alford, James	52
Alford, John	52
Alford, Mary	52
Alford, Matthias	52
Alford, Robert	52
Alford, Thomas	52
Alford, William	52
Allaby, Anne	250
Allaby, Peter	124
Allen (Allin), Francis	116, 136, 165, 172, 191, 245
Allen (Allin), Isabella	165
Allen (Allin), John	23, 165
Allen (Allin), Mary	172, 191
Allhallows Parish	34, 45, 46, 73, 82, 133
Allison, Barbary	118
Allison, John	85
"Allison's Park"	85
Alloy, Abraham	195
Alnutt, William	93
Alsten, Thomas	105
Alvey, Arthur	126
Alvey, Elinor	126
Alvey, Joseph	40, 126
Alvey, Leonard	126
Alvey, Margaret	126
"Ambrosia"	231
Ambross Elizabeth	90
Ambross, Mary	90
"Amsterdam"	23
"Anchovis Hills"	97
Anderby's Ck.	46
Anderson, Benjamin	43
Anderson, Charles	130
Anderson, Eliza	43
Anderson, Grace	130
Anderson, Hannah	43
Anderson, John	43, 128
Anderson, Martha	95
Anderson, Thomas	43
Anderson, William	43
Anderson, Zarah	151
Anderton, Francis (Frances)	158, 183
Anderton, James	158
Anderton, John	158
Anderton, Sarah	158, 183
Andrew, John	155
Andrew, Sarah	39
Andrew, William	39
"Andrew's Fortune"	192
Andrews, Markus	243
Andrews, Thomas	55
Andrews, William	44
"Angellica"	128
Angell, William	76
"Angels Lott"	153
Annamessex	45, 165, 211
Annapolis	15, 51, 53, 86, 113, 131-134, 150, 201-204, 207, 234, 238, 239, 241
Anne Arundel Co.	41-44, 46, 53, 81-86, 132, 134-136, 142, 150, 162, 169, 170, 201-204, 207, 234, 237-	240
Annis, Elizabeth	235
Annis, Thomas	235
"Aqueteth"	34
"Arcadai"	88
Archer, Jacob	88, 224
Archer, Mary	224
"Archibald's Desert"	181
"Archibald's Lott"	85
Arey, David	96
Arey, Easther	96
Arey, Jane	90, 91, 106, 139
Arey, Jonathan	91, 96
Arey, Joseph	91, 96, 139
Arey, Mary	96
Arindill, Richard	129
Armstrong, Mary	62
Arnill, John	174
Arnold, Mary	28
Artobarey, Thomas	97
Asbrook, Hannah	217
Asfurd, John	18
"Ashby"	214
Ashcom, Charles	20
Ashcom, Elizabeth	20
Ashcom, John	20
Ashcom, Judith	20
Ashcom, Martha	20
Ashcom, Samuel	20
"Ashcom's Mary Greenfield"	20
Ashcom, Susannah	20
Ashcraft (Ashcroft), Thomas	47, 108
Ashcroft, Susannah	242
Asher, Anthony	130
Ashman, John	58
Ashworth, George	143
Askew, Michall	173
Asmuth, Thomas	143
"Aspinnall's Chance"	51
Atchison, Thomas	168
"Athy's Folly"	111
Atkey, Anne	17
Atkey, John	17
Atkinson, Angelo	116
Atkinson, John	116, 136
Atkins, Stanton	116

INDEX

	PAGE		PAGE
Attwell, Joseph	185	Austin, Henry	120
Attwood, Henry	132	Austin, John	12, 60
Attwood, Jane	132	Austin, Sarah	137
Attwood (Atwood), Peter	29, 40, 58, 134, 148	Austin, William	137
"Augustine Mannor"	16	"Ayno"	133
Auld, Edward	144	Ayres, James	129

B

"Bachelder's Folly"	53	Baltimore Co., 11, 15, 16, 27, 28, 39, 46, 51, 52, 54, 64, 71, 89, 92, 93, 98, 100, 112, 120, 128, 130-133, 149, 151, 157, 162, 163, 169, 172, 180, 192, 200, 202, 203, 207, 214-217, 232-235, 253	254
Black Ck.	95, 246		
"Backland"	16		
Back R.	51		
Bacon, John	245		
"Bacon Hall"	169		
"Bacon Point"	99		
Bactson, John	219		
Bages, Mary	38	Banbury, Esther	141
Baggley (Bagley), Ralph	105, 110	"Bank, The"	223
		Banning, Phil	106
Baggley, Samuel	105	Banning, William	189
Baily, Elias	146	Bannister, John	193
Baily, James	143	Barbadoes	65, 100, 113, 157, 204
Baily, Sarah	146		
Baily, Stephen	146	"Barbados Hall"	125
Baily, William	146	"Barber and Dison"	7
Baker, Charles	24	Barber, Elizabeth	170
Baker, Elizabeth	119, 157	Barber, James	110
Baker, Henderson	186	Barber, John	170
Baker, Henry	100	Barber, Macdillion	170
Baker, James	186	Barber, Mary	110, 170
Baker, Jeremiah	100	Barber, Samuel	170
Baker, John	68, 162	Barber, Sarah	170
Baker, Mary	100, 162, 186	"Barber Rest"	7
Baker, Nathan	100	"Barber's Addition"	170
Baker, Samuel	11	Barclay, John	239
Baker, Sarah	26, 100	Barclay, Grace Hay	239
Baker, Thomas	186	"Bare Hole"	117
Baker, William	186	Baren Ck.	7, 71
"Balding's Addition"	81	"Bare Neck"	254
Baldwin, James	81	"Bare Ridge"	56
Baldwin, John	54, 81	Barker, Margaret	12, 107
Baldwin, Mary	81	Barker, William	12, 63
Baldwin, Susannah	81	Barke, William	112
Baldwin, Thomas	81	Barkhust, Ann	197
Baldwin, Tyler	81	Barkhust, Charles	197
"Ball"	128	Barkhust, Elizabeth	197
Ballard, Anne	61	Barkhust, James	197
Ball, Benjamin	59, 105	Barkhust, Jane	197
Ball, Elizabeth	59, 207	Barkhust, John	197
Ball, John	59	Barkhust, Mary	197
"Ballehack"	21	Barkhust, Rachel	197
Balleston, Deborah	201	Barkhust, Rebeckah	197
Ballew, Johannah	250	Barkhust, Sarah	197
Bally, William	1	Barkhust, Suanah	197
Baltimore, Charles, Lord	241	Barkus, Elizabeth	24

INDEX

Name	Page
Barkus, George	24
Barkus, Hannah	24
Barkus, James	24
Barkus, Mary	24
Barkus, Rebecca	24
Barkus, William	24
Barneby, William	250
Barnen Thomas	13
Barnes, Barbara	37
Barnes, Bethia	193
Barnes, Charles	242
Barnes, Charlton	90
Barnes, Henry	40
Barnes, Isaac	168
Barnes, Johanna	180
Barnes, John	242
Barnes, William	90, 221
"Barnet Purches"	13
Barnett, Christiana	89
Barnett, Thomas	63, 89, 112
Barneyeat, John	1
Barneyeat, William	1
Barney, Francis	123
"Barnobie"	29
Barnsbee, William	65
Barns, Godshall	161
Barran, Mary Ann	108
"Barren Ridge Addition"	59
"Barrell Green"	242
Barrett, Phillip	195
"Barros Lott"	19
Barrow, Margaret	236
Barrutt, Benjamin	96
Bartley, John	92
"Barton"	103
Barton, Abigal	162
Barton, Ann	162
Barton, Elizabeth	162
Barton, James	162
Barton, John	162, 188
Barton, Richard	50
Barton, Thomas	162
Barutt, Denis	108
Barweek, James	70
"Barwick Upon Tweed"	29
"Batchelars Adventure"	104
"Batchelers Rest"	5
"Batchelor's Harbour"	29
"Batchelour's Good Luck"	235
Bateman, George	39
Bateman, Lawrence	39
Bateman, Mary	39
"Bath"	228
Bather, John	79
Battel, Samuel	43
Bayer, William	125
Baynard, Thomas	189
Bayne, Walter	1, 36
Bazenbe, Joseph	146
Bazzell, James	83
Bazzell, John	83
Bazzell, Joseph	83
Bazzell, Ralph	83
Bazzell, Robert	83
Bazzell, Rose	83
Beacham, James	128
Beachham, William	34
Beal, Catherine	218
Beale, Elizabeth	16, 208
Beale, John	16, 117, 135, 207, 234
Beale, Richard	90
Beall, Benjamin	154
Beall, Dryden	154
Beall, George	85
Beall, Ninian	154
Beall, Thomas	154
Beall, William	154
Beavans, Caleb	187
Beavans, John	37, 136, 187
"Beaver Dam Range"	206
Beaverlye, George	219
"Beaver Neck"	107
"Beavour Dam Mannour"	5
Beck, Ann	252
Beck, George	129
Beck, Isabella	122
Beck, James	199
Beck, John	80, 209
Beck, Mary	190
Beck, Samuel	156
Beck, Vivian	228, 252
Beck, William	122
Beckingham, William	134
Beckles, Maud	65
Beckles, Thomas	65
"Becksley's"	248
Beckwith, Charles	112
Beckwith, Dorothy	158
Beckwith, Elizabeth	158
Beckwith, Frances	158
Beckwith, Nehemiah	158
Beddoe, Griffith	204
Bedeson, Thomas	51
Beesly, Eliza	132
"Begining"	216
Beherd, Richard	226
"Belfast"	164
"Bell"	254
Bell, Adam	211
Bell, James	189
Bell, John	62
Bellitior, Sarah	66
"Bell's Purchase"	194

INDEX

	PAGE		PAGE
Belt, Benjamin	170	Bishop, William	59
Belt, Joseph	170	"Bitt-by-Chance"	179
Benham, Benjamin	140	Black, William	236
Benham, John	140	Blackburn, William	3
Benham, Mathew	140	Blackiston, Ann	98, 110
Benham, Thomas	140	Blackiston, Ebinezer	197
"Benjamin's Mass"	20	Blackiston, John	98
Bennett, John	250	Blackiston, Priddocks	57
Bennett (Bennet), Mary 108, 109, 145		Blackiston, Susanna	98
		Blackitt, John	138
Bennett, Peter	109	Blackledge, Benjamin	153
Bennett, Richard 166, 213, 230, 234		Blackledge, Hannah	153
		Blackledge, Rebecca	153
"Bennett's Island"	235	"Black Ridge"	188
"Bennett's Lowe"	113	"Black Wall"	254
Benny, James	127	Blackwater R., 14, 68, 157, 174, 207, 243	
Benny, John	127		
Benny, Katherine	127	Blackwell, Joseph	232
Benny, William	127	Blackwood, John	26
Benson (Benston), John 62, 166, 225, 245		Bladen, Thomas	15
		Blaides, John	141
Benson, Rachel	166	"Blakeburn"	199
Benson, Susannah	27	Blake, Elizabeth	144
Benston, Benjamin	186	Blake, John	144
Benston, George	62	Blake, Peter	144
Benston, Mathew	62	Blake, Philemon	189
Benston, Rebecca	62	Blake, Richard	84, 173
Bentham, Richard	1	Blake, Susannah	84
Benton, Comfort	117	Blakison, Ebenz.	49
Benton, Mary	7	Blakston, William	152
Benton, Peter	117	Blanchet, Honnere	190
"Berry"	29	Blanford, Thomas	155
Berry, Ann	175	Blangey, John Wells	104
Berry, Elizabeth	175	Blangey, Sarah	104
Berry, James	91	Blangy, Jacob	104
Berry, John	175, 192	Blansett, Henry	181
Berry, Thomas	175	Blare, John	18
Berryman, Benjamin	39	Bleckhynden, Thephelet	168
"Bessington"	82	Blew, Richard	36, 56
Beston, Nicholas	203	Blisard, John	34
Beswicke, George	79	Blockson, Ann	76
"Betty's Delight"	117	Blunt, Richard	59
Bevans, Charles	10, 155	Boarman, Benjamin	118
"Beverdam"	201	Boarman, Elizabeth	118
Bevins, John	187	Boarman, James	118
Bickardike, Amos	237	Boarman, Joseph	148
Bickerton, John	173	Boarman, Mary	148
Biddeson, Thomas	28	Boarman, Thomas James	148
"Biggs' Purchase"	234	Boarman, William	118
Biggs, Seth	234	Bodfeild, Begnegoe	106
"Bin"	133	Bodfeild, Elizabeth	106
Birckhead, Francis	218	Bodfeild, Ellinor	106
Birckhead, Nehemiah	218	Bodfeild, John	106
Birckhead, Sarah	218	Bodfeild, Levi	106
Bishop, Charles	35	Bodfeild, Mary	106
Bishop, David	35	Bodfeild, Meshach	106
Bishop, Joseph	35	Bodfeild, Shedrach	106

INDEX

Name	PAGE
Bodfeild, Zadock	106
Bodien, Anne Elizabeth	168
Bodien, Frances Lucia	168
Bodien, Francis Ludolph	168
Bodien, Hannah	168
Bodien, Henry Augustus	168
Bodien, Sophia Sidonia	168
Body, Stephen	11
"Bohemia Mannor"	236
Boice, Mary	202
Bolch, Isaac	253
Bonner, Francis	251
Bonner, Theodorus	62
Booker, John	70
Booker, Margaret	70
Booker, Robert	70
Boon, John	155
"Boon's Delight"	216
Booth, Abraham	210
Booth, Ann	210
Booth, Basil	97, 147
Booth, Isaac	90
Booth, Jacob	210
Booth, John	24, 97, 147
Booth, Mary	147
Booth, Sarah	171
Boram, Thomas	173
Bordley, Ariana	16, 129
Bordley, Elizabeth	16
Bordley, John	15
Bordley, Mary	16
Bordley, Matthias	16
"Bordley's Beginning"	15
"Bordley's Choyce"	16
Bordley, Stephen	15, 88
Bordley, Thomas	15, 184
Bordley, William	15
Bordman, Elenner	71
Bordman, Groves	71
Bordman, Sarah	71
Bostick, James	122
Bostick, Margaret	122
"Boston Clift"	221
Bouchelle, Peter	195
Bouger, Frances	86
Bouger, James	86
Bouger, John	86
Boughton, Verlinda	40
Boulling, Edmond	105
Boulton, Daniel	24
Boulton, Elizabeth	24
Boulton, John	103
Bound, Jonathan	9
Bourk, Edward	95
"Bourne"	232
Boussell, John	140
Bowdidg, Richard	179
Bowdle, Joseph	22
Bowdle, Mary	22
Bowdle, Thomas	22
Bowen, Ann	92
Bowen, Benjamin	92, 253
Bowen, David	205
Bowen, John	92
Bowen, Jonas	71, 92
Bowers, Ann	122
Bowers, Thomas	122, 123, 229, 252
Bowes, George	79, 176
Bowin, Elizabeth	120
Bowin, George	61
Bowin, John	61, 97
Bowin, Joyce	61
Bowin, Littleton	61
Bowin, Luke	61
Bowin, Priscillia	61
Bowin, William	61
Bowles, Elinor	48
Bowles, George	48
Bowles, James	30, 48, 174
Bowles, Jane	48
Bowles, Mary	48
Bowles, Rebecca	29, 48
Bowles, Tobias	176
Bowling, Benjamin	15
Bowling, John	12
"Bowling's Plains"	117
Boyce, John	46
"Boyce's Adventure"	248
Boyd, William	227
Boye, John	194
Boyer, Ann	160
Boyer, Daniel	161
Boyer, Hannah	66, 160
Boyer, John	66
Boyer, Mary	66
Boyer, Nathaniel	160
Boyer, Peter	66
Boyer, Thomas	160
Boyer, William	160
Boyin, John	248
Boyle, Patrick	40
Bozman, Ann	19
Bozman, Blandina	19
Bozman, Bridgett	19
Bozman, Catherine	32
Bozman, Frances	156
Bozman, George	32
Bozman, Risden	150, 156
Braban, Hugh	74
Braban, Margaret	74
Braben, John	194
Brace, William	64
Brachaw, Margaret	58

INDEX

Name	Page	Name	Page
Bradbury, Precello	96	"Brewsly Hall"	238
Bradford, John	164	Brewton, Thomas	32
Bradford, William	11	Briant, Richard	132
Bradley, Francis	224	Brice, John	42
Bradley, James	224	Brice, Rachell	42
Bradley, Josiah	61	Brice, Sarah	42
Bradly, Richard	207	Brickenden, Thomas	69
Bradly, Robert	60	"Bridges"	63
Bradly, William	25, 127	Brigdell, Daniel	136
Bradshaw, Elinor	107	Brigdell, Helen	136
Bradshaw, Thomas	151	Briggs, John	183
Brady, John	107	Bright, Elizabeth	159
Brady, Patrick	199	"Bright Seat"	133
Brain, Samuel	74	Bright, Thomas	231
Bramble, Peter	149	Brightwell, Peter	2
Bramell, James	60	Brimer, William	54
Bramell, Mary	60	Briscoe, John	144
Bramell, Rebecca	60	Briscoe, Philip	142
"Branfield"	38	Brissett, John	123
Brannock, John	53, 144, 183	Brissett, Mary	123
Brannock, Thomas	53, 169, 247	Brissett, Sarah	123
Brascup, Joseph	22	Brissett, William	123
Brasier, Thomas	215	"Bristow"	153
Bratten, Hannah	211	"Britain"	183, 223
Bratten, James	34, 211	Brittingham, Isaac	62
Bratten, John	34	Broadaway, Sarah	114
Bratten, Joshua	211	Broadaway, William	114
Bratten, Mary	211	Broad Ck.	108, 111, 114, 225, 246
Bratten, Quanton	34, 211	"Broad Lane"	107
Bratten, Samuel	211	"Broadnox"	145
Bratten, William	34	"Broad Oak"	87, 229
Brawner, John	67	Brocust, Jane	108
Brayning, Edward	151	Brocust, Samuel	108
Bredell, Elizabeth	61	Brogden, William	48
Bredell, Isay	18	"Broken Islands"	215
Breding, Mathew	181	Brome, Elizabeth	97
Brent, Henry	167	Brome, (Brooms) Henry	97
Brent, Jane	167	Brome, John	97
Brent, William	167	Brome, Sherridine	97
Brereton, Mary	47, 86	Brome, Thomas	97
Brereton, Richard	86	Bronard, James	110
Brereton, Sarah	86	Broner, Abigail	56
Brereton, Thomas	47, 86	Broner, Edward	56
Brerewood, Charlotte	241	Broner, Elizabeth	56
Brett, George	118	Broner, Henry	56
"Brett's Hope"	197	Broner, John	56
Brewer, Deborah	150	Broner, Thomas	56
Brewer, Dinah	150	Broner, William	56
Brewer, Ferdinando	150	Bronor, John	1
Brewer, Henry	150	Broockes, John	118
Brewer, John	150	Broocks, Peternallo	94
Brewer, Joseph	150	Brooke, Ann	218, 231
Brewer, Mary	210	Brooke, Baker	175
Brewer, Nicholas	150	Brooke, Benjamin	175
Brewer, Sarah	150	"Brooke Chance"	175
"Brewer's Chance"	150	Brooke, Clement	231
"Brewerton"	150		

INDEX

Name	Page
Brooke, Elinor	155
Brooke, John	71
"Brooke Land"	233
Brooke, Lucy	175
Brooke, Mary	147, 231
Brooke, Rachel	231
Brooke, Richard	175
Brooke, Robert	147, 218
Brooke, Thomas	12, 147, 175, 233
Brooke, Walter	175, 231
"Brookfield"	175
"Brook Place Manner"	218
Brooks, Ann	94
Brooks, Catherine	87
Brooks, John	203
Brooks, Phillip	87
"Broom's Bloom"	214
"Brotherhood"	186
"Brother's Joynt Interest"	29
"Brothers United"	187
"Brough"	119
Broughan, Patrick	149
Brown, Abel	85
Brown, Andrew	224
Brown, Ann	87
Brown, Benjamin	85, 173
Brown, Calup	146
Brown, Charles	50, 239
Brown, Daniel	173
Brown, Elizabeth	66, 71
Brown, Francis	3
Brown, Gustavus	48
Brown, James	50, 169, 212
Brown, Jean	146
Brown, John	25, 37, 50, 59, 85, 90, 173, 183
Brown, John Elliot	135
Brown, John Richard	173
Brown, Joseph	2, 85, 99
Brown, Letitia	23
Brown, Mary	23, 85, 158, 169
Brown, Mathew	23
Brown, Naomy	146
Brown, Nicholas	127, 210, 214
Brown, Rhoda	59
Brown, Robert	71, 85, 238
Brown, Sarah	215
"Brown's Meddows"	211
Brown, Stephen	87
Brown, Thomas	25, 50, 76, 211, 246
Brown, William	86, 125, 146
Browne, John	124
Browne, Margaret	124
Browne, Mary	114, 188
Browne, Matthew	188
Browne, Rachel	124, 230
Browne, Robert	203
Browne, William	114
Broxon, Ann	170
Broxon, John	170
Broxon, Mary	170
Broxon, Thomas	170
Broxon (Brockson), William	170
Bruff, James	166
Bruff, Richard	166
Bruff, Susanna	166
Bruff, Thomas	166, 213
Brunsdon, Benjamin	96
"Brushy Neck"	81
"Bruton's Hope"	55
Brutt (Barutt), Denis	108
Bryan, Jennet	182
"Bryan Dayley"	233
Bryley, Eliza	102
Bryley, Mary	102
Bryley, William	102
Bryon, Dennis	70
Bryon, Elizabeth	70
Buce, Dinah	173
"Buckingham"	228
Buckingham, Henry	222
Buckingham, Rebekah	222
Buckinham, Mary	203
Bucknam, Thomas	148
Buckner, William	51
Bullenbrook Hundred	1
Bullen, John	63
Bullen, Joseph	38
Bullen, Margaret	63
Bullen, Mary	38
Bullen, Thomas	63, 156, 189
Bull, Jacob	180
Bullock, Benjamin	161
"Bunhill Fields"	67
Burbage, Edward	18
Burbage, John	18
Burch, Barbary	118
Burch, Benjamin	117
Burch, Edward	117
Burch, Elinor	118
Burch, George	5
Burch, John	4, 118
Burch, Jonathan	117
Burch, Justinian	118
Burch, Oliver	117
Burch, Thomas	118
Burchfeld, Mary	131
Van Burkeloo, Abell	100
Van Burkeloo, Catherine	100
Van Burkeloo, Harmen	100
Van Burkeloo, Margaret	100
Van Burkeloo, William	100

	PAGE		PAGE
"Burk's Purchase"	254	Bush, William	221
"Burned Marsh, The"	96	Busick, James	183
Burnell, Jane	131	Busie, Charles	27
Burneyat, John	1	Busie, Clare	27
Burneyat, William	1	Busie, Daniel	27
Burn, James	27	Busie, Dinah	27
Burn, Thomas	251	Busie, Elizabeth	27
"Burnt Marsh"	72	Busie, Paul	27
"Burnt Wood Common"	56	Busie, Samuel	27
Burn, William	109	Busie, Sarah	27
Burrar, William	58	Busie, Vilinder	27
Burridge, William	83	Butcher, Jame	42
Burroughs, Thomas	220	Butler, Henry	149
Burroughs, William	197	Butler, Joseph	110
Burt, Henry	66	Butler, Patrick	15
Burton, Benjamin, 45, 73, 74, 75		Butler, Thomas	140, 141
Burton, Elizabeth	75	Butters, John	180
Burton, John	52, 75, 217	Butterworth, Esther	100
Burton, Josiah	129	Butterworth, Hannah	101
"Burtton's Chance"	75	Butterworth, Isaac	100
Busey, John	189	Butterworth, Mary	100
Busey, Joshoa	189	Butterworth, Sarah	100
Busey, Paul	189	"Buttington"	16
Busey, Samuel	189	Buttler, Henry	60
Busey, Sarah	189	Buttrum, John	50
Bushaw, Anne	165	Butts, Christian	24
Bushaw, Elinor	165	Butts, John	97
Bushaw, Garret	165	Byrn, Ann	254
Bushaw, Giles	165	Byrn, Elizabeth	254
Bushaw, Thomas	165	Byrn, Jane	254
Bushaw, William	165	Byrn, John	254
"Bushey Neck"	51	Byrn, Martha	254
Bush, John	221	Byrn, Mary	254
Bush R.	11, 215, 234	Byrn, Thomas	254

C

Cabbin Ck. (br.), 127, 172, 251		Calvert, Margaret	150, 241
Cade, Elizabeth	118	"Calverton"	247
Cain, James	243	Camble, Elizabeth	211
Cairns, John	246	Camble, John	211
Caldcleugh, John	223	Cambridge	3, 62
Calder, James	206, 252	Cameron, John	244
Caldwell, Thomas	245	Cammell, Fillis	200
Calvert, Benedict Leonard	150, 241	Cammell, Quiller	200
		Cammell, William	200
Calvert, Cecilius	241	Campbell, James	223
Calvert, Charles	51, 150, 241	Campbell, Martin	193
Calvert Co., 2, 6, 12, 13, 20, 24, 27, 30, 68, 69, 76, 83, 85, 93, 97, 120, 121, 128, 129, 133, 142, 161, 169, 173, 174, 178, 185, 194, 195, 205, 218, 219, 235, 253		Campbell, Mary	193
		Campbell, Walter	143
		Camperson, Leonard	156
		Camperson, Mary	156
		Camperson, Sarah	156
		Camperson, Stephen	156
Calvert, Edward Henry	150, 241	"Canaan"	55
		"Cane's Purchase"	148
Calvert, Elizabeth	241	"Cannaday"	62

INDEX

	PAGE		PAGE
Cannon, Frances	159	Cash, John	224
Cannon, Henry	159	Cassey, Darby	88
Cannon, James	212	"Castle Carey"	58
Cannon, Thomas	25	"Castle Green"	186
"Canon's Delight"	54	Castles, John	39
"Canton"	29	Caswell, Richard	214
Canty, Gilbert	177	Catlin, Thomas	87
Capshaw, Hope	65	Caulk, Isaac	58
Carberry, John Baptist, 199,	210	Caulk, Jacob,	125
Carmichall, Walter..47, 59,	141	Caulk, Oliver	125
Carpenter, George	77	Cave, Dorothy	46
Carpenter, John........23,	140	Cavenough, John	18
Carpenter, Mary	140	Caves, Charles	34
"Carpenter's Square"	23	Cawood, Stephen	28
Carpenter, William	23	"Cay's Folley"	73
Carr, Ann	95	Cecil Co., 4, 15, 17, 22, 26,	
Carr, Elizabeth	248	50, 54, 58, 60, 66, 78, 83,	
Carr, John 22, 94,	95	94, 95, 100, 104, 113,	
Carr, Mary	95	120, 129, 130, 151, 152,	
Carr, William	95	170, 180, 195, 212, 222-	
Carraway, John	53	224, 232	236
Carrew, Henry	168	Cecil Meeting	183
"Carrolburgh"	133	"Cedar Swamp"	4
Carroll, Anthony	133	Cemperson, Frances	108
Carroll, Charles		Chaimberlin, Thomas	51
133, 135, 175, 203,	207	Chaires, Benjamin	103
Carroll, Daniel 133,	240	Chaires, Elizabeth	103
Carroll, Dominick 95,	133	Chaires, James	104
Carroll, James	133	Chaires, John 103,	104
Carroll, John 11,	26	Chaires, Mary	104
Carroll, Michael	133	Chaires, Nathaniel	103
Carroll, Peter	162	Chaires, Thomas	104
Carroll, Wliliam	41	Chalmers, John....29, 167,	203
Carry, Thomas	76	Chamberlain, Henrietta	
Carry, William	67	Maria	236
Carslake, Edward	185	Chambers, Ann	82
Carsy, Timothy	53	Chambers, Jane	82
Carte, Katherine	11	Chambers, John	18
Carter, Ann	14	Chambers, Joseph	190
Carter, Edward	132	Chambers, Nicholas	82
Carter, Elizabeth	14	Chambers, Olive	87
Carter, James	13	Chambers, Richard	
Carter, John	13	32, 46, 47,	87
Carter, Margaret	60	Chambers, Samuel	82
Carter, Mary 14,	179	Chambers, Sarah	87
Carter, Rachel	14	Chambers, Thomas	93
"Carter's Inheritance"	141	"Chance,"	
Carter, Solomon	132	57, 71, 128, 160, 174, 219,	231
Carter, Sparrow	132	Chandler, John	48
Carter, William	132	"Chandler's Addition"	167
Carty, Margaret	5	"Chandler's Hills"	167
Carty, Mary	5	"Chandler's Hope"	167
Carty, Maurice	5	"Chandler's Invention"	58
Carty, Susannah	5	"Chandler Town"	167
Carty, Timothy	22	Chandler, William	
Carvile (Carville), John	184	29, 40, 58,	167
Carvill, Phebe	184	Chapman, Ann	25

INDEX

Chapman, Edward..... 178, 188
Chapman, Henry 83
Chapman, John 152, 178
Chapman, Nathaniel 26
Chapman, Rebecca 82
Chapman, Richard 178
Chapman, William 82
Chappell Poynt 29
"Chaptico Manor" 51
Charles Co., 3-5, 10, 13, 20,
 23, 24, 28, 29, 37, 39, 40,
 48, 51, 58, 59, 65, 87, 90,
 97, 98, 113, 117-119, 128,
 134, 139, 142, 148, 152,
 155, 160, 161, 167, 177,
 178, 181, 182, 190, 193,
 196, 213, 220, 232, 233, 248
"Charles' Delight" 174
"Charles' Gift" 27
"Charles his Lott" 69
"Charles' Hills 55
"Charles' Lott" 122
Charles Town 213
"Charles Walker's Land".. 166
"Charlwell" 114
Chartur, Thomas 10
Chase, Douglas 241
Chase, Elinor 241
Chattell, William 232
"Chedle" 152
"Chelton" 2
Cheny, John 239
Cheny, Mary 239
"Cheney's Adventure" 150
"Cheney's Plantation" 133
Cheshire, Mathew 119
Cheshire, William 119
Chesley, John 221
"Chesterfield" 141
Chester Point 228
Chester R., 5, 95, 123, 204, 231
Chester Town
 125, 205, 208, 251, 252
Chetham, Edward 212
Chetham, Mary 212
Chew, Ann 83, 84
Chew, Benjamin 84
Chew, Joseph 83
Chew, Mary....... 83, 84, 237
Chew, Nathaniel 83, 84
Chew, Samuel
 83, 84, 85, 129, 133, 134, 173
Chew, Sarah 84
"Chezom's Prevention" ... 179
Chezum, Ann 179
Chezum, Judith 179
Chezum, Samuel 179

Chezum, William 179
"Chichester" 29
Chick, John 236
Chiconocomoco (Chickacone)
 R. 149, 206, 207, 212
Chidley, Richard 182
Childs, Abraham 202
"Chilton" 54
Chilton, Stephen 184
Chinton, Elinor 54
Chipley, William 52, 179
Chivens, William 58
Chocke, George 44
Chocke, John 44
Chocke, Margaret 44
Choptank R., 1, 13, 46, 158, 227
Christfeild, Philip 160
Christiana Ck. 130
Christian, Ann 88
Christian, Elizabeth 88
Christian, James 88
Christian, John 213
Christian, Mary 88
"Christian Milford" 23
Christian, Rachel 88
Christian, Rebecca 88
"Christian Temple Mannor" 98
Christian, Thomas 70, 88
Christopher, Clement 146
Christopher, John 146, 232
Christopher, Samuel 232
Christopher, Sarah 232
"Christopher's Camp" 128
Christopher, Thomas...... 232
Christopher, William 232
Chunn, Joseph 59
Church br. 74
Church of Christ 130
Church of England, 22, 30,
 35, 45, 46, 53, 55, 60, 72,
 82, 85, 93, 107, 117, 125,
 131, 168, 174, 175, 205,
 207, 210, 227.......... 239
Church of Scotland........ 208
"Churnell's Neck" 123
"Cilly" 104
Clagett, Charles 27
Clagett, Richard 16
Clagett, Sarah 218
Clalan, Martha 10
Clapan, Abigail 195
Clare, Elizabeth 6
Clare, Hannah 185
Clare, John 6, 185
Clark, Edward 37
Clark, Elizabeth 253
Clark, Henrietta 37

INDEX

	PAGE
Clark, James	37
Clark, John	52
Clark, Rachell	24
Clark, Robert	101, 253
"Clark's Enlargement"	55
"Clark's Folly"	43
"Clark's Purchase"	55
Clark, Thomas	131
Clark, William	24
Clarke, Adam	51
Clarke, Benjamin	51
Clarke, Caleb	139
Clarke, Edward	139
Clarke, Edward Kane	139
Clarke, Elections	51
Clarke (Clerk), Elizabeth	251, 240
Clarke, George	79, 219
Clarke, Hannah	139
Clarke, Henry	139
Clarke, Jane	139
Clarke, John	46, 51
Clarke (Clark), Joshua	38, 91, 139
Clarke, Luke	51
Clarke, Phillip	147
Clarke, Thomas	51
Clarke, William	190
Clarkson, Rachel	211
Clarkson, Richard	212
Clarkson, Robert	211
Clarkson, Sarah	211
"Clarkson's Forest"	211
Clarkson, Thomas	211
Clarkson, William	181, 211
Clayland, John	209
Clayland, Roger	70
"Clay's Hope"	107
Clayton, Edward	141
Clayton, Joan	157
Clayton, Joseph	157
Clayton, Mary	141
Clayton (Claytan) Rachel	141
Clayton, Solomon	140, 141
Clayton, William	70
Cleaver, John	123
Cleaves (Cleve) Nathaniel	140, 227
Clelan, Grace	20
Clement's Bay	5, 118, 119
Clements, Charles	148
Clenten, Ann	178
Clerk (Clarke), Elizabeth	240
Clift, Joseph	38
Clift, Susaney	242
Clifton, Daniel	248
Clifton, Jonathan	248

	PAGE
"Clifton's Chance"	248
Clifton, Thomas	248
Clifton, William	248
Clinkscales, Adam	51
Clothier (Clother), Lewis	197
Clouds, Benjamin	104
Clouds, Nicholas	104
Clove, John	153
"Clover Fields"	59
Club, Jennat	182
Coal, Elizabeth	193
Coale (Cole, Coole), John	180, 199
Coale, Thomas	172
Coale, William	10
Coape, George	65
Coarson (Courson), David	158, 159
"Coate's Retirement"	117
Cobb, James	253
Cobreath, Aron	235
Cobreath, John	235
Cock, John	110, 153, 154
Cocken, John	216
Cockett, James	156
Cockey, Elizabeth	203
"Cockmore"	87
"Cockold's Point"	26
Coffe, Daniel	13
"Coffer's Chance"	161
Coffer, Elizabeth	161
Coffer, Gerrard	161
Coffer, Henry	161
Coffer, John	161
Coffer, Mathew	161
Coffer, Richard	161
Cogghill (Coghill), Anne	111, 155
Cogghill, Lidia	111, 155
Cogghill, Mary	111, 155
Cogghill, Smallwood	111, 155
Coghill, William	111
Cogwill, Mary	1
Cogwill, William	1
Cohune, Margaret	236
"Cold Comfort"	157
"Cold Rain"	221
Cole, Ann	40
Cole, Charles	132
Cole, Edward	6, 31, 40, 113, 175, 250
Cole, Henry	253
Cole (Coale), John	15, 159, 180
Cole, Mary	102
Cole, Rachel	159
Cole's Ck.	10
Coleman, John	168

INDEX   xiii

	PAGE		PAGE
Colhoon (Colhone), John..	211	"Come Unto Him"	26
Collahone, Timothy	134	Comings, Dinah	196
Collens, Edmund	71	Comings, Elizabeth	196
Collens, John	71	Comings, Mary	196
Collick, Cornelius	34	Comings, Michael	196
Collick, Jacob	34	Comings, Nicholas	196
"Collier"	201	Comings, Sarah	196
Collier, Alice	59	Comings, Thomas	196
Collier, Mary	59, 101	Comings, William	196
Collier, Mathew	59	Compton, Mary	51
Collier, Peter	61	Conaly, John	99
Collier, Thomas	71	"Conant's Chance"	234
Collier, William	59	Conaway, Catherine	135
"Collier Tone Mannor"	4	Conaway, Charles	135
"Collierby"	150	Conaway, Jane	135
Colligan (McCallagan), Hugh	243	Conaway, John	135
		Conaway, Joseph	135
Collings, Amey	217	Conaway, Sarah	135
Collings, Anthony	51	Conen, James	137
Collings, John	74	"Coney Warren"	32
Collings, Mary	194	Conneley, Patrick	167
Collings, Price	46	Conner, David	226
Collings, Rebecca	46	Conner, James	14
Collings, Samuel	46, 217	Conner (Connard), John..	35
Collings, Simeon	217	Conner, Patrick	223
Collings, Solomon	46	Connor, Nathaniel	23
Collings, William	74	Connor, Sarah	23
Collington	188	Contee, Alexander	175
Collins, Andrew	116	Conway, Dennis	67
Collins, Catherine	103	Coocklin, Sarah	47
Collins (Colins), Charles..	226	Coocklin, Timothy	47
Collins, Elijah	226	Coode, William	110
Collins, Esther	226	Cook, Alexander	143
Collins, Jerome	221	Cook, Elizabeth	217
Collins (Collens, Collince), John	71, 116, 165	Cook, Francis	47, 107, 242
		Cook, Jeremiah	217
Collins, Levin	116	Cook, John	77, 143, 207, 217
Collins, Mary	45, 116	Cook, Robert	143
Collins, Michael	248	Cook, Sarah	217
"Collins' Pasture"	71	"Cook's Dubble Purches"..	217
Collins, Thomas, 35, 45, 116, 226		Cook, William	52, 65, 184, 217
Collins, William	116	Cooke, Dianna	142
Collison, George	144	Cooke, Edward	71
Collyer, Frederick	221	Cooke, Johannah	142
Colman, Thomas	86	Cooke, Sarah	65
Colston, Elizabeth	107	Cooke, Thomas	142
Colston, Henry	107	Coole (Coale), John	199
Colston, James	107	Coole, Joseph	199
Colston, Jeremiah	107	Coole, Margaret	199
Colston, Rose	107	Coole, Rosamund	199
Colston, William	107	Coole, Sarah	199
Combes, Richard	177	Cooley, George	242
Combs (Combes), Enoch..	192	"Cool Spring"	23
Combs (Coombes), Sarah..	213	Cooly, Benjamin	153
Combs, William	151	Cooly (Cooley), Daniel	153
"Come by Chance,"	186, 215, 225	Cooly (Culle), William	170
Comegys, William	110	Cooper, Grace	197

INDEX

	PAGE
Cooper, Henrietta	119
Cooper, Henry	119
Cooper, Mark	154
Cooper, Nathaniel	119
Cooper, Richard	79, 176
Cooper, Samuel	61
"Cooper's Mistake"	244
Coot, Mary	170
Coot, Robert	170
Copeland, Barbary	22
Copeland, Catherine	22
Copeland (Copland), Hugh	94
Copeland, Samuel	22
"Cope's Hill"	194
Copner, Burgis	239
Copper, John	253
Copper, William	121
Copping, Sarah	198
Coppins (Coppens) Angelico	18
Coppins, John	18
Copson, John	26
Coram, Henry	41
Corbitt, Daniel	165
Cord, Abraham	215
Cord, William	243
"Cork"	165
Cork, Charles Cartwright	108
Cork, Francis	108
Cork, James	108
Cork, John	108
Cork, Larance	108
Cork (Corke), Peter	108
Cork, Sarah	108
Corkett, Jane	254
"Cornelius"	6
"Cornoner"	50
"Cornwall"	183
Cornwall, William	203
Corricke, James	65
Corricke, Jone	65
Corricke, Patrick	65
Corse, Michael	123
Corsica Ck.	104
Corwen, Isaac	4
Cosden, Alphonso	128, 170
Cossey, Leonard	83
Coston, Benton	117
Coston, Mathias	117
Cottman, Benjamin	9
Cottrell, Elizabeth	162
Cottrell, Isabella	162
Cottrell, John	162
Cottrell, Sarah	162
"Cottrell's Purchase"	162
Coughlan, William	197
Countess, Catharine	227
Countess, Hannah	227
Countess (Countiss), James	227
Countess, Peter	227
Countess, Rachel	227
Countess, Sarah	227
Countess, William	227
Coursey, Arraminta	103
Coursey, Elizabeth	7, 103
Coursey, Henry	103
Coursey, John	7
Coursey, Juliana	103
Coursey, Mary	7, 103
Coursey, Otho	89, 103
"Coursey Point"	111
Coursey, Thomas	7, 177
Coursey, William	7, 103
Courson (Coarson), David	158, 159
"Courtney's Fancy"	219
Courts, John	177
Coventry, Parish of	35, 118, 187, 243
Covington, Abraham	212
Covington, Ann	152
Covington, Jacob	7
Covington, Sarah	7
Coward, Anne	125
Cowley, Elex	41
Cowley, Thomas	41
Cowman, Capt.	132
Cowman, Joseph	202, 238
Cowman, Sarah	237
"Cow Raing"	30
Cox, Benjamin	203
Cox Ck.	59
Cox, Daniel	247
Cox, Elizabeth	65
Cox, James	82
Cox, Joseph	197
Cox, Lazarus	141
Cox, Mary	107
Cox, Samuel	65
Cox, William	223
"Coxes Choice"	136
"Coxes Fancy"	223
"Coxes Performance"	225
"Coxes Prevention"	223
Coyle, Ann Burton	203
Coyle, Edward	203
Coyle, Elizabeth	203
Coyle, John	203
"Coy's Folly"	73
Cozen, John	170
Crabb, Marg.	176
Crabb R.	16
"Crabbtree"	118
Crabin, Alexander	168
"Crab Island"	159

INDEX xv

	PAGE		PAGE
Crabtree, Robert	136	Croxall, Richard	11
Crackan, William	146	"Crucked Ridge"	212
Craford, Samuel	236	Crudgenton, Roger	142
Craghill, George	137, 184	Cruickshank, James	252
Crapper, Ebenezer	46	Crump, Adam	220
Crapper (Craper), Nathaniel	47, 73	Cryer (Crayer), Mary	68, 179
		Cuchin, Robert	64
Crapper, Nehemiah	47	Cullason, Peter	41
Crapper, Rodah	73	Cullen, Catherine	216
Cratcher, Mary	207	Cullen, Francis	216
Craxson (Craxon), John	178	Cullen (Culling), Thomas	216
Craycroft, Charles	4	Cullen, William	132
Craycroft, John	4	"Cullin's Lott"	233
Crayer (Cryer), Mary, 68,	179	Cully, Christian	252
Crecian, Giancet	182	Culver, Ann	155
Creed, Bennett	234	Culver, Catherine	155
Crichard, John	161	Culver, Elinor	155
Criger, Eleanor	190	Culver, Henry	155
Critswell, John	128	Culver, Margaret	155
Crockett, Alice	115	Culver, Mary	155
Crockett, Gilbert	200	Culver, Monica	155
Crockett, John.94, 115, 172,	200	Culver, Sarah	155
Crockett, Richard	115	"Culver's Chance"	155
Crockett, Robert	115	Culver, William	155
Cromwell, John	203	"Cumberland"	46, 136
Crongelton, James	100	"Cumberstone"	237
Crongelton, Mary	100	"Cumberton"	237
Crooke, Charles	151	Cumming, William	
Crooke, Cloe	51	135, 201, 203, 237,	239
Crooke, James	51, 54	Cummins, Elizabeth	103
"Crooked Wik"	47	"Cumpass Hills"	97
Crookshankes, Robert	124	Curbe, John	51
"Cross Cloth"	175	Currant, Elizabeth	194
Cross, John	131	Currant, Hannah	194
Crouch, John	186	Currant, James	27
Crow, William	89	Currant, Jeremiah	27
Crowly (Crowley), David	152	Curtis, Ann	131
Crowly, Mary	152	Curtis, Daniel	104
Crowly, Rebecca	152	Cutchin, Robert	94, 216
Crowly, Sarah	152	"Cut Short"	169
Croxall (Croxell), Joanna (Johanna)	11, 133	Cuttance, Josias	48
		Cypress Swamp	32, 71
Croxall, Mary	11		

D

Dacens, James	202	Dallam, William	214
Daffan, John	25	Dallas, Walter	2
Dafft, Mathew	99	Dame Quarter Ck	13
Daft, Charles	99	Danenlen, Judith	42
Dail, John	195	Dangerman, Christopher	27
Daine, Ann	177	Dangerman, Elizabeth	27
Daintry, Richard	224	Dangerman, Rennis Renard	27
Daintry, William	36	Dangerman, Sufeer Renard	27
Dainty, Ann	86	Daniel, Elizabeth	11
Dalby, John	12	"Daniells"	9

INDEX

	PAGE		PAGE
"Daniel's Addition"	166	Davy, Sarah	47
"Daniel's Quarter"	23	Dawkins, Ann	2
Danin, Elizabeth	198	Dawkins, Bennet	2, 69
Dansey, Martha	20	Dawkins, Elizabeth	2, 69
"Darby"	128	Dawkins, James	2
"Darby Island"	99	Dawkins, Joseph	69
"Darly"	207	Dawkins, Penelope	2, 69
Darnall, Elizabeth	113	Dawkins (Dawkings), William	2, 69, 218
Darnall (Darnell), Henry	36, 83, 113	Dawlan, William	59
"Darnell's Grove"	43	Dawley, John	180
Dartt, Anne	176	Dawsey, John	247
Dasheron, Michall	33, 94	Dawsey, William	247
Dasheroon, John	33, 94	Dawson	109, 149
Dashiell, Ann	166	Dawson, Edward	224
Dashiell, George	166	Dawson, Elizabeth	109
Dashiell (Dasheill), Hast.	92, 166	Dawson, James	156
		Dawson, John	126
Dashiell, James	166, 244	Dawson, Mary	63, 224
Dashiell, Mathias	166	Dawson, Nicholas	63
Dashiell, William	166	Dawson, Obediah	109
Daughty, Absolom	68	Dawson, Ralph	63
Daughity, Amy	68	Dawson, Richard	63, 109, 156
Daughity, Charles	76	Dawson, Susannah	14
Daughity, Dorkas	68	Day, Edward	11, 233
Daughity (Daugity), George	67	Day, Francis	133
Daughity, Herodias	67	Day, John	174
Daughity, James	67	Day, Mary	113
Daughity, Jane	67	Day, Nicholas	200, 217
Daughity, John	67	Day, William	6
Daughity, Mary	76	Daynes, William	66
Daughity, Rebecca	68	Deacon, John	26
Davelen, Judith	42	Deacon, Richard	128
David, Evan	17	Deale, Alexander	185
Davidson, Patrick	87	Deale, Jacob	185
"David's Ridge"	96	Deale, James	185
Davies, James	182	Deale, John	185
Davies, Jona	4	Deale, Martha	12
"Davis' Chance"	242	Deale, Richard	12, 185
Davis, David	91, 214	Deale, Sarah	185
Davis, Edward	118	Deale (Deal), William	185
Davis, Elizabeth	91, 124, 200, 214	Dean (Deane), Ann	14, 31
		Dean, Charles	169
Davis, George	123, 124	Dean, Elizabeth	193
Davis, John	19, 49, 129, 145	Dean (Deane), William	57, 123, 193
Davis, Katherine	140		
Davis, Mary	26, 124	Deane, Henry	63
Davis, Nathaniel	89	"Deane's Choice"	123
"Davis' Pasture"	54	Dear (O'Dear), John	249
Davis, Peter	104, 234	Deaton, Mary	40
Davis, Richard	121, 161	Deaver, Antill	215
Davis, Robert	49	Deaver, Hannah	101, 215
Davis, Sarah	32, 206	Deaver, John	215
Davis, Simon	140	Deaver, Mary	215
Davis, Tamberlin	91	Deaver (Deavour), Richard	20, 215
Davis, Thomas	116		
Davis, William	116	Deaver, Samuel	101, 215

INDEX xvii

Name	Page
Debrular, George	88
Deer Ck.	232, 235
Deet, Sarah	64
Dehinayassa, Alex.	54
"Delabrooke Mannor"	113, 175
"Delahaye's Chance"	23
Delan, Jacob	210
"Delaroy"	139
Delaware R.	17, 38
Delfe	79
Delihunt, Mary	175
Demall, John	36
Demall, Mary	36
"Demby"	206
Demelion, Anne	93
Dement, Elizabeth	118
Dement, George	118
Dement, John	118
Dement, William	118
Demiliane, Ann	174
Demiliane, Elizabeth	174
"Denises Choice"	130
Dennis, John	245
Denny, Ann	102
Denny, Christopher	102
Denny (Denney), John Earle	102, 106
Denny, Rachel	102, 126
Denny, Susannah	126
Denson, Elizabeth	9
Denson, John	9
Denson, William	9
Dent, Anne	90
Dent, George	51
Dent, Peter	10, 30
Dent, Thomas	90
Denton, Anne	16, 42
Denton, Vachell	42, 81
Denton, William	130
Deptford	221
"Derrey"	225
"Desart"	165
Desmyniers, Elizabeth	103
Deson, William	216
Devil's Island	225
Deyne, Robert	139
Dicas, William	252
Dickenson, Samuel	221, 241
Dickeson, Charles	34
Dickeson, Cor.	116
Dickeson, Direeter	34
Dickeson, Hannah	34
Dickeson, John	193
Dickeson, Mary	34
Dickeson, Sarah	34
Dickeson, Sommersett	34
Dickinson (Dickenson), Charles	105, 207
Dickinson, Sophia	105
Digges, Eliz.	167
Diggs, Charles	36, 113
Diggs, John	113, 134
Diggs, Susannah	113
Dikes, John	234
"Diligent Search"	135
Dill, James	146
Dill, Mary	146
Dillehay, Thomas	151
Dillon, Martha	105
"Dinah's Beverdams"	238
Dirikeson, Samuel	34
"Discontent"	29
"Discovery, The"	15
Disheroon, John	33, 94
Disheroon, Mary	33
Disheroon, Michael	33, 94
"Divell"	75
Divideing Ck.	74, 205
Dixon, Robert	126
Dobson, Eliza.	156
Dobson, Nathan	38
Docwra's Tann Yard	202
Dod, John	127, 243
Dod, Joseph	127
Dod, Mary	127
Dod, Sarah	127
"Dod's Choice"	127
Dod, William	127
Dodson, John	235
Dodson, Walter	90
"Doggwood Ridge"	215
Dohaney, William	172
"Doncaster"	51
Donaho, William	34
Donahue, Henry	253
Donahue, Rachel	253
Donaldson (Donelson), John	65, 75
Donaway, Mary	178
Donohoe, Daniel	97
Donohoe, Eliza.	97
Donohaw, Teague	61
Dorchester Co., 3, 13, 14, 20, 21, 25, 28, 38, 50, 52, 53, 58, 63, 67, 68, 76, 77, 80, 96, 109, 111-113, 115, 126, 127, 143, 144, 149, 157-159, 169, 172-174, 178, 179, 183, 190-192, 197, 199, 206, 207, 211, 212, 231, 232, 242, 243, 247	248

INDEX

	PAGE		PAGE
Dorey, Ann	185	Drovine, Peter	24
Dorey, Philip	143	Drury, Robert	199
Dorman, Mathew	27	"Dryar's Inheritance"	54
Dormott, Charles	60	"Dubelfork"	53
Dormott, Rachell	60	"Dublin"	227
Dormott, Sarah	60	Duck Ck. Road	251
"Dorrington"	2	Duckett, Richard	194, 224
Dorrumple, John	218	"Duck Swamp"	157
Dorsett, Thomas	57, 128	Duckworth, Ann	240
Dorsey, Caleb	131	Dudley, Deborah	38
Dorsey, Edward	180	Dudley, Ellinor	107
Dorsey, Joshua	180	"Dudley Incloser"	107
Dorsey, Richard	208	Dudley, Rebecah	107
Dorsey, Samuel	55	Dudley, Richard	214
"Dorsey's Addition"	56	Dudley, Samuel	107
"Dorsey's Chance"	15	"Dudley's Beginning"	106
Dossey, James	129	"Dudley's Chance"	79
Double Ck.	95, 122	"Dudley's Clifts"	214
"Double Purchase"	187	"Dudley, Thomas	107
Dougherty, Walter	252	Dudley, William	107
Doughty, Thomas	241	Duggens, Daniel	219
"Douglas' Addition"	37	Duhadway, Edward	42, 43
"Douglas' Adventure"	37	Duhadway, Elizabeth	42, 43
Douglas, George	104	Duhadway, Jacob	42, 43
Douglas, John	104	Duhadway, Margaret	43
Douglas, Mary	105	Duhadway, Mary	43
Douglas, Thomas	248	Duhadway, Thomas	43
Douglas, Valentine	104	Duke, Andrew	218
Dove, William	44	Duke, Benjamin	218
Dover	162	Duke, James	218
"Dover's Clifts"	193	Duke, Martha	218
Dowdall, Andw.	95	Dukes, John	61
Dowdall, Christopher	146	Dukes, Mary	61
Dowdall, John	95	Dukes, Melven	61
Dowdall, Richard	95	Dukes, Robert	61
Dowding, Joseph	122	Dukes, Thomas	61, 222
Dowdle, William	237	Dukes, William	61
Dowlen, David	146	Dulany, Daniel	135, 175, 208, 234
Dowlin, Mordock	204	"Dumfreeze"	186
Downes, Charles	102	Dunand, Tamer	38
Downes, Edward	141	Dunaway, Timothy	3
"Dowsdale"	234	Dunawin, Frances	192
Doyne, Dennis	29	Dunbar, Jane	111
Doyne, Ethelbert	29, 148	Dunbar, William	111
Doyne, Ignatius	59	Duncan, James	249
Doyne, Jane	148	Duncarter, Josina	211
Doyne, Jesse	29, 167	"Dundee"	65
Doyne, Joseph	29	"Dunghill"	189
Doyne, Joshua	29	Dunkan (Dunkin), George	1, 184, 206, 229
Doyne, Mary	148	"Dunnington Manor"	36
Doyne, Robert	29, 139, 193	Dunn, Jane	145
Doyne, William	29	Dunn, Martha	121
Dreden, David	18	Dunn, Mary	145
Drew, James	215	Dunn, Robert	121, 145
Drewitt, Benjamin	108	"Dunn's Range"	114
Driskill, Moses	76		
Driskill, William	38		

INDEX

	PAGE		PAGE
Dunn, William	121, 145	Dusey (Ducey), Daniel	30
Durbin, Samuel	39	Dusey, Mary	30
Durbin, Thomas	39	Dyer, Elizabeth	22
"Durham"	117	Dyer, John	68
Durham, Elianor	253	Dyer, Martha	68
Durham, Samuel	232, 253	Dyer, Thomas	22
Durnford, Henry	170	Dyor (Dyre), Mary	102, 126

E

Eaden, Henry	84	Egg Harbour	4
Eaglestone, John	92, 253	Eibbeck, Sarah	180
Eames, Joseph	45, 211	Elder, Eliza	196
Earle, James	47	Elder, Thomas	10
Earle, Mary	102	Elder, William	10
Easterling, Henry	27	"Elk Plaines"	120
Eastern Neck Island	227	Elk R.	17, 58, 66, 223
Eaton, Andrew	78	Elle, Benjamin	218
Eaton, George	91	Elliot, John	52
"Ebenezar's Lott"	232	Elliot, Mary	36, 56
Eccleston, J.	242	"Elliot's Addition"	140
Eccleston, John	158, 179	Elliot, William	36
Ecklees, John	242	Elliott, Ann (Anna)	13, 140
Edds, Henry	49	Elliott, Edward	91, 112
Edds, James	49	Elliott, George	13, 140
Edds, Mary	49	Elliott, John	140, 216
Edgar, Anne	149	Elliott, Mary Anne	140
Edgar, Henry	149	Elliott, Robert	113
Edgar (Edger) James	149	Elliott, William	39, 101, 140
Edgar, Johanna	180	Ellis, Alice	226
Edgar, John	180	"Ellis Lott"	8
Edgar, Margaret	180	Ellis, Merick	226
Edgar, Mary	182	Elmes, Sarah	230
Edgar, Susannah	149	Elmes, William	230
Edgar, Triphany	149	Elsbery, Margaret	66
Edgar, William	149	Elsbery, Thomas	66
Edlen, Elizabeth	40	"Elstone's Hazard"	63
Edinburgh	208, 239	Eltington, Martha	54
Edingfeild, Jonas	103	Elton, Thomas	46
Edmondson, Elizabeth	221	Emerson, John	138
Edmondson, Hester		Emerson, Mary	119
Edmondson, James	191, 205, 221	Emerson, Sarah	138
Edmondson, John	191, 221, 241	Emerson, Vincent	138
Edmondson, Joshua	247	Emory, Arthur	7
Edmondson, Mary	247	Emory, John	103
Edmondson, Solomon	241, 247	Emory, Sarah	7
Edmondson, William	119, 221, 241, 247	"Enclosure, The"	4
Edwards, Deborah	42	"End of All Strife"	53
Edwards, Edmond	94	"End of Contraversy"	247
Edwards, John	159	Engles (Engls, Inglish), Margaret	26
Edwards, Margaret	67, 109, 173	Engels, Thomas	26
"Edward's Neck"	83	England,	12, 53, 70, 122, 124, 134, 143, 155, 168, 213, 221, 223, 231	250
"Edwin"	8		
"Edwin's Addition"	57		
"Edwin's Affront"	57	England, Isaac	125

England, Joseph 162	Erickson, Mary 128
England, Margaret 162	"Erickson's Hazard" 128
England, Sarah 230, 250	Esgate, Caleb 222
English, Thomas 94	Esgate, Dorety 242
"Enlargement, The" 54	Esgate, Stephen 222
"Ennallses Ridges" 149	Evans, Ann 189
Ennalls, Ann 206	Evans, Butler 189
Ennalls (Ennals), Bartholomew 14, 206	Evans, Charles 189
Ennalls, Betty 207	Evans, David 72
Ennalls, (Ennals), Henry 14, 206, 248	Evans, Elizabeth 189
	Evans, Henry 125
Ennalls, John 206	Evans, John, 58, 66, 115, 206, 227
Ennalls, Joseph 206	Evans, Mary 212
"Ennalls' Lott" 207	Evans, Philip 99, 111, 189
Ennalls, Mary 206	"Evans' Purchase" 147
Ennalls (Ennals), Thomas 14, 206	Evans, Richard 55
	Evans, Thomas...120, 189, 212
"Ennalls' Timber Yard"... 206	Evans, Walter 189
Ennalls, William 206	Everest, Sarah 195
Ensor, John 131	Everett, John 5
Erickson, Casparum 232	Everett, Joseph 5
Erickson, Erick 232	"Evinses Adventure" 248
Erickson, Gunder 128	Evorrel, William 123
Erickson, John 232	"Exchange, The" 14, 33, 45, 73
Erickson, Martha 128	"Expedition" 194
	Eyter, Anne 139

F

Facer, Elizabeth 54	Falkoner, James 31
Facer, Henry 54	Falkoner, John 31
Facer, James 54	Falkoner, Sarah 31
Facer, Martha 54	Falkoner, Thomas 31
Facer, Thomas 54, 237	Falkoner, William 31
Fadry, Elizabeth 142	Fallen, Elinor 144
"Fairly" 205	Fallen, Redman 58, 80
"Fair Promise" 229	"Fall Hill" 233
Falconer, Burton Francis.. 209	"Fancy, The" 15
Falconer, Emmanuel 209	Farr, Clement 176
Falconer, Gilbert 230	Farr, Edmund, ... 176
Falconer, James 209	Farr, Mary 176
Falconer, John 209	Farr, Sarah 176
Falconer, Sarah 209	Farrell, Eleanor 201
Falconer, Temperance 209	Farrer, James 115
Falconer, Thomas 209	Farthing, Maria 113
Falconer, Thomas Ford ... 209	Farthing, Richard 119
Falkener, Ann 80	Farthing, William Maria.. 78
Falkener, Benjamin 80	Fassitt, Elizabeth 45
Falkener, Elenor 80	Fassitt, Franklin 45
Falkener, Isaac 80	Fassitt, William 45, 226
Falkener, Jacob 80	"Father's Care" 33
"Falkenor's Lott" 80	Faudry, Elizabeth 135
Falkner, Gilbert 204	Faudry, Moses 135
Falkner, Jane 204	"Faulkner's Square" 106
Falkoner, Ann 31	"Fearon Hills" 62
Falkoner, Emanuel 31	Fearson, Atwicks 248

INDEX

	PAGE		PAGE
Fearson, John	248	Flinn, Margaret	227
Feaston, John	95	Flood's Ck.	99
Feddeman, Shadreck	179	Floyd, Mary	106
Fells, Edward	89, 131	Floyd, Moses	156
Fendall, John	51	Floyd, Richard	156
Fenton, Agnes	18	Floyd, Rowland	107
Fenton, Margaret	18	Fogg, Ann	161
Fenton, Moses	18	Fogg, Thomas	161
Fenton, Naomi	18	"Foldland"	240
Fenton, Sarah	18	Follard, Mary	105
Fenwick, Bennet	147	"Folly"	156
Fenwick, Cuthbert	147	Fooks, Benjamin	33
Fenwick, Elizabeth	147	Fooks, Catherine	33
Fenwick, Ignatius	78	Fooks, Mary	14
Fenwick, Robert	147	Fooks, Sarah	33
Ferguison, Alexander	25	Forbes, Alexander	47
Ferguison, James	25	Forbes, Sarah	47
Ferguison, Katherine	25	"Force"	29
Ferrall, Robert	37	Ford, Hannah	238
"Ferry Point"	202	Ford, Ignatius	192
"Ferry, The"	232	Ford, Isaac	103
Ferson, Elizabeth	20	Ford (Foord), John	21, 68
Ferson, Jane	20	Ford, Mary	70
Ferson, Percy	20	Ford, Rachel	176
Ferson, Sarah	20	Ford, Rebecca	103
Ferson, Sophie	20	Ford (Foord), Robert 5, 70, 119, 192	
Feston, John	22		
"Fingaul"	133	Ford (Foord), Thomas, 103, 238	
"Finland"	95	Ford (Foard), William 44, 82, 132	
Finley, Andrew	156		
Finley, Jane	70	Fordham, Benjamin	55
Fish, William	83, 201, 240	Foreman (Forman), Elizabeth	103, 204
Fisher, Barkle	87		
Fisher, Frances	109	Foreman, John	252
Fisher, Henry	94	Foreman, Joseph	204
Fisher, Mark	144, 178	Foreman, Mary	252
Fisher, Mary	151	Foreman, Philip	204
Fisher, Rebecca	149	Foreman, Robert	123
Fisher, Sarah	107, 151	Foreman, William	204
Fisher, William	201, 239	"Forester's Neck"	93
Fishing Ck.	247	Forest, Patrick	231
"Fishing Island"	19	"Fork Neck"	159
Fitch, Joseph	162	"Forked Neck"	204
Fitzpatrick, Charles	195	"Forlorn Hope"	21
Fitzpatrick, James	195	"Forrester's Delight"	229
Fitzrandolph, Nathaniel	103	Forrest, Francis	219
"Five Brothers"	5	"Forest of Harvey"	78
Fizgerald, Garratt	170	"Forrest, The"	231
Flaman, John	149	Forster, Francis	100
Flanikin, George	178	Forster, James	100
Fleet, Elizabeth	42	Forster, Margaret	100
Fleming, John	245	Forster, Mary	100
Fleming, Lodowick	73	Forster, Sarah	100
Fleming, Leviner	73	Forster, Thomas	100
Fleming, Massey	73	"Fortune"	92
Fling, John	103	Foster, Barzealey	203
Flinn, Laughlin	227	Foster, Isaac	223

INDEX

	PAGE
Foster, James	222
Foster, Jeremiah	223
Foster, John	14, 223
Foster, Mary	14
Foster, Pheby	14
Foster, Rebecca	14
Foster, Richard	222
Foster, Sarah	14
Foster, Thomas	14, 223
Foster, William	222
Fottrell, Ann	235
Fottrell, Edward	58
Foudry, Elizabeth	235
Fountaine, Betty	19
Fountaine, Brichett	19
Fountaine, Estar	19
Fountaine, John	19
Fountaine, Marcy	19
Fountaine, Mary	19
Fountaine, Nicholas	19
Fountaine, Risden	19
Fountaine, Samuel	19
Fountaine, Thomas	19
Fountain, William	232
Fowke, Gerard	40, 193
Fowler, Abraham	85, 174
Fowler, Ann	96
Fowler, Catherine	85
Fowler, Elinor	174
Fowler, George	85
Fowler, James	201
Fowler, Joseph	85
Fowler, Patrick	96
Fowler, Rebecca	174
Fowler, Samuel	174, 201
Fowler, Sarah	201
Fowler, William	85
Fox, Aron	11
Foxson, George	145
Foxwell, Mary	199
Foy, Andrew	99
Foye, Anne	137
Framton, John	171
Framton, Robert	171
Framton, Sarah	171
Framton, Thomas	171
Framton, William	171
Francis, Tench	214
Franklin, Samuel	93
Franklyn, Artridge	201
Franklyn, Charles	73
Franklyn, Ebenezar	45, 73

	PAGE
Franklyn, Edward	45, 73, 75
Franklyn, Jacob	201
Franklyn (Franklin), John	45, 73, 161, 201
Franklyn, Mary	74
Franklyn, Peale	73
Franklyn, Richard	201
Franklyn (Franklin), Robert	201, 238, 239
Franklyn, Sarah	74
Franklyn, William	73
Franch, Elizabeth	98
Franch (French), Henry	98
Franch, Mary	98
Franch, William	98
Fraser, Alexander	234
Fraser, Anne	234
Fraser (Frasor), John	57, 220
Fraser, Stephen Samuel	234
Frasher, Hugh	160
Frazer, Benony	63
Frazer, Elizabeth	149
Frazer, John	149
Frazier Barbary	198
Freeman, Isaac	229
Freeman, John	55, 74
Freeman, Nat.	39
Freemon, William	116
Free School	241
French (Franch), Henry	98
French, John	5
"Friend Good-will"	75
Friends, 1, 14, 59, 123, 125, 129, 131, 133, 139, 140, 176, 183, 221, 229, 240, 247
"Friendship"	10, 29, 57, 229
"Frigg's Adventure"	245
Frisby, Augustina	16
Frisby, Margaret	16
Frisby, Nicholas	220
Frisby, Peregrine	220
Frisby, Sarah	16, 234
Frissel, Sarah	112
Fuller, Henry	181
Furnis, Ann	249
Furnis, Esther	249
Furnis, George	248
Furnis, James	248
Furnis, Nehemiah	249
Furnis, William	246, 248
Fursters, James	94

INDEX

G

	PAGE		PAGE
Gadd, Grace,	157	Garrett, James	53
Gadd, William	143	Garrett, Mary	71
Gail, John	49	Garrett, Richard	60
Gaither, Benjamin	16	Garrett, Sarah	53
Gaither, Edward	44	Garrett, Seth	54
Gale, Betty	35	Gary, Stephen	158
Gale, Levin	147, 187, 226	"Gash's Neglect"	214
Gallaway, William	39	Gassaway, Thomas,	150, 162, 236
"Gallaway's Fancy"	153	Gatinbe, Elizabeth	206
Gallion, Henry	200	Gatinbe, William	206
Gallion, James	200	Gauffe, James	167
Gallion, John	200	Geist, Christian	113, 201
Gallion, Joseph	201	Geist, Samuel	201
Gallion, Samuel	200	Geist, Sarah	201
Gallion, Sarah	200	"Gentile Craft"	55
Gallion, Solomon	200	Geoftree, Elizabeth	28
Gallion, Thomas	200	George, John	2
"Gallion's Addition"	200	George, Joshua	51, 212
"Gallion's Hazard"	200	George's Ck.	75
Galloker, John	134	"George's Hill"	11
"Galloway"	157	German, Robert	102
Galloway, John,	42, 135, 208, 237	Getchell, Benjamin	16
Galloway, Joseph	42, 43, 237	Gibbins, John	48
Galloway, Mary	237	Gibbs, Bartholomew	159
Galloway, Peter	237	Gibbs, George	35
Galloway, Richard	237	Gibson, Barbara	138
Galloway, Samuel	12	Gibson, Elizabeth	188
Galloway, Susannah	237	Gibson, John	188
Galwith, Elizabeth	182	Gibson, Rachel	138
Galwith, James	182	Gibson, Rebecca	138
Galwith, Jonas	182	Gibsone, George	35
Galwith, Mary	182	Gideons, Elizabeth	64
Galwith, Sarah	182	Gilbert, John	152
Galwith, Tamer	182	Gilbert, Mary	152
Gambell, Abraham	207	Gilbert, Phebe	152
Gambell, Mary	207	Giles, Anne Maria	172
Gambrell, Sarah	163	Giles, John	172
Gantt, Thomas	175	Giles, Mary	172
Ganyatt, Charles	171	Giles, Nathaniel	172
Gardiner, Bullet	119	Gilles, Bridgett	71
Gardiner, Christopher	150	Gilles, John	71
Gardiner, Clement	148	Gilley, Robert	2
Gardiner, Douglas Gifford.	119	"Gillingham"	54
Gardiner, Hugh	119	Gills, Elizabeth	44
Gardiner (Gardner), Joseph	148, 188	Gills, John	44
		"Gill's Land"	39
Gardiner, Luke	148	Gills, Mary	44
Gardiner, Mary	148	Gills, Rachell	44
Gardner, Benjamin	148	Gills, Rebecca	44
Garettson, Garett	233	Gills, Samuel	44
Garfet, Anne	49	Gills, Sarah	44
Garfet, Charles	49	Gilpen, Charity	160, 220
"Garies' Choice"	174	Gilpen, Edward	160, 220
Garrett, Amos	53, 202	Gilpen, Henry	160, 220
Garrett, Bennett	217	Gilpen, Isaac	160, 220

INDEX

	PAGE		PAGE
Gilpin, Jane	160, 220	Goof, Thomas	169
Gilpin, Mary Ann	160, 220	"Goose Creek"	167
Gilpin, Thomas	160, 220	Goostree, George	80
Gilpin, William	160, 220	Goostree, Rebecca	80
Gimber, Thomas	43	Goostree, Richard	80
"Gingeteague"	243	"Goostree's Delight"	80
Ginn, Elizabeth	53, 202	Gorden, Elizabeth	109
Gioles, John	238	Gording, Robert	193
"Gisburough"	29	"Gordon"	201
Gittings, Ann	17	Gordon (Gorden, Gording),	
Gittings, John	17	Robert, 86, 135, 201, 207, 239	
Gittings, Thomas	216	Gordon, Stephen	180
Givan, Robert	72	Gorsuch, Charles	1
"Gleanings, The"	29, 85	Goslee, John	8
"Gleave's Adventure"	230	Goslee (Gostea), Thomas, 8, 165	
Glen (Glyn), Cecily	41	Gostwick, Elizabeth	71
Glen, Jacob	123	Gostwick, Joseph	71
Glover, Richard	199	Gostwick, Nicholas	71
Glover, Thomas	199	Gostwick, Thomas	71
Glover, Weneford	199	Gott, Hannah	84
"Goaldsborough's Addition"	107	"Gott's Plantation"	238
"Goare, The"	97	Gott, Verlinda	84
Goddard, George	9	Gott, Walter	84
Godfrey, Ginnitt	37	Gough, Ann	131
Godfrey, John	125	Gough, John	157
Godman, George	244	Gough, William	103, 141, 157
Godman, Thomas	168	Gould, Edward	92
Goe, John	85	Gould, Thomas, 71, 110, 206, 229	
Goffe, James	167	Goulden, Grove	50
"Golden Grove"	113	Goult (Golt), George	
"Golden Springs"	119		90, 91, 96, 106
Goldring, Mary	161	Goult, Lydia	91
Goldsborough, Charles	207	Goult, Martha	209
Goldsborough, Nicholas	145	Goult, Thomas	90
Goldsborough, Robert	21, 166	Goult, W.	139
Goldsmith, Richard	208	Goult, William	90, 91
Goley, Ann	178	Govane, Elizabeth	204
Goley, Susannah	178	Govane, James	204
Goley, Thomas	178	Gover, Samuel	170
"Gollaways"	53	Grace, Elizabeth	108
Golt (Goult), George		Grace, Mabell	108
	90, 91, 96, 106	Grace, Mary	108
Goodhand, Marmaduke	188	Grace, Nathaniel	108
"Good Hope"	168	Grace, Rachel	108
Goodin (Goodan), Moses	74	Grace, Sarah	108
"Good Luck's Range"	38	Grace, Susannah	108
Goodman, Thomas	66	Grace, William	108
Goodrick, Ann	24	"Grafton's Mannor"	22, 144
Goodrick, Aron	24	Grainnan, Edward	182
Goodrick, Benjamin	24	Grame, Elizabeth	65
Goodrick, George	24	Grame, George	65
Goodrick, Robert	24	Granan, James	99, 210
Goodrick, William	24	Granger, John	231
Goodson, William	88, 160	"Grange, The"	121
"Good Speed"	52	Grant, Thomas	4
"Goodwill"	50	Graves, William	184, 230
Goodwn, Elizabeth	233	Gray, Isabel	149

INDEX

	PAGE		PAGE
Gray, Jacob	127, 149	"Grey Sands"	55
Gray, John	225	Griffen, Ezekiel	154
Gray, Joseph	116	Griffen, Pathena	154
Gray, Margaret	225	Griffen (Griffin), William	154
Gray, Martha	218	Griffin, George	157
Gray, Mary	116	Griffin, Hannah	28, 157
Gray, Rebecca	92, 116, 225	Griffin, John	28, 86, 157, 170
Gray, Sarah	116, 225	Griffin, Joseph	157
Gray, Simon	97	Griffin, Katherine Mary	170
Gray, Thomas	127	Griffin (Griffith), Lewis	149, 157
Gray, Westcot	116	Griffin, Mary	63
Gray, William	3, 116, 225	Griffin, Robert	157
Great Britain	22, 36, 54, 59, 62, 78, 103, 104, 136, 161, 241	Griffin, Samuel	170
		Griffin, Sarah	63
"Great Brushy Neck"	55	Griffith, Edw.	136
Great Choptank R.	1, 13, 46, 158, 227	Griffith, John	5, 227
		Griffith, Orlando	170
"Great Elton Head Mannour"	6	Griffith, Rachel	142
		Griffith, Sarah	136
"Great Hope"	246	Griffith, Susannah	66
Greaton, Joseph	134, 203	Griffith, Thomas	109
Greeme, James	239	Grimes, Ann	202
Green, Catherine	224	Grimes, Barbara	156, 198
Green, Elizabeth	224	"Grimes' Enlargement"	55
Green, John	25, 188	"Grimes' Stone"	55
Green, Leonard	184	Groom, Moses	64
Green, Marjory	132, 135	Groome, Richard	176
Green, Mary	58	Grover, George	130
"Green Meadow"	121	Grover, John	130
"Green Oak"	113	Grover, Magdala	130
Green, Rachel	223	Grugen, Paul	137
Green, Robert	206	"Grumble, The"	15
"Green's Chance"	116	Gudson, William	250
"Green's Inheritance"	5	"Gueist's Plains"	15
"Green Spring"	167	Guibert, Anne	110
"Green Spring Punch"	28	Guibert, Elizabeth	110
Green, Tecla	177	Guibert, Joshua	110
Green, Thomas	223	Guibert, Sarah	110
Greenfield, James	20	Guibert, Thomas	110
Greenfield, Martha	97	"Gullet's Advisement"	72
Greenfield, Thomas Truman	20, 147	"Gunder's Delight"	128
		Gunpowder R.	157, 216, 232
Greenhough, Thomas	47	"Gunterton"	128
Greenup, John	17	Gur, Daniel	48
Greenwell, John	79	"Gutheridge Addition"	28
Greenwood, Bartholomew	30	Guy, David	46
Greenwood, Eliza	230	Guyther, John	219
Gregory, William	102	Guyther, Owen	31
Grenaway, Thomas	68	Guyther, Sarah	31
Gresham, John	125, 202	Gwin, Sarah	216
Grew, Theophilus	118	Gwynn, William	38

H

"Hab-Nab"	246	Hackman, Ann	39
"Hacker's Forest"	79	Hackney, John	50
Hackett, William	95	Haddaway, Peter	242

INDEX

Name	Page
Haddaway, Rowland	242
Hadden, William	66
Hadder, Warren	164
Haddock, James	188, 234
Haddock, Sarah	188
Hagan, Mary	5
Hagan, William	5
Hague, Joseph	151
Hail, Margaret	76
Hailes, Ann	49, 121, 163
Hailes, Edward	49, 121
Hailes, Frances	163
Hailes, George	162
Hailes, Hannah	163
Hailes, Jane	49
Hailes, John	152
Hailes, Mary	163
Hailes, Millisant	163
Hailes, Neale	163
Hailes, Nicholas	162, 172
Hailes, Roger	49, 121
Hailes, Sabbiner	163
"Hailes' Addition"	163
"Hailes' Fellowship"	162
"Hailes' Folly"	163
"Hailstone"	123
Haines, Joyce	20
Haise, Peter	77
"Half Pone"	48
Haliewell, John	143
Haliewell, Lawrence	143
Haliewell, Richard	143
Haliewell (Holliwell, Holloway), William	143
Hall, Alexander	47, 87
Hall, Ann	111
Hall, Charles	166
Hall, Daniel	111
Hall, Edward	242
Hall, Eleanor	209
Hall, Elizabeth	47, 48
Hall, Francis	134
Hall, Isaac	127
Hall, James	19, 155
Hall, John	48, 78, 111, 156
Hall, Mabell	156
Hall, Margaret	111
Hall, Mary	48
Hall, Parker	184, 217
Hall, Phenix	19, 75
Hall, Richard	166, 173, 254
Hall, Robert	166
"Hall's Craft"	254
"Hall's Palace"	54
Hall, Thomas	19, 48
Hall, William	19, 48, 74, 111
Halladay, Anne	183
Hallam, John	199
"Halloway's Increase"	238
Hambleton, Edward	67
Hambleton, Grace	218
Hambleton, Margaret	67
Hambleton, Philemon	138
Hambleton, Sarah	67
"Hambleton's Marsh"	67
"Hambleton's Park"	173
Hambleton, William	138
Hambrook, Mary	179
Hamer, Ann	140
Hamilton, Alexander	177
Hamilton, Eliza	248
Hamilton, James	177
Hamilton, John	63, 177, 208
Hamilton, Mary	177
Hamilton, Patrick	177
Hamilton, Samuel	177
Hamilton, William	28, 177
Hamlyn, Francis	61
Hamm, John	100
Hammond, Benjamin	204
Hammond, Charles	42, 86, 238
Hammond, John	133, 204
Hammond, Lawrence	204
Hammond, Mordecai	135
Hammond, William	204
Hampton, John	247
"Hamton"	30
Hance, Benjamin	129, 169
Hance, Francis	218
Handrey, Thomas	195
Hands, Benjamin	90
Hands, Margaret	241
Handy, Benjamin	94, 166
Handy, Ebenezer	94, 166
Handy, John	186
Handy, Samuel	62
Handy, William	117
Hangline, Isabel	147
Hangline, William	147
"Hangman's Folly"	250
Hankin, Edward	192
Hankins, John	154
Hanley, Elinor	111
Hanley, Elizabeth	111
Hanley (Handley), Hugh	111, 115
Hanley, Marmaduke	111
"Hanley's"	223
"Hanley's Adventure"	111
"Hanley's Regulation"	111
Hannington, Elias	119
Hanson, Christina	49
Hanson, Frederick	49, 154
Hanson, George	48, 154

INDEX

	PAGE		PAGE
Hanson, Gustavus	49	Harris, Jone	63
Hanson, Hance	48, 154	Harris, Joseph	163
Hanson, Jane	49, 154	Harris, Lloyd	15
Hanson, Jonathan	150	Harris, Mary	17, 202
Hanson, Martha	49	Harris, Mathias	129
Hanson, Mary	49	Harris, Rachel	66
Hanson, Robert	58, 90, 213	Harris, Richard	35
Hanson, Sarah	49	Harris, Samuel	66
Hanson, William	48	Harris, Sarah	185
"Hap-at-a-venture"	178	Harris, Temperance	35
"Happy Addition"	174	Harris, Thomas	17, 66, 76
Harber, Rosanna	126	Harris, Wat	145
Harbert, Charles	151	Harris, William	
Harbut, Elinor	189		35, 47, 57, 163, 221
Harbut, James	189	Harrison, Daniel	21
Harden, Edward	247	Harrison, Elizabeth	105
"Hardisty"	128	Harrison, Hester	23
Hardisty, Caleb	254	Harrison, Hezekiah	23
"Hardisty's Choice"	254	Harrison, Joseph	23
Hardy, Ben.	7	Harrison, Margaret	60
Hardy, James	7	Harrison, Richard	
Hardy (Harddy), John	7, 9		13, 23, 65, 213
Hardy, Joseph	7	Harrison, Samuel	133, 235
Hardy, Mary	8	"Harrison's Plains"	23
Hardy, Phillis	7	Harrison, Tabathia	23
Hardy, Rachell	7	Harrison, Thomas	23
Hardy, Robert	7	Harrison, Verlinda	24, 193
Hargedon, Jane	103	Harrison, William	
Hargedon, Mark	103, 157		23, 105, 221, 241
Harington, Elizabeth	47	Harryman, George	92
Harington, John	47	Harryman, John	92
Harington, Richard	47	Harryman, Thomas	95
"Harman's Towne"	232	Hart, Richard	112
"Harmonton"	122	"Harton"	38
Harper, Ann	188	Hartsfield, Godfrey	129
Harper, John	207	Hartshorne, John	103
Harper, Margaret	232	Harvey, Ann	240
Harper, W.	140	Harvey, Elizabeth	121, 240
Harper, William	119, 138	Harvey, James	120, 173
Harr, Mary	224	Harvey, Jane	120, 121
Harr, William	224	Harvey, John	120
Harrett, Elizabeth	28	Harvey, Mary	121
Harrington, David	106	Harvey, Newman	120
Harrington, John	47	Harvey, Samuel	120, 121, 240
Harris, Amy	163	Harvey, Sarah	120
Harris, Ann	163	Harvey, Thomas	120, 121
Harris, Aug.	129	Harwood, Pheby	219
Harris, Benjamin	66, 185	Hasbon, William	85
Harris Ck.	63	Haskin, Joseph	191
Harris, Edward	153	Haskin (Haskins), Mary	
Harris, Elizabeth	207		191, 235
Harris, George	35, 129	Haskin (Haskins), Thomas	
Harris, James	4, 16, 89, 145, 230		191, 235
Harris, Jane	207	Haskin, William	191
Harris, Jean	35	Haskins, Richard	52
Harris, John		Hassitt (Hassett), Robert	
	41, 117, 140, 165, 207		103, 104, 156

INDEX

	PAGE		PAGE
Hastwell, Thomas	64	Heatch, Catherine	186
Hatch, John	97	Heatch, Elgatt	186
Hatch, Mary	97	Heatch, Elizabeth	186
Hatch, Sarah	97	Heatch, Ezekiel	164
Hatch, Thomas	97	Heatch, John	164, 186
Hatchison, Vincent	152	Heatch, Mary	186
Hatfield, John	162	Heatch, Nehemiah	164
Hatton, Elizabeth	47	Heatch, Rachel	164
Hatton, Joseph	198	Heatch, Samuel	164, 186
Hatton, Mary	198	Heatch, Solomon	164, 186
"Hatton's Garden"	47	Heatch, Thomas	164
"Hawkins"	145	Heatch, William	164, 186
Hawkins, Ann	216	Heath, Adam	9
Hawkins, Elizabeth	90, 216	Heath, Charles	212
Hawkins, Ernault	90	Heath, Dormand	86
Hawkins, John	216, 220	Heath, James	212
Hawkins, Mary	216	Heath, James Paul	212
Hawkins, Robert	216	Heath, Mary	212
Hawton, Richard	257	Heath, Thomas	157
Hawton, Thomas	3	Hedges, Cathren	236
Haycock, John	214	Hedges, Charles	236
Hayle, John	25	Hedges, Dorcas	236
Haynes, Hezekiah	54	Hedges, Jonas	236
Hayes, Elizabeth	149	Hedges, Joseph	236
Hayes (Hays), James	50, 149	Hedges, Joshua	236
Hayes, John	11	Hedges, Ruth	236
Hayward, Ann	179	Hedges, Samuel	236
Hayward, Francis	13	Hedges, Solomon	236
Hayward, Henry	149, 179	Heighe, Ann	254
Hayward, Mary	179	Heighe, James	254
Hayward, Thomas	115	Heirs, Isabella	206
Hayward, William	115	Helborn, Elizabeth	103
Haywood, William	49	Helborn, Frances	103
"Hazard"	21, 28, 57, 96, 196	Helborn, John	103
Head, Adam	31, 147	Helborn, William	103
Head, Ann	31	Hellen, Ann	2
Head, Bigger	4, 86	Helsby, Elizabeth	178
Head, Edward	90	Helsen, Andrew	140
Head, Mathew	90	Hemingway, John	99
"Head of Mitchell's Choyce,"	35	Hemsley, Ann	141
Head, Priscilla	31	Hemsley, Vincent	7, 141
"Head Range"	183	Hemsley, William	31
Heard, Elioner	250	Hemsly, Mary	202
Heard, Elizabeth	250	Henderson, Bushap	188
Heard, Ignatius	250	Henderson, George	170
Heard, John	250	Henderson, Jacob	174
Heard, Luke	250	Henderson, Thomas	170
Heard, Marke	249	Hendricks, John	115
Heard, Mathew	250	Henly, Darby	13
Heard, Priscilla	250	Henly, Edmond	13
Heard, Susannah	250	Henly, John	13
Heard, William	249	Henry, John	18, 213
"Hearn Quarter"	86	Henry, Robert Jenkins	18
"Heart's Content"	174	"Henry, The"	99
"Heart's Delight"	233	Henwood, William	44
Heasy, Thomas	8	Hepburn, Patrick	30
Heatch, Adam	164, 186		

INDEX

Herbert (Herbertt), Elizabeth	31, 171, 240
Herbertt, Charles	171
Herbertt, Edward	171
Herbertt, James	171
Herbertt, John	171
Herbertt, Margaret	171
Herbertt, Mary Ann	171
Herbertt, Rachel	171
Herbertt, Sarah	171
Herly, Sarah	66
Herman, Augustus	16
Herman, Eph. Aug.	195
"Heron's Lott"	67
"Heereford"	55
Herring Ck.	82, 135, 234
Hervey Town	147
Hewes, Anne	50
Hewet, Elice	138
Hewet, Elizabeth	149
Hewet (Huet), John	138
Hewet, Mary	149
Hewet, Richard	93, 149
Hewet (Hewell), Robert	56, 138
Hews, Christopher	138
Hews, Richard	138
Hewton, Allon	213
Heyden, Susannah	24
"Hiccory Ridge"	55
Hickcock, Sarah	54
Hickee (Hickey), David	41, 110
Hickee, Mary	41
Hickman, Elizabeth	248
Hickman, James	25, 248
Hickman, Thomas	25, 248
Hickman, William	195, 246
Hicks, Denwood	212
Hicks, Elizabeth	174
Hicks, Henry	212
Hicks, John	212
Hicks, Liven	212
Hicks, Mary	174, 212
Hicks, Roger	174
Hicks, Sarah	212
Hicks, Sophia	3
Hicks, Thomas	174
Higgens, Nicholas	171
Higginbothom, Oliver	168
Higgins, John	161
Higgins, Mary	133, 161
Higgins, William	161
Higginson, Edward	221
Higgs, Elinor	166
Higgs, Sarah	21
High, Robert	27
"High Suffolk"	186
Hill, Agathia	179
Hill, Amy	179, 231
Hill, Charles	33
Hill, Clement	233
Hill, Comfort	226
Hill, Hannah	179
Hill, James	39
Hill, John	179, 222, 226
Hill, Johnson	226
Hill, Mary	62, 222, 223
Hill, Neomy	226
Hill, Rachell	65
Hill, Richard	134, 179, 201, 203, 231
Hill, Robert	226
Hill, Sarah	231
"Hill's Platt"	231
Hill, Thomas	94
Hill, William	179
Hill, William Stevens	226
Hills, George	145
Hillard, John	236
Hillard, Thomas	236
Hilleary, Elianor	93
Hilleary, Elizabeth	93
Hilleary, Henry	93
Hilleary, John	93
Hilleary, Sarah	93
Hilleary, Thomas	93
Hilleary, William	93
Hillen, John	11, 27, 131
Hillen, Mary	27
"Hillen's Adventure"	49, 229, 251
Hillen, Solomon	27
"Hinchman's Neck"	212
Hinckley, Francis	150, 163
Hincly, John	50
Hindman, Jacob	191
Hinds, Vincent	156
Hines, Thomas	28
Hinkson (Hington), John	29, 167
Hinsey, John	61
Hinton, Thomas	131
"His Lordshipp's Favour".	235
Hitch, Samuel	164
Hitchcock, George	131, 162
Hitchcock, John	122
Hobbs, Dorothy	203
Hobbs, John	203
Hobbs, Joseph	203
Hobbs, Margaret	203
Hobbs, Samuel	203
Hobbs, Susannah	203
Hobbs, Thomas	238

INDEX

	PAGE		PAGE
Hobbs, William	203	Holliday, William	132
"Hobson's Choice"	15, 97	Hollingsworth, Zebulon	151
Hodge, Robert	164	Hollinshead, Francis	12
Hodgkin, Thomas	98, 128, 163	Hollinsworth, John	227
Hodgkins, Charles	171	Hollon, Nehemiah	243
Hodgkins, Daniel	171	Hollyday, Edward	152
Hodgkins, Jane	171	Hollyday, James	214
Hodgson, Rowland	188	Holmes, Frances	106
Hodgson, Samuel	204	Holmes, William	151
Hodgston, Alexander	197	Holmond, James	85
Hodgston, Katherine	197	Holston, Charles	35
Hodgston, Samuel	197	Holt, Obadiah	195
Hodson, John	115, 149, 172	Holtham, Charles	78
"Hodson's Adventure"	149	Holtham, James	78
"Hog Harbour"	101	Holtham, John	78
"Hog Quarter"	71	Holtham, Joseph	78
"Hog Ridge"	211	Holtham, Katherine	78
Hogg, Andrew	74	Holtham, Mary	78
Hogg, Catherine	74	Holtham, Nicholas	78
Hogg, James	74	Holtham, William	78
Hogg, John	74	"Holy Spring"	23
"Hogg Neck"	48	"Honest Man's Lott"	55
"Hogg Quarter"	187	Honor, Edward	82
"Hogg Range"	157	Hood, William	132
Hogg, Sarah	74	Hook, Susana	105
"Hoggs Down"	165	Hooker, Roger	158
Holadgr, Elizabeth	252	Hooper, Henry	14, 127, 207
Holand, Larda	82	Hooper, John	11
Holand, Margaret	82	Hooper, Roger	126
"Holbourn"	149	"Hopewell"	51
Holeger, Philip	251	Hopewell, Ann	240, 249
Holland, Benjamin	19	Hopewell, Elizabeth	240, 249
Holland, Elizabeth	39, 191, 235	Hopewell, Francis	119, 249
Holland, Francis	234	Hopewell, Hugh	240
Holland, Israel	19	Hopewell, John	240, 249
Holland, John	31	Hopewell, Joseph	240, 249
Holland, John Frances	253	Hopewell, Mary	249
Holland, Joseph	17	Hopewell, Richard	41, 220, 240, 249
Holland, Leath	19		
Holland, Margaret	17	Hopewell, Susannah	249
Holland, Mary	235	Hopewell, Thomas Francis	240
Holland, Mary Elizabeth	19	Hopewell, William	240
Holland, Nehemiah	19	Hopking, John	242
Holland, Richard	79	Hopkins, Alice	244
"Holland's Addition"	235	Hopkins, Benjamin	106, 122, 222, 250
Holland, Sarah	17		
Holland, Thomas	192, 234	Hopkins, Dennis	44, 106, 221
Holland, Utie	235	"Hopkins' Destiny"	33
Holland, William	39, 161, 191, 234	Hopkins, Edward	242
		Hopkins, Elizabeth	52, 246
Hollaway, Mary	6	Hopkins, James	222
Holliday, Benoni	132	Hopkins, Jean	245
Holliday, Catherine	132	Hopkins, Jonathan	71
Holliday, Elizabeth	132	Hopkins, Joseph	106
Holliday, Leonard	194	Hopkins, Nathaniel	44
Holliday, Rachel	132	"Hopkins' Point"	106, 222
Holliday, Sarah	132	Hopkins, Rebecca	21

INDEX

xxxi

Name	PAGE
Hopkins, Richard	108
Hopkins, Samuel	226
Hopkins, Sarah	106
Hopkins, Stephen	246
Hopkins, Susannah	106
Hopkins, Thomas	70, 223
"Hopyard"	133
Horn, Edward	210
Horn, Henry	219
Horn, Patients	219
Hornbee, James	64
"Horne"	143
Horney, James	21
Horney, Solomon	138
"Horsepond Ridge"	67
Horsley (Horsely), James	23, 81, 197
Horsman, John	169
"Horton's Fortune"	15
Hoskins, Ann	77
Hoskins, Bennett	181
Hoskins, Elizabeth	13
Hoskins, Mary	13
Hoskins, William	13
Houchin, William	135, 203
Hough, Edmond	37, 187
Houlston, Joseph	37
Houston, Joseph	187
"Howard and Porter's Range"	55
Howard, Cornelius	55
Howard, George	34
Howard, James	176
Howard, John	8, 175, 176
Howard, Mary	176
Howard, Peter	176
"Howards"	254
"Howard's Inheritance"	42
"Howard's Interest"	55
"Howard's Mount"	56
Howard, Thomas	11, 35, 37, 176, 210
Howard, William	176
Howell, Ann	84, 224
Howell, Mary	185
Howell, Mordecai	26
Howell, Thomas	84
Howell, William	26, 224
Howes, William	213
Howgill, Elenor	151
Howgill, James	151
Howison, John	152
Hows, Harris	20
Howson, Elizabeth	78
Howton, Richard	167
Hoxon, James	199
Hoxton, Hyde	169

Name	PAGE
Hoy, Ann	57
Hoy, Dorset	57
Hoy, Isaac	57
Hoy, James	56
Hoy, Margaret	57
Hoy, Martha	57
Hoy, Mary	57
Hoy, Paul	56
Hubbart, Charles	53
Hubbart, Daniel	53
Hubbart, Mary	53
"Hubbart's Addition"	53
Hubanks, William	31
"Huckleberry Forrest"	55
Huddlestone, Margaret	88
Huddlestone, Rachel	88
Huddlestone, William	88
Hudson, Betty Holland	75
Hudson, Catherine	141
Hudson, David	75
Hudson, Frances	141
Hudson, John	75, 141
Hudson, Margaret	75, 226
Hudson, Mary	75, 141
Hudson, Peggy	75
Hudson (Hutson), Richard	29, 75, 141
Hudson, Robert	75
Hudson, Samuel	243
"Hudson's Desire"	77
Hues, John	2
Hues, Margaret	204
Huet (Hewet), John	138
Huff, John	206
Hugg, Jane	117
Hugg, Johana	117
Hugg, Mary	117
Hugg, Thomas	117
Hugg, William	117
Hughes, Anne	195
Hughes, Elizabeth	138
Hughes, James	173
Hughes, William	189
Hughs, David	95
Hughs, Jonathan	215
Hughs, Samuel	200
Hull, David	1, 153, 184
Hull, Ferdinando	5
Hull, Joseph	5
Humberstone, George	153, 154
Hume, Ann	12
Hume (Humes), James	12, 27
Hume, Sarah	12
Humes, Hercules	235
Humphrey, Richard	1, 204
Humphries Run	200

INDEX

Humphries (Humphry), Thomas..7, 8, 9, 71, 94, 164
Humphrys, John 44
Hungerford, Mary 134
Hunt, William 207
"Hunt's Chance" 235
Hunter, Rebecca 67
Hunter, Robert 171
Hunter, Roger 171
"Hunters-field" 67
"Hunter's Kindness" 56
Hunter, Thomas 67
Hunter, Walter 77
Hunter, William 67, 201
Hunting Ck., 77, 85, 172, 206, 254
"Hunting Fields" 206
Hurd, Robert 49
Hurley, Ann 53
Hurley, Darby 53, 112
Hurley, Elizabeth 112
Hurley, John 53, 112
Hurley (Hurly), Mary..53, 112
Hurley, Roger 53, 112
Hurlock, James 214
Hurlock, Mary 214
Hurst, Samuel 119, 143
Hussey, Michael 31
Hust, Emanuel 6
Hust, James 207
Hutchings, George 9
Hutchings, Mary 9
Hutchings, William 9
"Hutchins' Addition" 216
Hutchins, Ann 216
Hutchins, Elizabeth ...216, 218
Hutchins, Fran. (Francis, Frances) 24, 78, 218
Hutchins, John 216
"Hutchins' Lott" 216
"Hutchins' Neglect" 216
Hutchins, Nicholas 216
Hutchins, Susana 216
Hutchins, Thomas 216
Hutchins, William 77
Hutchinson, Michael 125
Hutchinson, Thomas 41
Hutchison, William 10, 148
Hutson (Hudson), Richard 29, 75, 141
Hutton, John 41
Hutton, Mary 41
Hyde, Jane 241
Hyde, John 36, 83, 84, 241
Hyde, John & Co. 167, 175
"Hyer-Dier-Lloyd" 62
Hyland, Nicholas 180
Hynson, Charles 206
Hynson, Isabell 58
Hynson, Richard 102
"Hynson's Haven" 206
Hynson, Thomas ..58, 123, 168
Hyws, Thomas 50

I

Idle, Ester 43
Ijams, George 133
"Indian Bones" 72
"Indian Field" 233
Indian Town 81
Inglish, Margaret 26
Inglish, Thomas 26
Ingram, Abraham 86, 92
Ingram, Peasley 86
Ingram's Ck. 143, 149, 158
"Inlargement of Dorrington" 2
Innes, Cornelius 62
Innes, John 62
Innes, Mary 62
Innes, Samuel 62
Ireland 19, 103, 133, 135
Ireland, Thomas 195
Iron, Hills 130
Irons, William 158
Irving, Briget 246
Irving, John 246
Isaac, Richard 169
Isaacke, Sutton 30
"Isaac's Addition" 245
"Isaac's Enlargement" 100
"Isaac's Folly" 116
"Isaac's Inheritance" 100
Island Ck. 58
"Island Neck" 13
Islenton 191
Iyds, Mary 110

J

	PAGE		PAGE
Jackson, Edward	100	Jarrard, James	169
Jackson, George	89, 156, 198	Jarrett, Graves	165
Jackson, Jacob	1	Jeames, John	170
Jackson, Joseph	90	Jeangaukin Neck	246
Jackson, Mary	136, 198	Jeffery, Josias	48, 117
Jackson, Rebecca	66	Jefferys, Ann	80
Jackson, Robert	119	Jefferys, Dorothy	80
Jackson, Thomas	90, 140, 156	Jefferys, Edward	80
Jackson, William	172, 198	Jefferys, George	80
Jacob, Benjamin	41	Jefferys, John	80
Jacob, Elizabeth	41	Jefferys, Mary	80
Jacob, John	41	Jefferys, Thomas	80
Jacob, Joseph	41	Jelly, Elizabeth	173
Jacob, Richard	41	Jelly, Francis	111, 159, 173
Jacob, Samuel	41	Jelly, Jonathan	141
"Jacob's Hope"	150	Jenifer, Daniel	77, 90, 117, 155
Jacob, Susannah	41	Jenifer, Daniel of St. Thomas	117, 155
Jacobs, Thomas	120	Jenifer, Elizabeth	155
Jaction, William	154	Jenifer, Mary	77
Jadwyn, Bartholomew	30	Jenifer, Michael	77
Jadwyn (Jadwin), Elizabeth	30, 106	Jenifer, Michael Parker	77
Jadwyn, Hannah	30	Jenkins, Ann	40, 139
Jadwyn, Isabel	30	Jenkins (Jinkins), Aves	216
Jadwyn, Jeremiah	30	Jenkins, David	152
Jadwyn, Joseph	30	Jenkins, Edward	40, 139
Jadwyn, Martha	30	Jenkins, George	40, 79
Jadwyn, Priscilla	30	Jenkins (Jinkins), Joseph	216
Jadwyn, Rachell	30	Jenkins, Mathew	151
Jadwyn, Robert	30	Jenkins, Richard	162
Jadwyn, Samuel	30	Jenkins (Jinkins), Sarah	216
Jadwyn, Solomon	30	Jenkins (Jinkins), Thomas	40, 193, 216
Jadwyns, Mary	30	Jenkins (Jinkins), William	40, 105, 139, 216
Jamaica	104	Jennings (Jenings), Edmund	208, 241
"James' Addition"	122	Jennings, Thomas	208
"James' Choice"	87	Jeromes, Michaell	70
James, Edward	104	Jessep, William	41
James, Evan	120	"Job's Fishing Hole"	164
James, Howell	236	Jobson, Thomas	16
James, Isaac	120	Joce, Nicholas	121
James Island	174	"John and Isaac's Lott"	100
James, Jonathan	45	John, Lewis	17
"James' Progress"	182	Johns, Abraham	217
James, Rachel	120	Johns, Ann	15
James, Sarah	130	Johns, Benjamin	15, 128
James, Walter	28	Johns, Charity	15
James, Watkins	28	Johns, Clary	15
James, Williabe	147	"Johns' Desire"	174
James, William	28	Johns, Eliza	128
Jameson, Thomas	5	Johns, Hannah	217
Janson, Henry	110	Johns, Hugh	15
Jarad, Mathew	76		
Jarboe, Peter	119		
Jarman, Henry	226		

INDEX

	PAGE
Johns, Isaac	68, 76, 93, 129
Johns, Kinsey (Kensey)	68, 128
"Johns' Lott"	50
Johns, Mary	15, 129
"Johns' Point"	174
Johns, Rachel	129
Johns, Richard	128
Johns, Samuel	128
Johnson, Ambrose	112
Johnson, David	249
Johnson, Edward	66, 180
Johnson, Elizabeth	80, 132, 136
Johnson, George	132
Johnson, Henry	21
Johnson, Jacob	151
Johnson, John	37, 58, 161, 230, 231
Johnson, Joseph	192, 232
Johnson, Mary	230, 231
Johnson, Nathan	69
Johnson, Richard	230, 231
Johnson, Robert	80, 83
Johnson, Ruth	112
"Johnson's Delay"	232
"Johnson's Forrest"	230
Johnson, Susannah	230, 231
Johnston, John	85
Johnston, Samuel	137
"Johnston's Lott"	166
Johnston, Susannah	137
"Joice's Plantation"	194
Joie, Jonas	244
Jolley, Jonathan	141
"Jonas' Chance"	81
"Jones' Adventure"	75
Jones, Alice	52
Jones, Ann	58, 130
Jones, Arthur	30, 254
Jones, Benjamin	71, 72, 110, 180, 215
Jones, Cadwallader	235
Jones, Cornealy	190
Jones, Daniel	238
Jones, Eleanor	72, 130
Jones, Elizabeth	127, 182, 251
Jones, Evan	54
Jones, Finch	164
Jones, Frances	102
Justice, Mary	243
Jones, George	61, 98

	PAGE
Jones, Griffith	64, 145, 251
Jones, Hannah	230
Jones, Jacob	199
Jones, James	52, 126, 206
Jones, Jennet	127
Jones, John	9, 19, 24, 130, 137, 142, 160, 174, 220, 249
Jones, Joshua	86
Jones, Leonard	244
Jones, Lewis (Lewin)	52, 57, 130
Jones, Margaret	72, 249
Jones, Mary	130, 145
Jones, Mitchel	72
Jones, Nicholas	251
Jones, Precious	193
Jones, Richard	60
Jones, Robert	19, 21, 63, 96, 102, 126
Jones, Samuel	32, 130, 254
Jones, Sarah	64, 127, 174
Jones, Savil	60
Jones, Thomas	69, 156, 205, 206, 229
Jones, William	1, 127, 169, 251
Jonson, Mary	118
Joppa	93, 232, 233
Jopson, Susannah	51
Jopson, Thomas	51
Jordan, Aaron	243
Jordan, Edmond	134
Jordan (Jordain), John	15, 134
Jordan, Jonas	238
Jordan, Justinian	110, 185
Jordan, Margaret	134
Jordan, Mary	134, 185
Jordan, Thomas	185
Jordan, Walter	134
Jordan, William	134
"Joseph His Place"	2
"Joseph's Lott"	92
"Joseph, The"	198
Jowles, Knellum Greenfield	176
Jowles, Rebecca	176
Jowles, Sybill	176
Joy, Elizabeth	39
Jubb, Helen	136
Jubb, Robert	42, 136
Justice, John	243

INDEX

K

	PAGE		PAGE
Kannerly, Thomas	173		162, 168, 183, 184, 205,
Karby, John	214		206, 208, 227-231, 250-252
Kay (Key), Robert	230	Kent, Elizabeth	12
Kearsey, John	130	Kent Island, 7, 39, 47, 59,	
Keating, William	137		101, 104, 141, 156, 168,
Keech, Courts	177		188, 197 ... 206
Keech, Elizabeth	177	Kent, Joseph	12
Keech, James	177	Kent, William	12
Keech, Mary	177	Kerby, Deborah	41
Keene, Ezekiel	149	Kerby, David	95, 114
Keene, Henry	143, 188	Kerby, Elizabeth	95, 114
Keene, Mary	143	Kerby (Kirby, Karby),	
Kees (Keese), Catherine	190	John	95, 214
Kellee, Benjamin	153	Kerby, Lemmon	95
Kellee, Joseph	123, 124, 153	Kerby, Michael	114
Kelly, Catherine	232	Kerby, Rebecca	95
Kelly, Dennis	232	Kerby, Richard	95
Kelly, James	64	Kerby, Thomas	41
Kelly, Joseph	199	Keron, David	76
Kelly, Mary	199	Kerry, William	161
Kelly, Michael	132	Kersey, Francis	69
Kemp, Constant	138	Kersey, Jane	69, 105, 143
Kemp, Elizabeth	138	Kersey, John	69
Kemp, Jane	138	Kersey, Mary	69
Kemp, John	22, 150	Kew, Susannah	250
Kemp, Martha	138	Key, Philip	20, 98, 113, 232
Kemp, Mathias	152	Key, Richard Ward	20
Kemp, Rachel	138	Keys, John	223
"Kemp's Lott"	138	Keys, William	174
Kemp, William	22, 138	Kibburne, Charles	54
Kenady, Ann	94	Kid, William	254
Kenady, Cathern	94	Kidder, James	14, 96, 179
Kenady, John	94	Kidder, Thomas	14
Kenady, Margaret	94	"Killglass"	73
Kenady, Timothy	94	"Killingsworth"	1
Kendall, James	60, 67, 181	Killiowe, William	126
Kendall, Robert	132	Killmenum	225
"Kendall's Delight"	54	King and Queen Parish	117
Kendrick, James	230	King, Arthur	72
Kenley, Ann	230	King, Benjamin	32
Kennard, John	228	King, Capell	92, 166
Kennard, Joseph	228	King, Charles	41, 78
Kennard, Phillip	124, 168, 228	King, Elenor	32, 72
Kennerly, Joshua	96, 179, 247	King, Elizabeth	32, 52
"Kennerly's Addition"	247	King, Ephraim	246
Kennerly's Mill	158	King, James	147
Kennerly, Sarah	247	King, Jesse	72
Kennerly, William	247	King, John	32
Kennett, William	226	King, Nehemiah	243
Kenny, John	221	King, Planner	72
Kenslaugh, Domk.	87	King, Richard	220
Kent Co., 1, 4, 5, 15, 24, 48,		King, Robert	32, 246
49, 57, 64, 71, 87, 88, 90,		"King's Chase"	72
95, 110, 113, 121-125,		King's Ck.	222
145, 146, 152-154, 160,		King, Susannah	240

INDEX

	PAGE		PAGE
King, Upshur	72	Kirby, Elizabeth	229
King, Whittington	32	Kirby, Mathew	222
King, William	110	Kirby, Thomas	249
King William School	241	Kirke, Alice	144
King, Zerebel	72	Kirke, John	169, 191
Kinghart, Thomas	254	"Knave, Keep Out"	196
Kingsbury, Elizabeth	12	Knight, Thomas	46
Kingsbury, James	12	Knock, Henry	251
Kinkey, James	66	Knott, Edward	184
Kinner, Sarah	236	Knott, George	126
Kinsey, Francis	88	Knowles, James	156
"Kinsey's Choyce"	28		

L

	PAGE		PAGE
Lake, Abraham	15	Laramur (Larimur), Thomas	147, 244
Lake (Leake), John	210	Large, Joseph	201
Lakey, John	86	Larimore, William	244
Lamb, Anthony	21	Larimur, John	244
Lamb, Francis	64	Larimur, Wenefret	244
Lamb, Mary	64	Larkin, Capt.	132
Lambden (Lamdin), William	22	Larkin, Elizabeth	202
Lambdin (Lambdon), Daniel	144, 197	"Larkin's Hills"	202
		Larkin, Thomas	202
Lambdin, Elizabeth	144	"Larkinton"	150
Lambdin, George	144	Larranc, Daniel	242
Lambdin, John	144	Larrimore, Thomas	244
Lambdin, Sarah	144	"Laste"	50
Lambdin, William	144	Latham, Joshua	152
"Lamberton's Addition,"	46, 69	Laurence, Benjamin	139
Lampton, Mark	119	Lawes, Thomas	19, 225, 226
Lanahan, Isabella	152	Lawley, Eliza	132
Lancaster, Benjamin	195	Lawn, Edward	161
Lancaster, John	181	Lawrance, Benjamin	65
Lancaster, Thomas	60, 134	Lawrance, John	46
Landin, William	108	Lawrence, Theodosia	241
"Land of Goshen"	54	Lawrence, Tobias	133
"Land Over"	16	Lawrenson, Lawrence	100, 195
"Land's Lane"	23	Laws, Bolitha	136
Lane, George	113	Laws, Elijah	136
Lane, John	31	Laws, Esther	136
Lane, Mary	87	"Laws His Last Chance"	136
Lane, Richard	238	Laws, John	136, 225
Lane, Samuel	239	Laws, Rachel	136
Lane, Timothy	189	Laws, Sarah	136
Lang, John	82	Laws (Lawes), Thomas	19, 225, 226
Lang, Robert	176		
Langake, George	186	Laws, William	136
Langford's Bay	4, 227	Lawson, John	90
Langham, George	193	Lawson, Samuel	58
"Langham's Rest"	193	Lawson, Thomas	182
Langly, Abraham	110	Lawson, William	182
Langly, John	41, 110	Layfield, George	186
Langly, Susannah	110	Layfield, Thomas	32, 165, 186
Lanham, Richard	60	Layton, Richard	53
"Lan's Chance"	38	Layton, Thomas	50

INDEX

	PAGE		PAGE
Layton, William	50	Levinis, Rice	50
Leach, Samuel	254	"Levin's Chance"	111
Leads, Danl.	4	Lewen, Eliza.	236
Leads, John	59	Lewin, Richard	84
"Leaf's Chance"	216	"Lewis"	108
Leake, Anne	210	Lewis, Charles	202
Leake, Catherine	210	Lewis, Elinor	132
Leake, John	210	Lewis, Elizabeth	132, 197
Leake, Katherine	210	Lewis, Francis	124
Leake, Richard	210	Lewis, James	135
Leake, William	210	Lewis, Johannah	159
Leaster, Peter	184	Lewis, John	66
Lecompte, Anthony	112	Lewis, Kely	132
Lecompte, Blanch	112	Lewis, Richard	66
Lecompte, Charles	112	Lewis, Sarah	104
Lecompte, John	112, 143, 190	Lewis, Thomas	159
Lecompte, Mary	115	Lewis, William	82
Lecompte, Philemon	63	Lidster, Abigail	245
Lecompte, Sarah	115	Lidster, Jane	244
Lecompte, William	115	Lidster, Jesse	245
Lee, Edward	69	Lidster, Leah	245
Lee, Elizabeth	220	Lidster, Thomas	244
Lee, Henry	254	Lidster, William	244
Lee, James	253	Lillingston, Susannah	204
Lee, Philip	175, 220	Linch, Cornelius	164
Lee, Robert	220, 254	Linch, James	253
Lee, William	81	Linch, Martha	92
Leeds, Esther	138	Linch, Mary	253
Leeds, John,	69, 105, 138, 197, 241	Linch, Patrick	92
Leghorn	162	Lindsay, Alice	181
Legrant, Charles	109	Lindsay, Anthony	181
Leigh, John	219	Lindsay, Samuel	181
Lemaister, Richard	117	"Lindsey"	40
"Lemaister's Delight"	117	Lingoe, Annsly	76
Lemaster, Catherine	161	Lingoe, Daniel	76
Lemaster, Thomas	161	Lingoe, Jacob	76
Lemmon, Hickford	220	Lingoe, John	76
"Lemster"	68	Lingoe, Nathaniel	76
Lenan, John	222	Lingoe, Rachel	76
Lenex, Elizabeth	11	Lingoe, Richard	76
Lenoir, Mary	90	Lingoe, Robertson	76
"Lently"	104	Lingoe, William	76
Leonard, Charles	146	"Linkhorn"	248
Leonard, Eleanor	146	Linthicum, Francis	203
Leonard, Elizabeth	146	Linthicum, Hezekiah	82, 237
Leonard, Henry	146	Litell, John	119
Leonard, James	146	Litell, Mary	119
Leonard, John	146	Littell, Assilla	194
Leonard, Katherine	146	Littell, Thomas	194
Leonard, Patrick	146, 173	Little Choptank	77
Leonard Town	210	"Little Harness"	239
Leonard, Winefrid	146	Little, Mary	215
Lesage, David	7	Little Run	201
Lester, Anne	120	"Littleton"	54
"Letchworth"	178	"Littleworth"	155, 189, 227
Levinis, Elizabeth	50	Liverpool	58
Levinis, Peter	50	Lizenbey, Charles	89

INDEX

	PAGE
Lizenbey, Jane	89
"Llewellin's Ridge"	70
Lloyd, Ann	235
Lloyd, James	235
Lloyd, John	22
Lloyd, Margaret	236
Lloyd, Philemon	22
Lloyd, Robert	235
Lock, Allen	17
Lock, Sarah	238
Lock, William	235, 238
Locker, Elizabeth	189
Locker, Walter	189
Lockhart, John	102
Lockwood, Mary	226
"Locust Thicket"	29
Loder, Richard	2
Lokey, John	86
Lomas, Elizabeth	163
Lomas, John	163, 237
Lomas (Lomax), Margaret	238, 248
"Lombey"	117
London, 3, 15, 36, 44, 59, 83, 84, 103, 124, 134, 142, 161, 162, 176, 204, 208, 231	236
London, Eleanor	189
London, James	189
London, Rebecca	189
London, Richard	189
London Town	82, 208
"Long Acre"	33, 45, 73, 99
Long, Anthony	60
Long, David	225
"Long Delay"	138
Long, Elizabeth	172, 207
Long, Jane	225
Long, Jeoffrey, 62, 166, 225, 245	
Long, John	172
Long, Mary	225
"Long Point"	141, 233
Long, Randel	45
Long, Samuel, 109, 111, 172, 225	
Long, Sewell	225
Long, Sollomon	248
Long, Thomas	172
"Longtown"	33
Loockerman, Dorothy	173
Loockerman, Elizabeth	173, 191
Loockerman, Govert	3, 173, 191
Loockerman, Jacob	172, 190
Loockerman, John, 172, 190, 247	
Loockerman, Magdalen	190, 205
Loockerman, Mary	191, 235
Loockerman, Nicholas	172, 191
Loockerman, Sarah	190
Loockerman, Thomas	172, 191
Lorde, Edward	142
"Lott"	33
Loveday, John	139
Lovel, William	89
Lowd, Charles	67
Lowder, Ann	89
Lowder, Charles	89
Lowder, Jane	89
Lowder, Joan	89
Lowder, Sarah	89
Lowe, Doroth	113
Lowe, Eleanor	29
Lowe, Elizabeth	22
Lowe, John	22, 144
Lowe, Margaret	7
Lowe, Mary	22
Lowe, Nicholas	7, 113, 236
Lowe, Thomas	22
Lowe, William	180
"Lower Bennet"	218
Lower Marlborough	254
"Low Ridge"	13
Lowry, Elinor	242
Lowry, Robert	242
Loyd, Ben	60
Loyd, Francis	79
Loyd, John	60
Loyd, Sarah	60
"Loyd's Triangle"	132
Loyd, Thomas	60
Lucus, Susana	178
Ludwigg, William	133
"Lundee"	170
Lurtey, John	63
Lurtey, Nicholas	63
Lurtey, Sarah	63
Lusby, Aaron	239
Lusby, Ellenor	239
Lusby, Jacob	239
Lusby, John	239
Lusby, Mary	239
Lusby, Rachell	239
Lusby, Robert	81
Lusby, Samuel	239
Lusby, Thomas	239
Lutheran Church	168
Lyle, Priscilla	121
Lyle, Robert	121
Lyle, Samuel	173
Lynch (Linch), James	253
Lynes, William	4
"Lynn"	37, 228
Lynn, Aaron	86
Lyons Ck.	10

M

	PAGE		PAGE
M'Callom, Mark	212	Mackdaniell, Daniel	150
McCallagan, Ann	243	Mackdaniell, Edward	150
McCallagan, Brigrett	243	Mackdaniell, Laughlin	150
McCallagan, Hugh	243	Mackdaniell, Mary	150
McCallagan, Moses	243	Mackeele, Thomas	112
McCarter, Alexander	222	Mackell (Mackeel), Thomas	77
McClean, James	227, 252	Mackemee, Roger	111
McClellum, Joseph	245	Mackeny, Alexander	27
McClester, George	246	Mackeny, Elizabeth	27
McClester, John	246	Mackeny, John	27
McClester, Neal	147	Mackeny, Sarah	27
McClester, William	246	Mackey, Isabella	152
McCormick, John	73	Mackinnys, Ann	24
McDaniel, Daniel	87	Mackinnys, Elizabeth	24
McDaniel, James	146	Mackinnys, Joseph	24
McDaniel (MacDaniell), William	43	Mackoy, Mary	197
McDonnell, Elizabeth	18	Mackoy, William	197
McDonnell, Margaret	18	Macky, Elizabeth	235
McDonnell, Moses	18	Macky, James	235
McDonnell, Naomi	18	Macleane, Hector	48
McGachan, Alexander	252	Macnemara, Michael	238
McGachan, Sarah	252	Maconchie (Maconokie), William	23, 40, 117
McIntosh, James	238	Madbury's Br.	209
McKnight, John	165, 195	Madcaff, Jane	142
McManus, John	95	Madcaff, William	142
McWilliams, Thomas	249	Madden, John	38
"Mabel Enlarged"	138	Maddocke, Edward	213
Macarthy, Ann	192	Maddocke, Jane	213
Maccarthy, John	192	"Maddox Folly"	29
Macclannahan, Thomas	126	Maddox, Thomas	9
Maccomus, Alexdr.	11	Maddux, Daniel	19
Maccubbin, Mary	43	Madkins, John	231
Macdanell, Brian	5	Madrey, William	1
Macdaniel, James	87	Magatee, Edward	148
Macdaniell (Maccdanill), John	30, 110	Magee, David	136
		Magee, Elizabeth	136
Macdaniell, Thomas	49	Magee, George	136
MacDaniell (McDaniel), William	43	Magee, John	136
		Magee, Moses	136
Mace, Anne	183	Magee, Peter	136
Mace, Elizabeth	183	Magee, Samuel	136
Mace, John	183	Magill (Makgill), David	48
Mace, Josias	14, 144	Magothy, R.	82
Mace, Mary	14	Magruder, Alexander	60
Mace, Nicholas	183	Magruder, Robert	176
Mace, Thomas	183, 231	Magruder, Samuel	17
Macey, Thomas	206	Mahone, Eliza	88
Macgill, James	174	Mahone, Mary	88
Mackalester, David	96	Mahone, Thomas	88
Mackalester (Mackcallister), John	96	"Maiden Fancy"	55
		"Maiden's Bower"	101
Mackalester, Patrick	96	"Maiden's Head"	83
Mackall, Benjamin	24	"Maidstone"	
Mackclanan, James	84	83, 84, 85, 129, 133, 134, 173	

INDEX

	PAGE
"Mair and Colt"	97
"Major's Choice"	55, 64, 120
"Major's Lott"	194
Makeel, Ann	77
Makeel, Clare	77
Makeel, Eliza	77
Makeel, John	77
Makeel (Mackell), Thomas	77
"Make Peace"	33
Makey (Macky), Elizabeth	235
Makey (Macky), James	235
Makgill (Magill), David (Daniel)	48
Makgill, Grace	48
Makmorie, Anna	137
Makmorie, James	92, 137
Makmorie, Margaret	249
Malane, Peter	200
Malden, Eleanor	218
Malden, Francis	218
Malden, James	68, 218
Mallard, Peter	108
Mallord, James	92
Mallooney, Martha	95
Mallooney, Mathew	95
Manaquicy	236
Manardo, Peter	94
Manering, Jane	80
Manhony, Eliza	89
Manhony, Mary	89
Manhony, Thomas	89
Maning, Cornelius	79, 99
Mankin, Eliza	152
Mankin, John	152
Mankin, Joseph	152
Mankin, Josiah	152
Mankin, Stephen	65, 152
Mankin, William	152
Manly, Peter	80
Manner, Jane	31
Mannery, Hannah	224
Mannery, John	224
Mannery, Thomas	224
Manning, Mary	37
Manoken	19, 165, 246
Mansell, William	193, 194
Mansfield, Robert	146
Marchant, John	21
Marchment, William	136
Mardrain, John	170
Marer, William	108
"Margaret's Delight"	87, 229
Mariarte, Anne	43
Mariarte, Arden	43
Mariarte, Daniel	43
Mariarte, Elinor	43
Mariarte, Margaret	43

	PAGE
Mariarte, Ninian	43
"Market Overton"	193
Markland, Charles	11, 113
Marlborough Town	188
Marles, Elizabeth	97
Marlow, Anne	128
Marlow, Edward	128
Marlow, Elinor	128
Marlow, Hannah	157
Marlow, James	128
Marlow, Joseph	128
Marlow, Mary	128
Marlow, Richard	128
Marlow, William	128
Marrill, Joseph	186
Marrish, Thomas	39
"Marsh Neck"	20
"Marsh Point"	72
"Marsh Range"	206
Marsh, Thomas	7
Marshaul, Mary	91
Marshy Ck.	80
Martin, Ann	220
Martin, Eliza	143
Martin, George	45
Martin, James	226
Martin, Nehemiah	18
Martin, Sarah	45
"Martin's Rest"	214
Martin, William	220
Martineaux, Nicholas	217
Maryland Point	23
"Mary's Widdower"	13
"Mason's"	48
Mason, Elizabeth	98
Mason, John	98
Mason, Mary	98
Mason, Mathew	98, 104
Mason, Rebeccah	80
Mason, Robert	98
Mason, Susannah	98
Masters, William	30
Massy, Daniel	6
Massy, Henry	57
Massy, James	6
Massy, Mary	6
Massy, Nicholas	6
Massy, Peter	6
Massy, Thomas	6
Massy, William	6
Massy (Mastin), Charles	51
Massy, Mastin, Charles	51
Mathewe, John	76
Mathews, Chidly	236
Mathews (Matthews), David	8, 47
Mathews, Elizabeth	8, 120

	PAGE		PAGE
Mathews, John	8, 217	Meo, Francis	26
Mathews, Martha	8	Mercer, Francis	165
Mathews, Mary	9, 193	Meredith, Humphrey	238
Mathews, Patrick	248	Merideth, John	177
Mathews, Rachel	8, 102	Merrifield, Jacob	134
Mathews, Roger	120, 215, 217	"Merrikeen's Branches"	11
Mathews, Samuel	8	"Merrikeen's Inheritance"	11
Mathews, Sarah	8	"Merrikeen's Outlet"	11
Mathews, Teague	8	Merriken, Ann	11
Mathews (Matthews), Thomas	23, 193	Merriken, Dianna	11
		Merriken, Hugh	11
Mathews (Mathewes), William	8, 11	Merriken, John	134
		Merriken, Joshua	11
"Mattapany Sewall"	220	Merriken, Mary	11
Mattawoman	29, 39, 98	Merrill, John	186
Mattenby, Charles	29	Merrill, Joseph	186
Mattison, Ann	113	Merryman, Johannah	163
Mauldin, Francis	100	Merryman, John	163
Mawdesly, John	189	Mersey, Alexander	61
Maxfield, Robert	103	Mersey, Comfort	61
Maxwell, Anne	64, 120	Mersey, Esther	61
Maxwell, Asael	64, 120	Mersey, Johnson	61
Maxwell, Hannah	120	Mersey, William	61
Maxwell, James	64, 120	Mezick, Jacob	245
Maxwell, Robert	103	Miars, Ann	6
May, John	200	Miars, Stephen	6
May, Peter	107	Michall, William	176
Mayhew, Mary	133	Michiell, John	132, 202
Maynadier, Daniel	11, 107	Micllbee, John	82
Maynard, John	224	Middalton, Mary	53
Mead, Mary	233	Midford, Bullin	49
"Mears"	128	Midford, Thomas	49
Mecandlis, Alexander	4	"Middle Branch"	57
Mecerthy, Ann	192	"Middle Ground"	171
Mecoy, William	74	"Middle Land"	174
"Medcalf Chance"	55	"Middle Neck"	54
Medcalf, John	81	"Middle Plantation"	248
"Medcalf's Mount"	55	Middlemore, Josias	64, 192
Medcalf, Thomas	81	Middleton, Eleanor	198
Medcalf, William	210	Middleton, Elizabeth	198
Medley, Ann	70, 192	Middleton, Hatton	198
Medley, Bennet	192	Middleton, John	5, 17, 188
Medley, Clement	192	Middleton, Luckner	5
Medley, George	192	Middleton, Penelope	198
Medley, Often	192	Middleton, Penelope Hatton	198
Meek, Christopher	202	Middleton, Sarah	198
Meek, Elinor	132	Middleton, Studly	5
Meek, James	202	Middleton, Susana	198
Meek, John	202	Middleton, Thomas	198
Meek, Ruth	202	Middleton, William	128
Meekes, Robert	228	"Might Have Had More"	92
Meekins, Isaac	183	Milburn, John	41
Meekins, John	14, 28, 143, 157	"Milerne"	51
Meekins, Mary	157	Miles, Anne	6
"Melborne"	99	Miles, Edward	6
Melowny, James	242	Miles, Elizabeth	6, 10
Melton, Richard	37	"Miles End"	118

INDEX

Name	Page
Miles, Henry	6
Miles, John	6, 10, 171
Miles, Margaret	6
Miles, Mary	6
Miles, Nicholas	6
Miles, Priscilla	6
Miles, Rachell	10
Miles, Thomas	10
"Milford Might"	91
"Mill Land"	55, 224
Millard, James	108
Millard, Mary	99
Miller, Arthur	57, 88
Miller, Elizabeth	233
Miller, Isaac	17
Miller, Michael	123, 233
"Miller Purchase"	95
Miller, Sarah	57
Miller, Theophilus R.	154
Miller, William	78
"Millford and Taylor's Lott"	55
"Millner"	193
Mills, Elizabeth	99
"Mills End"	88
Mills, John	25, 79, 98
Mills, Mary	79, 98, 179
Mills, Napper	25
Mills, Nicholas	98
Mills, Robert	18, 179
Mills, Susanna	99
Mills, William	117
Milton, Abraham	227
"Minges' Chance"	23
Minion, Robert	131
Minner, Peter	50
"Minor's Adventure"	234
Minskie, John Samuel	238
"Mistake"	194
Mitchell, Edward	154
Mitchell, John	48
Mitchell, Robert	116
Mockbie, Brock	36
Mohoney, Thomas	219
Moll, David	205
Moll, John	205
Moll, Mary	205
Mollikin, Ann	152
Mollone, John	78
Monocks, John	143
Monocosey R.	30
Monokin R.	174
Monrow, Alexander	243
Monrow, Daniel	73
Montague, William	208
Montigu, Ann	30
"Montserada"	232
Moorcock, John	15
Moorcock, Susannah	15
Moore, Ann	88
Moore, Archibald	85
Moore, Barbara	85
Moore, Edward	74
Moore, Elizabeth	52, 88
Moore, Euphen	85
Moore, James	85
Moore, John	88, 125
Moore, Richard	31
Moore, Robert	85
Moore, William	52, 88
Moore, Williamina	239
More, Edward	103
More, George	168
More, Joseph	180
More, Mary	31
More, Thomas	151
More, William	151, 244
Morey, John	29
Morgan, Charles	214
Morgan, Elizabeth	214
Morgan, Hugh	214
Morgan, James	214
Morgan (Morgain), John	127, 214
Morgan, Mary	214, 218
Morgan, Robert	214
Morgan, Samuel	214
Morgan's Ck.	168, 228
"Morgan's Resarve"	96
Morgan, Thomas	86
Morgin, Elender	70
Morgin, Elizabeth	70
Morgin, Mary	70
"Morgin's Choice"	96
Morgin, William	70
Morris, Elizabeth	5, 10
Morris, Daniel	248
Morris, Isaac	187
Morris, Jacob	33
Morris, Jemina	33
Morris, John	88, 183
Morris, Joseph	33
Morris, Mark	33
Morris, Mary	39
Morris, Randolph	147, 176
Morris, Temperance	33
Morris, Thomas	3, 39
Morris, William	62
Mosell, Thomas	110
Moses, Agnes	18
Moses, Fenton	18
Moses, Margaret	18
Moses, Naomi	18
Moses, Sarah	18
"Moses' Lott"	35

INDEX

xliii

	PAGE		PAGE
Mosgrove, Katherine	190	Muney, James	72
Mostin, James	125	Muney, Richard	72
Mostin, Thomas	125	Munk, William	153
"Mother's Gift"	81	Munn, Jonathan	238
Mouat, James	208, 237	Murdock, James	194
Moutlon, Lydea	12	Murdock, John	188
Moulton, Walter	12	Murdy, Alexander	63
Mount Calvert	10	Murdy, Margaret	114
"Mount Hope"	116, 140	"Murfey's Hazard"	131
"Mount Pleasant"	73, 163, 233	Murphey, Roger	90, 124
Movat, James	150	Murphey, Thomas	47
"Moxam"	115	Murphy, Edward	131
Mudd, Thomas	148	Murphy, James	123
Mugg, Peter	210	Murphy, John	131
Muir, Adam	247	Murphy, Margaret	123
Muley, Jane	195	Murphy (Murphey) Mary	
Mulikin, Ann	110		71, 124, 131
"Muling Field"	33	Murphy, Pryscilla	123
Mullen, Patrick	119	Murphy, William	95
Mullikin, Patrick	69	Murray, David	226
Mullinton, James	204	Murray, Henry	183
Mumford, Charles	72	Murray, John	177, 187
Mumford, James	72	Murray, William	
Mumford, Jemima	72		14, 115, 159, 169, 212
Mumford, Sarah	226	Murrett, Anthony	146
"Mumford's Lott"	72	Murrey, Richard	72
Mumford, Solomon	72	Muschamp, George	240
Mumford, Thomas	72	Muse, John	159
Mumford, William	72	Musgrave, Charles	182
Mumford Wricksam	72		

N

	PAGE		PAGE
Nairne, James	243	Neale, Henry	39, 167
Nairne, John	243	Neale, James	39, 181
Nairne, Mary	243	Neale, Jane	148, 181
Nairne, Robert	243	Neale, John	246
Nailer, Ann	79, 114	Neale, Margaret	40
Nailer, Deborah	79	Neale, Mary	113, 167, 246
Nailer, John	79	Neale, Mary Ann	181
Nailer, Mary	114	Neale, Mildred	40
Nailer, William	79, 114	Neale, Raphael, 20, 39, 118, 181	
Nanjemy	10, 40	Neale, William	39, 167
Nanticoke R.,		"Neck, The"	12
50, 72, 109, 111, 147, 158		Nedles, Edward	91, 96
"Narbrough"	102, 227	"Neglect, The"	67, 235
Narris, Mary	139	Nelson, Ambrose	112
Navarre, Mary	84	Nelson, John	112, 252
Neal, Ann	11	Nelson, Martha	112
Neal, Arthur	11	Nelson, Richard	112
Neal, Charles	11	Nelson, Sarah	190
"Neal's Lott"	99	Nelson, William	190
Neal, Susanna	11	Nesham, Mary	9
Neale, Benjamin	39	Nevett, Thomas	3
Neale, Charles	145, 167	Nevitt, William	126
Neale, Edward	148, 167	"New Design"	216
Neale, Elizabeth	39, 181	"New Holland"	58, 76

INDEX

	PAGE		PAGE
New Jersey	217	Nicholson, Mathias	36
"New Munster"	58, 195	Nicholson, Nehemiah	245
New Town, 80, 99, 135, 205,	234	Nicholson, Richard	8
New York	204	Nicholson, Roger	245
Newcastle	16, 17	Nicholson, Samuel	208
Newell, John	24	Nicholson, Sarah	36, 226
Newell, Mary	55	Nicholson, Susanna	226
Newell, Peter	179	Nicholson, William	207
"Newington"	195	Nickson, Mary	69
Newland, Sarah	188	Nicoll, James	58
Newman, Jonathan	151	Nicolls, Moses	207
Newman, Mary	151	Noads, Ann	55
Newman, Samuel	151	Noble, Ann	232
"Newman's Lott"	69	"Noble Desire"	232
Newman, Walter	151	Noble, Ellen	169
Newman, Daniel	89	Noble, George	30
Newport,	226	Noble, Grace	245
Newson, James	239	Noble, Isaac	245
"Newton"	99	Noble, James	136
Newton, Edward	109, 158	Noble, Jane	245
Newton, Frances	109, 159, 173	Noble, John	169, 245
Newton, John	76, 158	Noble, Joseph	220
Newton, Mary	109, 159	Noble, Mary	7
Newton, Richard	159	Noble, Robert	7
Newton, Sarah	159	"Noble's Chance"	69
"Newton's Purchase"	158	Noble, Susanna	245
Newton, Thomas	44	Noble, William	232
Newton, William	159	"Nod"	38
Nichalson, Er.	7	Noeland, Daniel	86
Nicholas, Abel	17	Noeland, Edward	86
Nicholas, Griffith	17	Noeland, Mary	86
Nicholas, Margaret	17	Noeland, Sarah	86
Nicholas, Mary	17	Noeland, Thomas	86
Nicholas, Tabitha	186	Noleman, Anthony	184
Nicholason, Abraham	195	"None So Good"	95
Nicholason, Martin	195	"None Such"	29, 75
Nicholls, Elizabeth	113	Nordrik, Richard	152
Nicholls (Nickolls, Nicols), Henry	113	Norman, Job	63
		Norman, Richard	63
Nicholls, Isaac	173	Norman, William	177
Nicholls, Mary	113	Norris, Caleb	154
Nicholls, Rebecca	63	Norris, Clare	27
Nicholls, Susannah	113	Norris, John	27, 162, 250
Nicholls, Thomas	113	Norris, Mary	40
Nichols, Jonathan	3, 20	"North Britton"	29
Nicholson, Anne	208	North East	17, 88, 160
Nicholson, Beale	207	North, John	190
Nicholson, Benjamin	208	North, Robert	253
Nicholson, Betty	8	Norton, Ann	15
Nicholson, Charles	36	Norton, Elizabeth	15
Nicholson, Edward	208	Norton I	93
Nicholson, Elizabeth	36, 208	Norton, John	15
Nicholson, Filles	8	Norton, Mary	15
Nicholson, James	8, 36, 187, 245	Norton, Richard	15
Nicholson, John	36, 204, 245	Norton, William	15
Nicholson, Joseph	33, 36, 208	"Norway"	128
Nicholson, Mary	8, 36	Norwood, Anne	208

INDEX

Name	Page
Norwood, Hannah	208
Norwood, Samuel	55
Norwood, Sarah	55
"Norwood's Beale"	208
"Norwood's Fancy"	55
Nottingham	97, 128, 175
Nowland, Denis	105
Noxon, Thomas	222
Numbers, Elizabeth	94
Numbers, John	66
Numberson, John	4
Nuner, Ann	14
Nuner, Mary	14
Nuner, Sarah	14
"Nuner's Lott"	14
Nuner, Thomas	14
Nuthall, Brent	245
Nutter, Ann	249
Nutter, Charles	53
Nutter, Christopher	137, 146, 249
Nutter, Elizabeth	249
Nutter, Margaret	137, 249
Nutter, Matthew	137, 249
Nutter, William	249

O

Name	Page
Oakley, John	233
Oarde, William	20
Oates, John	222
"Obligation"	82, 240
O'Brian, Rebecka	74
O'Bryon, Patrick	104
O'Bryon, Thomas	104
"Ocbrook"	99
O'Dear (Dear), John	249
O'Donnell, Owen	195
Offley, Robert	140
Oglesby, Thomas	6
Okane, Elizabeth	25
Okane, John	25
"Olbias Choyce"	99
Oldham, Edward	91, 139
Oldham, Hannah	91
Oldham, John	91, 139
Oldham, Martha	139
Oldham, Mary	139
Oldson, Henry	140
Old Town	38, 227
Oley, Sebastian	135, 136
Olfent, Thomas	176
Oliver, Ann	7
Oliver (Olifer), Cutbud	30
Oliver, Robert	214
O'Neale, Bryan	153
"O'Neal's Dezearts"	193
Opeckan	236
Oram, Jane	26
Oram, Robert	26
Orchard, Jacob	70
Orchard, John	231
Orchard, Mary	70
"Orchard's Neck"	153
Orem, Andrew	144
Orme, John	154
"Orphan's Gift"	16
"Orphan's Increase"	157
Orrell, Christopher	78
Orrell, Elizabeth	3
Orrell, Francis	3
Orrell, Glidwell	3
Orrell, John	3
Orrell, Martha	3
Orrell, Mary	3
Osborn, John	23
Osborn, Mary	85
Osborne, Benjamin	30
Osburn, Elizabeth	13
Osburn, Joseph	13
Osburn (Osborn), Thomas	13, 148
Ouldfilds, Sarah	30
Oulds, William	185
Outen (Outten), Abraham	8, 19
Outen, Elizabeth	8
Outen, John	8
Outen, Samuel	8
Outen, Thomas	8
"Outrange"	230, 231
Owen, Edward	188
Owen, James	178
Owen, Patrick	178
"Owen's Outland Plains"	214
Owen, Thomas	85
Oxford	91, 144
"Ox Head"	72
Ozborn, John	203
Ozburn, William	215

P

Name	Page
Paca, Aquila	232
Paca, Frances	232
Paca, Martha	184
Pacett, Jane	93
"Padget"	238
Page, Mary	57

INDEX

	PAGE
Page, Ralph	57
"Page's Purchase"	57
Pagett, Elizabeth	86
Pagett, Thomas	86
Pagget, Benjamin	28
Pagget (Paggitt), Mary	28, 128
"Pagget's Purches"	28
Pagget, William	28
Pain, Henry	199
Pain, James	199
Pain, Leonard	199
Pain, Mary	248
Pain, Susan	132
Pain, Tecla	199
Pain, Thomas	199
Paine, Edmond Bury Godfrey	182
"Painter's Rest"	15
Palmer, Oliver	64, 206
Palmer, Sarah	206
Pamunkey	9, 23
Panton, James	18
Pantry, Elizabeth	93
"Paradise"	98
Parandeor (Parandier), James	181, 190
Parandeor, John	181, 190
"Parander's Lott"	181
Parish, Elizabeth	68
Parish (Parrish), William	89
Parker, Charles	186
Parker, Elinor	186
Parker, Fielder	128
Parker, George	116, 186
Parker, John	186
Parker, Leah	186
Parker, Philip	186
Parker, Richard	21
Parker, Robert	51
"Parker's Adventure"	187
Parker, Samuel	186
Parker, Sarah	186
"Parker's Park"	96
"Parker's Range"	30
Parker, Tabitha	187, 226
Parker, Thomas	144
"Park Hall"	254
Parlett, Martin	92
Parlett, Thomas	114
Parlett (Parlot) William	114, 185
Parnham, Anna Maria	213
Parnham, Eliza	213
Parnham, John	167, 213
Parnif, Elizabeth	31
Parnif, John	30

	PAGE
Paromer, Elizab.	146
Parr, John	52, 145
Parran, Alexander	6
Parran, Esther	117
Parran, John	6
Parratt (Parrott), Aaron	38, 222
Parratt (Parrott), Benjamin	91, 96, 171
Parratt, Eliazor	91
Parratt, Hannah	91, 106
Parratt, Jane	91
Parratt, Leah	90
Parratt, Mary	91
Parratt, William	91
Parremore, Ann	63
Parrish, Edward	42, 89, 232
Parrish, John	89
Parrish, Mary	43
Parrish, Richard	89
Parrish, Sarah	89
Parrish (Parish), William	89
Parsons, Elizabeth	169
Parsons, Mary	122
Parsons, Solomon	122
"Partner's Desire"	33
"Partnership"	15, 156
"Part of Dundee"	65
"Part of Littleton"	54
"Part of Merryman's Lott"	163
"Part of Roper Gray"	55
"Part of Scotland"	119
"Part of Sewell's Increase"	54
"Party Chance"	230
Pasmore, John	234
"Pasqueum"	97
"Pass Watter"	53
Passons, Sarah	245
"Pasture, The"	9, 29
Patey, John	75
Patrick, Daniel	35
Patrick, John	244
Patrick, Mary	35
Patrick, Mathew	35
Patrick, Rodger	35
Patrick, Roger	35
"Patrick's Folley"	225
Patshall, Joseph	171
Pattason, Mary	2
Pattison, Gillbird	41
Patuxent Plantation	54
Patuxent R., 4, 15, 26, 133, 175, 199, 233	254
Paul, Eliza	199
"Paul's Folly"	33
Pavett, Jane	93
Peach, Joseph	169

INDEX

Name	Page
Peake, Peter	210
Pearce, Andrew	57
Pearce, Ann	250
Pearce, Benjamin	122
Pearce, Daniel	57
Pearce, Gideon	122
Pearce, Isabella	122
Pearce, Jeremiah	104
Pearce, Mary	57, 104
Pearce, Sarah	57
Pearce, William	228
Pearson, John	93
Pearson, Robert	57
Peck, Benjamin	108, 109
Peck, Daniel	108
Peck, John	108, 145
Peck, Sarah	145
Pecker, Hannah	190
Peele, John	162
Peers, Henry	65
Peers, Sarah	65
Peiott (Picott), Peter	50
Peirce, Edward	219
Peirce, Elinor	219
Peirce, John	219
Peirce, Robert	219
Peirce, Thomas	219
Peirpoint, Francis	44
Pell, Mary	146
Pemberton, Benjamin	139
Pemberton, Elizabeth	63
Penkinde, Michael	209
Penn, Mark	3
Pennewell, Anne	116
Pennewell, Charles	116
Pennewell, George	116
Pennewell, John	116
Pennewell, Richard	116
Pennewell, Thomas	116
Pennewell, William	116
Pennington, James	18
Pennington, John	222, 223
Pennington, Mary	18
Pennington, William	60
Pennsylvania	38, 251
Penoyre, Danet	18
"Penray"	117
Peper, Elizabeth	34
Peper, Mary	34
"Peper's Delight"	34
Peper, William	34
Perey, Sarah	159
Perey, William	96
Perkins (Pearkins), David	146, 152
Perkins, Elizabeth	162
Perkins, Francis	145
Perkins, Isaac	64
Perkins, Jacob	152
Perkins, Mary	162
Perkins, Sarah	110
Perkins, William	162
Perraro, Mary	230
Perre, John	194
Perrie, Samuel	188
Perrie, William	98
Perry, Daniel	141
Perry, Edward	224
Perry, John	141, 194, 224
Perry, Joseph	233
Perry, Margaret	141
Perry, Mary	141, 219
Perry, Robert	34
Perrymore, William	63
"Persimon Point"	174, 211
Person, Sarah	159
Peterkin, David	247
Pettey, James	60
Pettibone, Joseph	82
Pettibone, Phillip	82
Pettibone, Richard	82
Pettycoat, John	55
Phanton, William	156
Phelps, Mary	83
Phelps, Richard	83
Phelps, Ruth	83
Phelps, Susannah	202
Phelps, Walter	81, 83, 240
Phibble, Ann	201
Phibble, John	201
Philadelphia	21, 204, 238
Philips, Elizabeth	94
Philips, Manardo	94
Philips, Samuel	94
"Phillip and Jacob"	29
"Phillips' Adventure"	68
Phillips, Alice	68
Phillips, Anne	9, 118
Phillips, Anthony	157
Phillips, Betty	9
Phillips, Christopher	60
Phillips, Dorothy	9
Phillips, Hannah	143
"Phillips' Island"	157
Phillips, James	9, 68, 118, 157
Phillips, Jane	9
Phillips, Martha	157
Phillips, Mary	68, 157
Phillips, Michll (Mitchell)	13
Phillips, Philemon	60
Phillips, Phillip	68, 80
Phillips, Richard	9
Phillips, Robert	48
Phillips, Roger	8

INDEX

	PAGE
Phillips, Sarah	9
Phillips, Thomas....36, 56,	68
Phillips, William 142,	235
Phipps, Ann	246
Phipps, John	246
Pickum, Christian	161
Picott (Peiott), Peter ..50,	94
Pidgeon House Ck......21,	32
Pilbert, John	23
Pile, Joseph	213
Pile, Richard	194
Pile, William	194
Piles, Anne	26
Piles, Elizabeth	26
Piles, Francis	26
"Piles' Gift"	194
Piles, Hunter	67
Piles, James	26
Piles, John 26,	67
Piles, Leonard 11,	26
Piles (Pile), Mary......67,	194
Piles, Richard	26
Piles, William	67
"Pilgrim's Rest"	242
Pinder, Edward	143
Piner, John	124
Piner, Mathew 124,	205
Piner, Rachel	124
Piner, Thomas	124
"Piney Hedge"	43
"Piney Neck"	22
Pinkston, Martha	112
"Pinkstone's Fancy"	170
Pipe Ck.	133
Piper, Isaac	18
Piper, William	196
Pitca Ck.	61
"Pitchcroft"	155
Pitts, Andrew	203
Pitts (Pitt), John, 174, 221,	238
Pitts, Mary	174
"Pitts' Neck"	207
Pitts, Robert	19
Plafay, Phillip	16
"Planter's Delight"	69
Plowden, Edmund	48
Plummer, Abezar	65
Plummer, Elizabeth	65
Plummer, George	65
Plummer, James	64
Plummer, Jerome	64
Plummer, John	65
Plummer, Micajah	65
Plummer, Phebe	65
Plummer, Philemon	64
Plummer, Priscilla	65
Plummer, Samuel 10,	64

	PAGE
Plummer, Sarah	10
Plummer, (Plumber, Plumer), Thomas, 64, 70,	99
Plummer, Yate	65
Plunkett, Richard	62
Plunkett, Winnifritt	62
Plasstid, Susanah	242
Plater, Oxford 241,	254
Poalk, Robert	50
Pocomoke District	124
Pocomoke R. 73,	186
"Point Look-Out"	111
"Point Patience"	20
Polk, Ann 13,	32
Polk, David 19,	32
Polk, Elizabeth	32
Polk, Grace	21
Polk, Henry	32
Polk, James	32
Polk, Jane 13,	32
Polk, John 13,	32
Polk (Polke), Joseph ...19,	21
Polk, Margaret	32
Polk, Mary 21,	32
Polk (Poalk), Robert ..21,	50
"Polk's Folley"	13
Polk, Sarah	32
Polk, Thomas	21
Polk, William .....:.13, 21,	33
Polke, Charles	92
Polke (Pollock), Magdalen 19,	32
Pollard, Jeffry	204
Pollard, Tobias	242
Pollet, John 13,	33
Pollet, Mary	33
Pollett, Magdalen	19
Pollett, William	19
Polly, Edward	172
Pomankka	193
Ponteny, Ann	105
Ponteny, William	104
Poole, Basil	169
Poole, David 159,	173
Poole, Richard 41,	240
Poore, Nicholas	88
Poorter, Sarah	108
Pope, James	62
Poplar Hill Hundred	142
"Poplar Land"	68
"Poplar Neck"....191, 207,	223
"Poplar Ridge".......36, 50,	179
"Pork Hall"	133
Porter, Francis	245
Porter, Giles	64
Porter, Hugh	245
Porter, James	245

INDEX

	PAGE		PAGE
Porter, Jonathan	245	Presbury, James	172
Porter, Joshua	245	**Preston, Barnard**	130
Porter, Leah	245	Preston, Daniel	130
Porter, Mary	245	Preston, Elizabeth	215
Porter, McKemie	245	Preston, James	130
Porter, Nehemiah	245	Preston, Sarah	130
Porter, Richard	113	"Preston's Chance"	130
Porter (Poorter), Sarah, 61, 108		"Prevention"	29, 31
Porter (Pourter), William 35, 61, 245		Prewett, Andrew	60
		Price, Alexander	164
"Portland"	83	Price, Andrew	223
Portobacca 5, 134, 148, 161, 167, 213		Price, Ann	70, 164
		Price, Benjamin	131
Portobacca Parish..24, 160, 220		Price, Clare	105
Pottenger, Robert	36	Price, Crispin	164
Potter, Alee	35	Price, Elizabeth	70
Potter, Ann	35	Price, Evan	70
Potter, Catherine	35	Price, Eve	164
Potter, Henry	35	Price, Frances	105
Potter, Thomas	35	Price, Henry	70, 105
Potts, Maj.	49	Price, Hester	70
Pounce, William	57	Price, Johana	105
Pouncey, George	68	Price, John	186
"Pound's Second Addition"	149	Price, Mary	186
Pourter, William	35	Price, Rachel	164
Powel, Eleanor	149	Price, Richard	13
Powel, Henry	203	Price, Solomon	164
Powel, James	203	Price, Susannah	204
Powel, Josias	203	Price, Thomas Taylor	179
Powel, Richard	140	Price, William	70, 105
Powel, William	203	Prince Frederick Town	128
Powell, Charles 112, 143, 158, 232		Prince George's Co., 1-3, 9-11, 16, 17, 22, 26, 29, 36, 37, 41, 43, 55-57, 60, 64-67, 81, 85, 86, 93, 97, 99, 111, 113, 128, 133, 150, 154, 155, 163, 169, 170, 174, 175, 180, 181, 188, 189, 193-195, 198, 212, 213, 224, 231, 233, 236, 239	254
Powell, Daniel	107, 221		
Powell (Powel), Elizabeth 43, 203, 221			
Powell, Gary	112		
Powell (Powel), Howell 191, 221			
Powell, John	200, 221	Pritchard, Ann	178
Powell, Joseph	221	Pritchard, James	46, 178
Powell, Mary	43	Pritchard, John	178
Powell, Robert	180	Pritchard, Joseph	215
Powell (Powel), Sarah 140, 191, 221		Pritchard, Margaret	46
		Pritchard, Obadiah	46
Powell (Powel), Susannah 203, 221		Pritchard, Richard	178
		Pritchard (Pritchart), Samuel	46, 79
Power, John	148		
Power, Mary	148	Pritchard, Sarah	46
Power, Richard	126	Pritchard, William	178
"Poynton Manner"	193	Procter, Elizabeth	118
Pratt, Dinah	38	Procter, Hugh	174
Pratt, Elinor	79	"Prospect"	175
Pratt, Gemelin	69	"Providence"	55, 69
Pratt, Joseph	132	Pruet, James	60
"Pratts' Neck"	82		
Pratt, Thomas	38		

INDEX

	PAGE		PAGE
"Pryers"	122	Purnell, Martha	61
Pulling, Elenor	190	Pursell, John	70
Pullman, Richard	154	Pye, Alice	167
Purit, Elizabeth	52	Pye, Charles	40
Purit, William	52	Pye, Jane	167
Purnall (Purnal), Richard	78, 84	"Pye's Chance"	160
Purnall, Thomas	78	"Pye's Hardshift"	40
Purnell (Purnall), John	19, 244	"Pyney Plaine"	82

Q

Quaker Neck 5
Quakers, 1, 14, 59, 123, 125, 129, 131, 133, 139, 140, 176, 183, 221, 229, 240, 247
"Quantico" 137, 175
Quarry, Robert 54
"Quarter, The" 85
Quatermus, Isaiah 53
Quatermus, Margaret 112
Quatermus, Patrich ...53, 112

Queen Anne's Co., 5-7, 22, 23, 30, 31, 38, 39, 47, 59, 66, 80, 81, 89-91, 95, 101-104, 122, 125, 126, 139-141, 156, 157, 166, 177, 188, 189, 197, 198, 209, 227 231
Queen Ann Parish 174
Queen Ann Town......128, 134
Quick, Charles 209
Quinton, Walter 67

R

Rabbitts, William	156	Randolph, Thomas	22
Rabbling, Joseph	43	"Range"	55, 81
Rabeling, John	175	"Rantom"	194
Radford, Henry	99	Rasin, Abraham	229
Radford, John	99	Rasin, Benjamin	251
Radford, Sarah	99	Rasin, George	229
"Radford's Chance"	99	Rasin, John	252
Radford, Thomas	99	Rasin, Joseph	229, 251
Rage, Sarah	28	Rasin, Mary	183, 229, 251
Raily, Henry	31	Rasin, Philip	251
Raily, John	31	Rasin, Thomas 1, 153, 184, 208, 229, 251	
Raily, Michael	31	Rasin, William	229
Raily, Richard	31	Ratcliffe, Hannah	177
Raily, William	31	Ratcliffe, William	177
Rakes, Ann	209	Rathell (Rathall), John	106, 214
Rakes, John	209	"Rattle Snake"	254
Rakes, William	60, 209	"Rause"	29
Ralleigh, Frances	247	Raven, Luke	51
Ralleigh, Mary	247	Rawles, John	188
Ralleigh, Morries	247	Rawley, James	126
Ralleigh, William	247	Rawley, William	126
"Ramsey's Folley"	166	Rawlings, Ann	6
Randall, Aquila	28	Rawlings, Anthony 67, 68, 76, 207	
Randall (Randal), Catherine	28, 135	"Rawlings' Choyce"	6
Randall, Christopher	28, 169	Rawlings, Daniel	6
Randall, Hannah	28	Rawlings, Isaac	6
Randall, Roger	28		
Randall, Urith	28		

INDEX

	PAGE
Rawlings, John	44, 76, 157
Rawlings, Mary	76
"Rawlins' Chance"	140
Ray, Alexander	106
Ray, John	68, 70
Rayman, William	163
Raymon, Jonathan	90
Raymon, John	90
Raymon, Judie	90
Raymon, Priesley	90
Read, Clark	78
Read (Reade), George	78, 121, 153, 220
Read, (Reads), John	48, 78, 117, 245
Read, Mary	221
Read, Owen	48
Read, Peter	145
Read, Richard	163, 221
Reaves, William	92
"Recsom Plaines"	227
"Redding"	96
Reddish, John	33, 136
Redgrace (Readgrave), Alice	110
Redgrave, Abraham	64, 87
Redgrave, Isaac	64
Redgrave, Jacob	64
Redgrave, John	64
Redgrave, Joseph	64
Redgrave, Martha	64
Redgrave, William	64
"Red Lane"	47
Redman, Daniel	210
Redman, Elizabeth	210
Redman, Jeremiah	210
Redman, John	210
"Redman's Hardship"	137
Redman, Solomon	210
Redman, Vincent	210
Reech, William	64
Reed, John	245
Reed, Robert	58
Reed, Rosanna	126
Reed (Reede), William	58, 126
"Reerguard's Addition"	104
Rees, Thomas	17
Reeves, Jane	25
Reeves, John	83
Reeves, Thomas	24, 160, 176
Reeves, Ubgatt	199
"Refuse, The"	60
Regestor, Francis	91
"Regulation"	172
Reid, William	215
Relley, James	46
Rensha, Thomas	45
Rensha, Underwood	45
"Residue of Clark's Enlargement"	55
Revill, Randell	187
"Revisis Lott"	92
Reviss, Thomas	92
Rewark, Timothy	159
Rewastico Ck.	196
Rex, John	63
Reynolds, John	240
Reynolds, Mary	188
Reynolds, Robert	227
Reynolds, William	161
Rhine (Rine), Derby	128, 175
Rhoads, Richard	253
Rhodes, Nicholas	199
Ricards, Mary	90
Rice, Abraham	78
Rice, Catharine	180
Rice, David	180
Rice, Elizabeth	14
Rice, Mary	180
Rice, Thomas	180
Rice, William	180
"Rich Levell"	218, 251
"Rich Range"	79
"Rich Ridge"	50
Rich, Stephen	139
Richalls, Robert	52
Richards, John	9
Richards, Mary	90
"Richard's Pleasure"	23
Richards, Warner	204
Richards, William	164
Richardson, Anna	44
Richardson, Benjamin	105
Richardson, Charles	34
Richardson, Daniel	105
Richardson, David	44
Richardson, Eliza	44
Richardson, Hannah	44
Richardson, James	34
Richardson, John	34, 44
Richardson, Joseph	43
Richardson, Katherine	79
Richardson, Mary	34
Richardson, Mathew	88
Richardson, Nicholas	231
Richardson, Rebecca	43
Richardson, Richard	144
Richardson, Robert	34
Richardson, Ruth	105
Richardson, Samuel	34, 44
Richardson, Sarah	43
"Richardson's Outlet"	233
Richardson, Tabitha	34, 44

INDEX

Name	Page
Richardson, William	34, 44, 105, 134
Richeson, Benjamin	59
Richeson, Daniel	59
Richeson, Nathan	59
Rickco, Beniones	89
Ricketts, David	151
Ricketts, Edward	95
Rickits, Jane	121
Rickits, Philip	121
Riddle, Andrew	229
Riddle, Walter	127
Rider, John	212
Ridgaway (Rigaway), Samuel	71, 110
Ridgaway, Sarah	71, 110
Ridgaway, William	110
"Ridgely and Tylors Chance"	133
Ridgely, William	26
"Ridges"	72
Ridgley, Anne	42
Ridgley (Ridgely), Charles	89, 149
Ridgley, John	149
Ridgley, Nicholas	42
Ridgley, Pleasance	149
Ridgley, Rachel	42
Ridgley Rebecca	42
Ridgley, Ruth	42
Ridgley, Sarah	42
"Ridgley's Beginning"	56
Ridgway, Benjamin	141
Ridgway, Elizabeth	141
Ridgway, William	141
Rigby, John	171, 218
Rigdon, George	130
Right, Martha	247
"Righton"	85
Rigin, Samuel	34
Rilince, Files	31
Rimner, Edward	108
Rind, Abigl.	132
Ringgold, Elias	160, 252
Ringgold, James	57, 125, 168, 228
Ringgold, Mary	252
Ringgold, Thomas	57
Rix, Mary	254
Roach, Alice	33
Roach, Charles	33
Roach, Isaac	33
Roach, John	33
Roach, Michael	35
Roach, Sabarah	33
Roach, Stephen	33
Roach, William	33
Roberts, Alice,	114
Roberts, Ann	93, 144, 185
Roberts, Bartholomew	182
Roberts, Edward	32
Roberts, Elizabeth	45
Roberts, Frances	93
Roberts, George	133
Roberts, Isaac	68
Roberts, James	151
Roberts, Jane	68
Roberts, John	45, 64, 93, 132, 222
Roberts, Judith	222
Roberts, Kinsey	68
"Roberts' Luck"	201
Roberts, Lucinda	93
Roberts, Margaret	68
Roberts, Mary	94, 185
Roberts, Nicholas	182
Roberts, Patience	68
Roberts, Priscilla	68
Roberts, Rachel	45
Roberts, Rensha	45
Roberts, Richard	68, 182
Roberts, Robert	68, 185
Roberts, Stephen	93
Roberts, Thomas	45
Roberts, William	45, 91, 182, 240
Robertson, Andrew	61, 72
Robertson, Berbary	124
Robertson, Patrick	66
Robins, Bowden	243
"Robin's Camp"	54
Robins, Elizabeth	243
Robins, Ester	243
Robins (Robbins), George	69, 221
Robins, James	243
Robins, John	243, 244
Robins, Mary	243
Robins, Susannah	243
Robins, Thomas	165, 243
Robinson, David	11, 107
Robinson, Elinor	63
Robinson, John	47, 76, 107, 173
Robinson, Margaret	107
Robinson, Mary	76
Robinson, Richard	63, 112
Robinson, Sarah	63, 112, 210
Robinson, Solomon	63, 107, 112
Robinson, William	63, 74, 112, 151, 162, 171, 213
Robinsone, Jeanet	74
"Robotham's Raing"	67
Robson, David	96
Robson, Jane	143
Robson, John	106, 143

INDEX

	PAGE		PAGE
Robson, Mathew	169	Row, Sarah	225
Robson, William	143	Rowland, Samuel	218
"Robson's Outlett"	143	"Rowle Ridge"	87
Rock (Rocky) Ck., 10, 128,	195	"Royston's Creek"	125
"Rochester"	191	Rozer, Ann	36, 167
Rocks, Charles	39	Rozer, Elizabeth	36
Roe, Elizabeth	58	Rozer, Henry	36
Roe, Henry	100	Rozer, Katherine	167
Roe (Row), Thomas	225	Rozer, Notley	30, 36
Rogers, Isabella	250	Ruak, Margery	136
Rogers, John, 79, 122, 153,	250	"Ruerdon"	227
Rogers, Joseph	250	Ruff, Richard	215
Rogers, Nathaniel	125, 250	Rule, Elizabeth	79
Rogers, Nicholas	157	Rule, Peter	79
Rogers, Sarah	122, 250	Ruley, Ann	83
Roistern's Ck.	122	Ruley, Anthony	83
Roiston, Jone	194	Ruley, Elizabeth	239
Roland, Robert	24	Ruley, Michael	83
Rolph, Margrett	252	Ruley, Rebecca	83
Rolph, Thomas	252	Ruley, Seth	83
Roman Catholic	30, 78, 98, 167	"Ruley's Search"	83
"Roses Green"	101	Ruley, Thomas	83
Rose, Sarah	24	Ruley, William	83, 239
Rose, William	232	Rumball, Thomas	14
Ross, Catherine	144, 183	Rumsey, Edward	224
Ross, Charles	25	Ruork, Patrick	217
Ross, David	202	Russell, Cuthbert	244
Ross, James	25, 178	Russell (Russel), Luke	119
Ross, John	50, 109, 241	Russell, Mary	119
Ross, Mary	25	Russell, Nicholas	148
Ross, Parcill	50	Russell, Robert	119
Ross, Robert	25, 193	Russell, Thomas	119
Ross, Sarah	50	Russell, William, 210, 234,	235
Ross, William	196	Rutter, Ralph	152
Rosser, Eliza.	122	Rutter, Richard	152
Rosser, William	122	"Rutland's Discovery"	237
Rothery, Solomon	194	Rutland, Thomas	237
Round, Edward	61	Ry, Christopher	229
Round, James	46	"Ryhall,"	122
"Round Stone"	88	Ryland, John	223, 224
Rounds, William	247	Ryland, Rebecca	224
Rousby, John	78	Ryson, Daniel	211
Roux, Paul	79		

S

	PAGE		PAGE
Sadler, James	66	"St. Edmand's"	117
Sadler, Mary	66	"St. Elizabeth"	29
Saile, George	79	St. George's Parish	85, 131
Sails, Clement	79	"St. Giles"	5
Sails, Elizabeth	79	"St. James Enlarged"	235
Sails, Gabriel	79	St. James' Parish	135, 239
Sails, Jane	79	St. John's Ck.	143
Sails, Sarah	79	St. John's Parish	
St. Ann's	55, 241	93, 180, 200, 217,	233
St. Clement's Bay	37	St. Leonard's Ck.	6
"St. Dorrothy's"	118	St. Martins	61

INDEX

	PAGE
St. Mary's Co., 5, 6, 20, 25, 31, 37, 41, 48, 51, 70, 77-79, 98, 99, 105, 110, 111, 113, 118, 119, 126, 137, 142, 143, 147, 154, 155, 167, 171, 175-177, 181, 184, 185, 192, 199, 210, 219, 220, 231, 240,	249
St. Mary's C. H.	113
"St. Michals"	161
St. Michael's Parish, 65, 107,	138
St. Michael's R. 108,	182
St. Paul's 88, 125, 205,	253
St. Thomas'" 40,	181
St. Thomas' Ck.	48
Salem, Colony of	38
Salisbury, James	177
Salisbury, John	177
Salisbury, Mary	177
Salisbury, Sarah	177
Sallaway, John	59
"Sallop"	91
Salmond, Robert	25
"Salmon's Hills"	55
Salter, John	95
Salter, Sarah	95
"Samariea"	99
Sample, Charles	196
Sample, Frances	196
Sampson, Isaac	71
Samuell, Elizabeth	147
Samuell, Isabell	147
Samuells, Ann	246
Samuells, Martha	246
Samuells, Peter	246
Samuells, Richard	246
Samuells, Robert	246
"Samuels' Lott"	246
Samuels, Sarah	13
"Sand Down"	73
Sanders, Ann 148,	196
Sanders, Charles	29
Sanders, Edward	148
Sanders, Eleanor	196
Sanders, Elizabeth	150
Sanders, George	122
Sanders, Ignatius	213
Sanders, John .....▼....148,	213
Sanders, Katherine	196
Sanders, Mary	148
Sanders, Prudence	213
Sanders, R.	221
Sanders, Rachel	196
Sanders, Richard	213
Sanders, Robert	237
Sanders, Selanah	122
Sanders, Thomas ..122, 148,	213

	PAGE
Sanders, Valinda	213
Sanders, Williams 122, 148, 196, 213,	237
"Sand Gate"	15
Sands, Frances	43
"Sandwich"	174
Sanford, James	91
"Sankes Island"	196
Santee, Nathaniel	144
"Saplen Ridge"	117
Sappington, Thomas	237
"Sarah's Neck"	69
Sasser, Roger John	97
Sassafras R. 15,	64
Saunders, Aaron	102
Savin, Cornelius Augustine	105
Savin, Thomas	223
"Sawer's Addition"	38
Sawell, James	53
Sawell, Mary	178
Saxton, Absolom	67
Saxton (Sexton), John	67
Saxton, Sisly	67
Scandret, William	126
Scarbrough, Henry	186
Scarbrough, Matthew	44
"Scarbrough's Castle"	44
Scarf, Henry	129
Scarf, John	129
Scarth, James	129
Scarth, Jonathan	44
Schee, Harmanus	71
Schoolfield, Henry	243
"Schoolhouse Marsh"	106
Scobie, Jo.	221
"Scotch Neck"	48
Scotland 192,	234
Scott, Charles	125
Scott, Daniel 130, 232,	253
Scott, Deborah	45
Scott, Edward	125
Scott, Eliza.	45
Scott, Hannah	125
Scott, John ..45, 116, 125,	233
Scott, Thomas 25, 61,	143
Scott, William 45,	125
Scotten, James	141
Seager, John	240
Sealy, Ephram	236
Sealy, Henry	236
Sealy, Joseph	236
Sealy, Martha	236
Sealy, Mary	236
"Seaman's Delight"	65
Searson, Alice	185
Sehee, Rebekah	230
Selby, William	8

INDEX

	PAGE		PAGE
Semmes, Ann	58	Shephard, Thomas	254
Semmes, Ignatius	58	"Shepherd's Park"	215
Semmes, James	58, 213	Sheppard, Ezecale	230
Semmes, Joseph Milburn	58	Sheppard, Mary	230
Semmes, Juliana	58	"Sheppard Forrest"	141
Semmes (Simmes), Marmaduke	58, 119	Sheredine, Daniel	28
		Sheredine, Elizabeth	24
Semmes, Mary	58	Sheredine, Jeremiah	20, 24
Semmes, Susannah	58	Sheredine (Sheridine), Martha	24, 97
"Senequa Point"	83		
Sennott, John	123	Sheredine, Thomas	92
Sermon, Peter	179	Shierclieff, John	176, 184
Sescell, William	194	Shierclieff (Shurtliff), Peter	176, 184
Sewall, Charles	175, 220, 234		
Sewall, Elenor	175	Shierclieff, Thomas	184
Sewall, Henry	220	Shierclieff, William	184
Sewall, Nicholas	31, 167, 220	Shiless Ck.	115
Sewall, Nicholas Lewis	220	Shippard, Mathew	94
"Seward's Hope"	168	Shippin, Francina	129
Shacklet, Michael	59	"Shirt Come Off"	218
Shacklet, Tabitha	59	Shockley, John	136
Shahan, Catrin	151	"Shoomaker's Hall"	28
Shanks, Margaret	176	Shores, Thomas	82
Sharp, Henry	241	Shorter, Frances	239
Sharp, Isaac	241	"Showel's Addition"	72, 74
Sharp, John	50	Shurtliff, John	176, 184
Sharp (Sharpe), Peter	205, 241, 247	Shurtliff (Shierclieff), Peter	176, 184
Sharp, Samuel	241	Sikes (Sykes), Catherine	142
Sharp, Solomon	241	Sikes, John	70
Sharp, William	236, 241	Sikes, Joseph	184
Sharpe, Mary	65	Sikes, Mary	77
Sharter, Anthony	149	Sikes, Thomas	77
Shaw, Ann	248	Sikes (Sykes), Walter	142
Shaw, Christopher Durbin	232	Sill, Joseph	124
Shaw, Elizabeth	39	Sillwood, Sarah	102
Shaw, Richard	81	"Silver Street"	46
Shaw, William	25	Silvester, Benjamin	222
Shawhane, Daniel	88	Sim, Patrick	175
Shay, Thomas	101	Simcockes, William	125
Sheaffield, Mary	156	Simmes, Marmaduke	119
Sheaffield, Samuel	156	Simmons, Ainie	2
Sheehe, David	146	Simmons, Ann	2
Sheehe, Margery	146	Simmons (Symonds), Charles	172
Sheehe, Pottr.	146		
Sheehe, Sarah	146	Simmons, Elizabeth	2
"Sheffields"	95	Simmons, Jonathan	2, 99
Shehawn, David	247	Simmons, Joseph	2
Shehawn, Thomas	183, 247	Simmons, Marjory	2
Shehon, Eliza	194	Simmons, Mary	2
Sheldon, John	136, 245	Simmons, Rebecca	2
Shelley, Elizabeth	20	Simmons, Richard	2
Shenton, John	80	Simmons, Sarah	2
Shephard, Ann	215	Simmons, Winnefred	188
Shephard, Christopher	215	"Simpaltum"	8
Shephard (Shepherd), Rowland	215	Simper, Thomas	50
		Simpson, Archibald	244

INDEX

	PAGE
Simpson (Sympson), George	248
Simpson, James	161, 173
Simpson, John	161
Simpson, Mary	27
Simpson, Samuel	39
Simpson, Sarah	40
"Simpson's Hazard"	232
Simpson (Sympson), William	198, 232
Simpton, Andrew	58
Simpton, Juliana	58
Simson, Ann	104
Simson, James	104
Simson, John	104
Simson, Love	104
Simson, Mary	104
Simson, Thomas	104, 205
Simson, William	104, 205
Sinclar, Rachell	195
Sinclar, William	195
Sing, Margaret	131
"Sinnacor Landing"	99
Sinnott, Elineor	6
Skidmore, Judith	153
Skidmore, Rebecca	153
Skillitt, Mathew	114
Skinner, Ann	218
Skinner, Constance	51
Skinner, James	51
Skinner, Mary	51
Skinner, Sarah	139
Skinner, Thomas	51
Skinner, William	51, 139, 169, 185
Skirven, George	64, 87, 123, 205
Slade, Elizabeth	203
Slade, Ezekiell	203
Slade, Josias	202
"Slade's Camp"	203
Slade, Thomas	203
Slade, William	202
Slater, Ellis	20, 24, 205
Slater, John	222
Slater Susannah	222
Slaughter, John	91
Sligh, Thomas	253
Slimeedar, Mary	54
"Slip"	57
Slipper, William	160
Sloan (Slone), James	178, 179
Sloan (Slone), Jane	178, 179
Sloan, John Brown	212
Slye, Gerard	58
Slye, Thomas	92
Small, Robert	82
Small, Samuel	145, 222
Smallwood, Mary	111, 155
Smallwood, Mathew	155
Smart, Elizabeth	115
Smart, Jane	115
Smart, Rebecca	115
Smart, Richard	115
Smart, Robert	64
"Smart's Folly"	115
Smeaton, Marmaduke	204
Smeaton, Thomas	204
Smeaton, William	204
"Smith"	2
Smith, Abraham	46, 62, 219
Smith, Alexander	83
Smith, Alice	84
Smith, Anne	25
Smith, Anthony	39
Smith, Arthur	144
Smith, Basill	178
Smith, Daniel	84
Smith, Dorothy	41, 178
Smith, Edward	54, 131, 172
Smith, Elenor	69, 254
Smith, Elizabeth	84, 214, 219, 254
Smith, Eve	186
Smith, Frances	134, 238
Smith, Henry	66, 155
Smith, Isaac	84
Smith, Isabell	132
Smith, James	66, 78, 117, 124, 125, 153	219
Smith, John	12, 25, 46, 50, 69, 89, 132, 160, 161, 178, 224	235
Smith, John Addison	254
Smith, Joseph	66, 173
Smith, Levin	25
Smith, Mabel	66
Smith, Margaret	144
Smith, Martha	46, 114
Smith, Nathaniel	31
Smith, Nich.	49
Smith, Peter	46
Smith, Philip	89, 103, 173
Smith, Rachel	219, 254
Smith, Ralph	134, 238
Smith, Rebecca	254
Smith, Richard	76, 90, 254
Smith, Robbenist	69
Smith, Roger	178
Smith, Rose	50
Smith, Samuel	1, 125, 135, 206
Smith, Sarah	7, 84, 132, 160
Smith, Simon	160
"Smith's Point"	10
"Smith's Purchase"	69

INDEX lvii

	PAGE		PAGE
"Smith's Range"	5, 112	Sparkling, Richard	155
"Smith's Ridge"	141	Sparks, John	81
Smith, Stephen	50	"Sparks' Poynt"	101
Smith, Thomas, 22, 25, 27, 46, 50, 90, 95, 108	183	Speake, John	167, 213
Smith, Walter	219, 254	Speake, Mary	213
		Speake, Richard	213
Smith, William 25, 50, 65, 154, 214,	233	Speake, Thomas	213
Smith, Winston	214	Speeak, Elizabeth	37
Smithson, Ann	253	Speeak, Theodoshea	37
Smithson, Avarilla	253	Spearman, Charity	123
Smithson, John	18	Spearman, Francis	123, 153
Smithson, Martin	105	Spearman, Philip	123
Smithson, Sarah	253	Spearman (Spearmint), William	64, 123, 153
Smithson, Thomas	17, 253	Spence, Adam	34
Smitz, Thomas	144	Spencer, Elizabeth Shearnead	2
Smoot, Barton	48		
Smoot, Thomas	3	Spencer, Jonathan	126
Smoot, William	3	Spencer, John	2
Smothers, Blanch	184	Spencer, Zacharias	232
Smothers, Elizabeth	110	Spicer, Elinor	159
Smothers, James	110, 184	Spicer, James	159
Smothers, John	110, 184	Spicer, John	159
Smothers, Mary	184	Spicer, Mary	159
Smothers, Richard	184	Spicer, Phillip	159
Smothers, Thomas	110	Spicer, Rachel	159
Smothers, William	110	Spicer, Thomas	159
Smyth, James	57	Spicer, William	159
Snowden, Richard	237	Sping, Robert	82
Sollers, Sol.	173	Spratt, Stephen	27
Somerset Co., 8, 9, 18, 19, 31-35, 44-47, 50, 61, 62, 65, 71-76, 86, 87, 94, 115-117, 124, 133, 136, 137, 146, 147, 164, 165, 174, 186-188, 196, 211, 215, 225, 226, 234, 243-246, 248	249	"Spries' Hill	113
		Sprigg, Edward	16, 17, 194
		Sprigg, Elizabeth	194
		Sprigg, Richard	194
		Sprigg, Thomas	77
		Springar, Mary	52
		Springar, William	52
		Spry, Elizabeth	242
Somervell, James	185	"Spry's Inheritance"	192
Somnor, Anne	120	Spry, Thomas	222, 242
Sorden, Henry	182	Spurway, Edward	
Sorrency, Samuel	151	Stableford, Charles	143
Soslin, John	8	Stableford, Dorothy	143
Sothoron, John Johnson	51	Stableford, Thomas	143
Sothoron, Richard	51	Stack, Joseph	52
"Southampton"	9	Stack, Sarah	96
Southel, Edward	207	Stafford Co.	1
Southorne, John	176	Stagg, Rachell	106
South R.	41, 133, 237	Stalker, Thomas	153
Spalding, Bassell	5	Stalling, Mary	120
Spalding, Charles	4	Stallinges (Stallings), Jacob	12, 185
Spalding, John	4		
Spalding, Mary	5	Stallinges, Richard	12, 185
Spalding, Priscilla	4	Stallings (Stallins), Francis	68, 218
Spalding, William	5, 41		
Spaulding, Ann	40	"Stanaway's Forrest"	192
Sparkes, Thomas	39	Standish, Thomas	97

INDEX

Name	Page
Stanford, Augustin	21
Stanford, Charles	21
Stanford, Elizabeth	20
Stanford, James	172
Stanford, John	20
Stanford, Margaret	21
"Stanford's Addition"	20
Stanford, Samuel	178
Stanford, Thomas	98
Stanford, William	21
Stanley, Richard	211
Stanley, William	5
Stansbury, Bowen	253
Stansbury, John	11
Stanton, John	199
Stapeley, James	71
Stapelton, Henry	99
Stapelton, John	99
Stapelton, Margaret	99
Staplefort, Charles	179
Staplefort, George	28, 179
Staplefort, Thomas	179
Staples, Sarah	32
Staplesford's Ck.	157
Start, Ephraim	138
Start, Sophia	138
Steel, John	180
Steel, Sarah	180
Steele, William	84
Steelpone Ck.	145, 228, 251
Stennett, Benjamin	196
Stennett, Elizabeth	196
"Stepmother's Folly"	97
Stepney Parish	71, 72, 117, 137, 246, 249
Steuart, George	174, 239
Steven, Sarah	195
Stevens, Abel	153, 154
Stevens, Charles	69
Stevens, Elizabeth	63, 69
"Stevens His Addition"	69
Stevens, Katherine	69
Stevens, Mary	69
Stevens, Rebecca	33
Stevens, Richard	12
Stevens, Thomas	9, 209
Stevenson, Elizabeth	74
Stevenson, John	74, 154
Stevenson, Margaret	74
Stevenson, Mary	74
Stevenson, Robert	74
Stevenson, William	74, 208
Steward, Charles	133, 204
Steward, Eleanor	190
Steward, John	42
Steward, Kathrine	225
Steward, Sarah	201
Steward, William	225
Stewart (Stuart), Alexander	34, 166
Stewart, John	3, 165, 226
Stewart, Mary	3
Stewart, Patrick	147, 244
Stewart, Sarah King	166
Stewart, Steven	150
Stewart, Thomas	21, 190
Stewart, William	246
Stichbury, Stephen	161
Still, Robert	144
Still, Thomas	65
Stimton, Benjamin	10
Stimton, Elizabeth	10
Stimton, Jeremiah	10
Stimton, Mary	10
Stimton, Sarah	10
Stimton, Solomon	10
Stinchcombe, Anne	134
Stinchcombe, Nathaniel	134
Stirling, Archibald	147
"Stoakly"	218
Stockdell (Stocksdill), Edward	89, 225, 245
Stockett, Benjamin	240
Stockett, Damaris	240
Stockett, Lewis	240
Stockett, Sarah	240
Stockett, Thomas	65, 82, 240
Stoddert, Benjamin	10
Stoddert, Elizabeth	9
Stoddert, James	9
Stoddert, John	10, 180
Stoddert, Thomas	10
Stoddert, William	9
Stoker, Mary	109
Stokes, George	232
Stokes, Humphry	232
Stokes, John	160, 232
Stokes (Stoakes), Peter	179, 247
Stone, David	40, 193
Stone, Katherine	40
Stone, Mathew	139, 193
Stone, Mary	40
Stone, Richard	193
"Stone's Rest"	193
Stone, Theodosia	193
Stone, Thomas	15, 40, 193
Stone, William	23, 193
"Stony Hill"	189
"Stony Run"	163
Stoops, John	18
Storts, John	60
Story, Walter	40
Stoughton, William	226, 234

INDEX

	PAGE
Strahan, James	205
Strahan (Strahon), Alexander	21, 149
Strange, John	182
Strawbridge, James	62, 249
Strickland, John	129
Strickland, William	251
"Strife"	29, 98
Stringer, Samuel	86, 132, 150, 201, 240
Stuard, Elizabeth	237
Stuart, Alexander	166, 201
Stuart, James	201
Stuart, John	179
Stuart, Mary	202
Stuart, Sarah King	166
Stuart, Thomas	179
"Sturton's Rest"	55
Suel, William	138
"Suffolk"	71
Sulivan, Rhoda	102
Sullivan, Michael	245
"Sumerland's Lott"	55
"Summerfield"	6, 33
Summers, Anne	248
Summers, John	111, 115, 248
Summers, Sarah	248
Summers, Susannah	248
"Summerton"	144
Sumner, John	93
"Surveyor's Forrest"	143
Susquehanna	223
Suthell, Edward	109
Sutton, Ann	156
Sutton, Elice	138
Sutton, Ellicksander	156

	PAGE
Sutton, James	156
Sutton, John	109, 138, 156
Sutton, Josiah	129
Sutton, Sarah	138, 156
Sutton, Sophia	138
Sutton, Thomas	92
Swale, Mary	78
Swale, William	78
Swallowe, John	141
Swan, Anne	118
Swan Ck.	88, 98, 254
Swan (Swann), Edward	22
"Swan Harbour"	29
Swan, Katherine	118
"Swan Neck"	55
Swann (Swan), Thomas	22, 142
Swann, James	142
Swann, Judith	142
"Swanson's Lott"	65
Sweat, John	70
Sweat, Vertue	70
Sweeting, Edward	253
Sweeton, Edward	71
Swetnam, Edward	123
Swelvan, Ann	131
Swelvan, Owen	131
Swift, Richard	246
Swift, William	31, 197
Sword, William	79
Swormsted, Nicholas	23
Sykes, Catherine	142
Sykes, Walter	142
Symonds, Charles	172
Sympson, William	198
Syprus Swamp	71

T

	PAGE
Taile, Andrew	134
Talbart, Paul	10
Talbot Co., 1, 7, 11, 12, 21, 22, 30, 38, 46, 47, 52, 62, 63, 67, 69, 70, 78, 79, 90, 91, 95, 96, 105-109, 113, 114, 119, 127, 138, 139, 141, 144, 145, 150, 151, 156, 161, 171, 175, 182, 190, 191, 196, 205, 206, 213, 214, 221, 222, 235, 236, 241	242
Talbott, Edmund	200
Talbott, Elizabeth Elinor	200
Talbott, John	200
Talbott (Talbot), Mary, 93,	200
Talbott (Talbot), William	93, 200

	PAGE
Talley, Thomas	160
Taney, Mary	40
Taney, Thomas	40, 178
Tannehill, James	66, 212
Tannehill, William	212
Tanner, Anne	190
Tanner, Elizabeth	190
Tanner, Henry	190
Tanner, John	190
Tanner, Joseph	190
Tant, Mary	192
Tarlow, Edward	82
Tarman, Henry	187
Tarvin, Elizabeth	90
Tarvin, Richard	90
Tasker, Benjamin	30, 133
"Tasker's Camp"	254
Tasker, Thomas	175

INDEX

	PAGE
Taten, Richard	32
Tatlock, Edward	68
Tawney, Mary	40
Tawney, Thomas	40, 118
Taylor, Abraham	52
Taylor, Agnes	52
Taylor, Ann	131, 195
Taylor, Comfort	75
Taylor, Elizabeth	57, 143, 158, 179
Taylor, Frances	130
Taylor, George	75, 235
Taylor, Gilbert	187
Taylor, Henry	190
Taylor, James	52, 187
Taylor, John	62, 187, 200, 205
Taylor, Jonathan	62, 241
Taylor, Joseph	75, 130
Taylor, Lawrance	52
Taylor, Margaret	187
Taylor, Mary	179
Taylor, Mathias	75, 187
Taylor, Michael	133
Taylor, Peter	50
Taylor, Philip	205
Taylor, Rebecca	76, 205
Taylor, Richard	130
Taylor, Robert	9
Taylor (Tayler), Samuel	75, 97, 136, 226
Taylor, Sarah	52
"Taylor's Choice"	120
"Taylor's Discovery"	130
"Taylor's Folly"	158
"Taylor's Island"	158, 242
"Taylor's Joy"	27
"Taylor's Promise"	172
"Taylor's Range"	131
"Taylor's String"	130
Taylor, Tabitha	59
Taylor, Thomas	3, 59, 62, 77, 130, 163, 173
Taylor (Tayler), Walter	75, 226
Taylor, William	57, 179, 187, 205
"Taylorton"	97
Tayman, Benjamin	200
Tayman, John	200
Tennely (Tennerly), Philip	67, 113
Terry, Ann	170, 223
Terry, Augustine	122, 222, 223
Terry, Elizabeth	122, 223
Terry, Hugh	88, 222, 223
Terry, Rosamond	223
Terry, Thomas	170, 223
Thackary, John	152
Thackery, Elizabeth	66
Thackstone (Theckstone), Mary	230
Thackstone (Theckstone), Thomas	229, 230
Thalkstone, Thomas	64
Tharlow, Edward	82
Tharp, John	57
Thawloe, John	156
"Thirds"	249
"Thomas' Addition"	209
Thomas, Anne	102, 209
Thomas, Charles	223
Thomas, Edmond	209
Thomas, Edward	160
Thomas, Elisha	17, 130
Thomas, Elizabeth	130
Thomas, Frances	127
"Thomas Haddawayes Lott"	196
Thomas, James	209
Thomas, John	2, 4, 12, 151, 219
Thomas, Joseph	120, 122, 161
"Thomas' Lott"	50
Thomas, Martha	209
Thomas, Mary	160
Thomas, Mary Ann	209
Thomas, Phillip	142
Thomas, Rebecca	79
Thomas, Robert	119
Thomas, Samuel	124, 160
Thomas, Stephen	168
Thomas, Tilden	209
Thomas Thomas' Br.	199
Thomas, Thomas	120, 207
Thomas, Trustram	209
Thomas, William	1, 160, 235
Thompson, Augustin	23, 95
Thompson, Dowdall	95
Thompson, Elizabeth	109
Thompson, Isabella	61
Thompson, James	99, 110, 184, 199, 250
Thompson, John	207
Thompson, Joseph	109
Thompson, Michael	37
Thompson, Oswald	210
Thompson, Richard	119, 129
Thompson, Robert	148
Thompson, Sarah	23, 95
"Thompson's Islands"	174
"Thompson's Lott"	53, 207
"Thompson's Town"	160
Thompson, T.	196
Thompson, Thomas	109, 148, 192
Thompson, William	59

INDEX

Name	PAGE	Name	PAGE
Thompson, William Mathews	59	Todd, Ruth	193, 199
Thomson, Daniel	151	"Todd's Horse Pasture"	193
Thomson, Thomas	247	"Todd's Range"	55
Thorne, George	209	Tole, John	210
Thornell, William	109	Tollet, John	169
Thornlee, Mary	95	Tolley, James	233
"Thornton and Bateman's Farm"	230	Tolley, Mary	233
		Tolley, Thomas	41, 171, 220, 233
Thorold, George	118, 134, 167	Tolley, Walter	233
Threadhaven Ck.	47, 69, 107	Tolson, Ann	181
"Three Islands United"	99	Tolson, Frances	181
"Three Sisters, The"	93	Tolson, Francis	111, 181
Thurman, Joseph	28	Tolson, Henry	181
Thursby, Edward	163	Tolson, John	181
"Tibbet's Venture"	125	Tomson, Elizabeth	182
Tibbot, James	124	Tomson, George	169
Tibbot, Richard	124	Tomlinson, Ephraim	217
Tibbot, Samuel	124	Tomlinson, John	91
"Tibbott"	58	Tomlinson, Joseph	217
Tibbott, Thomas	206	Tomlinson, Magdalen	20
Tibbs, Ann	233	"Tossitter"	92
Tibbs, William	233	Touchstone, Christian	129
"Ticknell"	244	Touchstone, Andrew	129
"Tick Ridge"	32	Touchstone, Richard	129
Tilden, Charles	4	Toulson, Francis	1
Tilden, Jane	4	Toulson, John	1
Tilden, John	4	Tovey, Samuel	57, 228
Tilden, Marmaduke	4	Towers, James	157
Tilden, Martha	4	Towing, Elizabeth	145
Tilden, Mary	4	Townely, George	108
Tilden, Rebecca	251	"Town Hill"	135
Tilghman, Richard	47	"Town Neck"	20
"Tillington"	85	"Tracey's Level"	233
Tillman, John	249	Transquaking,	14, 158, 178, 207
Tillotson, John	140, 227	Traqueer, Alexander	224
Tilton (Tillton), John	4, 94	Traqueer, Mary	224
"Timber Neck"	55	Travers, Anne	212
"Timber Point"	77	Travers, Eliza	158
"Timber-well"	12	Travers, Mary	158
Timmans, Rebecca	164	Travers, Mathew	158
Timmans, Sarah	164	Travers, Thomas	126
"Timm's Neglect"	31	Travers, William	126, 158
"Timnah Sarah"	29	Tredhaven Ck.	47, 69, 107
Tingle, John	226	Tredway, Ann	215
Tipperary, County of	133	Treger, Elizabeth	211
Tippet, Butler	143	Treger, James	211
Tippet, Dennis	143	Treger, Mary	211
Tippet, Jane	143	Trickey, Thomas	140
Tippet, Phillip	143	Trippe, Edward	172
Tipton, Jonathan	132	Trippe, Henry	179
Toadvine, Henry	94	"Tripp's Horse Range"	179
Toby, Mary	132	Troth, Henry	221
Todd, James	192	Truelove, Thomas	17
Todd, John	38	Truett, Eleanor	226
Todd, Michael	159, 192	Truitt, Alice	164
Todd, Benjamin	192	Truitt, Benjamin	164
		Truitt, Cassiah	164

INDEX

	PAGE		PAGE
Truitt (Truett), George	8, 164, 226	Turbutt, Ann	7
Truitt, Job	164	Turbutt, Mary	7
Truitt, Joseph	61	Turbutt, Michael	7
Truitt, Leninah	164	Turbutt, William	7, 47
Truitt, Mary	164	"Turkey Range"	157, 232
Truitt, Nehemiah	164	"Turkey's Hills"	215
Truitt, Partheny	164	Turner, Ann	71, 234
Truitt, Rebecca	164	Turner, Edward	38, 80, 95, 114, 118
Truitt (Truett), Samuel	8, 226	Turner, Francis	17
"Truitt's Choyce"	164	Turner, Gilbert	79
Truitt, Thomas	116	Turner (Turnor), Henry	45, 75, 91
Trulock, Ann	229	Turner, John,	38, 53, 71, 87, 187
"Truman's Chance"	128	Turner, Jonathan	71
"Trustram"	209	Turner, Joseph	71, 171
"Trydant"	51	Turner, Loveday	230
Trygor, Thomas	211	Turner, Mary	71, 87
Tubman, Elener	28	"Turner's Hazard"	38
Tubman, Richard	28	Turner, Thomas	38, 139
Tuckahoe Ck.	30, 69, 102	Turner, William	38
Tuckahoe Meeting	106, 176	"Turnstile"	244
Tucker, Ann	58	Turpin (Turpen), John	62, 246
Tucker, Henry	48	Turpin, William	187
Tucker, John	174	Turrell, John	29
Tull, Esther	62, 165	"Turvey"	78
Tull, Grace	62	Turvile, William	45
Tull, Isaac	62	Turvy, Edward	3
Tull, John	31, 62, 165	Turvy, John	3
Tull, Joshua	31, 165	Turvy, Thomas	3
Tull, Mary	62, 165	Turvy, William	3
Tull, Rachel	62	"Tuscaroro Plains"	84
Tull, Richard	165	Tute, Christian	95
Tull, Samuel	62	Tweedie, William	239
Tull, Sarah	62	"Twifor"	56
Tull, Stephen	165	Twillee, Robert	196
Tull, Thomas	62	"Twittnam"	176
Tull, William	62	"Two Brothers"	198
Tully, Edward	133	Tyer, James	193
Tully, Michael	133	Tyler, Jonathan	222
"Tully's Neck"	209	Tyler, Robert	81
Tunhill, Elizabeth	184	Tyschow, Bastion	229
Tunhill, John	184		
Tunhill, Robert	184		
Tunhill, William	184		

U

Umberstone, George	153, 154	Urey, Honer	96
Underwood, Thomas	111	Urey, Margaret	96
Unick, Thomas	121	Urey, Mary	96
"Union, The"	29	Urey, William	96
"Upper Taunton"	56		

V

Vaine, John	95	Valliant, James	242
Vallete, Ann	104	Valliant, John	242
Vallete, Peter	104	Valliant, Joseph	242

INDEX lxiii

	PAGE
Vanburkeloo, Abell	100
Vanburkeloo, Catherine	100
Vanburkeloo, Harmen	100
Vanburkeloo, Margaret	100
Vanburkeloo, William	100
Vanderford, Rebekah	227
Vanderford, Vincent	126
Vanderheydon, Anna Margaretta	129
Vanderheydon, Matthias	129
Vandesant, Weniface	110
Vandever, Jane	163
Vansant, George	153, 154
Vansant, John	153, 154
Van Sante, Cornelius	17
Vanswerring, Mary	40
Vaughans, Richard	99
Vearing, Edward	95
Vearing, Rebecca	127
Veatch, John	12
Veazey, Lucia	60
Veazey, Mary	60
Veazey, Robert	60, 195
"Veil of Misery"	33
"Vening's Inheritance"	56
"Venture"	21, 68, 160

	PAGE
Venum, George	134
"Verina"	229
"Verlinda"	23
"Vernam Dean"	72
"Verona"	57
Vernon, Thomas	142
Vernon, William	135
Viana	247
Vickers, Ann	96
Vickers, Elizabeth	96
Vickers (Vickors), John	96, 114
Vickors, Sarah	114
Vickors (Vickers), Thomas	96, 114
Vickors, William	114
Vickors, William Browne	114
Vincent, Capt.	140
Vineing, Abram	204
"Vineyard"	175
Vinscent, George	188
Vinson, James	232
"Vinson's Chance"	53
Virginia, 1, 39, 98, 99, 148, 155, 186, 198, 199, 238, 243	
Vivian, William	230

W

Wade, Elizabeth	180
Wade, Mary	37
Wade, Richard	37
Wade, Robert	37, 56, 117, 181
"Wade's Adventor"	37
Wade, Zachariah	37, 67
Wadsworth, William	12
Wagstafe, John	215
Wailes, Benjamin	92
Wailes, Elizabeth	92
Wailes (Wales) Joseph	92, 166
Wailes, Levin	92
Waiman, Stephen	82
Wainoth, Mary	242
Wainwright, Hayford	169
Wainwright, Pleasance	169
Wainwright, Priscilla	169
Wainwright, Thomas	169
Waitt, Thomas	65
Waldy, Martha	40
Wale, Charles	73
Wale, Elias	73
Wale, Margaret	73
Wale, Mary	73
Wale, Nathaniel	73, 74
Wale, Rachel	73
Wale, William	73
Wales, Daniel	166

Wales, John	166
Walken, James	105
Walker, Ann	169
Walker, Charles	166, 169
Walker, Creecy	169
Walker, Elizabeth	169
Walker, George	15, 46
Walker, James	190
Walker, Jane	248
Walker, John	188, 190
Walker, Joseph	37, 65, 169
Walker, Mary	37, 169
Walker, Rachel	169
Walker, Rebecca	169
Walker, Robert	222
Walker, Ruth	169
Walker, Susanna	37
Walker, Thomas	37
Walker, William	3, 166, 216
Wallace, Thomas	73
Walles, Lodwick	73
Walley, Martha	139
"Wallnut Thicket"	28
Walls, Elizabeth	183
Walls, John	183
Walls, Martha	183
Walls, William	183
Wallter, Daniel	246

INDEX

Name	Page
Walter, Sarah	246
Walstone, Boez	31, 166
Walstone, Joy	31, 166
Walstone, London	31
Walstone (Wallstone), Mary	31, 32
Walstone, Thomas	31
Walstone, William	31
Walter, Catherine	84
Walter, John	84
Walters, Robert	141
Walton, Elizabeth	45
Walton, Sarah	73
Walton, William	73
Ward, Ann	161, 180
Ward, Camilla	180
Ward, Edward	180
Ward, Elizabeth	84
Ward, Hannah	217
Ward, Henry	222, 232
Ward, Jane	213
Ward, John	213
Ward, Mary Anna	217
Ward, Nathan	224
"Ward Oak"	95
Ward, Owen	248
Ward, Parthenia	213
Ward, Rosanna	217
Ward, Samuel	217
Ward, Sary	161
"Ward's Hope"	122
Ward, Thomas	151, 161
Ward, William	118, 143
Ware, Francis	213
Warfield, Richard	44
Waring, Ann	233
Waring, Basil	188, 233
Waring, Eleanor	233
Waring, James Haddock	188, 234
Waring, Lodwick	73
Waring, Marsham	188, 233
Waring (Warrin), Martha	137
Waring, Richard Marsham	233
Waring, Sarah	233
Warman, Stephen	202
Warner, Ann	184
Warner, Elizabeth	178, 213
Warner, George	1, 183, 229
Warner, Joseph	1, 124, 153, 183, 230
Warner, Mary	183
Warner, Samuel	213
Warner, Sarah	1, 213
"Warner's Levell"	183
Warring, William	128
Washington, John	254
Waters, Elizabeth	237
Waters, Walter	183
Watertons Ck.	64
Wathen, Hudson	119
Watkins, John	202
"Watson"	156
Watson, Bartholomew	70
Watson, Benoni	197
Watson, Comfort	188
Watson, Elizabeth	188, 197, 238
Watson, Francis	188, 197
Watson, James	2, 86, 188
Watson, Jane	2
Watson, Jugg	70
Watson, Lawrance	86
Watson, Leon	60
Watson, Luke	188
Watson, Margaret	60
Watson, Mark	132
Watson, Mary	60, 86
Watson, Mary Ann	197
Watson, Peter	188
Watson, Sarah	188
"Watson's Swine Range"	197
Watson, Thomas	86, 154
Watson, Urias	188
Watson, William	2, 197
Watton, Ann	234
Watts' Branch	199
Watts (Wattz), Daniel	36, 79
Watts, Edward	253
Watts, Elizabeth	79
Watts, Frances Holland	253
Watts, Grace	63
Watts, Joshua	79
Watts, Mary	253
Watts, Naomy	63
Watts, Stephen	210
Watts, Thomas	79
Watts, Winneford	71
"Wattses Lodge"	79
Wattson, Hugh	26
Wayman, Ann	237
Wayman, Jean	237
Wayman, Stephen	82
"Waymouth"	44
Weall, John	72
Weamoth, John	222
Weasly, John	11, 217
"Weatherill's Hope"	145
Weatherlee, James	196
Weatherlee, John	196
Weatherlee, William	196
"Weatherley's Marshes"	196
"Webb"	230
Webb, Edward	230
Webster, Ann	179

INDEX

Name	Page
Webster, Elizabeth	172
Webster, Isaac	101, 253
Webster, Margaret	253
Webster, Michael	39, 101, 172, 179, 214
Webster, Richard	21, 179
Webster, Thomas	5, 163
"Wedge"	175
Weeden, Elizabeth	3
Weeding, James	146
Weeks, John	11
Weems, David	238
Weems, James	238
"Welley"	69
Wells, Charles	28, 89, 163
Wells, Elizabeth	185
Wells, Humphrey	81, 89
Wells, John	88, 188
Welsh, Catherine	137
Welsh, James	135
Welsh, John	18, 134
Welsh, Robert	135
West, Ann	187
West, Anthony	187
West, Benjamin	199
West, Catherine	187
West, Elinor	170
West, Elizabeth	170
West, Jersey	38
West, John	24, 199
West, Joseph	86, 195, 198
West, Mary	127
West, Priscilla	170
West, Randall	187, 246
West, Rebeccah	199
West, Stephen	170
West, William	187, 198
"Westfield"	6
"Westmoreland"	192
"Weston"	188
"Westward"	183
Wetherell (Wetherall, Wetherill), George	64, 145, 206
Wetherell, John	145
Wetherell, Samuel	145
Wetipkin	166
Whaley, William	213
Wharton, Ann	222
Wharton, Anstes	114
Wharton, Henry	114
Wharton, Mary	114
"What You Will"	67
Wheatley, Edward	137
Wheeler, Charles	53
Wheeler, Henry	149
Wheeler, Isaac	94
Wheeler, James	149
Wheeler, John	94, 149
Wheeler (Wheeler), Margaret	94, 176
Wheeler, Mary	126
Wheeler, Sarah	149
Wheeler, Solomon	149
Wheeler, William	94, 176
Wheller, Robert	161
Wherrit, John	79
Wherrit, Mary	79
Wherrit, Thomas	79
Wherrit, William	79
Whetenall, Henry	36
Whetenall, John	36
Wheyland, Benjamin	242
Wheyland, Elizabeth	242
Wheyland, Lurana	242
Wheyland, Sarah	242
Wheyland, William	242
Whips, Elizabeth	142
Whislor, Thomas	137
Whitaker, Thomas	203
White, Alice (Alce)	67, 101
White, Benjamin	10
White, Elliner Haththorne	181
White, Francis	101, 141, 216, 253
"White Hall"	238
White, James	1, 101, 231
White (Wighte), John	57, 99, 140, 178, 197, 219
White, Letteshey	101
White, Margaret	67, 245
"White Marsh"	248
White, Mary	101
White, Rebecca	52
White, Richard	181
White, Samuel	10, 101
White, Sarah	231
White, Thomas	77, 232
White, Timothy	113
White, W	151
White, William	1, 10, 22, 67, 101, 171, 219, 231
"Whiteacres Ridge"	200
"Whitehaven"	29
Whitehead, F	39
Whitegreave, James	148
Whitley, (Whitely), Anthony	100, 195
Whitley, C	60
Whitley, Richard	78
Whitley, Sarah	78
Whitmore, Humphry	189
Whitmore, Margaret	189
Whitmore, Mary	189
Whitter, William	160

INDEX

	PAGE		PAGE
Whittington, Elizabeth	35	Willcocks, James	158
Whittington, Southy	36	"Willenbrough"	179
Whittington, William	35, 187	Willer, Edward	168
"Whittles Rest"	128	Willes, John	47
Whitworth, John	5	Willes, Susannah	47
Whitworth, Mary	5	"William and Marie's Addition"	144
Wiatt, James	121, 152	"William Heard's Purchase"	250
"Wiatt's Addition"	122	William, John	120
"Wiatt's Chance"	122	William, Joseph	104
"Wicconies Neck"	186	Williams, Aldren	119
Wickes, Ann	228	Williams, Ann	182
Wickes, Benjamin	228	Williams, Anthony	119
Wickes, Francis	227	Williams, Benjamin	239
Wickes, Joseph	228	Williams, Cicelia	214
Wickes, Lambeth	228	Williams, Edward	238
"Wickes' Marsh"	228	Williams, Elleanor	240
Wickes, Martha	228	Williams, Harry	140
Wickes, Rebecca	228	Williams, Hugh	3
Wickes, Samuel	227	Williams, James	68
Wickes, Simon	228	Williams, John, 27, 30, 46, 121, 123, 129, 159	227
"Wicklief"	227	Williams, Jonathan	116
Wicocomoco R.	9, 35	Williams, Joseph	41, 239
"Widdow's Purchase"	158	Williams, Katherine	68, 203
"Widow's Folly"	197	Williams, Magdalen	66
Wight, Ann	97	Williams, Margaret	239
Wight, Innocence	97	Williams, Mary	50, 119
Wight, John	57, 97	Williams, Rachel	74
Wight, Jonathan	97	"Williams' Range"	239
Wight, Mary	97	Williams, Rebecca	179
Wight, Richard	97	Williams, Richard	240
"Wight's Forrest"	97	Williams, Sarah	50, 101
Wilbourne, Ann	180	Williams, Thomas 68, 93, 119, 188, 203, 210	
Wilbourne, Edward	180	Williams, William 37, 68, 119, 182, 190, 203	
Wilbourne, Elizabeth	180	Williamson, Alexander	153
Wilbourne, Thomas	180	Williamson, George	122
Wilbourne, William	180	Williamson, Henry	28
Wilcocks, Daniel	140	Williamson, Judith	142
Wilcocks, Henry	140	Williamson, Mary	210
Wilcox, George	74	Williamson, Samuel	142
Wilde, Mary	17	Williamson, William	202
Wilde, Samuel	17	Willington, Elizabeth	7
Wilde, Sarah	17	Willmot (Wilmott), John	46, 150
Wilde, Thomas	17	Willmot, Ruth	46
Wilder, John	3	Willis, Andrew	80
Wilgus, Phillis	234	Willis, Elizabeth	25
Wilgus, Thomas	204	Willis, Jennet	127
Wilkins, Thomas	5	Willis (Willes), John	47, 109
Wilkinson, Christopher	125	Willis, Mary	109
Wilkinson, Elizabeth	7	Willis, Rebecca	80
Wilkinson, Francis	3, 219	Willis, Richard	109, 173
"Wilkinson's Choice"	141	Willis, Susannah	47
Wilkinson, Sibella	126	Willocy, Phillip	3
Wilkinson, Sophia	3		
Wilkinson, Susanna	3		
Wilkinson, Thomas	7, 125		
Wilkinson, William	3, 48		
"Wilkshear"	44		

INDEX

lxvii

	PAGE
Willson, Ester	38
Willson, Giles	118
Willson, Jemima	38
Willson, John	38, 101
Willson, Nathan	38
Willson, Phineas	38
Willson, Sarah	38
"Willson's Addition"	38
"Willson's Chance"	38
"Willson's Fancy"	38
Wilmer, Ann	4, 251
Wilmer, Francis	251
Wilmer (Wilmore), Lambert	125, 251
Wilmer, Martha	251
"Wilmer's Arcadia"	251
Wilmer (Wilmore), Simon	4, 123, 124, 140, 206, 251
Wilmott, Anna	150
Wilmott (Willmott), John	46, 150
Wilson, Abraham	86, 211
Wilson, Agnes	189
Wilson, Ann	195
Wilson, Catherine	228
Wilson, David	37, 225, 246
Wilson, Elizabeth	16, 211
Wilson, Ephraim	187, 246, 248
Wilson, Frances	12, 246
Wilson, George	87, 124, 189, 211, 229
Wilson, George Augusta	252
Wilson, Henry	16
Wilson, James	87, 188, 228, 252
Wilson (Willson), John	38, 101, 137, 195, 211, 228, 252
Wilson, Jonathan	176
Wilson, Jos.	155
Wilson, Josiah	16, 195
Wilson, Margaret	16
Wilson, Martha	16
Wilson, (Willson), Mary	38, 87, 137, 252
Wilson, Rebecca	252
Wilson, Richard	160
Wilson, Samuel	246, 253
Wilson (Willson), Sarah	38, 187, 211
Wilson (Willson), Susannah	38, 195
Wilson, Thomas	137
Wilson (Willson), William	45, 59, 105, 211, 234
"Winchester"	75
Windsor, Elizabeth	139
Windsor, William	97
Wineet, Henry	79

	PAGE
Wingate, Henry	159
Winifrett, John	37
Winkinson, Christopher	60
"Winslow's Range"	202
Winsor, Ann	182
Winsor (Winser), Elizabeth	182
Winsor, Garvis	182
Winsor, James	225
Winsor, John	182, 225
Winsor, Joseph	182
Winsor, Lazarus	225
Winsor, Thomas	97, 182
Winsor (Windsor), William	97, 182
Wintersell, Catherine	70
"Winterton"	144
Wist, Richard	1
"Witherall's Last Addition"	93
Withers, Thomas	175
Withington, John	122, 152
Withington, Mary	110, 152
Wolf, Johannes Ghsonsas	86
"Wolfpitt Ridge"	95
"Wolf's Harbour"	32, 93
"Wolf's Hook"	168
"Wolleston Manror"	39, 181
"Woolidge"	225
Wood, Eliza	180
Wood, George	162
Wood, Rachell	137
Wood, Robert	170
Wood, Thomas	36, 137
Wood, William	130, 243
Woodall, Abraham	21
"Woodberries' Hope"	23
"Woodbridge"	155
Woodcock, Grace	112
"Woodcock's Nest"	55
Woodin, Robert	128
Woodland, Blackledge	153
Woodland, Mary	229
Woodland, William	229
Woodland, Wilson	229
Woodward, Achsa	237
Woodward, Amos	55, 237
Woodward, Elizabeth	54
Woodward, Garrett	55
Woodward, Hannah	55
Woodward, Henry	54
Woodward, Mary	53, 202
Woodward, William	54
"Woodyard"	56
Woolland, John	143
Woollehan, Ann	101
Woollehan, Ealse	101
Woollehan, Elizabeth	101
Woollehan, Morris	101

INDEX

	PAGE
Woollehan, Susannah	101
Woollford, Elizabeth	173, 174
Woollford, Grace	21
Woollford, James	3, 169
Woollford, John	173, 174, 190
Woollford, Roger	173, 174
Woollford, Roseannah	174
"Woollfords"	174
"Woollford's Foresight"	174
"Woollford's Inheritance"	174
"Woollford's Meadows"	174
"Woollford's Outlet"	174
"Woollford's Pasture"	174
Woollford, Thomas	174
Woolman, Alice	138
Woolman, Sarah	138
"Woolver Hampton"	95
Wooten, Agnes	82
Wootton, Edward	117
Wootton, John	117
Wootton (Wooten), Turner	82, 134
Word, Benjamin	118
Word, Mary	146
Wordie, Alexander	147
Wordie, Hannah	147
Wordie, John	147
Wordie, Susannah	147
"Workinton"	113
Workman, Anthony	145
"Workman's Hazard"	101
"World's End"	157
Worrell, Edward	153
Worsley, Thomas	16
Worthington, Charles	42
Worthington, John	42
Worthington, Thomas	42, 44, 207
Worthington, William	42, 204
"Worthless"	8
Wray, Joseph	1
Wright, Charles	140
Wright, Edward	102
Wright, Hannah	26
Wright, John	26, 227
Wright, Mary	7, 102, 168, 177, 227
Wright, Nathaniel	101, 140
Wright, Robert Norrest	102, 104
Wright, Samuel	168
Wright, Sarah	101
Wright, Solomon	101, 177, 227
Wright, Solomon Coursey	177
Wright, Susannah	168
Wright, Thomas Hynson	7, 23, 177, 227
Wrightson, Elinor	144
Wrightson, Francis	145
Wrightson, John	69, 150, 182
Wrightson, Mary	105
Wroth, James	222
Wyatt, Elizabeth	121
Wyatt (Wiatt), James	81, 121, 152
Wyatt, Jane	81
Wyatt, John	81, 122
Wyatt, Joseph	121
Wyatt, Judeth	81
Wyatt, Mary	121
Wyatt, Ruth	81
Wyatt, Solomon	81
"Wyatt's Ridge"	55
Wyatt, Thomas	81, 122
Wyatt, William	81, 121
Wye R.	7

Y

	PAGE
"Yapp"	64
Yarde, George	177
Yarde, William	177
Yates, Richard	4
Yeamans, Musgrave	104
Yoe, John	205
Yoe, William	174
"York"	183
Yorkson, John	88, 224
Yorkson, Thomas	88, 160, 224
Young, Benjamin	68
Young, Constance	129
Young, David	89
Young, Edward	89
Young, Elizabeth	89
Young, Henry	205
Young, Humpry	252
Young, Jacob	223
Young, John	205, 223
Young, Joseph	223
Young, Katherine	223
Young, Mary	113
Young, Mathew	25
Young, Philemon	205
Young, Rebecca	185
Young, Richard	113
Young, Robert	241
Young, Samuel	205, 223
Young, Sarah	49, 89
"Young's Desire"	205
Young, Thomas	242
Young, William	205, 223

www.ingramcontent.com/pod-product-compliance
Lightning Source LLC
Chambersburg PA
CBHW070721160426
43192CB00009B/1264